Hendrik Petrus Berlage

Complete Works

Hendrik Petrus Berlage

Complete Works

Sergio Polano

Essays by
Giovanni Fanelli
Jan de Heer
Vincent van Rossem

RIZZOLI
NEW YORK

First published in the United States of America in 1988 by
Rizzoli International Publications, Inc.
597 Fifth Avenue, New York, NY 10017

Originally published in Italian under the title
Hendrik Petrus Berlage: Opera completa

Copyright © 1987 by Electa Spa Milano
English translation copyright © 1988 by
Rizzoli International Publications, Inc.

"Modern Architecture" first appeared in 1912 in *The Western Architect*

ISBN 0-8478-0901-3
LC 87-43252

Translated by Marie-Hélène Agüeros and Mayta Munson
Text layout by Blackpool Design
Printed and bound in Italy

Contents

Foreword

Sergio Polano

Hendrik Petrus Berlage is the most important figure in modern Dutch architecture. His career spans more than fifty years, between the end of the nineteenth and the beginning of the twentieth century.

He studied at the Zürich Institute of Technology, where he came under the lasting influence of Gottfried Semper. After graduating, he traveled in Italy and Germany. On his return to the Netherlands at the beginning of the 1880s, he entered into a partnership with Theodor Sanders and quickly started on a busy career, producing such extraordinary works as the office buildings for the insurance companies De Nederlanden van 1845 and De Algemeene, the Henny Villa, the headquarters of the Diamond Workers' Union, the Amsterdam Stock Exchange, the London House, the fantastic St. Hubertus hunting lodge, the Church of Christ Scientist, and, finally, the Municipal Museum at The Hague. He also created a remarkable series of designs which clearly show a desire to combine new forms with ancient values—the Monument Historique, the Beethoven House, the Wagner Theater, the Pantheon of Humanity, and the Lenin Mausoleum. Berlage's many ventures in the field of urban planning, whether on a large scale or on a limited one, are also of historic significance. He drew plans for the development of The Hague, Utrecht, the south of Amsterdam, and the Hofplein in Rotterdam—to name only the major projects. Finally, Berlage took an active part in the debates on architecture in the Netherlands as a lecturer and writer. He helped to spread the latest developments in international culture, in particular the recent ones in Germany. He formulated a body of theories which were to inspire different movements in Dutch architecture—albeit with some possible oedipal consequences—whether De Stijl and the School of Amsterdam in the 1910s and 1920s, or the Nieuwe·Zakelijkheid of the 1930s.

However extensive the existing literature on Berlage may be, a book was still needed which would encompass his whole work and present the analytical tools necessary to carry out subsequent research. The present book was planned with such an objective, after a long period of research and with contributions by Dutch and Italian specialists. The main purpose was to bring the lesser known areas to the fore. Consequently, the first part of the book is devoted to essays on some crucial points in the career of the Dutch master. Giovanni Fanelli studies the range in Berlage's designs, especially the works fol-

lowing the Amsterdam Stock Exchange: Between 1900 and 1930 Berlage's production was not without contradictions; as a consequence it is usually neglected in the specialized literature. Vincent van Rossem analyzes the composite roots of Berlage's philosophy regarding urban life and planning. He dwells on his connection with the German theoreticians in the field and outlines the often fruitful exchanges between the two countries. Jan Dé Heer explores Berlage's designs, which were strongly influenced by his political and social beliefs, and by which he tried to resolve problems arising from a growing demand for housing in cities. This first part ends with the text of a classic lecture Berlage gave in 1911 in the United States.

The second part of the book presents a complete analytical list of his works, with a catalogue and a bibliography. New archival and iconographic research, including derivative and secondary sources, produced over one hundred and forty items outlining Berlage's career as an architect and urban planner. The existing critical literature was taken into account in the treatment of each item, in order to separate major works from minor ones and to highlight the lesser known works which merited re-assessment. A catalogue raisonné of Berlage's writings completes this second part, with a bibliography including close on four hundred titles.

The book is richly illustrated with a wide selection of pictures found in archives and many new photographs of existing buildings. Most of these illustrations have never been published before. The essays feature extraordinary drawings, and each item in the catalogue of his works is accompanied by designs and mainly period photographs. This endeavor was made possible by the openness and great competence of several Dutch institutions, without whom new illustrations could not have been found. Mention should first be made of the Nederlands Documentatiecentrum voor de Bouwkunst in Amsterdam, which provided full access to the greatest existing collection of documents on Berlage. The other sources were the Rijksmuseum Kröller-Müller at Otterlo, the Municipal Museum and the Nationale Nederlanden at The Hague, the archives of several Dutch municipalities and in Amsterdam in particular, the Institute for Social History, several corporations, many libraries, and private collections. We extend our thanks to all who have helped us in our research work. Unfortunately, for reasons of space, we cannot name here all the institutions and individuals in the Netherlands who have generously given us assistance and information. Even if those already mentioned above were omitted, the list would be very long indeed. This project was also made possible by a grant from the Department of Architectural History at the Venice Institute of Architecture.

The Complete Works of Berlage is the result of a patient labor of love. It must be added that it would not have been possible to start this project, overcome many unexpected obstacles, and complete the book without the advice of a few good friends. We are grateful for their loyalty and unstinting support.

My work is dedicated to Cesare, *alea jacta*.

"Unity Within Diversity"
The Architecture of Berlage

Giovanni Fanelli

Berlage "should not be judged by standards of 'rationalism,' but with a subtle understanding of his role as a mediator between the 'ancients' and the 'moderns.'"[1] Fifty years later, and in the euphoric excitement of post-Modernism, we must again admit that Edoardo Persico was right. In spite of its apparent simplicity, Persico's approach seems most appropriate for the writings of the Dutch master, his buildings, and his relationship with both contemporary Dutch and international culture. Berlage's restraint and his gift for bold moderation, so to speak, has kept his works relevant. In a monograph that is still one of the most perceptive studies on Berlage, J. Havelaar wrote in 1927, "Every true revolutionary has proven to be likewise a traditionalist; he is the one who takes tradition seriously again."[2]

Berlage wanted to ensure a continuity between past and present. While he wished to be attuned to his time and to contemporary problems, he envisaged solutions geared toward an ideal society. This combination of realism and idealism led to a duality in his work that could not be solved on a general cultural level. This duality inherent in modernity was solved at the level of forms: Berlage found a subtle idiom to express a difficult balance that was made possible—albeit precariously—by an inner consistency.

The same approach characterizes each work by Berlage and ties all his works together. This approach reflects both an ideology and a basic choice in design: Berlage sets himself the task of understanding and interpreting the situation, needs, and aspirations at the time when a building is raised on a specific site, but he foresees also possible changes in circumstances, even in the building itself. When his work is examined as a whole, it becomes clear that each design, whether it is one on which he worked for a long time—such as the Amsterdam Stock Exchange or the Museum at The Hague—or one that was completed quickly—such as the church at The Hague or the town hall at Usquert—evolved from a process, which needed at a certain moment to take material form as a building, and is not a definitive solution. The town hall at Usquert, for example, is a small building that was planned, designed, and erected in a very short time. There were, nevertheless, at least five stages in the design as well as modifications during construction.

The construction itself was part of the design. It was not a coincidence that Berlage liked to collect photographs of the different stages in the construction of his buildings.

However carefully designed and built, the work was never regarded as completed and could always be changed, even after construction work was finished. This accounts for successive alterations in the office buildings for De Algemeene in Amsterdam (1892–94 and 1901–05) and for De Nederlanden van 1845 in Amsterdam (1894 and 1910–11) and The Hague (1895–96, 1901–02, and 1908–09).

Manfred Bock understood very well Berlage's approach—the importance he gave to the present and to the relationship between lasting and temporary values in architecture—when he wrote, "The lecture 'Architecture and Impressionism' (*Bouwkunst en Impressionisme*) given in November 1893 was a good example of [Berlage's] new formulation of a theory. . . . The date matters. It could not have been formulated a few years earlier, and it would no longer have held good a few months later, when social reality was to catch up with his precursory theory. The Stock Exchange is a good example of a new architectural idiom; its form seemed so revolutionary at the time that this monumental construction was not regarded as 'architecture' by contemporaries. This as well could not have been built earlier or later either."[3]

Because he absorbed with great intelligence typologies and forms belonging to a more or less distant past and displayed an extraordinary ability to link up with history, Berlage successfully created works striking a difficult balance between past and present.

He himself thought that the Amsterdam Stock Exchange was neither a starting point nor a point of arrival, but a milestone.[4] It bears witness to his ability to assimilate components of contemporary culture and work them out in a continuous process. It makes little sense, therefore, to underline the possible influence of the ideas and architecture of Karel Petrus Cornelis de Bazel, Johannes Ludovicus Matteus Lauweriks, and Jan Hessel De Groot, but it also makes little sense to deny that Berlage was aware of them and made them a part of his work. Beyond acceptance and rejection, beyond the criticism expressed by De Bazel and Lauweriks, and later by Jacobus Joohannes Pieter Oud, Johannes Bernardus van Loghem, and Jan Duiker, the Stock Exchange stands as an irreplaceable presence because it achieves a dynamic synthesis between different cultural currents.[5]

Berlage was trained at the height of nineteenth-century historicism. The evolution of the Dutch master's style can be compared to that of the Viennese Otto Wagner, because both explored every aspect of historicism and went beyond when they gave their experiments another orientation. We cannot discuss here the similarities in the development of the two architects, which have been analyzed elsewhere and confirmed by Berlage himself. Suffice it to mention that it was rooted in the theories of Gottfried Semper. In a major text written in 1912, Berlage recounts his trip to the United States and mentions Wagner's name next to that of Frank Lloyd Wright. Berlage and Wagner arrived at a different relationship with period forms because these forms by themselves were not suitable for the characteristics and new conditions of the industrial civilization. Both men, however, searched for a new style without breaking with the architecture of the past. It is, therefore, necessary to note again that the complexity of their major works cannot be understood without taking into account their roots in eclectic historicism.

P. Singelenberg dates the renewal of Berlage's architecture to the early 1890s, and he regards the Pijzel House, built in 1891–92, as "the first expression of Berlage's new style, when he begins to eliminate such ornaments that he knows from experience to be superfluous and to 'smooth out' surfaces."[6] More recently, Bock challenged this interpretation, arguing that in the 1890s Berlage's theories and buildings still showed inconsistencies and confusion, influenced as they were by contemporary political events.[7] At the end of 1893, in his lecture "Architecture and Impressionism," Berlage came to criticize eclectic historicism as a threat to creative architecture. In 1892, however, he still advocated eclecticism as a style suitable for monumental works, while such buildings as middle-class private houses required a simpler and more rational idiom. Bock reviews Berlage's whole eclectic period of the 1880s and 1890s in terms of typology and content. He shows how they are related to a social and political context, and he can therefore explain why the eclectic designs of monumental buildings coexisted with the rational simplicity of townhouses and villas.

From 1893 on, and above all between 1896 and 1898, Dutch graphic art and architecture evolved toward stylization, and such designers as De Bazel and Lauweriks championed a new approach to negative and positive space. The design for the Stock Exchange, and the dematerialization of the wall mass in particular, mirrors such development. The office building for De Nederlanden van 1845 in The Hague, dated 1895–96, and the headquarters of the Diamond Workers' Union in Amsterdam, dated 1897–1900, already featured openings in the smooth masonry—niches, loggias, and perforations—and railings used as a coping or in a wall. But there were clear variations in Berlage's idiom during those years, as can be seen in the houses in Groningen and Bussum and the office buildings on the Sophiaplein in Amsterdam and the Kerkplein in The Hague.[8] As a designer—of furniture in particular—he combined even more rationalism with the purely decorative, such as in ornamental patterns based on oriental motifs and in the graphic treatment of the ironwork.

The Henny Villa at The Hague, dated 1898, is typical of Berlage's style at the time. The very skillful plan is reflected in the arrangement of masses, which features a deceptively free, but in fact restrained, grouping of perfectly designed solids. The rational interior layout is highlighted by original detail inspired by Nieuwe Kunst.

The Stock Exchange is characterized by a search for "unity within multiplicity," to use Berlage's own definition, and the result is one of "quiet" clarity. The exterior design is both monumental and simple; everything, from the general to the particular, is arranged in a carefully balanced composition. The massive unity of the whole is set against the rich variations in the outer shell—Berlage called them impressionistic—which are attuned to variations in the urban landscape, in accordance with the precepts of Camillo Sitte. The rhythmic continuity of the outer shell is counterpoised by the free arrangement of its components; the modular treatment of the façade, by a painterly composition.[9] The asymmetrical general composition is balanced by the symmetrical arrangement of elements; symbolic decorative details by the expressive building logic; a desire to dematerialize by the significance imparted to mass.[10]

In the interior design, the plan clearly dictates the form. Several rooms on different levels are connected to one central room; galleries are set against the unity of vast rooms; the continuity of the walls contrasts with the woven design of bricks, with the structure, and with the architectural details. In the end, the quotations from past styles and the reinterpretation of period forms reach beyond historical references. The grand hall is shaped like a great square, with walls resembling façades ennobled by the severity of the design. Art historians have rightly suggested such different references as the Renaissance Stock Exchange in Amsterdam, Sant'Ambrogio in Milan, the Broletto in Pavia, P.J. Cuypers's Rijksmuseum in Amsterdam, the Bargello in Florence, the Stock Exchanges in Antwerp and Bremen, the Basilica in Vicenza, a palace in Madura, the town hall in Amsterdam, and the cathedral in Modena.[11] All these possible examples, however, are assimilated into an extraordinary "superhistorical" style which is therefore deeply rooted in contemporary times. Berlage avoids eclecticism. He successfully controls all his references and creates a dynamic synthesis based on a basic principle, "unity within diversity," a synthesis of structure and whole.[12] Artistic form and construction, expression and structure, solutions dictated by the psychology of perception and those derived from a desire for symbolic meaning, all these elements are blended into an indissoluble combination. This is not a mere arrangement of revived historical elements. In order to invent a uniquely decorative idiom, Berlage carefully selects some existing elements of style, assessing their material or aesthetic function, and he highlights that function.

In a text written in 1912, Berlage explained the long gestation of the Stock Exchange, during which he finally chose a design derived from the Romanesque and went past it into the ahistorical. "The outline of a solid mass . . . is the pride of architecture. . . . Today, the art of building cannot be other than that of arranging masses. The problems that need to be solved and the manner in

1. *Entry in a competition for an artist's studio and house, 1888, view from the street.*

2. *Design for a Mausoleum, 1889, cross-section.*

1

PROJET D'UN MAUSOLEE

COUPE.—ÉCHELLE 1: 500

2

ONTWERP VAN EEN SPQZ RAADHUIS TE ZUTPHEN

HET RAADHUIS VAN HET 's GRAVENHOF GEZIEN

3

4. *De Algemeene Building, Amsterdam 1892–94 and 1901–05, elevation on Damrak, drawn by J. Hessing in 1893.*

5. *De Algemeene Building, Amsterdam, 1892–94 and 1901–05, the hall in the first extension, 1901–02, section published in* De Architect, *in 1905.*

4

5

6. *Villa Heymans, Groningen,*
1893–95, general view and outline of
the floor plans.

which they are stated point in one direction: The architect recognizes that his most ambitious objective is to create a grandiose and dynamic distribution of masses. . . . The Romanesque is consistent with basic modern concepts because of its simplicity, its structural disposition of masses, and the role given to decoration. There is the danger, however, of being snared in this style."[13] Clearly, Berlage regards the Romanesque not simply as a style but rather as an exemplary precedent for a modern idiom in architecture.

The extraordinary felicity of the period around 1898—the last phase of the period of the Stock Exchange—is attested by such other significant works as the Diamond Workers' Union Building and the Henny Villa. However, the deliberate and miraculous balance in the Exchange was not intended to—and could not—provide solutions to every problem in subsequent designs. By definition, the type of dynamic balance that Berlage sought needed to be defined anew with each design. The variations characteristic of the period until 1911, when Berlage traveled in the United States, can be understood if the Stock Exchange is regarded not as a point of departure or arrival, but as a point in a process, a work completed but neither definitive nor conclusive. During that time there is a surprising dichotomy between Berlage's commissioned works and his routine works. It is a dichotomy between simple pragmatic solutions to professional problems and architecture as an expression of higher aspirations, between private and monumental architecture. Berlage was very active then, both in the Netherlands and abroad, but he built few monuments. He was commissioned mostly to design office buildings, hotels, villas, and houses and apartments for cooperatives or corporations. In such works as the apartment buildings in Amsterdam, on Hobbemastraat (1903–04) and Linnaeusstraat (1905), Berlage achieved balance and puritan consistency by relying solely on precisely drawn surfaces and lines—the edges in particular—and on architectural detail reflecting the building logic. The alterations and additions to the office buildings of De Nederlanden van 1845, in Amsterdam and The Hague, and of De Algemeene, in Amsterdam, show a significant desire for simple clarity. The architecture of these buildings is so sparse as to seem "without qualities." The headquarters of the Voorwaarts cooperative in Rotterdam (1906–07), the post office and a hotel at Bergen (1908–13),[14] the headquarters of De Nederlanden in Rotterdam (1911), and other works in Leipzig, Soerabaja, and Batavia are even sparser. General explanations left aside—and given that Berlage's works struck a difficult balance between different elements related to a social and economic context that played an increasingly determinant role in his designs—this architecture without qualities remains problematical to this day. It already seemed problematical to his contemporaries. On the occasion of the architecture exhibition organized by the association "Architectura et Amicitia" at the Stedelijk Museum in Amsterdam, the young architect Johannes B. van Loghem wrote a major article published in the daily newspaper *Nieuwe Amsterdammer*, on December 11, 1915. Van Loghem was to become one of the

7. *De Nederlanden van 1845 Building,*
   Amsterdam, 1894–95 and 1910–11,
   façades, plan of the second floor, and
   architectural details of the extension,
   1910–11.

8. *De Nederlanden van 1845 Building,*
   Amsterdam, 1894–95 and 1910–11,
   elevations and floor plans, 1894–95.

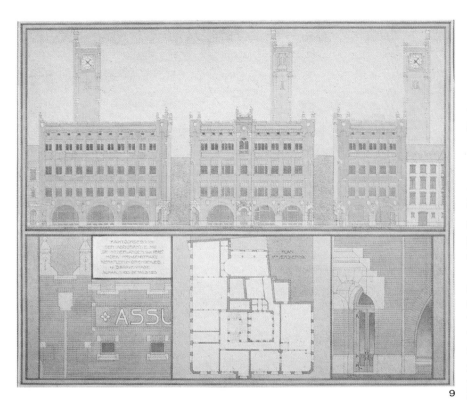

9

10

major proponents of *Nieuwe Zakelijkheid* (New Objectivity) as well as one of the most articulate interpreters of Dutch rationalism in architecture. In his article, he correctly analyzed the significance and contemporary relevance of Berlage not as a pure artist producing finished works, but as a man involved in a process of experimentation. According to Van Loghem, modern architecture cannot afford the beautiful harmony of the Antiquity; it must find its own characteristic beauty, "in which there is an element of ugliness." Van Loghem set modern equilibrium against classical harmony: The architect must accept what is ugly and make it a part of his design; only then can he experiment and be open to something new. He made a distinction between imagined architecture as an idea or an ideal and the actual architecture of an existing building. In Berlage's design for the Pantheon of Humanity, "the idealist surpassed the artist." The result is a "tragic contradiction" with the contemporary world, which lacks a common general culture. This tragic expression succeeds in "breathing life into others," who either support or criticize Berlage. "Berlage never reaches his goal," Van Loghem continued, "either his instinct or his intellect prevents him from doing so. . . . He always stumbles on the new paths on which he travels; then he grows, but again he fails to reach his goal."[15] Jan Gratama—an engineer, professor of architectural history at the Academy of the Hague, and director of the weekly *Bouwkundig Weekblad* from 1908 to 1914—was aware of Van Loghem's article when he wrote his own article in the 1916 issue of the journal published on the occasion of Berlage's sixtieth birthday. His assessment of the master's work was to become a reference for future studies on Berlage. Gratama emphasized Berlage's search for *Zakelijkheid*, for rationalism. He regarded this explicit honesty of purpose as the explanation for Berlage's "continuing evolution." A member of the so-called Amsterdam School, Cornelis J. Blaauw, reviewed in *Architectura* the special issue honoring Berlage. He echoed the criticism voiced by Van Loghem: "One is aware of a certain lack of beauty in Berlage's works, which borders on ugliness. However, one must instinctively respect his heroic spirit. His surprising sparseness may be almost ugly, but it is the expression of a great spiritual victory. This very sparseness, resulting from a spiritual struggle, is characteristic of modern man."[16]

On March 21, 1923, J.J.P. Oud, one of the most intelligent members of the De Stijl group, gave a now famous lecture in Berlin, "The Development of Modern Architecture in the Netherlands: Past, Present, and Future," which was repeated on several occasions and published. He also echoed Van Loghem's critical appraisal of Berlage's work, calling it an architecture in transition, "more tragic than beautiful." He made a crucial distinction between Cuypers's work, in which "rationalism is of an aesthetic nature," and Berlage's brand of rationalism, the consequences of which have a wider range. "[His rationalism], Oud noted, refers as solidly as possible to all aspects of life directly or indirectly connected with ar-

11. *The Amsterdan Stock Exchange, 1896–1903, preliminary sketch of the southern view for the second design of 1897.*

12. *The Amsterdam Stock Exchange, 1896–1903, detail of the elevation drawn by H.J.M. Walenkamp and published in 1901 in* De Architect, *main entrance.*

13. *The Amsterdam Stock Exchange, 1896–1903, detail of the interior drawn by H.J.M. Walenkamp and published in 1901 in* De Architect, *the eastern arcade of the Commodities Exchange.*

14. *The Amsterdam Stock Exchange, 1896–1903, detail of the exterior drawn by H.J.M. Walenkamp and published in 1901 in* De Architect, *corner of the tower and the Gijsbreght van Aemstel.*

11

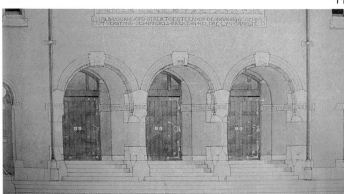

12

13

14

*15. The Amsterdam Stock Exchange,
1896–1903, detail of the interior
drawn by H.J.M. Walenkamp and
published in 1901 in* De Architect,
*beams of the ceiling of the Commodities
Exchange.*

chitecture. Rationalism becomes a rational mental attitude, so to speak."[17]

In November 1911, Berlage traveled for two months in the United States. There he acquired first-hand knowledge of the works of Henry Hobson Richardson, Louis Henry Sullivan, and, most important of all, Frank Lloyd Wright.[18] The trip clearly marked a turning point in his career. He felt an intellectual and cultural affinity with Wright. They shared ideas on classical art, the Gothic style, and the Renaissance; they both accepted the rise of industrial society and perceived modern technology as a development consistent with democratic ideals. Berlage also recognized in his American colleague "a man who had freed himself from tradition without severing his ties with the past, who does not imitate the past but understands it as a historic phenomenon."[19] He found further confirmation of this intellectual affinity in Wright's works and idiom. Berlage was interested mostly in the works combining technological and formal experiments with a monumental vision. He also regarded the prairie house as following implicitly the program Wright formulated himself in his article written in 1908, "In the Cause of Architecture." It must be pointed out, however, that Berlage did not find an unexpected revelation in American architecture, nor a reason to change his own ideas. What he found was a confirmation of what he was searching for and an illustration of his own experiments. Like him, American architects were proceeding from the inside to the outside; they gave pride of place to the inner layout; they aimed for a clean geometry and an outline made of modular lines. Like him, they favored contrasts between large central areas and galleries. Finally, both Sullivan and Wright used ornament to highlight clarity of construction and space. In his comments on Sullivan's architecture, Berlage noted that "ornament is entirely subordinate to the true structure of the construction."[20] He used the word "fabric" to describe the wall surface, the same word that Wright had used. He happily recalled a visit to a Dutch manufacturer of bricks in Minneapolis, whose wide range of samples made it possible to build beautiful walls.[21]

Berlage produced several designs and buildings before he went to the United States that suggest that his direct acquaintance with Wright's architecture brought about less a discovery than a meeting of two minds. His approach in these designs is quite similar to that of his American colleague. And in some places his memoir of his trip to America ("Amerikaansche Reisherinneringen") reads like quotations of himself. The Vredespaleis, dated 1906, and the Kunstenaarhuis, dated 1911–12, show a fundamental correspondence between form and simple solids, a relationship between the square central part of the building and the corner parts built on the Greek-cross plan. The openings are rhythmically spaced. Great value is given to lines, and stones are used to highlight the unity created by brick walls. Here Berlage went beyond academicism and the Beaux-Arts style, putting forward types of form that are similar in concept to the ones Wright and Wagner were also proposing in the same period. His

15

private houses, such as the Salomonson country house in Baarn, dated 1909–10, seem to be laid out according to a rigid symmetry, but some components suggest a resemblance to Wright's designs. The layout and arrangement of masses are in the shape of a cross; the living room runs into the terrace and, on the second floor, the bedrooms into balconies, in a system of tiers; the corner windows are at an angle of 45 degrees to emphasize the diagonal orientation of the house.

It may be that Berlage already knew Wright's work from the report and documentation supplied by William G. Purcell in 1906. This is difficult to prove, however, and it must be noted that signs of an affinity with Wright can be detected in much earlier works. Suffice it to mention the entrance hall in the Henny Villa, built in 1898, which is two stories high, laid out in the shape of a cross, and placed diagonally at the center of the first floor. The villa is also remarkable for the free disposition of masses, the interlocking flat and pitched roofs, and an arrangement of terraces, verandas, and loggias at different levels. The kitchen and one bedroom are placed diagonally. The inner walls are made of exposed bricks. The Heymans Villa in Groningen, built in 1893–95, also features a free layout, a combination of solids including terraces and verandas, and a wall fitted with cabinets separating the dining room from the living room.

Berlage's works for the Kröller-Müller family are clearly influenced by his trip to the United States and his discovery of American architecture. A.G. Müller, the magnate and chairman of a multinational corporation, and his wife, Hélène Kröller, were unhappy with a design by Peter Behrens for a villa-museum to be built at The Hague. After a competition of sorts between Ludwig Mies van der Rohe—who was then Behrens's assistant—and Berlage, they took Bremmer's advice and offered Berlage a ten-year exclusive contract. Berlage had just lost hope for a much sought-after public commission when he was barred from competing for the design of a new town hall in Rotterdam. His first commission for the Kröller-Müllers was the company's offices in London. He had become interested in designing office buildings even before his trip to the United States, and while there he had carefully studied such buildings.[22] In "Amerikaansche Reisherinneringen," written on his return to Europe, he singled out office buildings as the type of architecture that would replace the great buildings typical of ancient cities. He wrote that commercial buildings can have "a spirit that might be defined as religious. . . . Office buildings and commercial buildings are ideal types of modern architecture, while in Antiquity temples represented the loftiest cultural values."[23] Therefore Berlage regarded it as logical that "an office building be the most typical work by Wright or Sullivan."[24] He referred admiringly to Wright's Larkin Building in Buffalo, pointing to "the beautiful windows separated by pillars rising along the whole façade."[25] They evoke buildings by Sullivan and also Berlage's own De Nederlanden van 1845, built in Rotterdam in 1911. The latter design was perfected in the Kröller-Müller London House, achieving even greater clarity and Zakelijkheid. The vast floors of the building

are subdivided by movable partitions. The steel frame is visible in the façade and covered by glazed terracotta tiles, size and grayish-green color of which are determined by the design. This solution takes into account fire regulations in London, the smog, and Berlage's own aesthetic considerations. The same tiles cover the inner walls and the spaces between the glass columns and the pilasters. The rhythmic arrangement of the façade as well as the tile cladding clearly show the influence of Sullivan's Wainwright Building in St. Louis, dated 1890–91, and his Guarantee Building in Buffalo, dated 1895.

The Holland House is correctly regarded by specialists as one of Berlage's most finished and refined works. He brilliantly juxtaposes two contradictory themes, continuity in the façade and voids prevailing over masses. A solid marble fascia runs along the base and the sides, separating the building from its neighbors. This fascia stops at the last floor of the other buildings and allows the ceramic cladding to expand above. Details of measured beauty, which cannot be appreciated from photographs, provide the high points of the façade and set the logic of the structure against that of the cladding. The design is entirely focused on the value of surface and line. The uninterrupted base and the pilasters form a clean surface; the visible joints between the tiles covering the pilasters create a precise and regular pattern. Chamfered architectural components always play an important role in Berlage's designs; here they become a key element. Above the second floor, the surface of each pilaster evolves into the chamfer of a triangular prism. The pilasters follow a quick rhythm; the elements in the space between the pilasters—glass, full panels, etc.—are stepped down to five different depths. A narrow cornice separates the architrave of each window of the parapet from the solid panel above, and merges with the chamfered edge of the pilasters. There is only one purely decorative element, and it is very consistent: the solid panels under the windows feature a square lacunar that controls and reduces their mass in relation with the vertical space between the pilasters. To finish the façade, the pilasters are extended a little and a railing contrasts with the vertical element between the pilasters. Above the railing there are two more floors set back from the façade.

Before he undertook the commission for Kröller-Müller, Berlage had already experimented with some design elements of the London House, especially in the Meddens store in Hofweg at The Hague, dated 1913–15. There were three versions of the Meddens design, and the final building is more monumental in style than the Holland House, with sculptures by Lambertus Zijl.

The objectivity (Zakelijkheid) and noble style created by the refined design of the Holland House suggests several interpretations. It could be seen as a logical conclusion to Berlage's quest for realism combined with rationalism, which had come to fruition when he discovered American architecture. It could also be his answer to the requirements of idealism when applied to the contemporary theme of actual office buildings. It might be more accurate to regard it as a further expression of the dualism between realism and idealism. In his 1915 article quoted above,

16. Berlage and his team on the construction site of the Stock Exchange, 1901.

17. The Amsterdam Stock Exchange, 1896–1903, southern view when almost completed.

18. The Amsterdam Stock Exchange, 1896–1903, northern view of the Commodities Exchange hall before the laying of the floor.

19. *The Amsterdam Stock Exchange,*
1896–1903, southern view of the
Commodities Exchange hall, present
state.

20. *The Amsterdam Stock Exchange,*
1896–1903, the trusses of the roof of
the Commodities Exchange hall, present
state.

19

20

21. *The Amsterdam Stock Exchange, 1896–1903, detail of the gallery on the second floor of the Commodities Exchange hall, present state.*

22. *The Amsterdam Stock Exchange, 1896–1903, detail of the baluster of the stairs on the south-west side, present state.*

23. *The Amsterdam Stock Exchange, 1896–1903, detail of the static reinforcement of the arches on the ground floor of the Commodities Exchange (1906–09), present state.*

21

22

23

Van Loghem wrote that "the building for the Müller company in London is another significant example of the beginning of a period, with all the flaws related to such a stage. It is *zakelijk*, but not enough. While Berlage 'wants' to achieve objectivity, as an idealist he is unable to do so. This is how a dualism is born." Later, Havelaar saw the Meddens store and the Holland House as works "expressing something both inevitable and relentless. They are a tragic and firm protest against romanticism, a tragic and firm acceptance of reality." And he defined the Holland House as a "commercial fortress."

While Sullivan was the main source of inspiration for both the Meddens store and the Holland House, Wright's influence is more clearly felt in the works Berlage designed for the Kröller-Müllers between 1915 and 1917. In 1914 they commissioned a hunting lodge in Veluwe, halfway between Otterlo and Hoenderloo.[26] In this design Berlage used many themes characteristic of Wright's architecture: the articulate arrangement of masses and free-flowing spaces; the combination of horizontal, highly pitched, and conical roofs; and the windows grouped in series. They come together in a refined design highlighted by the logical texture of the walls. The "lodge" was to be called St. Hubertus. Hélène Kröller wished the layout and the front view to express the deep meaning of the legend of St. Hubert and extol the unity of matter and spirit. The building is shaped like the antlers of the legendary stag that appeared to the hunter Hubert. A tower, ninety feet high, stands at the center between the two branches and is reflected in the lake, a symbol of the cross on the deer's head.

This shape creates an inner courtyard facing the main entrance. In the spaces designed around the lodge, the structural components are arranged close to the ground; each component excludes the other in a succession of vistas, thus bringing out with maximum intensity the characteristics of each element. The tall tower is the only consistent point of reference for the arrangement of the lower parts of the building. The tower develops its full height when seen from afar and it appears as the only possible vertical element in the flat countryside, denying—so to speak—the presence of the low part of the building. In order to enhance this effect, the lower body is made even lower, almost disproportionate when compared to the tower. The expressive combination of differently shaped roofs reflects the structure of the building as a compact grouping of parts. The layout, lighting, decoration, materials, and colors of the rooms are planned as an intricate symbolic representation of the legend and spiritual life of St. Hubert. Everything must express the saint's road from doubt to wisdom, revelation, and peace. Whether inside or outside, Berlage used his favorite material—bricks—and played on its range of textures and colors. The brick becomes the basic element in the design of masses and details. The small columns in the windows, made of travertine, bring another touch of color. The lodge itself is only one part of a larger complex including a garage, stables, lodgings for the staff, and offices. Wright's influence can also be detected in these ancillary

buildings, as well as in the landscaping of the grounds and the design of an artificial lake.

By 1915 Hélène Kröller had decided to build her house-museum—which had first been planned for The Hague—at Hoenderloo in Veluwe. Berlage was then involved with the construction of the hunting lodge. It was only between 1917 and 1918 that he could undertake the design of a house-museum on a site in the Fransche Berg. This design still needs further study. It went through three phases, one dated May 1917, another December 1918, and the third January 1918. It is most significant for two reasons: it leads to a better understanding of the role played by Wright in Berlage's development, and it also offered Berlage an opportunity to combine the pragmatism of prior commissions with the idealism of his grand designs that were never built. He skillfully played on the varying levels of the site and developed different visual possibilities according to the double function of the building as a residence and a museum. The layout features recurring square shapes, inscribed crosses, and angles of 45 degrees, which allow the main areas to flow into the secondary ones. A distinction is created between spaces according to their function. Passageways, amenities, and baths form narrow rings around square spaces designed for important functions, some of which are two stories high and lit from above. On the outer edge, jutting triangular prowlike shapes are paired at the corners of the building through a diagonal arrangement of terraces on the second floor and hexagonal balconies on the third. Terraces complement the closed masses; solid horizontal strips are balanced by bands of glass. The traditional relationship between the horizontal and the vertical is superseded; and the accent on the horizontal is emphasized by linear cornices. The articulated arrangement of floors, made possible by a system of lighting from above and the pergolas around the main building, increase the structure's complexity. In the last version of the design, Berlage highlights the articulation of the construction and the different levels by developing the trellised terraces that run more closely along the building. He eliminates the pitched roofs and gables, and chooses square shapes for the entire building. He also introduces one of his favorite symbolic structures, the spire-tower-beacon, placed at the corners of the highest part of the central body. In this last version, he makes significant changes to the square main hall circled by a ring of galleries on each floor. He adds one floor, making the room almost a cube. He develops the continuous vertical structure, simplifying the relationship between vertical and horizontal components, and creates a continuity between the empty space at the center and the galleries surrounding it behind the vertical structure. Horizontal strips form cornices around the hall, cutting through the vertical elements. The walls of the ground floor are decorated by a series of sculptures and create a closed shell interrupted only by four entrances placed on two intersecting axes; the corners are bisected at an angle of 45 degrees by prismatic shapes bearing decorations and massive urns that reach to the second floor. The ceiling of the hall is made of a prismatic ar-

24

24. *The Amsterdam Stock Exchange, 1896–1903, detail of the gate in the passageway between the Exchanges, present state.*

rangement of surfaces, combined with a central square containing a small cupola in colored glass, which evokes the shape and symbolic meaning of a diamond.

The whole building is designed as scaled, interlocking volumes with wide terraces and wings radiating from the center. These long narrow parts feature porticoes or pergolas. On the south side of the building, they merge with the landscape; on the north side, they enclose a courtyard and form the wings of the library. The decorative fascia on the surface and the uninterrupted cornices play an important role. The flow of rooms creates an inner continuity. All these solutions betray Wright's influence, in particular that of the Midway Gardens in Chicago, built in 1913. Other details such as the cantilevered terraces above the pergolas on the south side of the building seem to be taken directly from Wright's Imperial Hotel in Tokyo. There are also precedents, however, in Berlage's own work: The progressively set-back terraces, for example, are already a major component of his 1908 design for an exhibition hall.

It was an uneasy collaboration between Berlage and Hélène Kröller, which came to an abrupt end in 1919, after six years. Just as Berlage's contract with the Kröller-Müllers had come at a propitious time, when he had no prospect of public commissions, the break occurred when he was finally about to be commissioned for a major public building. The director of the municipal art collection at The Hague, H.E. van Gelder, was a friend of long standing; they had met in the late 1890s through the socialist circle around the journal De Kroniek. He succeeded in persuading the municipality to commission Berlage for the design of a municipal museum. Between 1919 and the end of 1920 Berlage produced a first series of designs, which were variations on the same layout. He expanded the proposal of the municipality to include a museum of modern art, with a drawings and prints department; a museum of arts and crafts; a building for temporary exhibitions; a congress hall; and a hall for chamber music. His design for the Kröller-Müller museum was rich in idealistic implications. These became even more marked as he envisaged a public museum. He imagined a complex program necessitating the integration and collaboration between architecture, figurative arts, and music in a space devoted to meditation. The result is a layout based on a modular design, in which Berlage displayed his usual skill for diagonal arrangements and articulation of masses in harmony with the surrounding urban landscape. Although the architecture seems academic at first glance, it creates a complex sequence with calculated irregularities. Here Berlage renewed the whole concept of a museum from the point of view of urban design, typology, function, and aesthetics.

The interior layout of the museum takes into account the theories of museologist Benjamin Ives Gilman.[27] Rooms for special exhibitions and the permanent collection vary in shapes and grouping to avoid the monotony of traditional museums. The building is made up of wide wings forming a trapezium around a large central basin.[28] Side rooms of different sizes flow into the open central rooms; the latter are either rectangular or shaped on the Greek-cross plan. In the exterior design, each side room has a different shape, height, and roofing. The entrance halls are grand spaces crowned by a noble cupola; they encompass wide rooms varying in height and, on each floor, galleries that lead to the different parts of the museum. Once again, the outer design is ruled by an inner layout for which the word *functional* is too weak to convey its complex implications, both symbolic and formal.

This first series of designs for the museum in The Hague was rejected, and the office building for De Nederlanden van 1845 at The Hague was the first major work to be built after Berlage's contract with the Kröller-Müllers ended. He worked on the design between 1920 and 1922, and the building was put up between 1924 and 1927. Since 1904 Berlage had regarded the technique of reinforced concrete as crucial for the development of a new style, because it allowed for uninterrupted surfaces or "seamless walls." But it was not until the De Nederlanden building that he left the concrete structure exposed; he also freed the brick external walls of their loadbearing function and used concrete-framed glass bricks. He designed a modular structure, the logic of which is not mechanically ruled by function or size. While experimenting with new materials, he found a new freedom and a more complex relationship between the horizontal and the vertical. He created a system of linear elements to highlight both the structural framework and the different spaces that are filled with masonry. Double pilasters tightly line the ground floor facing the streets. On the second floor, a row of single pilasters are equal to half that of the pilasters on the floor below. The hall of the Stock Exchange had already featured such unusual relationship between the first and second floors. The same theme appears inside the De Nederlanden building: On two sides of court-like spaces, the narrow span between the pillars of the second floor is staggered on the other two sides.

The use of reinforced concrete did not eliminate decoration, but the ornaments consist of details of the structure and the finishings rather than elements added to the structure. Both the structure and some details in the finishings are in reinforced concrete. The pilasters are connected to the beams by an entablature of staggered overhangs, in a design that Berlage had explored earlier for the interior architecture of the museum in The Hague, the façade of the Voorwaarts Building in Rotterdam, and, even earlier, the hall of the Stock Exchange. From a purely structural point of view, this staggered entablature is redundant, mostly a device to highlight a building technique. It is therefore a decorative element, echoed in the thin vertical segments connected to a continuous narrow cornice housing the exterior shades. The concrete was mixed with a very coarse gravel imparting a unique texture to the finished surface. The boards of the forms in which the concrete was set imprinted vertical and horizontal lines on the exposed surface, creating patterns on the walls of the great court-like rooms. The light red bricks filling the reinforced-concrete frame are arranged in different patterns, and a black strip of glazed bricks outlines the structure. These decorative elements are

25. *Headquarters of the Diamond Workers' Union, Amsterdam, 1897–1900, drawing by J. Brié for* Studies over bouwkunst, stijl en samenleving, *Rotterdam 1910.*

26. *De Algemeene Building, Soerabaja, 1899–1900, view drawn by H.J.M. Walenkamp and published in* De Architect, *in 1902.*

27 *Headquarters of the Diamond Workers'*
Union, Amsterdam, 1897–1900, view
of the board room (mural paintings
by R.N. Roland Holst will cover the
white panels), 1912.

BESTUURSKAMER IN HET GEBOUW VAN DEN ALGEMEENEN NEDERLANDSCHEN DIAMANTBEWERKERSBOND TE AMSTERDAM

27

28. De Algemeene Building, Leipzig, 1901–02, view drawn by H.J.M. Walenkamp and published in De Architect, *1905.*

carefully distributed. The lines created by the casting forms appear only on some walls, generally the ones that are the least exposed to weathering, while the strips of black bricks are featured only on the ground floor.

The horizontal theme in the façade is reinforced by a division in two bands, one overhanging the other, and by the flat roof. Massive prisms made of concrete-framed glass bricks jut out around and above the main entrance: The ground floor is recessed and shaded by the second floor, and the glass walls form oriel windows with chamfered sides. The second floor is in full light; it creates an effect of continuity scanned by the rhythmic lines of cement. The structure housing the shades constitutes the only three-dimensional element. The clarity of the modular structure is set off by the recessed ground floor, the diagonal lines of the oriel windows, the chamfered edges, and the staggered entablature over the pilasters. The result is a refined geometry without rigidity, showing great stereometric precision in components of a strong general order.

Pilasters in the rear facing of the building are not differentiated from the architrave; they create an elaborate and linear structure of different right-angled modules. The surface of the clean, square volumes resembles beautiful pages of typography.

In his essay presenting the building, Berlage describes the interior layout as ruled by clear functions.[29] The unusual arrangement clearly echoes Wright's Larkin Building, but it is also derived from Berlage's experiments with the interior layout of the municipal museum in The Hague. It consists of a central hall in the shape of a cross, contrasting with two vast wings designed for open office space; these wide areas resemble inner courts and are set off by smaller rooms and individual offices. The relationship between main and ancillary spaces is similar to that in Wright's buildings. Finally, technical problems of lighting and microclimate are given remarkable attention.

In the De Nederlanden van 1845 building Berlage offered a new interpretation of themes that are constant in his architecture, the relationship between structure and decoration in particular. It was the beginning of a new phase that was to last until his death, and this creative approach found further expression in the work that immediately followed, the Church of Christ Scientist in The Hague.

Aside from the obviously symbolic tower, the design of the church did not feature the monumentality of Berlage's ideal designs. After Wright's Unity Temple and Wagner's Steinhof Church, the Church of Christ Scientist stands as another great lay interpretation of a religious theme. Rather than a house of worship, it is a public building, a meeting place for members of a rationalist religion. Here again, the structure in reinforced concrete is not mechanically functional. Unlike the De Nederlanden van 1845 building, the concrete is exposed in some places and in others is absorbed in the continuous cladding surface. The exterior arrangement is ruled by the function of each part of the building. The vast church, with a capacity of 700, is preceded by low horizontal buildings:

at the center, an entrance hall with a coat-room; on the left-hand side, the janitor's lodgings; and on the right-hand side, a monumental door separating the entrance hall from the wing designed along the canal for a Sunday school. Berlage made skillful use of the site, on dunes and water, giving different heights to the solid masses: The floor of the church is at the level of the terrace-roof of the school. For a better control of the design, Berlage drew elevations with a modular structure, outlining vertical rectangles and their diagonals, as he had done for the Stock Exchange. In the exterior design, the theme of seamless walls is interpreted anew and pushed to the limit. Horizontal and vertical strips of cement-framed glass bricks replace windows; they become part of the wall surface, and this integration of the windows into the walls is new. There are no ornaments. The decorative element lies in the relationship between cladding and structure, such as on the edges of the "wall-windows,"[30] where the luminous gray glass is in a composition with the strong green line of the cement frame and the light yellow of the brick walls. These "wall-windows" impart a new value to seamless walls, which become wide, clean surfaces. As a result, the church creates an effect of extraordinary precision. The careful calculation of the shearing stress molds all the details, and this is especially clear in the corners of the solids. The great hall combines the shapes of the square and the triangle (the latter pointing to the tower), and its corners are cut at an angle of 45 degrees. The resulting outline is unusual, calling to mind the cross-section of many solids in Berlage's designs, which are beautifully shaped by stereometric shearing, from the pilasters in the Holland House to the tower of the church itself.

The structure inside the church is partially covered. When structural elements are exposed, such as load-bearing slabs and carried elements, they become elements of design highlighting a structural logic. In the hall, where the passageways on different stories converge at the level of the tower, square ceramic tiles create a subtle play between the logic of the structure and that of the covering: The precise proportions of the modular concrete structure interact with the tiling, which covers the reinforced-concrete structure on the ground floor and leaves the separators exposed in the railings of the cantilevered landings. Linear elements and bare surfaces define different areas in the hall according to their function: altar, organ, stalls, and balconies. The ceiling brings out a structural arrangement based on the shape of the triangle; the skylight forms a ten-pointed star inscribed in a decagon, which may be seen as a two-dimensional interpretation of the facets of a diamond. The interior design is the result of a freer relationship between the exterior, the structure, and the covering, featuring both linear and flat elements. The cement-frame glass offers new possibilities for one of Berlage's favorite designs, diffused lighting from above; literally, light "comes from the walls."

Here again, these briefly outlined characteristics must be seen as the result of Berlage's exceptional ability to further his own experiments and absorb cultural and his-

LANDHUIS VAN DEN HEER ROLAND HOLST TE LAREN NOORD HOLLAND EN EDERLAND

29

PERSPECTIVE   PROJET POUR LE PALAIS DE LA PAIX   AVEC ENTOURAGE

30

31. *Hingst House, Amsterdam, 1907, general view.*

32. *Villa Salomonson, Baarn, 1909–10, perspective sketch.*

33. *Furnishing and decoration of a small meeting room for the World Fair in Brussels, 1910, plan of the design.*

PERSPECTIVISCHE SCHETS VAN EEN LANDHUIS VOOR DEN HEER SALOMONSON AAN DE BEAUFORTLAAN TE BAARN

32

HUIS AAN DEN KONINGINNEWEG TE AMSTERDAM 1907

31

33

*34. De Nederlanden van 1845 Building,
Rotterdam, 1911, perspective sketch.*

34

torical references. Bock has pointed to the significance of two designs preceding the Church of Christ Scientist: Victor Schröter's Protestant Church in St. Petersburg, dated 1873, and C. Börgemann's Notkirche in Hanover, dated 1891.[31] As for the example of Sullivan's St. Paul's Church in Cedar Rapids, Iowa, Berlage noted in "Amerikaansche Reisherinneringen": "Sullivan showed me a reproduction of a sketch for a Protestant church. . . . He started with the correct premise that a Protestant church must be an ideal meeting place, and he designed a semicircular shape, placing the tower in the center, above the pulpit."[32] For his church in The Hague, Berlage drew his inspiration both from Sullivan's church and from Wright's Unity Temple. The chunky shapes and the galleries circling a multistoried main hall are clearly reminiscent of Wright, as is the design of the main entrance and the furniture. Wright's layout divides large groups of people into smaller ones, and Berlage skillfully adopted the same approach for the hall of the church and the school; the latter is divided in small stands along its long side.

Constructed in the mid-1920s, the church stands as a significant work illustrating the complex relationship between Berlage, Wright, and rationalism. Some elements in its design are simplified according to a rationalist idiom, but they have their roots in past works by Berlage. It is also clear, however, that Piet Zwart played an important role in the final design, the interior design in particular. Zwart worked with Berlage from 1921 until 1927. There are many sketches bearing his signature for such details as the skylight of the portico, the lamps, and the pulpit. They are a splendid functionalist reinterpretation of similar elements in Wright's Unity Temple. It would also be interesting to establish how decisions were made to use such new materials typical of aesthetic functionalism as concrete-framed glass bricks, rubber tiles for the floor in the hall, and iron for the edges of the furnishings. Some purely decorative elements remained and were absorbed in a consistent totality, such as the stained-glass skylight in the hall, another reference to the Unity Temple, or—in the exterior design—the bell tower, the lamp post at the corner of the school, and the small majolica tiles on some edges. These are elements belonging to Berlage's mature style, with roots in his early works, and they are also his personal interpretation of the geometry in the *Nieuwe Kunst* culture.

Although Berlage produced several significant works in the 1920s, this period in his career has its share of shadows as well as light. Around 1926, Berlage fell victim to some of the worse mechanisms of his profession, as can be seen in the Mercatorplein. He accepted a commission for the Rijksverzekeringbank in the south of Amsterdam, on a site provided by the municipality, and the press voiced protests against the selection of that site for the erection of such a monumental building. The office building of the Amsterdamsche Bank, designed with W.B. Ouëndag, is a dull and heavy work—in spite of skillful alignments—and it was not well received. It is also surprising that in 1929 Berlage should enter the competition for the development of the area around Allebéplein in Amsterdam.[33]

Berlage's design for a new bridge on the Amstel, a commission he received in the beginning of 1926, is more interesting. It is on the axis of his Y shaped development plan for the south of Amsterdam. Showing his full measure as an urban planner, Berlage integrated the bridge in a design wider than this mere stretch of the Amstel. The new bridge was to be fairly close to the existing Scholen Bridge; for this reason, he decided not to build an incline and to raise the area along the canal and between the two bridges, the Weesperzijde, with terraces over moorings. He created a great basin for water sports, with walls, arches, and pilasters, which could make the architectural transition between the city and the open countryside. Stairs on either end of the bridge lead to walks along the water, under the walls of the banks. On the side of the Amsteldijk, the walk leads to a beautifully designed pavilion reminiscent of Wright.

Berlage's ambitious designs of 1919–20 for the museum in The Hague did not come to fruition. He was able to prepare another design between the end of 1927 and 1929. Construction started in March 1931, and the work was completed after his death by his son-in-law, the Swiss architect Emil E. Strasser. Berlage had to eliminate from his new design the multifunctional complexity of the previous one. In 1919 he had conceived of a larger system of buildings arranged on the edge of a wide irregular site. Now the museum is placed in the middle of the site, and for this reason it does not try to become part of the urban landscape. It follows two basic rules of distribution of space:[34] The administrative building is separate from the museum itself; and the rooms for temporary exhibitions and the permanent collection are regrouped as they were in the previous design, in order to avoid the boring succession of rooms typical of traditional museums. A shorter gallery encircles an inner courtyard; passageways at a right angle from the gallery cross two series of rooms, and the visitor is not obliged to walk through too many rooms in order to find the one that interests him.

The entrance is a glassed-in pergola leading to a vestibule, with, on either side, a basin in the garden. Beyond the vestibule, a hall, two stories high, leads to three series of contiguous and often connected rooms. In the center of each series of rooms, free-standing pilasters with a square or chamfered section create a Greek-cross design as well as an uninterrupted flow through the museum. If the stairs and air shafts in the corners are taken into account, the whole design is based on the shape of the Greek cross inscribed in a square or a rectangle. Two characteristics are carried over from the 1919 version: the lateral lighting from above, and the different height and size of the rooms according to their function. First there is a passageway with benches and showcases along the sides; small rooms are connected to the passageway, and they lead to larger exhibition rooms. The passageway is thus connected to five groups of three small rooms.

The hall has great dignity. It is divided into three areas and crossed by passageways on different levels. The concept of space remained fairly constant from the first to the second design, but Berlage's architectural idiom evolved toward a beautifully clear rationalism and a rigorous simplicity of volumes, reminiscent of Wright's geometry. The different views of the hall that were drawn for the second design chart this evolution: The exposed concrete structure creates a simple arrangement of vertical and horizontal lines; there is a continuity between the different areas and levels; the careful distribution of the sources of light above gives a scansion to the structure and the arrangement of space; and finally, linear elements—in the floor, the walls, the ceiling, and the uninterrupted plinth at the base of the vertical structures—highlight this clean geometry.

The exterior design is again ruled by the interior layout and the distribution and articulation of the different functions. When compared to the 1919 version, the later design adds balconies, pergolas, glass walls and cases, and jutting or recessed volumes. It presents an arrangement of square, stepped solids, a subtle play between symmetry and asymmetry, and it is related to the basic interior layout on a Greek-cross plan. The volumes are either grouped or separate, in a logical relationship clearly inspired by Wright's Unity Temple. The drawing of the elevations is regulated by a modular grid made of squares and isosceles triangles. The chimneys of the heating unit and the lamps at the entrance are shaped like towers, as a reminder of the more ambitious symbolism in the first design.

The facing on the cement structure constitutes the main element of style in the exterior design. The size of the module used throughout the building is 43″ x 43″, based on the size of the bricks used for the facing. Exposing the structure, as it is done in the interior design, could result in a dichotomy between the interior and the cladding. In order to avoid such contradiction, the bricks do not highlight structural elements. They are used as a textured covering, creating abstract patterns. Obviously the wall surfaces are not loadbearing, and their function lies in their texture. Bricks laid in bed and bricks laid in edge form alternate courses. On the higher part of the walls, cracks left in the arrangement produce an effect resembling that of quilting. On the ground floor, where the showcases stand, the wall juts out and the horizontal and vertical courses of bricks become the weft and warp of a weaving pattern. The continuity and texture of the brick surfaces are the more effective because Berlage eliminated cornices and frames from the glazed surfaces. Instead, he carefully designed the edges: The distance between the wall and the slightly recessed glass is broken by a narrow strip of horizontally laid bricks.

In the second half of July 1928, the small municipality of Usquert, near Groningen, with a population of 1700, commissioned Berlage for a new town hall to be built on a site away from the center of the village.[35] This is a small building, in which Berlage successfully avoided any rhetoric and combined the traditional needs of a town hall with a clearly functional program. With great mastery, his design took the urban landscape into account while it consistently expressed the organization of the different functions contained in the building. In spite of the very short time—the first drawings are dated Feb-

35

35. *Holland House, London, 1914–16, perspective view.*

36. Meddens en Zoon Department Store,
The Hague, 1913–15, view dated June
1914.

MAGAZIJN DER FIRMA MEDDENS EN ZOON AAN DEN NIEUWEN VERKEERSWEG SPUI-BUITENHOF TE 's GRAVENHAGE

MEDDENS EN ZOON HIGH ART CLOTHING MEDDENS EN ZOON HEERENMODES

36

37

38

37. *Hunting lodge St. Hubertus, Hoenderloo, 1914–20, view dated 1916.*

38. *Hunting lodge St. Hubertus, Hoenderloo, 1914–20, present view of the inner courtyard with the kennel.*

39. *Hunting lodge St. Hubertus, Hoenderloo, 1914–20, A.G. Müller's study, interior, 1917.*

40. *Hunting lodge St. Hubertus, Hoenderloo, 1914–20, Hélène Kröller's study, interior, 1917.*

ZITKAMER VAN DEN HEER DES HUIZES IN HET LANDHUIS ST. HUBERTUS.

39

ZITKAMER VAN DE VROUW DES HUIZES IN HET LANDHUIS ST. HUBERTUS.

40

41. Municipal Museum, The Hague, 1919–20 and 1928–35, view of the main entrance in the first design, 1920.

PLAN voor het GEMEENTE MUSEUM HOOFDINGANG

41

ruary 1929; construction started in March of the same year, and work was completed at the beginning of 1930—there is a series of drawings developing his initial intuition. We know of at least five stages in the design. Berlage started with the idea of a cubic shape with a tower in the center, corresponding to a core connecting the different functional areas fitted into the building. This evolved into an arrangement of independent solids, the individual shapes of which are clearly responding to their respective function. The core—halls on the ground and first floors—is displaced to the west, while a wing on the east side of the building is designed for official functions: on the ground floor, the offices of the mayor and the secretary, and on the second floor, the council room. This wing is higher than the other part of the building by one module, that is, 43 inches. The less important functions are located in the corner of the west side of the building, which is therefore smaller and simpler in detail. In the third version of the design, the tower is moved from the center of the cube to the façade on the south side of the building. It becomes a separate solid, rising from the ground, and one of the faces of its clock looks toward the center of the village. Such a tower in the center of the façade was already featured in the church in The Hague and again in 1929 in the design for the town hall in The Hague, done with J. Limburg, the tower of which is flanked on either side by tall lamp posts or beacons. The angle of the oblique side of the tower in the Usquert building is parallel to the alignment of the corners of the buildings on the two adjacent lots (this alignment is featured in the drawing on a scale of 1:500). Berlage also designed a garden with a wall and two entrances on either side, and a lawn in the continuation of the entrance and the tower. In December 1929, the tower was already built when Berlage wanted to raise it by two modules, or seven feet. When the municipal administration argued that this was financially difficult, he even offered to take charge of the additional expenditures. P. Karstkarel and R. Terpstra noted that Berlage wanted the town hall to stand out from the surrounding villas, which were more or less of the same size. For that reason he made the tower disproportionately tall when compared with the lower part of the building, as he had done in the hunting lodge St. Hubertus. For the same reason, the first drawing already featured symbolic decorations expressing the official role of the building: the light on the tower, the coat of arms, the flagstaff, and the weathervane. The entrance is almost at the center of the façade. It is anything but monumental: Sheltered by a slab awning, it is a recessed and narrow opening between the tower and the prowlike projection of the east wing. The shape of a prow inscribed in an octagonal layout occurs frequently in Berlage's work, from the Henny Villa to the museum in The Hague. It characterizes the more official part of the façade and echoes the chamfered upper part of the tower. The bicycle shed and the treasury form a smaller solid added to the building. Like the ancillary building in the Church of Christ Scientist, the treasury is covered by a pergola. In the

42. *Municipal Museum, The Hague,*
    1919–20 and 1928–35, view of the
    courtyard with gallery and basin in the
    first design, 1920.

42

43. Municipal Museum, The Hague, 1919–20 and 1928–35, view of the central hall in the first design, 1920.

exterior design, the wall surface is very simple but just as rigorous as in preceding works, with special care given to the edges. Like the museum in The Hague, on which Berlage was working at the time, the walls are based on a 43″ x 43″ square module defined by the size of the bricks, but the walls are loadbearing. Inside, the hall and the stairs form a truncated cross with three arms. On the ground floor, the arms of this cross contain respectively, the entrance on the south side, a waiting room on the north side, and the stairs on the west side; in the center, the hall is defined by four free-standing pilasters connected to the stairs above. On the second floor, the central hall is connected on either side to symmetrical coat rooms; it gets light from a central stained-glass skylight and high windows in the back of these rooms. This layout of the hall and the double volume of the open stairs create a flowing space compensating for the apparent rigidity of the floor plan and reminiscent of the church in The Hague. The exposed structure of the roof, the floor and wall covering, and the railings also recall the sparse inner geometry of the church. Doors to ancillary rooms are set in the trimmed corners of the hall, thus outlining the diagonal axes that are featured in the first sketches.[36]

From the beginning of his career on, Berlage consistently explored the possibility of an architectural idiom based on a dialectic relationship between mass (as the product of the building process), and function on the one hand, and dematerialization and decoration on the other. His work is deeply rooted in this relationship and it should be regarded as pioneering, although it was often criticized as insufficiently daring by architects belonging either to Expressionism or Rationalism, to the Amsterdam School or the *Nieuwe Zakelijkheid*. Berlage himself always kept at a distance from either school. He recognized their importance but also rejected all excesses, as can be seen from an analysis of his behavior during the "affair" of the competition for the Society of Nations building in Geneva or his participation in La Sarraz's CIAM.

It is significant that the most radical architects in the *Nieuwe Zakelijkheid*, such as Mart Stam, should take the most consistent position against Berlage in 1927. Other radicals with a more complex experience, however, and whose ideology was less narrow, such as Van Loghem and Duiker, formulated more subtle criticisms. The relationship to Berlage became particularly important at the beginning of the 1930s, when the first signs could be felt of an approaching crisis in the rationalism of the *Nieuwe Zakelijkheid*. In 1931, Berlage commented favorably in *Bouwkundig Weekblad Architectura* on Wijdeveld's initiative to start "a new international laboratory"; he wrote that the spiritual development of the modern world runs the risk of "falling into constructivism."[37] In an interview published on February 13, 1932, in *Vooruit*, he criticized the rationalists for their lack of feeling, the limitation of their attention to technical considerations, and their rejection of decoration. "I do not see the *Nieuwe Zakelijkheid* as a means," he said, "but as an end. It is the symbol of the end of bourgeois society. . . . Problems cannot be resolved with such slogans as the ones Germans are so

44. *Municipal Museum, The Hague,
1919–20 and 1928–35, view of an
exhibition room in the second design,
1929.*

44

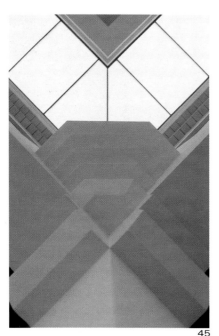

45

46

keen on. The supporters of the *Nieuwe Zakelijkheid* claim that 'Architecture starts where ornament ends.' . . . This is sheer arrogance, because it is tantamount to saying, 'Before us, nothing good was built.' . . . I should like to answer, 'Art begins where technique ends.' The summit in architectural style is reached when complete harmony is achieved between rationality and feeling. . . . Capitalism has no spiritual content. . . . Only after the end of capitalism can a new style of life be possible."

In an article published in *De 8 en Opbouw*, Duiker includes Berlage's whole interview and tries to respond to his criticism. He makes a distinction between "financial economy" and "spiritual economy": The latter "pushes the building to the limit, it depends on the materials used, and it always develops toward dematerialization and spiritualization." Using this distinction, Duiker offers a new approach to Berlage's work: "Dr. Berlage, why is the grouping of openings in your buildings so different from that in the designs of your imitators? Because of a thin brick pilaster. One could speak of a contrast; the small pilaster speaks for the architectural potential of bricks. And why did you design the lower arches in the hall of the Stock Exchange as a loadbearing structure, the shape of which shape is so taut that it needed to be 'materialized'? Because inspiration, intuition, feeling, artistic ability—however you wish to call it—has brought you to the supreme technical possibilities and defined the spiritual value of the resulting architecture. It is incorrect to say that 'Art begins where technique ends.' Because in the history of technology as elsewhere, inspiration, etc. . . . precedes material definition. . . . But *the development of an impulse has a cultural value only if the laws of economics are followed.*"[38] Duiker differentiates between functionalism and its poor imitations. His arguments, however, and even his distinction between financial and spiritual economy, could be regarded as a logical development of Berlage's ideal principles rather than a criticism.

In 1935 the first signs of divergence appeared in the group around the review *De 8 en Opbouw*. In 1938 Sybold van Ravesteyn, followed by Arthur Staal and other young architects, left the group and claimed that it was necessary to return to monumental architecture, ornaments, and symbolism, as a protest against the dryness of the Functionalists' theses and their rigid architecture. Van Loghem and Van Tijen tried to stem the crisis. They claimed to have their roots "in the pioneering work in which the younger generation did not take part and of which they know only the last phase."[39] Van Loghem's writings, from the above-mentioned commentary of 1915 to the book *Bouwen* of 1932, show him to be the one among the critics who has reflected the most on his relationship to Berlage. In a major article on the crisis within the group De 8, he wrote, "In order to understand the differences of opinion in our group, it is necessary to understand that art has and always will oscillate between realism and symbolism."[40]

We must note that at this dramatic time in the history of Dutch modernism, Van Loghem refrained from taking a dogmatic and exclusive position. He recognized the dualism in Dutch architectural culture, and particularly in such architects as Berlage and himself. This recognition, however, did not mean that he did not choose one or the other term of the duality. He claimed that the "realism" of *Nieuwe Bouwen* responds to a moral awareness of contemporary conditions, which do not allow for symbolism. "Really great architecture should be symbolic, but our times do not have any great common symbols, therefore no contemporary monumental architecture can be created. We should be grateful that this century has seen such innovators as Berlage, De Bazel, later the group De Stijl, the *Nieuwe Zakelijkheid*, and CIAM. Our switch from individual to group work is proof that realism has become a common value in present architecture; a first step, however tentative, has been taken toward the creation of a common orientation."[41]

48. De Nederlanden van 1845 Building,
    The Hague, 1920–27, the construction
    site.

49. De Nederlanden van 1845 Building,
    The Hague, 1920–27, advertisement
    drawn by H.J.M. Walenkamp, 1930.

48

49

50. *De Nederlanden van 1845 Building, The Hague, 1920–27, detail of the oriel window on the lower floor with the protective railing, present state.*

51. *De Nederlanden van 1845 Building, The Hague, 1920–27, main entrance, present state.*

50

51

52

52. Glazed wall elements for Mercatorplein, Amsterdam, 1924–27, photograph of the construction site.

53. Church of Christ Scientist, The Hague, 1925–26, elevation.

54. Church of Christ Scientist, The Hague, 1925–26, aerial view.

55. Church of Christ Scientist, The Hague, 1925–26, present state.

1. E. Persico 1935, p. 7.
2. J. Havelaar 1927.
3. M. Bock 1983, p. 16.
4. Ibid., p. 71.
5. Berlage wrote in "P.J.H. Cuypers" in 1917, paraphrasing Goethe, "The value of a work is not derived from the manner in which someone does something, but from the fact that others can draw from this work elements for their own fruitful creation."
6. P. Singelenberg 1972, p. 63.
7. M. Bock 1983, pp. 124–ff.
8. M. Eisler 1919, pp. 10–11.
9. For the significance of geometry in Berlage's work, see M. Bock 1983, pp. 69–70.
10. This combination of mass and immateriality is evident in the texture of the inner brick walls and the openings pierced in the outer railings, which can be found in several works of the same period. It is not a coincidence that Gerrit Thomas Rietveld, in an article published in *De 8 en Opbouw* and written on the occasion of Berlage's death in 1938, added to his brief text a drawing of the openings in the railing of the Stock Exchange. The significance of this testimony by Rietveld was noted in G. Fanelli 1978, p. 490, and M. Bock 1983, p. 22.
11. A.W. Reinink 1970, *American Influence on Late Nineteenth-Century Architecture in the Netherlands*, p. 165; P. Singelenberg 1972, passim; M. Bock 1983, passim.
12. A.W. Reinink 1970, *Berlage en Viollet-le-Duc*, pp. 156–63.

13. H.P. Berlage 1912, "Amerikaansche Reisherinneringen."
14. Berlage's works at Bergen deserve to be studied more and documented better. Only the post office is usually mentioned in the chronologies. Liliana Grueff was so kind as to bring to my attention designs for the train station, the hotel "Nassau-Bergen" (in collaboration with J.C. van Epen), and a few private houses.
15. In this article, Van Loghem's aesthetic theory of ornament seems related to post-Hegelian philosophy and to Goethe. For a more detailed analysis of Van Loghem's text, see G. Fanelli 1978, pp. 33–35.
16. C.J. Blaauw 1917, p. 10.
17. Quoted in G. Fanelli 1978, p. 231.
18. For Wright's influence in the Netherland, and on Berlage in particular, see G. Fanelli 1968; G. Fanelli 1978; E. Godoli, *Jan Wils, Frank Lloyd Wright e De Stijl*, Florence 1980.
19. H.P. Berlage 1912, op. cit., p. 157.
20. Ibid., p. 149.
21. Ibid., p. 151.
22. A 1910 drawing for the façade of the offices of De Nederlanden van 1845 in Rotterdam follows a design that is closer to American models than the actual building was to be. It emphasizes a rhythmic division of surfaces and verticality.
23. H.P. Berlage 1912, op. cit., p. 130.
24. Ibid., p. 158.
25. Ibid., p. 159.
26. See S. van Deventer 1956, and M. Gunnink 1985, for notes on this work.

27. See P. Singelenberg, "Het Haags Gemeentemuseum, De geschiednis van Berlage's museumbouw," in AA.VV. 1975, *H.P. Berlage 1856–1934. Een bouwmeester en zijn tijd*. Useful data on the museum can also be found in H.E. van Gelder 1921, "Bij de Museum-ontwerpen."
28. The idea of a pool of water as part of the design may have come from Wright, from his Coonley House in particular. However, Berlage used it also for the hunting lodge St. Hubertus and his design of a museum for the Kröller-Müllers.
29. Quoted in C.M. van Moorsel 1927, "Het nieuwe gebouw van de Nederlanden in Den Haag," p. 153.
30. To use J. Havelaar's terminology, 1927.
31. M. Bock, 1983, pp. 134–35.
32. H.P. Berlage, 1912, op. cit., p. 151.
33. G. Fanelli 1978, pp. 306, 320, 400–01, 458.
34. H.E. van Gelder, *Toelichting tot de ontwerpen van Dr. H.P. Berlage voor het nieuwe museum*, The Hague, n.d.
35. P. Karstkarel and R. Terpstra 1980.
36. Ibid., p. 32.
37. Quoted in G. Fanelli 1978, p. 423.
38. J. Duiker 1932, p. 45.
39. J.B. van Loghem, "Beschouwing," in *De 8 en Opbouw* X, 1939, 1, p. 17.
40. J.B. van Loghem, "Sticht 'De 8' verwarring?" *De 8 en Opbouw* X, 1939, 1, p. 17.
41. Ibid., p. 19.

53

54

55

Berlage and the Culture of City Planning

Vincent van Rossem

Berlage stated throughout his career that urban planning should approach "the urban character as a whole" and not an "isolated designs of streets and squares." In other words, one should not limit oneself to an allotted site; one must think out what will be built. With such a premise, Berlage designed his first plan of the south of Amsterdam; while it still belonged to the nineteenth century in its general lines, it also aimed at protecting "the urban character as a whole" from the unpleasant view of poor architectural quality. Indeed it was a thoughtful design, another proof that by 1900 Berlage was an experienced urban planner.[1] His 1893 lecture "Bouwkunst en impressionisme" and his 1895–96 design for the "Museumplein" in Amsterdam had already shown that he was fully aware of contemporary issues in planning, that he had thought of some solutions, and that he could be innovative.

He presented his first plan for the south of Amsterdam in a lecture given in November 1904, and he had clearly embraced a theory of urban planning that was as realistic as possible. He explained that Amsterdam could not be further developed in concentric circles, and he demonstrated the same realism and understanding of urban conditions as he had ten years before, when he was advocating "impressionistic" building. By 1900 Berlage had subscribed to Joseph Stübben's pragmatism. This had not come easily to him, and it put a stop to his impetuous ideas of the early 1890s. He had to come to terms with politically conservative constraints and the fact that the average architect was still working in the spirit of the nineteenth century. His obvious unhappiness with such compromise led him to a new approach, with the possible prodding of J.H.W. Leliman's criticism of his 1904 plan.

After 1904, Berlage incorporated the history of urban planning into his own theory—and it should be noted that this gave him an opportunity to return to the theme of "Bouwkunst en impressionisme." He began with a fairly neutral but sweeping overview of the city's history, in which he saw persuasive arguments for the outline of blocks. Therefore the history of planning itself, rather than one "reformer of the arts," appeared to point prophetically to the building of "impressionistic" blocks of edifices.

Berlage's theory of urban planning found its definitive form in the lecture "Stedenbouw" he gave in the fall of 1908, in Delft, in which he included elements of an essay, also dating from 1908, on the theory of architectural styles, "Grundlagen und Entwicklung der Architektur."

Clearly, Berlage took an avant-garde stance in "Stedenbouw." A few months later, when he was in Düsseldorf to give the same lecture in German, he discovered that he was not alone in preferring a geometric plan—or, in historical terms, a Baroque plan. The German historian A.E. Brinckmann had come to the same conclusion in his book *Platz und Monument*, in which he dwelled on the idea that European urban planning had reached new heights during the Baroque period. This aesthetic and historical approach was to be widely adopted in the following years. It even became the dominant approach, until pioneering theoreticians of the 1920s rebelled in the name of functionalism in urban planning. In his fourth "Stedenbouw" lecture, delivered in the winter of 1913–14, Berlage clearly took into account the most recent German literature, and Brinckmann's ideas in particular.

In March 1892, Berlage had already put forward his interpretation of a fundamental book by the Austrian architect Camillo Sitte, *Der Städtebau nach seinen künstlerischen Grundsätzen.*[2] It is almost certain, however, that Berlage was prompted by the review of another book to discuss Sitte's work.[3] In 1890, Stübben published *Der Städtebau*, a substantial handbook in which he discussed the complexities of urban planning as well as its technical problems.[4] Karl Henrici reviewed Stübben's book in the *Deutsche Bauzeitung*, a journal that Berlage read regularly.[5] This review, and Stübben's answer, provoked a discussion that was to last until the end of the 1890s. In order to bring his book up to date, Stübben had considered Sitte's most recent ideas. In his review, Henrici noted that there were two contradicting approaches to urban planning: on the one hand, Sitte's modern "system," and on the other, obsolete nineteenth-century principles, to which Stübben was still attached in spite of some effort toward innovation. Therefore Henrici and Stübben propounded two different interpretations of Sitte's book. According to Henrici, Sitte was a revolutionary because he placed ideal goals above speculation and a preoccupation with traffic. Stübben noted that Henrici could propose such an interpretation because he was free from "the worry and experience of actual urban planning;" he himself read Sitte's book as an eloquent and persuasive argument for more aesthetic components in the design of realistic urban plans.

In all likelihood, this discussion induced Berlage to reconsider the content of Sitte's book. He did not mention this in his lecture, strangely enough, as if he were not

45

aware of the polemics between Henrici and Stübben. He had no taste for methodological discussions, and his thinking pertaining to Sitte took another orientation. Berlage was less interested in urban planning as such than in architecture's function in urban planning. The heart of the matter was formulated by Sitte and was repeated by Berlage in 1892: "In modern urban planning the relationship between built and open space has been reversed. In the past, open space—streets and squares—created a closed and expressive design. Today the building plots are arranged as regular self-contained shapes, and whatever is left becomes street or square."[6] Sitte alluded to the aesthetic problems and possibilities of urban space, an aspect of planning that played only a secondary role in the eighteenth century but acquired an increasing importance in the nineteenth century. To regard public space as an architectural problem implied that the façade of each building be designed to integrate elements that are part of the design of streets and squares. When he again turned his attention to this issue, Berlage showed that he had more insight into the nature of Sitte's ideas than his German colleagues, who had heated arguments over the issue.

Sitte's proposal hinged on a correct assessment of the role played by squares. He suggested that the first step in an urban plan was the design of "several main squares, with their precise respective shape and size." In a second step he determined "the fillers between the high points thus created."[7] Berlage advocated the same method. In the summer of 1893, however, he came to the conclusion that the design of open spaces is less problematic than that of the "fillers," the buildings between these open spaces.[8] Since traditional urban planning limited itself to monumental squares, new solutions must be found for the residential areas between squares. In November 1893, Berlage spoke of "Architecture and Impressionism" before an audience that must have listened with disbelief and growing surprise. In his opening remark, he noted that low-priced housing units needed to be built on an enormous scale in modern cities, with efficient allotments and blocks. He spoke of an urban character in which conventional architectural detail had become inappropriate. Residential blocks—mass buildings—forced the architect to think in terms of great units and ample lines. Berlage's prophetic statements regarding "blocks of buildings" found few sympathetic ears at the time. Only later did it become clear that the elimination of one-family houses and their individual façades was an essential element of modern urban character, and more years were to pass before the concept of a single design for a whole street gained ground. In 1903, in Germany, Karl Scheffler came up against a wall of incomprehension when he put forward similar ideas.[9] In 1904 Berlage ridiculed the anachronism of "buildings designed for pomp" and "boulevards where façades compete with each other." Architects were reluctant to accept the idea of residential massing in city blocks, and they were persuaded only by historical arguments, especially Brinckmann's appreciation—solidly based on art history—of the grand order of Baroque cities.

It is necessary to go back to the beginning of the century to better understand the lecture Berlage gave on November 14, 1904, before the association "Het Koggeschip," in which he presented his first development plan for the south of Amsterdam. In a secret meeting on March 8, 1900, the municipal council of Amsterdam shot down the plan designed for the south of the city by the director of public works, a civil engineer. The council felt that the new development must be more attractive and that, being both a commercial city and an art center, Amsterdam must maintain its cultural image. Public opinion was bemoaning the monotony of new developments, and this caught the attention of public administrators. It was well known that an increasing number of people were leaving the city for the 't Gooi and the dunes. A development plan was needed that would induce the well-to-do classes to remain and pay their taxes in the city. The new neighborhood had to have a stylish design and greenery that would attract those who were leaving the center of town and seeking refuge in a more natural surrounding. The plan prepared by the office of public works did not satisfy such requirements; it included some open space, but it was merely a development of the ugliest neighborhood of the city, known as the "Pijp." The council was pressed for time and, on March 28, it commissioned Berlage for another plan.

The new plan was presented to the public in the summer of 1904. It was badly received. The most articulate criticism was voiced by Leliman, who felt that Berlage's design resembled that of a "medieval neighborhood" because it was inspired by "some of Sitte's theories." He thought that it was not realistic to center a plan around a monumental square, thereby echoing Stübben's objection to Henrici's plan of Munich.[10] Leliman noted also that other models than the medieval one could achieve a dense urban texture, such as cities of the seventeenth and eighteenth centuries. "We know from everyday experience the seventeenth-century layout," Leliman wrote, clearly thinking of the belt of canals around Amsterdam. "Let us hear what Sitte thinks about the artistic quality of urban planning inherited from the much disparaged Baroque period."[11] He then quoted Sitte's remarks on the functional aspect of Baroque urban planning and criticized Berlage for ignoring them: "Berlage's plan does not foresee any thoroughfare; almost all the streets, even the most important one, are contrived, with arbitrary twists and turns. There are turns even in streets that are only one block long."[12] All this, Leliman added, surprised the critics, who could not believe that it was Berlage's work.

On November 14, Berlage defended himself in the face of such harsh criticism. He addressed himself to historicists who depict the growth of Amsterdam as an unlimited development of the concentric belt of canals. Gosschalk, H. Walenkamp, and J.H.W. Leliman all agreed: The seventeenth-century concentric system of canals had to be the point of departure for any new plan. Berlage disagreed. While he admired past urban planning, he claimed that there were now fewer historical reasons for such a type of planning. In those days wide canals

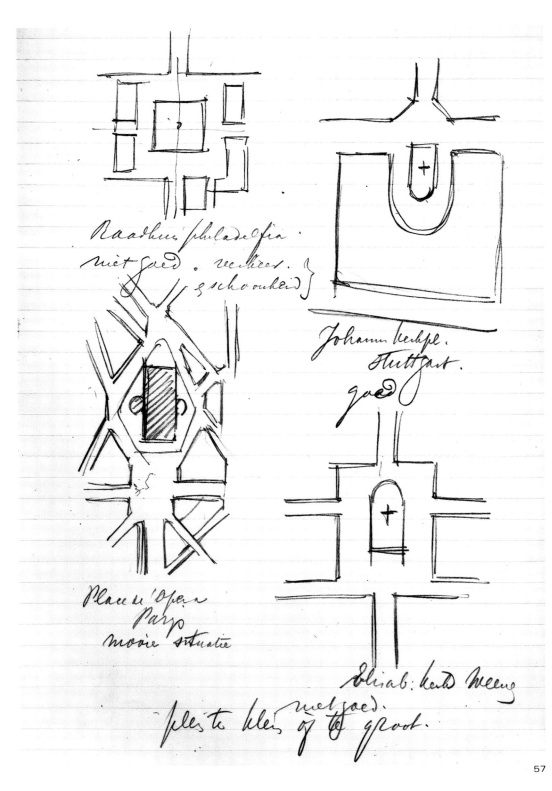

57. *Sketches of squares, manuscript of the
lecture "Straten en pleinen," drawn
from Stübben's* Der Städtebau.

Raadhuis philadelfia.
niet goed. rechtees.
[gschoonheid]

Johann verkfl.
Stuttgart.
goed

Plaan Open
Parp
mooie situatie

Elisab: kerk weeng
niet goed.
plei ti kleen of te groot.

were created, separated by long blocks; the streets radiating from the canals had a secondary role and were not the structure of the neighborhood. Now everything has changed, Berlage stated. Streets radiating from the canals have developed into the city's thoroughfares. Modern cities become monotonous when they develop according to a concentric plan and feature a modern architecture with short blocks and narrow streets. Moreover, the concentric streets south and southeast of the city run from east to west, and houses have the least favorable exposure. Finally, these streets are inevitably long and allow the wind to stir up a lot of dust.

These were concrete and irrefutable arguments that Berlage found in Stübben's book. He also had arguments of an aesthetic nature. In 1883 Berlage had said that he particularly liked the Herengracht, which was the shortest and most central canal in the seventeenth century part of the city. In 1904 he observed that the outermost canal, the Prinsengracht, "was long enough." In other words, the "picturesque" architecture, which was acceptable along the Herengracht, created an unpleasant impression of chaos along the Prinsengracht. A new concentric development would require a "monumental" architecture. This was the heart of the aesthetic problem that Berlage had to confront in his plan for the south of Amsterdam: The architecture of such a development would respond mostly to real estate speculation and could not be suitably monumental for a grand plan. Moreover, Berlage noted, "the Dutch by temperament prefer the picturesque; the monumental never flourished in our country."[13] This is the reason why he gave up, albeit reluctantly, what he called "a systematic plan."

We may question the validity of Leliman's criticisms and wonder whether Berlage's plan really resembled that of a medieval neighborhood or which theories of Sitte he ignored. As a matter of fact, Berlage's plan had little in common with a medieval layout; it featured a low-density architecture that belongs more to the nineteenth century than the Middle Ages. Sitte had enclosed his open spaces in the blocks of apartment houses, while Berlage's parks and open spaces determined the whole urban character. The general philosophy behind the plan has its origins less in Sitte's ideas than in English models, as they were described in Stübben's article, "Die Einseitigkeit im Städtebau und ihre Folgen." Berlage had always been partial to designs with parks and trees. In 1881, on a hot July day in Venice, he perhaps was feeling some nostalgia for cool Dutch cities when he compared the Grand Canal with the Herengracht in his diary: "An impartial judge might still award the prize to the Herengracht, although the palaces on the Grand Canal would, of course, win, and life on the Venetian waters is much more fun. But a Venetian might perhaps envy the somber gravity of the majestic row of trees which overshadow the patrician houses of Amsterdam and mirror themselves in the water."[14] Berlage returned to this theme in the lecture "Amsterdam en Venetië," when he remarked on the monumental possibilities of trees. A great tree by itself is a monument, he stated, but a forest is not. A forest is

57

"an extremely picturesque group, because the trees seem to be arranged according to no discernible rule. Then comes man. Man takes the trees that are made available to him by nature and he aligns them in two rows. He creates a lane, hence a monumental group."[15] Although the Herengracht did not have monumental buildings, Berlage judged it to be more beautiful than the Grand Canal because it featured majestic trees, and he linked up with Stübben's observations on open spaces in the city.

Berlage did not use the term "garden city" in his 1904 lecture, but he said explicitly that an area for countrylike walks is "the cornerstone of the whole plan." The remark is strongly underlined in the manuscript of the lecture. This objective statement revealed the aesthetic center of Berlage's design: The form of the plan hinges on its open spaces. Naturally, like the Baroque planners, he created a general plan for his new urban development but, unlike Leliman, Berlage asked himself some questions on how other architects would build within this general plan. Indeed, in 1893, he had referred to his fellow architects as the "art proletariat."[16] This may be the reason why Berlage renounced the Baroque urban plan and used trees to create the monumental effect he could not expect from other Dutch architects. He also did not trust them with the building of villas and noted with a certain pleasure that the land for one-family houses was scattered between wide-open spaces in order to preclude a "monotonous expanse of villas."

Berlage used open spaces to outline a plan in which he designed a system of low-density buildings along the Schinkel, the Amstel, the Boerenwetering, and the southern canal. He followed Stübben's advice in *Der Städtebau* and included several basins for aesthetic pleasure.[17] A pedestrian mall linking the Vondel Park to the Amstel is given a significant structural role and becomes the east–west axis of the plan. This *corso*—the very word also came from Stübben—continues along the southern canal; both are lined with low-density buildings. Thus a wide stretch of open space connects the large area near the Amstel that was designed for low-density buildings with the remaining sites for villas and the park southwest of the plan. High-density buildings are also planned on both sides of this *corso*; some are adjacent to the buildings constructed south of the Ceintuurbaan boulevard and others, on the south side of the *corso*, stand between the open space along the Amstel and the park. The green banks of the Boerenwetering cut through this area of high-density buildings. These do not play a structural role in the plan; they are a secondary element embedded in a structure of greenery.

The street plan designed for the high-density construction shows Sitte's influence or—more precisely—that of the Sitte School, as Leliman noted. There were streets and lanes which Leliman criticized because they twisted even when they were very short. In his lecture, Berlage presented several arguments drawn from Henrici's plan for Münich to explain his approach. "The design a street plan must take into account," he paraphrased Henrici, "that one cannot command a view of the whole urban panorama when crossing a street, one can only see a stretch of a street or a square at a time. As a result, each stretch of a street, each square deserves an artistic and varied treatment."[18]

Leliman's criticism did not address itself to the essence of Berlage's plan, because he did not fully understand it. He was more to the point, however, when he noted that the abundance of open spaces and the low-density buildings showed little understanding of a need for housing. But this criticism should be directed at Amsterdam's municipal building policy rather than the urban planner. Berlage's commission was to modify a modest urban plan, merely technical in nature, in order to attract a share of the middle-class wealth and culture into a new neighborhood. The municipal authorities and Berlage both insisted on the role of open spaces, but Leliman noted that it might be more reasonable to try and stop the exodus of the well-to-do classes with designs for cultural and urban functions. Berlage conceived of an intelligent plan, full of walks and greenery, which could not be easily spoilt by real estate development. Only at first glance are the twisting streets and lanes of the "Sitte School" dominant. Leliman calculated that "in the northern sector, only 41.5% of the land is suitable for building and in the southern sector barely 38.8%. From that percentage, only 30.1% and 17% are available for high-density building."[19] These figures unveil the real nature of the plan. Berlage resorted to "some of Sitte's theories," as Leliman had noted "only when he dealt with the problem, which he deemed secondary, of high-density building."[20]

He revealed his own judgment on his plan at the end of the lecture. He was prepared to be accused of extravagance, and he said in his own defense that "he had not wanted anything impossible, and he could have made a very different plan had he so wanted. He was not been allowed to do so, and it also had not been necessary, since Amsterdam did not need to become exotic."[21] In other words, he would have preferred to take Paris as a model, but in view of the circumstances, he chose another solution.

The plan was favorably received by the municipal council, apart from some protest about costs. The majority at the council was ready to support this "grand plan," which was approved by a wide majority.[22] The plan that Berlage presented on November 14, 1904, was really a compromise in style. The reasons for the compromise were understandable, but the lecture showed that he was not completely satisfied with his own work. Earlier that year, he had given a lecture in Krefeld, with the sonorous title of "Gedanken über Stil in der Baukunst."[23] On this occasion he openly expressed his thoughts on contemporary issues of planning. There was no trace yet of the halfhearted optimism to be found in the following lecture given in November. He made no mystery of the fact that a good urban plan is a difficult task. Interestingly enough, he made no differentiation between urban plan-

58. *Urban plan for the south of Amsterdam, 1900–05 and 1914–17, first version, general plan, 1904.*

59. *Urban plan for the south of Amsterdam, 1900–05 and 1914–17, study for the second version, 1915.*

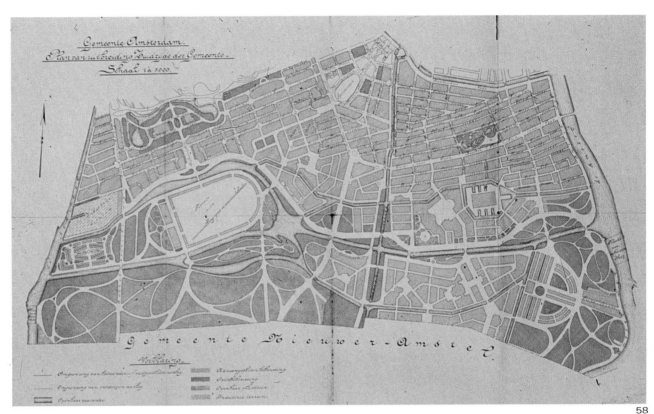

58

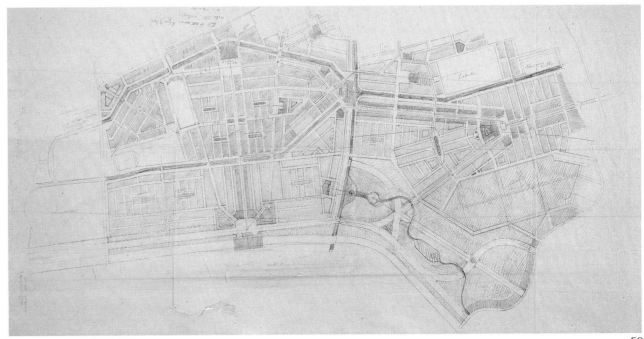

59

60. *Urban plan for the south of
Amsterdam, 1900–05 and 1914–17,
second version, bird's eye view from the
railway station, 1915.*

AMSTERDAM ZUID GEZIEN VAN BOVEN HET ZUIDERSTATION.

61. Urban plan for the south of
Amsterdam, 1900–05 and 1914–17,
second version, bird's eye view from the
bridge on the Amstel, 1915.

AMSTERDAM ZUID GEZIEN VAN BOVEN DE ZUIDERBRUG.

ning and architecture, the problem being the same: "We urgently need a new style, a monumental style,"[24] and he asserted that this style was lacking because of "a total lack of an ideal of life, a general collaboration toward a common purpose."[25] While he stated such a negative view of the contemporary world, Berlage indicated that there were also reasons for hope: A new movement was developing in the arts as the social democracy was growing.[26] The existing order, whether social or aesthetic, deserved to be condemned—"the great struggle had begun." What was needed was to find the correct strategy to fight against "pseudo-art." "The fashionable clothes will be torn away to show the naked body, the healthy nature, and the truth."[27] This truth—in other words, "naked architecture"—would be the point of departure for a new style, once "pseudo-art" was routed. Berlage was convinced that this coming style would be born in big cities. Nothing good could arise from a return to nature or the simplicity of the countryside. Modern culture could develop only in cities, and "architecture alone will be able to represent symbolically the greatest endeavors and the most sacred feelings of man; and such monuments could be erected only in a spiritual center, in other words a city, a city of the future."[28] Three years later Berlage was to revise his ideas on style and create a comprehensive theory.[29] He presented it in a course on architecture he taught in the fall of 1907 in Zürich, which was published in 1908 as a book, *Grundlagen und Entwicklung der Architektur*. The book's reasoning bears a striking resemblance to that of "Stedenbouw," a lecture Berlage gave in the winter of 1908, which was to influence urban planning in the Netherlands for the next twenty years. In more than half of the 120-page book, he discusses the benefits of a design based on geometry. He then turns to another problem: "Now that we have a basis, a method, we must proceed and consider the building process. What will be the form of the architecture of the future?"[30] Historicist architecture of the nineteenth century was out of the question. Reproductions of grand past styles had not produced good results because these styles need to be studied for their "spirit." And "this spirit lies in *objectivity*, which means *clarity of construction*."[31] There he concluded his strictly architectural theory of styles: "First, the architectural composition will be based on a geometric grid. Second, characteristic forms of past styles will not be copied. Third, architectural forms will develop according to objective needs."[32] Next to the geometric order, the taboo against historicist forms, and the honesty of construction, Berlage defined a fourth pillar of his theory of styles. He referred to Karl Scheffler's *Konventionen der Kunst*, in particular to a remark that seemed to go to the heart of the matter: "It is essential for the fine arts that a universal consensus be founded on the fundamental concept of life."[33] The "Stedenbouw" lecture presented similar reflections on the theory of urban planning. Berlage started with a statement of an aspiration toward a modern, metropolitan culture, as he had described it earlier in 1904. He went on to defend geometric urban planning with historical arguments. The regular structure of the Baroque

city was presented as the clearest example of a classical tradition successfully applied to modern times. He then turned his attention to the aesthetic errors committed in the nineteenth century. He concluded with remarks on the social conditions necessary for good planning—and here he was influenced by Fritz Schumacher, as he had been by Karl Scheffler before.

Berlage prepared three other lectures before "Stedenbouw," which may shed light on his intellectual development between 1904 and 1908.[34] The third one is a sort of preparatory draft for "Stedenbouw"—although it does not bear the same title—and it must date from 1908. It is more difficult to give a date for the other two lectures, but they must precede "Stedenbouw." The preparatory draft for "Stedenbouw" is simply called "Inleiding" (Introduction) and was presented as a preface to the lecture called "Straten en pleinen"; both texts are paged separately. "Straten en pleinen" was written almost certainly before "Inleiding." It is a revised, more detailed presentation of the second part—concerning the aesthetic aspect of streets and squares—of the lecture Berlage gave in November 1904. If Stübben's influence was already apparent then, it became more so in the revised text. "Straten en pleinen" could be called a smaller, paperback edition of Stübben's book. Aside from the sixth chapter and a few paragraphs that he did not use, Berlage closely followed *Der Städtebau*; the ninth chapter, more theoretical, was briefly outlined. He even used the book's illustrations for his lecture. It should also be noted that in the margin of the first chapter, "Geschichtlicher Rückblick," Berlage wrote, "See the lecture on urban planning." Berlage was referring to a course he had taught, "Cursus stedenbouw," in which he both agreed and differed with Stübben's historical vision. At a certain point he felt that the handbook he knew so well left something to be desired, and he tried to complete it with elements drawn from his own "Beschouwingen over stijl" of 1905. He did not limit himself to a chronological presentation and considered historic forms of urban planning as problems to be be clarified in the light of a theory of styles. "The concept remains the same," he wrote, "the form must change because of new constraints." Unlike Stübben, Berlage noticed the influence of architecture on urban planning: "When there was a great architecture, there were also beautiful cities." He added, "The beauty of a city is closely related to the beauty of its architecture and, ultimately, the beauty of all the arts. When there is a great architecture, there is also great art and a universal style." He referred again to Scheffler on the social basis of a universal style when he observed about medieval and classical cities that "in both cases, the city had a religious structure; there was a concept of universal beauty, hence its great attraction."

After the 1904 lecture, which owes so much to Stübben's ideas, Berlage developed a more personal view of urban planning based on his research on the history of styles. He kept Stübben's methodology, but he added a historical and cultural framework. In "Inleiding," this framework was extended to contemporary culture.

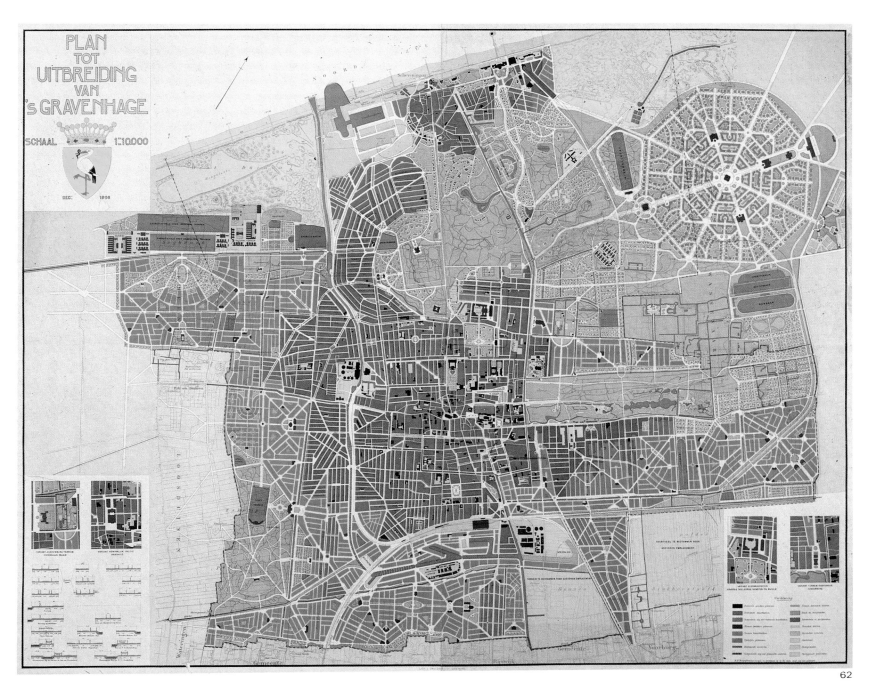

62. Urban plan for The Hague, 1907–11, general plan, 1908.

62

Berlage quoted poetic texts on the city and referred to the theories of Hermann Muthesius, Cornelius Gurlitt, and Fritz Schumacher. The main difference between "Inleiding" and the later version entitled "Stedenbouw," published in 1909, is that in the earlier text Berlage did not insist on the stylistic superiority of the "geometric plan." His preference for geometry came after he wrote *Grundlagen und Entwicklung der Architektur* and it became part of his theory of urban planning only in the winter of 1908.

The history of the 1907 development plan for The Hague resembles that of the development of Amsterdam seven years earlier.[35] In 1903 a plan was drawn for The Hague by the director of Public Works, obviously a civil engineer. This plan stirred a wave of protest among leading citizens of The Hague, who compared it unfavorably with Berlage's plan for Amsterdam. The municipal council agreed with the critics: The plan of the Bureau of Public Works was rejected on March 17, 1907, and a week later Berlage was called in as an consultant. At first sight, the plan he proposed strongly resembled the one that had just been scrapped. The most obvious difference was the creation of a large park southwest of the city. Upon closer scrutiny, however, Berlage's main contribution was in the details of the new plan. With a few aesthetic improvements and well-designed public buildings, he succeeded in imparting a new spirit to the structure of the old plan. Guided by contemporary development in urban planning, he turned a prosaic street plan into a design that adapted technical requirements to political ones. Urban life was conceived as a feast celebrated by a classless population appreciative of the arts. This was the point of view he set himself to defend when, in the winter of 1908, he was invited to discuss urban planning and artistic theory before a student association, "Praktische Studie," in Delft. He often quoted his favorite texts on such occasions, and mostly from *Die deutschen Städte*,[36] a book featuring essays by Gurlitt and Schumacher, which he had come to know at the beginning of November 1904. The German *Denkmaltage* were also an important source of ideas. They were yearly meetings of art historians, urban planners, and other specialists, in which great attention was given to the issue of historic monuments in the city. Stübben was an active participant in these meetings, which had the merit of dealing with urban planning and included such prominent art historians as Gurlitt and Brinckmann. The proceedings of these *Denkmaltage* were published in the *Deutsche Bauzeitung*.

In 1908 Berlage opened his lecture with an "elegy of the city," and he clearly distanced himself from those who regard the modern city simply as an ugly agglomeration of ugly popular architecture. Quoting several poets, Berlage showed that the city has always been more than a problem of popular architecture: It is a work of art as well as a functional construction. Following this lyrical introduction, Berlage described the historic and artistic circumstances of the birth of ancient cities. He dwelled on the origins of two types of cities: "the free-form city and the city based on a geometric plan."[37] In other words,

he contrasted the medieval city with that of the Renaissance, which later developed into the Baroque city. In his wish to be thorough, or perhaps to give the seal of art history to the geometric plan, he used a lengthy German quotation on the regular street pattern of classical times.[38]

After this cultural and historic introduction, Berlage proceeded to demonstrate that the geometric plan was the most practical for modern urban planning. Quoting Muthesius, he acknowledged that after Antiquity, the Middle Ages were another peak of our Western culture.[39] The medieval city, however, presented some serious practical drawbacks: "The architecture and street plan both have one characteristic in common, they aim at a maximum concentration."[40] "This very concentration," Berlage continued, "this intimate atmosphere often creates a certain fascination; it is pleasing, easy to grasp, but we know this has little to do with beauty." With this argument he rejected a fundamental doctrine of the Sitte School. Unlike Henrici, who chose the medieval urban plan, Berlage preferred formulas drawn from the Renaissance and the Baroque because "this type of urban planning proves the point I was referring to earlier, that a sense of space combined with a regular street plan can create great beauty, as long as it satisfies a primary need for high density in the urban character. One could thus claim that the geometric plan becomes more compelling as the need grows for a sense of space."[41] While the need for ample space is a consequence of historic evolution, the break with the Middle Ages and the switch to a regular urban plan can be explained by a practical argument: increasing traffic. As a consequence, streets become straight, blocks are built at a right angle, and "diagonal streets serve the traffic between these angles."[42] Naturally, Berlage did not ignore that geometry had been discredited by nineteenth-century planning, but he felt that the errors of the nineteenth century were not inherent in geometric plans. The point was not to set two extremes against one another, "the ugliness of today and the beauty of yesteryear," without the possibility of considering that "the powerful obstacle to the development of beauty, namely commercialism, can be reduced."[43]

Some of the errors of the nineteenth century were discussed, and above all the so-called *Freilegen* of old monumental buildings, by which they were made to stand free and stripped of everything surrounding them. Sitte himself had criticized the concept of *Freilegen*. "The mistaken opinion still endures," he wrote, "that everything must be visible, and that the only correct solution is a monotonous empty space all around [each monument]."[44] Berlage referred to another authority, the "famed Gurlitt." Gurlitt was indeed an authority on contemporary German urban planning, and in the circles of the *Denkmaltage* in particular. Berlage quoted from Gurlitt at length—directly in German, since he did not translate his quotations in this lecture—and claimed that this "stripping" derived from a total misunderstanding of that which creates monumental city buildings. However, Berlage continued, although this misunderstanding may have been a leading

*63. Urban plan for The Hague, 1907–11,
perspective study for Gevers Deynoot
Square in Scheveningen, 1908.*

*64. Urban plan for The Hague, 1907–11,
perspective study for a* Volksplein *in
the southwest, 1908.*

63

64

65. *Urban plan for The Hague, 1907–11,*
perspective study for an exhibition
center in Nieuwe Parkland, 1908.

66. *Urban plan for The Hague, 1907–11,*
perspective study for the square of the
three cemeteries (Roman-Catholic,
Jewish, non-denominational) on the east
side, 1908.

principle in the nineteenth century, the "empty space" decried by Sitte could also be justified. "The modern age must take into account the requirements of traffic and hygiene. These are so compelling that the planner must keep them in mind before he can think of anything else."[45] According to Berlage, the writings of German authorities in the field point to the geometric plan. "Today more than ever, designs in the spirit of classicism are needed, featuring stylization and regularity. In the confusion of ideas characteristic of our times, one reality cannot be denied: There is a trend toward more regular, more simple social relations, marked by the greatest possible practicality, in other words, stylized."[46]

The arguments against the "picturesque" plan ended here. Berlage returned to his earlier point, the most elementary geometric plan, and he quoted Stübben: "Today as before, the right-angle grid should be the basis for a street plan, which leaves integrations and expansions to future needs."[47] Berlage wished to prove that a plan could be made beautiful, once basic practical needs were satisfied. After all, it was during the much decried nineteenth century that such beautiful plans were achieved as that of Paris—"the most beautiful modern city in the world"—or that of Gottfried Semper in Dresden and, above all, Vienna. The secret of Baron Haussmann and Semper was that they worked in the wake of Baroque urban planning. "Since the Baroque plan is so germane to the modern spirit, it must still be held in high regard. The traffic of today, however, creates another constraint; right-angled streets do not suffice, there remains also the problem of diagonal streets, which is so difficult to solve. But as far as art is concerned, the Baroque design provides all the necessary elements, with its high-density structure, long straight boulevards, and great vistas."[48] An unimaginative usage of such techniques could lead to monotony, but the urban planner will forestall boredom by including in his design the natural and historic variations existing in the area to be developed. "A neighborhood will be designed according to a geometric plan," Berlage stated, "unless there are some natural obstacles to prevent it. When the area presents such natural unevenness in the terrain as a body of water, a hill, or a forest, these are integrated in the plan. If nature is artfully combined with rigorously designed areas, the plan should present pleasing variations and avoid the monotony resulting from an overly systematic regularity."[49] Finally, details also contribute to the beauty of the whole.

Berlage's last point concerns the aesthetic aspects of modern planning. The planning in each period was related to a specific architectural order. The medieval urban plan was unthinkable without medieval architecture, just as the principles of classical architecture were implied in the geometric plan. "There has always been good architecture," Berlage observed, "until it became a basely eclectic art."[50] Now the opportunity has come to give the city a new and artistic aspect. "In a very interesting article," Berlage wrote, "Prof. Schumacher outlined the responsibilities of the authorities in this regard."[51] The

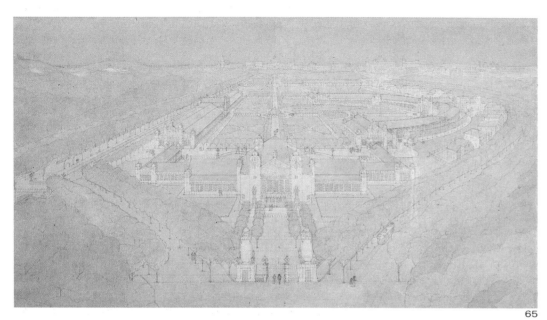

65

66

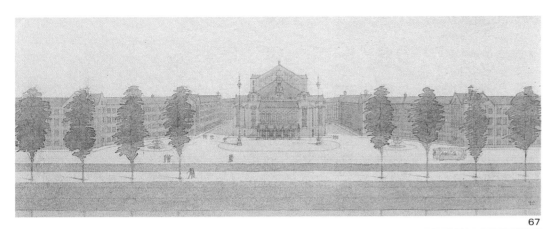

67

68

article he quoted claimed that "the accumulation of economic power in some specific areas in the social structure has always found its significant expression in the development of the arts."[52] Schumacher observed sharply that public authorities are the modern expression of social power. "Since time immemorial, consciously or unconsciously, power expresses itself through the arts."[53] Historically, therefore, public authorities have certain duties in the field of the arts, which are not limited to the construction of public buildings. Just as the Gothic, Renaissance, and Baroque styles are *Parallelbegriffe*—parallel concepts of church, bourgeois, and court art, respectively—contemporary public authorities must promote the birth of a new style and bring to life "an art of public power." Berlage quoted from Schumacher's frank views on the aesthetic quality of such art: "At the core of a modern approach to architecture, there is an objective style rather than an imitation of period forms; this style should try and develop purely objective solutions that are as practical as possible; finally it should address itself to the problem of shaping and grouping rather than that of decorating."[54] This coincided with Berlage's own ideas on architecture and also with his assessment of the concept of space in Baroque planning. As for the architecture of the future, Berlage noted that "the issue itself of greater size requires a completely different solution. Because of this greater scale, the problems regarding the grouping of buildings tend to be completely different. The philosophy of architecture, like the rest, must change. Classical architecture made loadbearing structures visible; medieval architecture eliminated this load and aimed at a sort of dematerialization of matter; the architecture of our times should represent symbolically the outline of spaces."[55]

The quotations from Schumacher helped Berlage resolve two problematic aspects of planning. He gave a political dimension to his theory by defining urban planning as "an art of public authorities." At the same time, he made his first step toward an architectural solution to problems created by "wide spaces" in modern urban planning. He chose a quotation from Brinckmann, "To build a city means to create space with housing material," and made it the motto of his "Stedenbouw" lecture. The quotation was from Brinckmann's *Platz und Monument*, which Berlage came to know early in the spring of 1909, when he was preparing his lecture for Düsseldorf. He was translating the text of his lecture into German when he read with great pleasure Stübben's review of Brinckmann's book in the February 24, 1909, issue of *Deutsche Bauzeitung*.[56] He observed that Brinckmann firmly presented many ideas he himself had formulated in 1908 in a more tentative manner, and that he supported his theory with a solid study of art and history. In the German version of his lecture, Berlage quoted excerpts from that review, thus showing that he had moved a step further from the position he had taken in Delft. Not only did he differ with the Sitte School, but he also sided with the critics of that school. The Dutch edition of his lecture, however, did not contain these new quotations; the original text was maintained, although a great many illustrations were taken from *Platz und Monument*.

Unlike Stübben, who showed no particular interest in the nature of urban space, Berlage did not limit himself to a polemical exchange with the Sitte School. He even ignored some superficial problems of form, which were remarked on by Stübben. Instead, he developed his own vision of the cardinal problem put forward by Sitte and reformulated it in a creative manner in 1908. He followed Sitte inasmuch as he gave pride of place to the problem of urban space, but he tried to qualify it: Modern planning must find aesthetic means to control the vast urban areas created by practical contingencies. In the German lecture, he quoted at length from Stübben's review of *Platz und Monument* and his comments on the "new sense of space" that came with the Baroque. Berlage believed that twentieth-century planning should also bring about a "new sense of space." In 1908, he still did not know precisely which were the determinant factors of this new sense of space, nor the means to give it a shape. Five years later, in the winter of 1913–14, he gave another lecture entitled "Stedenbouw," again before the association "Praktische Studie" in Delft, on which occasion he confronted this crucial issue and brought several new elements into the discussion.

In 1908 Berlage's approach was essentially different from Stübben's. The latter conceived of urban planning as a total sum of its parts: The planner starts from an elementary structure; he resolves problems one by one and combines the solutions in the best possible manner, inserting them into his basic structure. Berlage showed his appreciation of Stübben's methodology by quoting him extensively in his lecture, but his own preference for the Baroque led him in another direction. A Baroque plan is not designed on the basis of an abstract structure; such plan is determined from the beginning to the end by a visual concept of unity and order, and urban space is perceived as a whole. The main difference with Stübben's approach is that he regarded the aesthetic aspect as only one of the factors involved. In the Baroque plan, which Berlage championed, visual qualities determine the whole design—even its structure—from the very beginning.

The concept of planning as a sum of its parts shows how much Stübben's handbook belonged to the nineteenth century, grounded as it was in the positivism of nineteenth-century engineering. Berlage found such a relationship between the part and the whole unconvincing. Surely this was not how a work of art was created. He was searching for an approach in planning in which the concept of the whole is reflected in the parts just as the parts are reflected in the whole. Once he had understood that the Baroque city fit such an approach, Berlage could be persuaded by Brinckmann's argument that the modern urban planner can learn from the Baroque. In 1908, Brinckmann's formula "das neue Raumgefühl" (a new sense of space) gave an effective characterization of one of the dominant themes of modern planning. Brinckmann

was a subtle art historian and an even more subtle critic, but his thoughts and writings on the Baroque also belonged to a particular time in history, the years around 1910. It was significant that he should have dedicated *Platz und Monument* to Heinrich Wölflin and, three years later, *Deutsche Stadtbaukunst in der Vergangenheit* to Otto March and Hermann Muthesius, both pioneers of a new architecture. In 1911 Brinckmann observed about the process of planning that "the whole cannot be built up from its parts; in fact, whenever there is unity in style, the artistic process goes the other way around. A new fundamental concept will guide to the new particular values of new times."[57] In his review of Brinckmann's second book, Werner Hegemann called it "a milestone and also a road sign in the tumultuous flux in which present aesthetic concepts of urban planning are developing—this is a practical contribution, not the work of an antiquarian."[58]

Berlage achieved full maturity with his new lecture "Stedenbouw," which had become so extensive that it was presented in four evenings.[59] The tone had changed; it had become professorial. The presentation had also changed; it was ruled less by classical rhetoric than by methodology. The tone he adopted is understandable. He was not alone in his enthusiasm for *Platz und Monument*.[60] Brinckmann had a great following in Germany and his other book, *Deutsche Stadtbaukunst*, was well received. Berlage also consulted a book by Walter Curt Behrendt, *Die einheitliche Blockfront als Raumelement im Stadtbau*, published in 1911 and dedicated to Karl Scheffler. The latter's own book, *Grosstadtarchitektur*, was in many ways a prophetic work; it was published in 1913 and quoted by Berlage in the same year. Berlage perused these four German books and Gustav Langen's system for "unity in urban planning" to write the final long version of the "Stedenbouw" lecture.[61] Like the lecture given five years earlier, the 1913 "Stedenbouw" opened with a historical overview, to which Berlage devoted the first evening. History, however, was presented here as more coercive: It was less an arsenal of aesthetic possibilities, from which the urban planner could choose, than an inescapable development. The logic of this evolution was brought to the fore, while less attention was given to aesthetic achievements. The second evening was devoted to the study of squares and the third evening to the discussion of streets and, above all, "the unity of blocks." The fourth evening opened with a brief summary and discussed the possibilities offered by "unity in urban planning."

In December 1913, Berlage opened the first evening of his lecture by strongly advocating ideas and concepts drawn mainly from Scheffler's recently published *Grosstadtarchitektur*. From the first page on, the book described the city as the center of the industrial world but also as the dominant force in man's life in society. "The city is the result," Berlage noted, "of man's social life—and in a sense it is also its means and its end. It is born from man's aspirations as a group."[62] Without naming Scheffler, from whom he had borrowed the idea, he concluded that "we must keep in mind that, as far as we can foresee, the architecture of the future will be the art of the city. This art must follow the development of the city and can only be middle-class and the product of a democratic culture."[63] The dominant theme of the four evenings was this connection between architecture and urban development in the modern world.

After this brief and innovative introduction, Berlage presented a history of the city, from two different angles: first, the city and its architecture in connection with his vision of Western social and cultural history; then, the history of the parallel development of forms. Practical, general history came before the history of art, hence the formula "practical-aesthetic solution" that Berlage used to describe modern urban planning. He seemed unable, however, to prove the actual link between urban developments and the historical facts he mentioned. He used Baumeister's book and the three volumes by H. Brugmans and C.H. Peters[64] to outline the economic development of the city, but the data had little connection with the arguments that followed. The link between history and forms was elsewhere: "The type of housing is the factor that molds the character of a city."[65] A reference to Brinckmann gave his statement the necessary authority; Brinckmann had noted that "there is a very close link between the architectural style of house construction and the construction of cities. The urban character changes as housing changes. As a consequence, the city is perpetually changing, since every progress in housing brings about a different urban character."[66]

Berlage did not dwell on the economic phenomena he had just described, but he invoked "three great cultural periods" to examine this link between housing and planning: classical times, the Middle Ages, and the Renaissance, which he defined in a fairly conventional manner, according to their respective cultural and social spirit. Berlage was pursuing different goals under the guise of a historical presentation: Clearly, the "practical" and the "aesthetic" aspects of planning could not be simply linked; a mediating factor was needed. Berlage processed and distilled the practical factors to make them into a transcendental idea necessary for his theory. The mediating idea was also the point of departure for some aesthetic observations. The Renaissance had reintroduced regularity in the urban plan and marked the modern beginning of "the real art of urban planning."[67] The Renaissance was a revolutionary movement against the religious and spiritual dogma of the Church and against a collective spiritual idea,[68] but it also created the basis for "excessive individualism" and "that which is harmful in nineteenth-century culture."[69] Architecture and the city became middle-class facts. The religious factor that held the Middle Ages together was lost and with it, slowly but surely, the "objective beauty" characteristic of that period, which could exist only when there was a powerful "universal spiritual idea." Even during the Baroque period, when urban planning and architecture reached new peaks,

the decline of European culture could not be reversed. "There was then a type of beauty that could be regarded as universal because it was linked to a culture, but not a beauty created by the community, as it had been in classical times and the Middle Ages."[70] Such considerations on the history of culture differed from Brinckmann's vision, although Berlage drew freely from Brinckmann for data, which were interesting from the point of view of art history. There were few changes compared to his 1908 lecture. The main theme remained the same: The classical city was built according to a regular plan, the medieval city was not; in the Renaissance, the city plan was again regular. Now the book *Platz und Monument* provided him with the arguments necessary to complete this historical overview.

The second evening of the lecture, in February 1914, developed the theme of city squares. According to Berlage, Sitte had the merit of noting that the beauty of medieval squares was related to their enclosing walls: The square is "closed," even if this is only an optical effect. Eighteenth-century French architects first described how squares could seem closed while in reality they were open. Brinckmann discovered these theoretical texts and analyzed them in *Platz und Monument*, when he studied the historic origins of Parisian squares. Following his lead, Berlage became interested in the ideas of Marc-Antoine Laugier and Patte. The principle of enclosure is valid, he noted, but "it must be kept in mind that the concept of the enclosed square is very flexible. Sitte showed that one need not be rigid on this point; suffice it to secure very small openings on the sides and to design preferably curving streets leading to the square. In the Middle Ages it was easy achieve this impression of enclosed space because the city was small."[71]

French theoreticians regarded "city squares not as enclosed spaces as in the Renaissance, nor as 'squares-vestibules' as in the Baroque, but as independent spaces, regular and central, to which streets converge, thus giving an orientation to the plan. Squares are born from the confluence of several streets. The natural position of a square, Laugier argued, is at the intersection of several streets, and its size should be calculated to insure that increased traffic resulting from the convergence of streets be absorbed."[72] "The concept of the enclosed square," Berlage concluded, "in its widest sense, has therefore its place in modern urban planning."[73]

On the evening of March 2, 1914, Berlage offered more quotations: again from Brinckmann, but also from Behrendt's *Die einheitliche Blockfront*. At the previous meeting, he had observed after Brinckmann and Patte that "enclosed" squares were not created by uninterrupted buildings but by a marked harmony in the façades and a unity of vistas. Now Berlage set out to explain how such harmony is achieved, and he pointed to the role of rhythm. In *Deutsche Stadtbaukunst*, Brinckmann gave a major place to rhythm, that is, the scansion of architectural elements that determine and give life to urban spaces. The aesthetic enjoyment of space becomes dynamic; it is not something

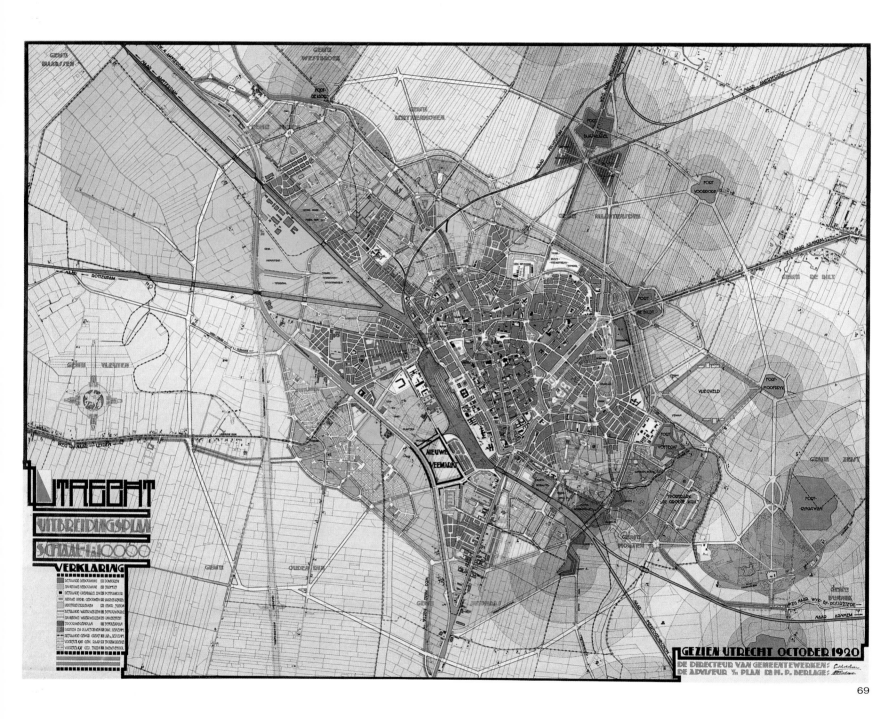

69

static as in Sitte's theory, because the organization of vast spaces implies movement—to use Brinckmann's formula, a *Bewegungsstrom*, a current.

Squares and other open spaces have a rhythm, but so do streets. "Rhythm," Brinckmann explained, "lies in the segmentation of movement. A street can create a sense of space; it can even create a continuous deep movement through vistas; but it will have rhythm only through the definition of distinct segments."[74] Berlage went one step further when he observed that "streets have become more important than squares in today's planning."[75] He then gave a summary of the whole introduction to Brinckmann's chapter on streets (with the exception of the paragraph on village streets), in which he briefly explained that streets should be viewed as historical and aesthetic phenomena. Brinckmann stated most significantly that "the development of streets depends on the design of the blocks. Only the unity of buildings gives shape to streets—whether these are straight or curving—and creates a sense of space."[76] Behrendt had already developed this idea in his book, *Blockfront*. Berlage elaborated on that, quoting Scheffler and Laugier, and examining Haussmann's works in Paris and John Nash's in London.[77] There is a very significant passage from Behrendt: "The mass and façade of a building are also a consequence of the artistic structure of the space; it is only with this mass that the modern avenue with its heavy traffic, the monumental street for parades, and the boulevard of great cities can create an effective spatial effect. Great monumental architecture dominating the wide space of streets can be guaranteed only through the integration of each façade into the unity of a block."[78]

What are the rules for such streets? Laugier gave them in his *Essai sur l'architecture*. Behrendt presented Laugier's theory, but partly in his own words. Berlage used Behrendt's text without going to the source. "For a city to be well built," Laugier asserted, "the exterior of buildings cannot be left to the wishes of private citizens. Everything in a street must be approved by public authorities and abide by general rules established for the design of streets. It is necessary to establish by law the sites on which buildings can be erected, but also the manner in which this should be done." There is a risk of monotony, and "excessive uniformity is a very grave error." Laugier proposed—and Behrendt and Berlage both agreed—that "for a street to be well designed, uniformity is needed only for corresponding and parallel façades. The same design should be valid for a street until it crosses another one; in other cases, the solutions should be different. Designs may be changed by giving a different shape to buildings, applying more or less ornaments, combining differently the components of buildings. With these three resources—each of which contains endless possibilities—the same façade need never be repeated, even in the greatest city."[79]

As for the sociological aspect of street vistas, Behrendt and Berlage both let Scheffler speak: "There is nothing more petit-bourgeois than the old idea of a 'house' at a time when such a house is not a unit anymore. Today we live in apartments and not in houses."[80] Berlage added, "The apartment house is an investment for real estate speculators," but this does not necessarily bear negative consequences for planning. On the contrary, the planner who accepts the facts of the market place and recognizes that "overly personal approaches have become unacceptable because they have spoiled our cities in all their articulations" also shows a growing insight into the art of building, which could bring about a new and better architecture.[81] Berlage concluded by answering a question about the future aspect of housing as a mass product. To give more weight to his argument, Berlage called on "the new book by the famous Karl Scheffler, one of the most cultivated and sharply perceptive men of our times."[82] Scheffler wrote about "a product of contemporary necessity." "Big cities were born at the same time as industry. Since industry is international, big cities took an international orientation, they became centers for commerce and manufacturing, reflecting world economic expansion."[83] He called the phenomenon *Grosstadtgeist*, the spirit of the big city: "This spirit has created new types of architectural blocks. There is no modern provincial, small-town, or rural architecture. Wherever such architecture can be found, it is either the last manifestation of an ancient tradition or an attempt at a new folk art that refers to trends originating from big cities. We must, therefore, keep in mind that, as far as we can foresee, the architecture of the future will be the art of the big city. This art must follow the development of the city and can only be middle-class, upper middle-class, and the product of a democratic culture."[84] Berlage "could not but respect someone who conceived of the development of modern cities in this way, as connected with a new architecture. Industry, which was regarded with such scorn by all artists, was undeniably the determinant force in the present evolution of cities."[85]

The fourth and last evening was devoted to the unity of the urban plan, which was also the theme of the final chapter in Brinckmann's *Deutsche Stadtbaukunst*, entitled "Die Stadt als künstlerisch einheitlicher Organismus" (the city as an artistic organic unity). For each city, Berlage stated, a particular relationship can be established between form, place, and history. The question is, how? In 1913, Berlage thought he had found the answer when he visited the international Building Trade Exhibition in Leipzig. There he met Gustav Langen, whose work he found very interesting.[86] Langen's system consisted of drawing the plans of several cities on the same scale and inscribing specific symbols to indicate various data on land ownership, traffic, industry, and other elements of note. Berlage already knew how difficult it was to establish the relationship between form, place, and history. Statistics are of no real use to designers. Their data only make sense when they are presented in a manner making their connection with urban reality evident. This was where Berlage saw the utility of Langen's maps: "All these data illuminate the connection between the various elements, their cause and effect relationship; the successive stages of development can thus be reconstructed." A short paragraph further, he added, "such maps identify and examine the evolutionary process of cities. It is a method in which single cases are viewed within a whole framework."[87] Berlage interpreted Langen's method as a method by which to reconcile abstract scientific data with the spatial reality to be controlled by urban planning. This was the first step to indicate graphically, on a map, the determinant factors of a plan. "Thus," Berlage explained, "the scientific groundwork is established for urban expansion," and the first step toward "a grand composition" is made.[88]

This third version of "Stedenbouw" completed Berlage's theoretical contribution to the Dutch school of urban planning. His 1918 lecture, "Normalisatie in de Nederlandse woningbouw," did not bring any changes to his approach to planning. His lectures between 1883 and 1914 may be the swan song of nineteenth-century urban planning, but they are also an introductory chapter to the history of "functional cities." In 1914 he received an honorary doctorate in the liberal arts for his role in the development of Dutch architecture. Shortly thereafter, one of his biographers proposed to place his works and honors in a broad cultural perspective: "Also, and above all, he has rendered justice to his own time, which was an extraordinary time. This is the major significance of Berlage's work—greater perhaps than the individual talent that created it. His work—its purity, intelligence, and clear insight—was at the heart of a great period, during which we have witnessed near revolutionary progress in all fields."[89]

1. M. Bock 1983, part 2.1. *Stadtentwicklung und Stadtbaukunst*, pp. 85–120; see also M. Bock, "Stedenbouw," in M. Bock, K. Broos, P. Singelenberg 1975, pp. 51–72.

2. H.P. Berlage 1892, "De Kunst in stedenbouw," in *Bouwkundig Weekblad* XII, 1892, 15, pp. 87–91; 17, pp. 101–02; 20, pp. 121–24; 21, pp. 126–27.

3. M. Bock 1983, p. 104 and p. 192, fn 94.

4. J. Stübben, *Der Städtebau, Handbuch der Architektur*, Darmstadt 1890.

5. M. Bock, op. cit., p. 149 and p. 213, fn 319.

6. C. Sitte, *Der Städtebau nach seinen künstlerischen Grundsätzen*, Vienna 1965 (1901 ed.), p. 93.

7. C. Sitte, op. cit., pp. 142–43.

8. J. Stübben also noted the one-sided aspect of Henrici's solutions. See J. Stübben, "Die Einseitigkeit im Städtebau und ihre Folgen," in *Deutsche Bauzeitung* XXVII, 1893, 57, pp. 349–50; 61, pp. 373–74; 68, pp. 415–18.

9. K. Scheffler, "Ein Weg zum Stil," in *Berliner Architekturwelt* V, 1903, 9, pp. 291–95.

10. In his 1893 text, page 415, Stübben noted that "we would be deluding ourselves if we thought that we could choose one hundred monumental buildings, regroup them in twenty different locations on the outskirts of town, chosen at random, and believe that future generations would comply."

11. J.H.W. Leliman 1904, p. 376.

12. Ibid.

13. H.P. Berlage, *De Uitbreiding van Amsterdam*, ms, p. III, Berlage Archives, N.D.B.

14. Quoted in P. Singelenberg 1972, p. 41.

15. H.P. Berlage, "Amsterdam en Venetië," in *Bouwkundig Weekblad* III, 1883, 34, p. 217. For an analysis of this lecture, see M. Bock, 1983, pp. 92–3.

16. H.P. Berlage, "Bouwkunst en impressionisme," in *Architectura* II, 1894, 24, p. 106.

17. J. Stübben, op. cit., p. 210.

18. H.P. Berlage, *De Uitbreiding van Amsterdam*, p. X.

19. J.H.W. Leliman, op. cit., p. 390.

20. In his lecture, Berlage reviewed chapters 4, 8, and 9, part two, of Sitte's book.

21. H.P. Berlage, "Architectonische toelichting," in *Gemeenteblad* 1904, I, p. 1725.

22. "Verslag van het raadsdebat op 11-1-1905," in *Gemeenteblad* II, 1905, pp. 14–57.

23. The Dutch version was used here, "Beschouwingen over stijl," published in the 1922 edition of *Studies over Bouwkunst, stijl en samenleving*, Rotterdam.

24. Ibid., p. 81.

25. Ibid., p. 62.

26. Ibid., p. 68.

27. Ibid., p. 72.

28. Ibid., p. 81.

29. H.P. Berlage, *Grundlagen und Entwicklung der Architektur*, Rotterdam 1908. On page 14, he refers to *Gedanken über Stil*: "I hope to go here into that which I could not discuss then as I would have wished to."

30. Ibid., p. 71.

31. Ibid., p. 98.

32. Ibid., p. 100.

33. Ibid., p. 109.

34. H.P. Berlage, "Cursus stedenbouw," "Straten en pleinen," and "Inleiding," mss, in the Berlage Archives, N.D.B.

35. R. Blijstra "Stedenbouw 1900–1940 in 's Gravenhage," in *'s Gravenhage* XXV, 1970, 12.

36. R. Wuttke, ed., *Die deutschen Städte, geschildert nach den Ergebnissen der ersten deutschen Städteausstellung zu Dresden 1903*, Leipzig 1904.

37. H.P. Berlage, "Het Uitbreidingsplan van 's Gravenhage," in *Bouwkunst* I, 1909, 4–5, pp. 97–144.

38. Ibid., pp. 102–04.

39. Ibid., p. 105. H. Muthesius, *Stilarchitektur und Baukunst*, Mülheim a/d Ruhr, 1901, p. 9. Berlage used the same quotation in *Grundlagen der Architektur*.

40. H.P. Berlage, op. cit., p. 105.

41. Ibid.

42. Ibid.

43. Ibid., p. 106.

44. C. Sitte, op. cit., p. 31.

45. H.P. Berlage, op. cit., p. 108.

46. Ibid., p. 110.

47. Ibid., p. 111.

48. Ibid., p. 113.

49. Ibid., p. 115.

50. Ibid., p. 101.

51. Ibid., p. 118.

52. R. Wuttke, ed., op. cit., p. 46, fn 35.

53. Ibid., p. 47.

54. Ibid., pp. 52–53.

55. H.P. Berlage, op. cit., p. 119.

56. J. Stübben, "Der Städtebau in der Kunstgeschichte," in *Deutsche Bauzeitung* XLIII, 1909, 16, pp. 102–06.

57. A.E. Brinckmann, *Deutsche Stadtbaukunst in der Vergangenheit*, Frankfurt a/Main 1911, p. 3.

58. W. Hegemann, "Brinckmann über deutsche Stadtbaukunst in der Vergangenheit," in *Der Städtebau* VIII, 1911, p. 105.

59. H.P. Berlage, "Stedenbouw," in *De Beweging* X, 1914, 3, pp. 226–47; X, 1914, 4, pp. 1–17; X, 1914, 5, pp. 142–57; X, 1914, 6, pp. 263–79.

60. Second edition, Berlin 1912.

61. W.C. Behrendt, *Die Einheitliche Blockfront als Raumelement im Stadtbau. Ein Beitrag zur Stadtbaukunst der Gegenwart*, Berlin 1911; K. Scheffler, *Die Architektur der Grosstadt*, Berlin 1913; G. Langen, *Erläuterungen für die Herstellung der städtebaulichen Einheitspläne*, Internationale Baufach-Ausstellung, Leipzig 1913.

62. H.P. Berlage, *Stedenbouw I*, p. 226.

63. Ibid., p. 227; K. Scheffler, op. cit.,

70

70. *Development of the Hofplein,*
Rotterdam, 1921 and 1926, view
of the model of the first design, 1921.

71. *Development of Mercator Square, west*
of Amsterdam, 1924–27, preliminary
study for the square with
Volksgebouw, *1924.*

p. 3, fn. 60.

64. H. Brugmans and C. Peters, *Oud Nederlandse steden in haar ontstaan, groei en ontwikkeling*, Leiden 1908–12.

65. H.P. Berlage, op. cit., p. 230.

66. A.E. Brinckmann 1911, p. 23.

67. H.P. Berlage, op. cit., p. 234.

68. Ibid., p. 232.

69. Ibid.

70. Ibid., pp. 236–37.

71. H.P. Berlage, "Stedenbouw II," pp. 8–9.

72. Ibid., p. 9.

73. Ibid., p. 10.

74. A.E. Brinckmann, op. cit., pp. 56–57, fn 56.

75. H.P. Berlage, "Stedenbouw III," p. 143.

76. A.E. Brinckmann, op. cit., p. 82; H.P. Berlage, op. cit., pp. 143–44.

77. W.C. Behrendt, op. cit., pp. 63–65; H.P. Berlage, op. cit., pp. 147–48.

78. W.C. Behrendt, op. cit., p. 64.

79. W.C. Behrendt, op. cit, pp. 40–41; H.P. Berlage, op. cit., pp. 152–53.

80. W.C. Behrendt, op. cit., p. 73; H.P. Berlage, op. cit., p. 153.

81. H.P. Berlage, op. cit., p. 154.

82. Ibid., p. 155.

83. K. Scheffler, op. cit., p. 4.

84. Ibid., p. 3; H.P. Berlage, op. cit., pp. 155–56.

85. H.P. Berlage, op. cit., p. 156.

86. Berlage himself took part in the Leipzig exhibition. The Berlage Archives contain the blueprints of "unitary plans" and a list of the symbols used.

87. H. P. Berlage, "Stedenbouw IV," pp. 267 and 269.

88. Ibid., pp. 272 and 273.

89. T. Landré, *Dr. H.P. Berlage Nzn*, Baarn, 1916, p. 3.

*72. Urban plan for Groningen, 1927–28,
general plan, 1928.*

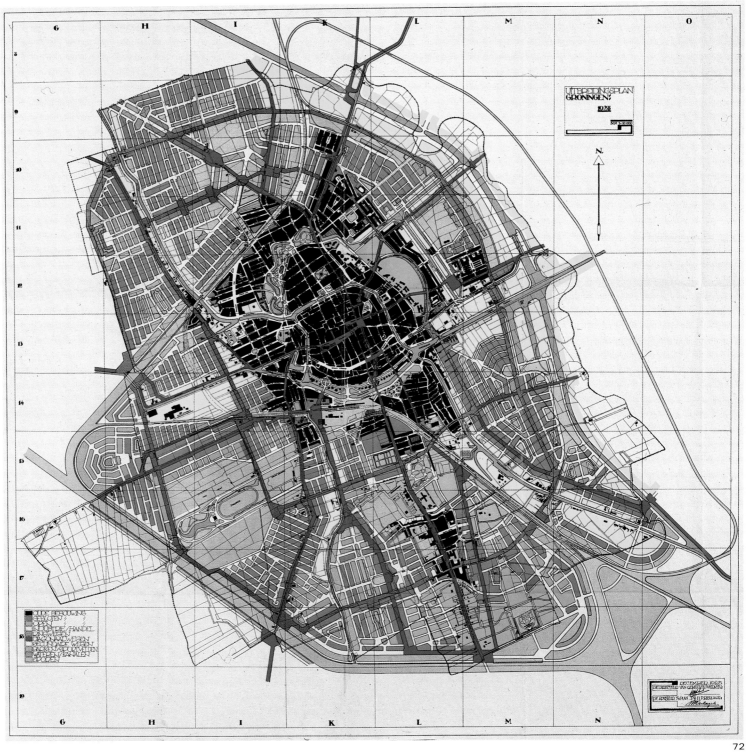

Style and Dwelling Type: Berlage's Housing Projects

Jan de Heer

To build a city means to create space with housing material.
—Brinckmann

The scope of Berlage's interests in the field of housing can hardly fit in a brief outline. Neither M. Bock nor H. Searing[1] could illuminate fully the complexity of the topic, although both give an overall picture of Berlage's designs for housing between 1908 and 1918. In itself, the picture they give is not inaccurate, but it fails to show the full aesthetic significance of housing in Berlage's concept of urban planning. Since his development plan for The Hague in 1908, Berlage clearly regarded housing as the fundamental component in the building of a city. It is therefore important to analyze the nature of a relationship between city and housing that remains valid to this day. The difficulty lies in finding an acceptable definition of housing, beyond a description of styles and forms. Berlage viewed the architect's interest in housing—and, to a certain extent, urban planning—as a part of the institutional system, and for that reason he was always interested in doing both. In his eyes, this strong connection with institutions illustrated the organic link between architecture and society. The design of both housing and cities was the clearest example of architecture as "a social art."

It is generally thought that Berlage's most significant ideas on housing were published in *Normalisatie in woningbouw*,[2] which was his response to the report on standardized housing given by the engineer J. van der Waerden at the Woningcongres, a conference on housing held in Amsterdam in 1918.[3] Everybody felt that Berlage's paper did not quite keep to the topic. He was criticized for not addressing himself to the core of Van der Waerden's presentation and limiting himself to that which he called the "psychological and aesthetic aspect" of standardization. Van der Waerden advocated a massive intervention of central authorities in the field of housing, since private enterprise seemed unable to resolve the problem of housing shortage. He also proposed the mass production of nine types of housing. Local architects would not be called upon to design these types. Their task would be to resolve problems of planning regarding such standardized housing and to decide on groupings, heights, and colors of buildings.

On closer consideration, nothing suggests that Berlage did not share the premise of Van der Waerden's report. He agreed that the enormous shortage in housing called for mass production. This would limit the number of dwelling types, but it would also, among other benefits, reduce costs and construction time. Assessing the discussions at the congress on housing, Berlage came to the conclusion that the criticisms were consistent on one point: the psychological and aesthetic aspects of the problem. "The workers," he stated, "regard the frightful monotony of an endless succession of identical buildings and houses as an attempt against their personality, freedom, and humanity." He added, "The architects also regard it as an attack against their personality, artistic prerogatives, and creative freedom."[4] He intended, however, to soften such criticisms, because he wished to support Van der Waerden's program.

Berlage did not expect a protest on the part of workers, "because it is not humiliating for people of the same social origins to live in the same type of building, if this housing is—as it should be—free of technical and practical flaws."[5] He pointed to the fact that standardized housing is in keeping with social and economic evolution, and moreover that it reflects a concept of democracy. The workers' best guarantee of a good standardization is their involvement, their participation and cooperation with architects and political authorities. He noted, however, with some skepticism that "the Dutch are hopeless individualists and the Dutch workers would be probably no exception."[6]

Standardization, Berlage argued, is nothing more than bringing order, rules, and regularity to disorder. In the face of the architects' egotism and artistic subjectivity, he claimed that, in the field of art, "regularity—i.e. objective stylization—comes first, while irregularity—i.e. individual stylization—comes second."[7] He referred to historic examples of urban development with a regular street plan and regular blocks, made of uniform houses. Cities and housing complexes have always existed, and the present development does not reflect any aesthetic decline. Rather, it could be said that "we are struck chiefly by the repetition of the same type of housing. The beginning of every style, the whole of architecture even, is nothing but rhythm creating order and connections between similar units, which is essentially the basis for ornamentation."[8] Architects could demonstrate their social commitment by conceiving and designing units grouped in great masses. This is precisely how, Berlage claimed, his 1915 development plan of the south of Amsterdam should be architecturally interpreted.

One may wonder about the expectations of Berlage's supporters and opponents at the conference on housing when they asked for his views after a heated debate on

Van der Waerden's report. Berlage's ideas on mass-produced housing had been well known since he gave his lecture on "Bouwkunst en impressionisme."[9] His designs for the housing corporations De Arbeiderswoning and Algemeene Woningbouwvereeniging were also known. Van der Waerden used these designs as examples to illustrate his point during the discussion.[10] In his "Memorie van toelichting," Berlage noted that housing complexes were necessary to carry out his development plan for the south of Amsterdam.[11] As a consequence, housing would be mass-produced and the types of dwellings would be rationalized and limited in number. The other consequence was that the shape of the whole housing complex would play as important a role in the aesthetic unity of the city as the shape of streets and squares. It would have been unreasonable, therefore, to expect Berlage to disagree with Van der Waerden. More accurately, Van der Waerden mostly generalized from the ideas Berlage had submitted in his presentation of the development plan for the south of Amsterdam. Finally, Van der Waerden himself—who was director of the Amsterdam Bureau of Inspection of Construction and Housing since 1915—was responsible for the execution of Berlage's development plan, with the directors of Public Works and the Housing Administration. The plan had been discussed at the municipal council a few months before the conference, in October 1917.

The Amsterdam conference on housing provoked the same heated controversy as the congress of the Deutsche Werkbund had done in Cologne in 1914. Hermann Muthesius had stated in Cologne that the architecture and all other activities of the Werkbund pointed to standardization, although there was no discussion on the normalization of housing and the limitation of types of dwellings. His position provoked a sharp debate between supporters and opponents of standardization. The latter, led by Henry van de Velde, defended the primacy of the individual artist. Berlage attended the Cologne Congress, where he gave a paper but did not take part in the debate.[12] Consequently, Berlage was well aware of the arguments. His contribution to the Amsterdam conference and the discussion on standardization could be interpreted as his rejoining, albeit belatedly, Muthesius's standpoint.

Considerations after the conference on housing drew a distinction between Berlage's and Van der Waerden's ideas. "The intentions of Van der Waerden," Z. Gulden commented, "are clear. He wants unified housing." Gulden thought that Berlage's paper was significant because of his preoccupation with the aesthetic composition of a housing complex. He concluded, "the battle at the conference on housing, however, was not waged on the notion of housing complexes."[13] A.E. Brinckmann was even called to Amsterdam from Düsseldorf to explain that the idea of standardization presented at the conference was wrong. Of course, Berlage knew that his paper did not deal primarily with the technical aspects of standardization. "Take note," he told the audience, "building is a social activity that is not practiced foremost for art's sake. It is meant to create housing, the purpose of which is to be useful. Even when such activity becomes art, as it should, it should reflect the fact that this is not art for oneself, but art for and with the community."[14] Almost inevitably, Berlage concluded that urban design provided the analysis and resolution of aesthetic problems created by standardized housing. But he did not make himself heard. In his commentary, Gulden wrote that Berlage went around the question. Berlage confronted the problem again in his *Schoonheid in samenleving*,[15] published shortly thereafter, in which he took a completely different approach. He did not limit himself to discussing the issue of standardized housing, and he also presented arguments drawn from philosophy and art history.

Published in 1919, *Schoonheid in samenleving* is not easy to read. It takes exception with both the "naturalism" of ancient art and the degenerate "subjectivity" of new art. By ancient art, Berlage meant the nineteenth-century imitations of past styles, and by new art, he meant the first forms of abstract art. The only serious response to his book came from Theo van Doesburg.[16] Van Doesburg's reaction is the more remarkable since Berlage's ideas on standardization had been received positively in *De Stijl*.[17] Clearly, the tone of *Schoonheid in samenleving* is not that of a program of standardization. Moreover, Van Doesburg was piqued by Berlage's rejection of modern abstract art, and discussing Berlage's book helped him rapidly develop his own ideas on architecture. He presented Berlage's text as an architectural theory of form and type, in which the abstract character of an architectural type should be symbolized by a form in order to become art. What is really important, he wrote, "is to transpose the abstract and metaphysical into reality, to *shape* it rather than *symbolize* it."[18] Van Doesburg was contrasting an architecture of form and type with an architecture *without forms*.[19]

Berlage's line of reasoning was unusual. He followed the nineteenth-century theory of architecture and distinguished between two poles, "a utilitarian object" and "an artistic form."[20] The former is the raw, natural state of architecture—the result of purely functional demands—while the latter is the result of artistic work and spiritualization. The utilitarian aspect of architecture revolves around the objective spatial form and the resulting manner in which type/form is built. The artistic aspect revolves around the architect's subjective participation, the symbolic form. Utilitarian buildings have no intrinsic artistic value; at the most, their natural beauty can move the viewer. This is as true of nineteenth-century steel buildings as it is of a Bushman's shelter. A building becomes a work of art only when the architect's personal experience makes it rise above its natural state.

Berlage's argument for standardized housing is based on a similar notion that there are universally accepted, primordial forms of architecture and a personal act to create symbols without which these forms are not art. He conceived of urban development as the field for the artistic form of standardized housing, thus showing that the utilitarian aspect of this architecture could be institutionalized without forfeiting aesthetic requirements.

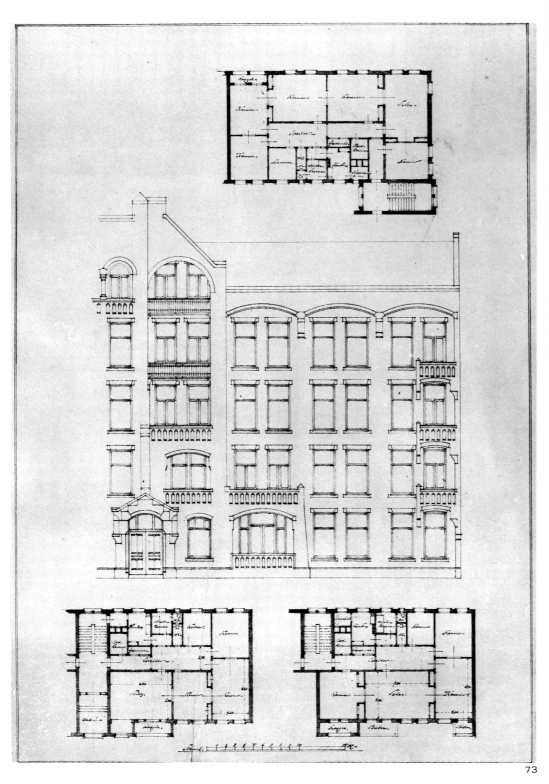

73. *Building plan for the museum area, Amsterdam, 1895–1896, ground plans and elevation for a portion of a building on the south side.*

In his considerations on the historic development of architecture, Berlage regarded the utilitarian object as the material basis for the history of artistic forms and the artistic form itself as the superstructure. Consequently, Berlage did not view the succession of styles as a valid moving force in the history of architecture. What comes first is the history of the material basis, the utilitarian aspect of architecture, and techniques of construction. The history of artistic forms and outer stylistic characteristics comes second, as a result of the former. Berlage imagined an architectural prototype, which was built in different manners in the course of history and changed specific aesthetic configurations according to building techniques and historic circumstances.

This architectural prototype is closely linked to the purpose of the construction: "Building means creating space to provide man with a shelter." He then proceeded to explain.[21] The prototype is a square box: four walls, a floor, and a roof. To be usable, this box gets a window and a door, both indispensable elements. Without a door, the space has no meaning and cannot be inhabited. The window is the first additional element that is, in a sense, an antithesis to the wall: It lets in light, which allows the space to become visible. While the interior of the box is space, the exterior is a mass, which gives a visible shape to space. The window is the first opportunity to introduce rhythm in this mass: and so the façade is created. The window, therefore, is the first clear artistic form. And volumetric relationships are the first aesthetic achievement directly derived from architecture's most objective forms, which are close to architectural prototypes. Berlage concluded that consciously satisfying volumetric relationships alone can create art and make artistic forms superfluous. Should the architect decide to use ornamentation, this should be limited to the structural parts so as not to blur the volumetric relationship.

Van Doesburg's reaction was both simple and effective. He simply rejected Berlage's dialectical relationship between utilitarian objects and artistic forms. His argument for an architecture *without forms* was not aimed at artistic forms per se, but at an artistic form tied firmly to a rigid prototype of architecture. Berlage used the self-contained characteristics of the prototype to create the visual aspect of a building as an independent artistic form, but also to define the basic units of great complexes. It made little difference whether they were complexes in history or in a city. Van Doesburg rejected precisely this rigid prototype. Berlage viewed the nineteenth-century steel building only as another manner to build a basic architectural form that remained the same but was devoid of intrinsic artistic value. Unlike Berlage, Van Doesburg regarded it as a new form without any preestablished concept of architectural form: "A form without purpose, preconception, or artistic pretensions, but real, purely based on geometry, without intention other than to control and shape space with steel, glass, and reinforced concrete."[22] A new architecture confined in a rigid prototype bears directly on the issue of repetition. "Modern architecture has done away with symmetry's monotonous

74. *Design of an apartment building for Eigen Haard, Amsterdam, 1902, study of ground plans.*

75. *Apartment building with stores on Hobbemastraat, Amsterdam, 1903–04, ground plan of the second floor and section, September 1904.*

76. *Apartment building with stores on Hobbemastraat, Amsterdam, 1903–04, building plan, September 1904.*

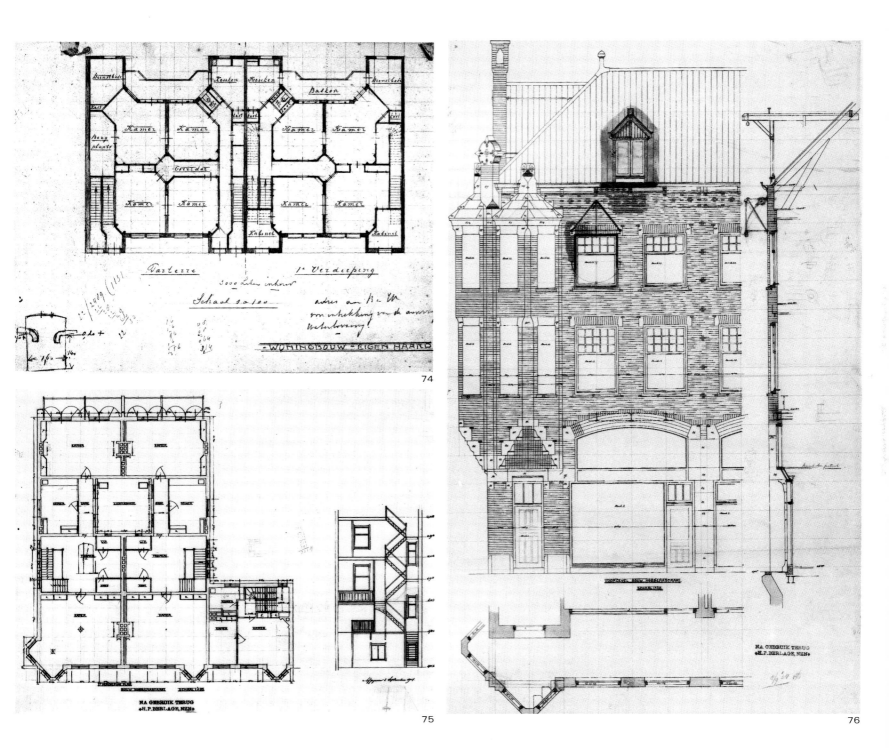

74

75

76

repetition, the stiff similarity of two halves, the mirror image. It does not know repetitions in time, vistas of unified street fronts, and standardization. A group of buildings is as much of a unit as a single house. The rules applicable to single houses are also valid for groups of buildings or cities. To symmetry, the new architecture contrasts a *balanced relationship between dissimilar parts.*"[23] Van Doesburg rejected the notion of a preconceived utilitarian object; he took the exactly opposite stand and sought to give an independent reality to the means to artistic forms. He proposed to use the purity of plastic means rather than artistic forms as symbols or individual creations. Clearly, he did not take Berlage's ideas into account and included among these means the moments in the development of forms which Berlage had predetermined for the objectivity of utilitarian objects. Consequently, what Berlage called the utilitarian objects of architecture, making them into social institutions (types of housing, housing complexes, streets, and squares), became for Van Doesburg the object of an ever renewed architectural process.

Clearly, Berlage preferred to use a proportional geometric system to define architectural forms, without resorting to decorative artistic forms. In "Beschouwingen over Stijl," in 1905, he asked himself whether such a system was not the best to bring order into architecture.[24] The strength of the proportional system is that the aesthetic unity of a building is achieved through such inner stylistic means as dimensional relationships, rather than the external, overlaid means of classical architecture. The dimensional system becomes a constant yardstick, on the basis of which the building is rhythmically developed. If the selected module is correctly used, the proportions of the building are almost automatically correct.

The best known examples are Berlage's designs of plans and elevations of the Amsterdam Stock Exchange, which were drawn with a modular system. A proportional grid can also be seen in other designs: the Villa Henny in The Hague (1898); and, in Amsterdam, the designs for townhouses at the corner of Hobbemastraat and Jan Luykenstraat (1891), an apartment building (1898), the Villa Parkwijck (1900), four apartment buildings on Frans van Mierisstraat (1902), and three residential buildings with commercial space on Hobbemastraat (1904).

The buildings on Hobbemastraat reveal the details of a modular system. The floor plan was designed on a grid based on a square module measuring 47⅞" x 47⅞" (1.21 x 1.21 meters); the elevations were designed on a grid based on a module 47⅞ inches wide (1.21 meter) and 39⅜ inches high (1.00 meter). The whole building rests on this modular grid. Whenever possible, the walls follow the module's straight line and pilasters stand at the points of intersection. The axes of the openings for windows and doors coincide with a modular line or a line between two modular ones. The size of the space outlined by walls, floors, and ceilings is visibly ruled by the module, while the position of the openings and the pilasters, stairs, closets, fireplaces, and light fixtures marks the rhythm of this modulation.

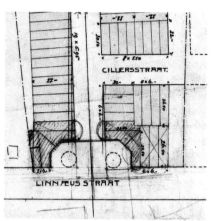

77

77. *Twin apartment buildings with stores on Linnaeusstraat, Amsterdam 1905, plan study.*

This modular system rules the interior as well as the exterior decorations. On the façade, the grid between two dwellings is marked by masonry crosses, which reveal the vertical modular line and help to measure the height of the building in meters. Even the rhythm in the frieze under the cornice and the projection of the oriels are regulated by the module. This modular system has aesthetic as well as practical reasons. While it rigidly structures the floor plan, it intervenes less in the vertical development of the building. The relationship between vertical and horizontal systems is not due to an aesthetic preconception. Berlage did not use the so-called Egyptian triangle or the golden section. His choice seemed dictated by practical reasons; this is the most evident in the horizontal grid, since the 47⅞" x 47⅞" module is related to the dimensions of the brickwork. In the drawings, measurements are not given in centimeters but in heads; the 47⅞ inch module corresponds to eleven heads, each head being the end size in a brick of the Waal type. The same for the elevations: The 39⅜ inch module corresponds to sixteen courses of bricks. It can be correctly assumed that the significance of the modulation is related first to the building's brickwork. The modular system, however, does not include the carpentry work—closets and fixed fixtures,—the work in lighter building materials, and the varying height of the floors. Pride of place is given to brickwork, which follows Berlage's statements about "the architecture of the wall," according to which a flat wall is architecture's essential means of expression.[25]

It so happens that Berlage did not use a modular system in his large residential projects for De Arbeiderswoning and the Algemeene Woningbouwvereeniging, although he did not pay less attention to proportions. And we know from *Schoonheid in samenleving* that he regarded spatial proportions as the first artistic form in architecture. Instead of a modular relationship, he used a system of dwelling types for these residential developments. These types were even more far-reaching than the proportional grids, because they were not limited to a single building. Types have a bearing on the whole structure of a plan, the distribution of the building components, and the specifications of the main measurements in each building.

Created in 1906, De Arbeiderswoning was a sort of affiliate of the Social-Technical Association of Democratic Engineers and Architects. Its president, G. Van Gelder; secretary, A. Keppler; and one board member, J. van Hettinga Tromp, were board members of the Social-Technical Association. The most active member of De Arbeiderswoning was Keppler, who worked as a volunteer at the Bureau of Inspection of Construction and Housing. He was involved in every initiative and negotiation. On October 2, 1907, H.P. Berlage, D. Hudig, and F.M. Wibaut were asked to be trustees of De Arbeiderswoning.[26] Berlage accepted, at least for a year.

In February 1908, De Arbeiderswoning took a decisive step that was to influence the rest of its activity until it closed in 1918. It submitted a request to the municipal administration of Amsterdam for the funding of the building and management of low-income housing. Since

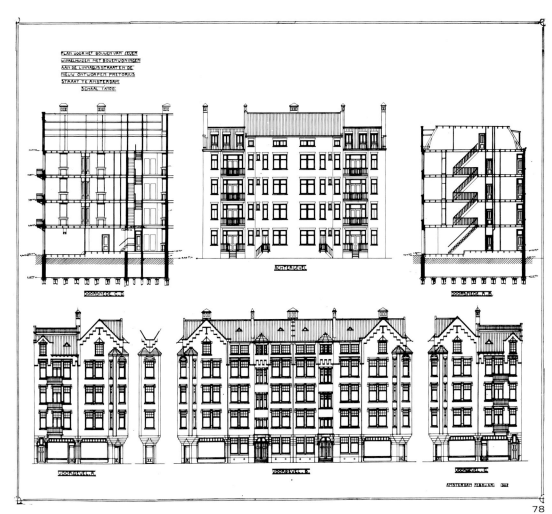

the establishment of the Woningwet (housing law) in 1902, building corporations could ask the State, through the municipal authorities, for low-interest loans to build low-income housing. De Arbeiderswoning's application was different: The municipality was asked not only to finance the construction but also to subsidize the corporation because the income from the rental would not be sufficient to break even—the rents were to be low and stabilized. This initiative was a variation of the amendment to the housing law proposed by the Social-Technical Association and the Housing Council of Amsterdam:[27] They had proposed to extend the mortgage from fifty to eighty years in order to reduce the rents, which required an amendment of the law. De Arbeiderswoning's request, however, was covered by the regulations in force, which made provisions for loans and, in some cases, subsidies.

The correspondence between Keppler and Wibaut—who was both a board member of De Arbeiderswoning and a Social-Democratic councilman of the City of Amsterdam—shows that the consequences of this application had not been entirely considered. Keppler wondered whether the income of the future tenants of the low-cost apartments of the corporation should not be subject to some conditions: "Will families with many children have a reduction? Should we encourage them to rent the apartments?"[28] Even J.W.C. Tellegen, the director of the Bureau for Construction and Housing, who considered Wibaut's request, wondered with dismay how the corporation could be sure that such low rentals would end up with the families that were rightly entitled to them.[29] The Bureau's report for 1909 reveals that the previous year De Arbeiderswoning had applied for a loan and subsidies for 225 housing units, arguing that "this proposal was linked to measures to combat the overcrowding of apartments."[30]

Not surprisingly, such a request could not be answered quickly. Meanwhile, De Arbeiderswoning modified its plans and, in 1911, sent another proposal for 720 housing units. The design of the plans presented several interesting aspects. The initial proposal was for twin buildings with a staircase leading to eight apartments. The name of the designer is not known, but it was probably Keppler. In the Berlage archives, there is an undated "floor plan for low-income housing." It bears resemblances with both sets of plans of De Arbeiderswoning, and, presumably, it was done during the time between the two proposals. This could mean that Berlage was involved with the designs of De Arbeiderswoning at a very early stage, not only as a trustee of the corporation but also as an architect. It is almost certain, however, that the plans of the second proposal were made by Keppler, who published them in a brochure of the Amsterdam Housing Council in 1911, together with the first plans.[31]

In June 1911, Berlage and K.P.C. de Bazel were asked to design housing for De Arbeiderswoning. De Bazel was put in charge of a first site on Van Beuningenplein and Berlage, a second site on Zaagmolenstraat and a third one on Javaplein. Keppler gave them a ground plan as a point of departure: It was an exact copy of a model designed

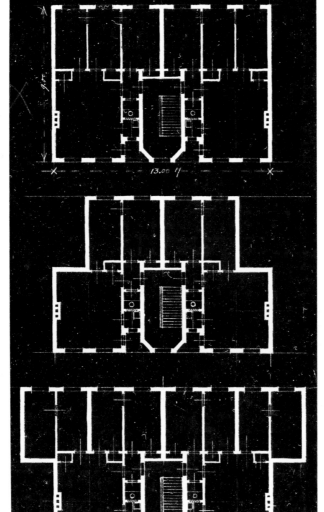

79

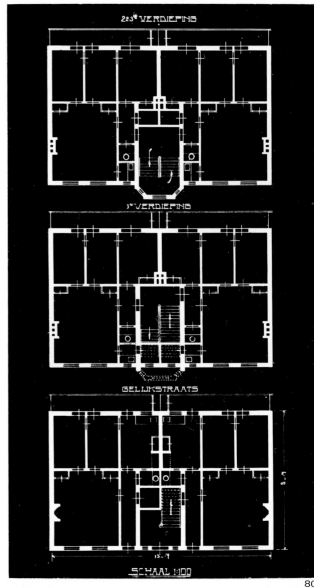

80

79. A. Keppler, housing type for De Arbeiderswoning, 1910.

80, 81. Berlage's development of Keppler's model, 1911, drawings, section, attic, and foundations.

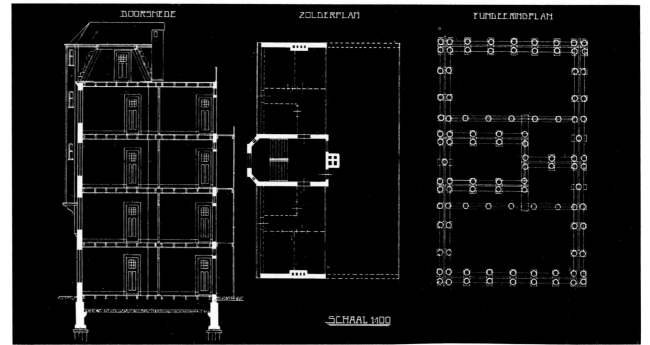

81

by Robert Henry for the London World Fair of 1851, known in the Netherlands in the slightly modified form given by the *Verslag aan den Koning* of 1855.[32] Keppler judged it to be worth considering: Its main feature was a central staircase leading to eight apartments; as a consequence, the arrangement of the buildings was not based on a single dwelling but on a pair of symmetrical dwellings around the stairs. The bedrooms faced an interior courtyard, and the living area and stairs were on the street side of the building. Instead of a kitchen, there was a scullery for washing dishes, and the cooking was done in the living room.

Since Berlage and De Bazel were given similar assignments, their designs make for an interesting comparison. On Zaagmolenstraat, Berlage kept to the prototype of a housing complex, while on Javaplein he divided it into three small attached buildings. De Bazel did precisely the opposite. On Van Beuningenplein, each of his two complexes is built on two combined lots. His treatment of the corners is noteworthy, and the diagonal position of the stairs in those corners ensures the continuity of the building. By contrast, Berlage just cut off the corners of his buildings. There are remarkable resemblances between Berlage's façades on Zaagmolenstraat and De Bazel's first building on Van Beuningenplein: They both emphasize the stairwells and corners. The second building by De Bazel features a central part deeply recessed from the square; the corners of the recessed part are treated like the outer corners of the building. The elevation of the roof at the corners and the strong pediment above the stairwells make the complex even more sculptural. In his municipal housing on Spaarndammerbuurt (1917), De Bazel's huge projecting roof creates an even stronger effect. Berlage designed much plainer roofs. On Javaplein, he simply relied on the strong sculptural effect of the staircases, open corners, and rhythmic succession of the three buildings. Neither Berlage nor De Bazel regarded the housing complex only as a model for developing a site. They used the opportunity to define the housing complex as an architectural unit by relying only on a simple selection of dwelling types, simple arrangements and repetitions of these types, simple architectural means for the façade, and the shape of the roof.

The specifications for the housing complexes on Javaplein were ready in July 1912; the ones for the building on Zaagmolenstraat, in November of the same year. Meanwhile, the Social-Democratic Party, SDAP, submitted a proposal to the municipal council that housing be built within the frame of the existing housing law and rented below the cost of construction and management. The answer to this request was given only in 1913. The socialist Wibaut, recently elected councilman, intervened energetically to help resolve the administrative difficulties between the municipality and the State due to a combined request for a loan and subsidies. On October 1, 1914, the request was officially approved; Berlage's building on Zaagmolenstraat and De Bazel's buildings on Van Beuningenplein were inaugurated on October 16, 1915.

Before getting the commission from De Arbeiderswoning, Berlage also became the architect of the Algemeene Woningbouwvereeniging. This corporation was founded by active leaders of the Nederlandsch Verbond Vakvereenigingen, the association of Dutch unions. Leaders of the different union movements were invited to its first meeting.[33] Keppler spoke and explained the purpose of the corporation, which was independent of religious denominations and trade groups. A provisional board of directors was elected at the same meeting; it included Keppler, L. Soesan, A. Kan, M.J. Meijers, J.C. Mebius, and E. Kupers; F.M. Wibaut and Jan A. van Zutphen volunteered as trustees.[34]

In October 1910, shortly after the corporation was ratified, Berlage received his commission. The leadership thought it had made a good choice and was convinced that Berlage could "provide our members with good housing, within the limits of the construction costs, which could be exemplary from an aesthetic point of view." They felt also that they should thank Berlage for their growing membership, especially after the meeting of June 14, 1911, during which Berlage presented his design.[35] The permanent board was elected at that same meeting. Keppler resigned from the board because of his appointment with the municipal Bureau of Inspection of Construction and Housing, but he then returned to the board as a trustee representing the municipality. The selection of Berlage as the corporation's architect was also due to the fact that diamond workers, who played a leading role in the trade-union movement, were widely represented in the executive committee of the Algemeene Woningbouwvereeniging and made up 20 to 25 percent of the membership. In the late 1890s, two leaders of the diamond workers' union, Jan A. van Zutphen and Henri Polak, had commissioned Berlage for a union headquarters building that would be "the symbol of the working class, the beauty and strength of which it was to express."[36]

Berlage designed five housing complexes, to be built on Tolstraat, Transvaalbuurt, Spreeuwenpark, Nieuwe Tolstraat, and Staatsliedenbuurt. The last two projects were finally built after the designs of J. van Epen, in which Berlage's hand can be felt. Berlage and the Algemeene Woningbouwvereeniging regarded the buildings on Tolstraat and Transvaalbuurt as a single design on four sites. Only for the contracts were the four building complexes treated separately. By mutual agreement with Berlage, the corporation proposed a series of dwelling types of different sizes, for large and small families, which would be rented for between 2.50 and 6.50 florins a week. One of the corporation's objectives was to create different types of apartments: If it wanted to be true to its name of "General Corporation for Housing," as opposed to "sole-purpose corporation," it had to open its doors to all and take into account the size and income of families.[37]

The types of apartments still showed a strong link with the single-family "Dutch house." There is no common stairwell and each apartment, whenever possible, has its

82. *Study for low-income housing,
cross-sections, elevations, ground plan,
1911 (?).*

own stairs—at a minimum, the ground-floor apartment is separate from the upper floors. Each apartment is made of a wide and a narrow bay. Theoretically, the wide bay includes two adjoining rooms separated by a sliding door, one room of which can be used as a second living space or a large bedroom or be divided into two narrow bedrooms. The narrow bay includes the foyer, corridor, stairs, bathroom, and kitchen and, sometimes, another bedroom. The large bay is more or less of the same size in every type of apartment, and it is, in a way, the single constant element throughout the series. The variations are to be found in the narrow bay, which can extend the front or back of the building to create another room. In the types C, D, K, and L—as well as F in the Spreeuwenpark building—the variation consists of the addition of a second small, narrow bay containing bedrooms. Another theme in these series is the combination of two types. C and D, as well as K and L, are always designed in pairs so that both can use the additional bay between them. Types A, B, and F, for low buildings, are more complex. They are variations of J.H.W. Leliman's apartments "2 on 3," designed on Zeeburgerdijk in 1913 for the Eigen Haard corporation. They each group five apartments: two small ones on the ground floor and three larger ones on the second floor, each with additional bedrooms in the attic. The purpose of this grouping is to create, even in the smaller combinations, the widest possible range in the size of apartments in order to suit either large or small families, in accordance with the institutional views of the Algemeene Woningbouwvereeniging. The five-story buildings feature mainly apartments with three or four rooms, with an additional double living area in the type L. The lower buildings, where the attic is used, feature combinations of three-, four-, five-, and six-room apartments.

The corporation's annual report shows that the initial designs for Tolstraat and Transvaalbuurt must have looked different.[38] The site allotted for the apartments on Tolstraat was smaller than that which had been requested. After a first and limited part of the complex was built, the rest was completed only in 1918. The design for the Transvaalbuurt was radically modified upon the request of the municipal Bureau of Public Works. Two small complexes of nine apartments each were supposed to be built on Transvaalplein; they were rejected by the municipal authorities on the grounds that a street planned within the housing complex would create "back streets." The Bureau of Public Works ruled that the square be left unbuilt to be equipped as a playground. Later, the Smitstraat was extended in a straight line, and later still, a small rectangular complex was erected on the west side.

Berlage made the designs between April 1 and June 14, 1911, and drew up a preliminary cost specification, on the basis of which the Algemeene Woningbouwvereeniging decided to take a long-term lease on the sites. Construction work started in 1912 on Tolstraat and Transvaalbuurt. Berlage had designed two different versions, the first one dated June 1911 and the second, which was executed, dated March–April 1912. The main dif-

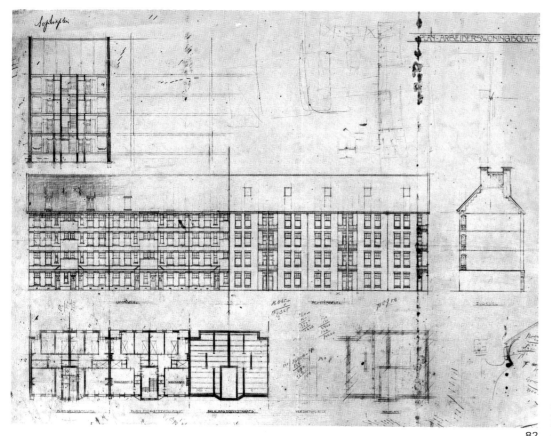

82

ference between the versions is in the façades. Let us take the Tolstraat complex as an example: Horizontally, there is little difference between the 1911 and 1912 versions of the façade other than in the role of the windows. In the first version, the design of the openings is austere; there are two types of windows: small ones, always in pairs, to light up the stairs; and large windows for the bedrooms and, when they adjoin, the living rooms. In the second version, the design becomes more complex. The overhang jutting out over the street entrance to the types H and L is also designed over the street entrance of the type F. It is important to note that the design of these overhangs has no functional relationship with the space behind them: In the type F, this space is used for the stairs; in L, for a bedroom; in H, for a kitchen. It stems from a wish to enliven the façade of the building. In the narrow bay, which is easily modified, the floor plan can add projecting elements. The living rooms on the upper floors feature a large window and a French window opening onto a balcony; in the type K, the living rooms on the upper floors get oriel windows. The initial severity of the façade is alleviated by the variety created by compact stone overhangs, wooden balconies and oriels, which stand out against a regular brick wall featuring a simple pattern of windows. The design for the Transvaalbuurt underwent a similar evolution. Initially very simple, the treatment of the corners on the northern side becomes much more sculptural. The whole complex is a majestic composition combining a low, recessed central part and higher, projecting wings; the architect plays skillfully with sloping and flat roofs, cornices, and the harmony between the oriels, roofs, balconies, and overhangs, which conclude with a towerlike part on the corner.

In fact, the façades for the Algemeene Woningbouwvereeniging are quite remarkable. Berlage never designed a general view of the elevations for each of the building complexes; on the contrary, he gave each type of apartment its own façade while he was developing his dwelling types. The façade of the whole building is a construction of several interconnected types. Berlage did not use a fixed rule for the precise location of each apartment type in the building—with the exception of the type J, the store, which is always on the corner—nor for the location of each façade type in the general design of the whole façade. He followed only an elementary rule for the horizontal connection of the apartments: Pairs of apartments are always placed in a mirror image of one another, and some types are grouped in more complex combinations. All other types of apartments are distributed arbitrarily, whether in the low or the five-story buildings. The sequence of apartment types on the ground plan of the housing complex determines the composition of the façade. Simple rules in the combination and connection, together with preestablished façade types, provide a sufficient guarantee for the architectural quality of the entire façade. A conclusion then prevails: What seems to be a single house—because it has been designed as such—in fact combines four superposed dwellings, and the respective type of each dwelling cannot

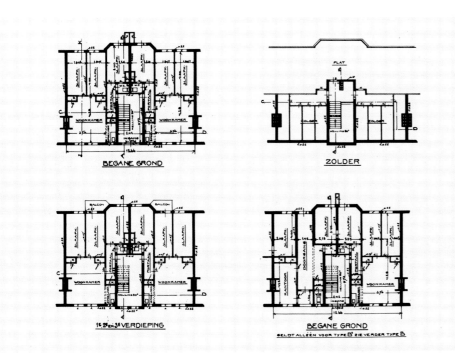

83

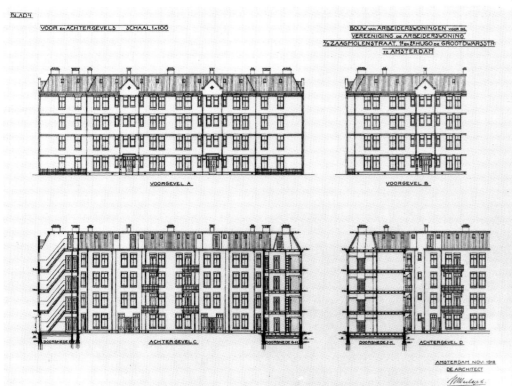

84

85. Three buildings of low-income housing for De Arbeiderswoning, east Amsterdam, Indischebuurt, 1911–15, draft plan.

86. Three buildings of low-income housing for De Arbeiderswoning, east Amsterdam, Indischebuurt, 1911–15, distribution of the types and sketch plan, July 1912.

87. Three buildings of low-income housing for De Arbeiderswoning, east Amsterdam, Indischebuurt, 1911–15, floor plans of the type A, July 1912.

88. Three buildings of low-income housing for De Arbeiderswoning, east Amsterdam, Indischebuurt, 1911–15, floor plans of the types B and B', July 1912.

89. Three buildings of low-income housing for De Arbeiderswoning, east Amsterdam, Indischebuurt, 1911–15, elevation of the street front and the inner courtyard, July 1912.

90. Three buildings of low-income housing for De Arbeiderswoning, east Amsterdam, Indischebuurt, 1911–15, building plan.

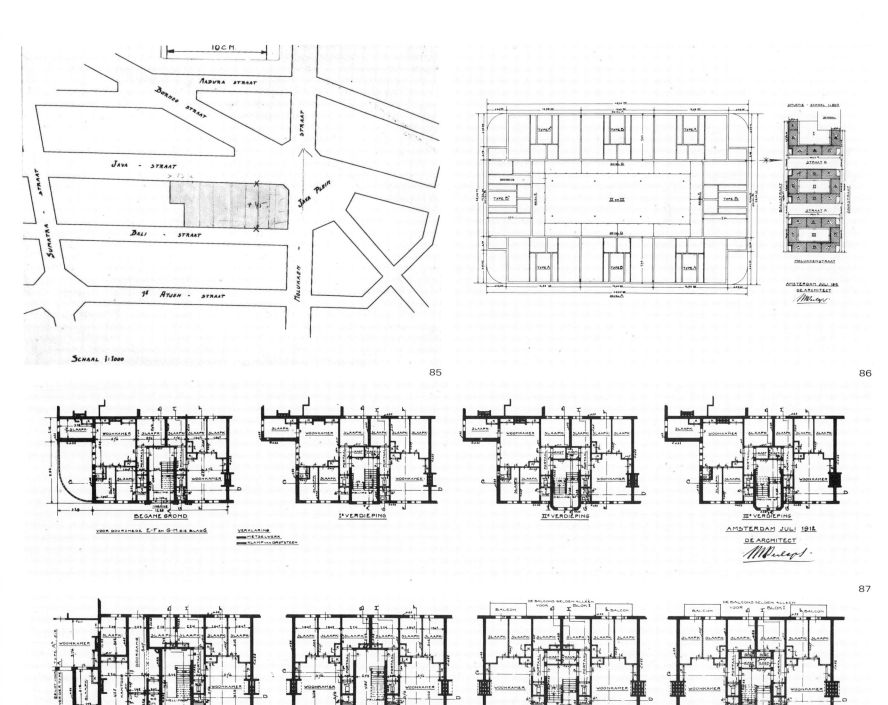

VOORGEVEL A

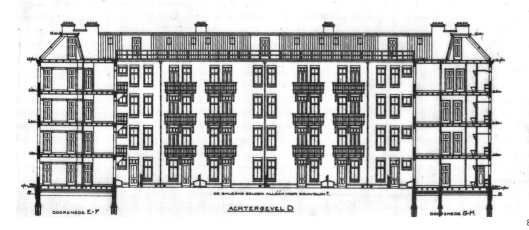

DOORSNEDE E-F   DE BALCONS GELDEN ALLEEN VOOR BOUWBLOK II   DOORSNEDE G-H
                              ACHTERGEVEL D

89

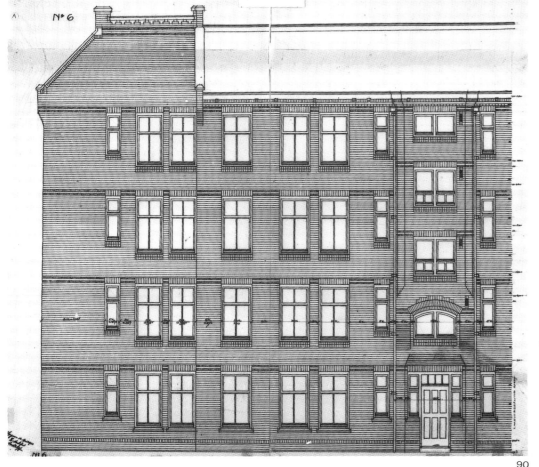

90

be recognized from the façade. In his design of a housing complex, Berlage makes the "Dutch house" vanish in a mirror arrangement of single houses. The greater size created by symmetrical arrangements focuses the attention on the entire building, while the single apartment type—the nucleus of the building—does not have its own expression. Even in the low buildings, Berlage achieved the same result in an arrangement of "free-standing little houses." His transformation of the "Dutch house" into "Hausmaterial" (housing material), to use A.E. Brinckmann's term, is decisive. On the one hand, the different types of dwellings respond to the different requirements of different social classes; on the other, the specific spatial structure of these types is ruled first by the character of the building in which they are placed—in this case, a high-density complex. Single dwellings are conditioned by the new architecture of grouped buildings, and they lose their individual style.

The Algemeene Woningbouwvereeniging's annual report for 1912 mentioned the housing complexes of Staatsliedenbuurt and Spreeuwenpark. While waiting for a decision on the land, it also discussed plans for the extension of the Tolstraat complex on Nieuwe Tolstraat; that part of the complex was to be completed only in 1918. Pride of place was given to the issue of the housing on Spreeuwenpark, north of the IJ river. According to the housing regulations of 1912, buildings north of the IJ could not be more than four stories high. The influential Keppler was the main proponent of the idea of "free-standing little houses," and the 1914 development plan for this area reflected this preference for low buildings. The complicated arrangement "2 over 3" low buildings proved, however, that not every family could live on the ground floor. Berlage's design is somewhat different from the others. His two housing complexes each have an inner public area: One is a communal garden, next to small private gardens, and the other is occupied by school buildings. The smaller and cheaper houses face the small street between the two complexes, with very little view. Otherwise, the housing complex presents architectural characteristics similar to that of the Tolstraat and the Transvaalbuurt. The only notable difference is at the intersection of two rows of houses at the corner of the complexes, where he designed a low and simple connecting element usually housing the kitchen or the scullery, which increases the architectural quality and sculptural effect of the corners.

The 1914 designs bear at the bottom, next to Berlage's signature, that of J.C. van Epen, and the word "architect" is changed to "architects." Under the line "Amsterdam: January 1914," the line "Amsterdam: October 1912" is faintly visible. Berlage moved from Amsterdam to The Hague at that time, to work for Wm. H. Müller & Co. According to P. Singelenberg, he moved on September 1, 1913.[39] The terms of the contract stipulated that he settle in The Hague and also that he work exclusively for the Müller company. Berlage was to divest himself of all his current design commissions, and the Müllers made an exception only for the revision of the develop-

91. *K.P.C. de Bazel, two buildings of low-income housing for De Arbeiderswoning on Van Beuningenplein, 1914–18, elevation and floor plan of the first building on De Kempenaerstraat, October 1913.*

92. *K.P.C. de Bazel, two buildings of low-income housing for De Arbeiderswoning on Van Beuningenplein, 1914–18, elevation and floor plan of the second building on Van Beuningenplein, December 1915.*

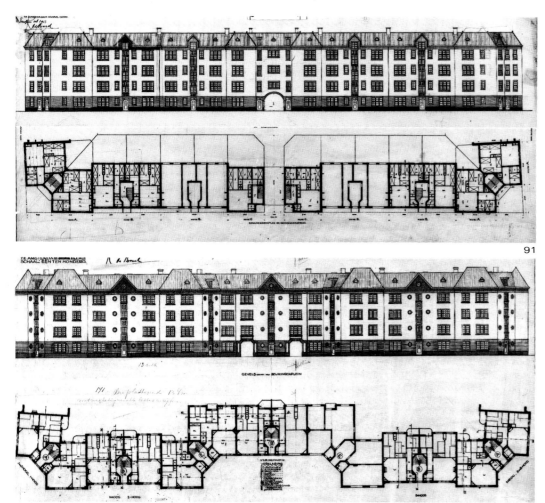

ment plan for the south of Amsterdam. The contract with the Müller company lasted until 1919, and it is not quite clear how things went during that period. As an independent architect, Van Epen had already designed housing. His work was widely appreciated and he was a friend of Wibaut. These may have been the reasons why the Algemeene Woningbouwvereeniging chose him as Berlage's successor. Consequently, from January 1914 on, the work was done in Van Epen's studio in Amsterdam and not at Berlage's in The Hague. It was Van Epen who came to be in charge of the execution of the designs on Spreeuwenpark.

In a certain sense, the designs for the housing complexes on Staatsliedenbuurt and Tolstraat/Nieuwe Tolstraat are variations of the three first designs submitted to the corporation. The January 1913 designs for the buildings on Staatsliedenbuurt, on Van Hallstraat and De Kempenaerstraat, are very close to that of the Transvaalbuurt. The rectangular complex on the corner of Smitstraat is clearly a model for that on De Kempenaerstraat, and the same is true of the recessed building on Transvaalstraat respective to that on Van Hallstraat. The small complexes on De Kempenaerstraat are exact copies of the ones on Transvaalstraat. In June 1913, the designs were changed because the street plan was modified; there was also a change in the distribution of sites on Van Hallstraat. The designs were submitted in October 1913, followed by new discussions on the land and the street plan. Construction work began only in 1917, under the direction of Van Epen. For the first time, he designed a housing type with a stairwell for the Algemeene Woningbouwvereeniging. The second portion of the Tolstraat/Nieuwe Tolstraat project also featured such a stairwell, unlike the portion built earlier. For Tolstraat/Nieuwe Tolstraat, Van Epen continued along the lines of Berlage's façade. For the Staatsliedenbuurt project, however, he created a much more personal design.

On Saturday, October 16, 1915, tenants were given apartments in the first housing complexes built by De Arbeiderswoning on Van Beuningenplein and Zaagmolenstraat and designed respectively by De Bazel and Berlage. In his speech, councilman Wibaut emphasized the pioneering role of the corporation in its program to rent apartments "below cost."[40] With these two housing complexes, De Arbeiderswoning created a precedent that opened the way to a plan for 2,000 units, presented by the SDAP to the municipal council on June 1911. This plan was the first step toward the municipality's more general housing policy. The role of the corporation had been carefully planned. In 1908, Wibaut emphasized the significance of De Arbeiderswoning's first proposal, which he regarded as a premise for the SDAP's policy of low-income housing in the different municipalities. In the magazine *De Gemeente*, Wibaut argued repeatedly for special subsidies to build housing for slum-dwellers and large families, as well as for a wider action on the part of building corporations and municipal administrations.[41] He claimed that such initiative was necessary because the low-interest loans granted within the existing framework

93. K.P.C. de Bazel, two buildings of low-income housing for De Arbeiderswoning on Van Beuningenplein, 1914–18, period photograph of the corner.

93

of the housing law were inadequate in the face of the city's need for low-income housing: The rents were still too high. Moreover, the state had once before allocated extra subsidies against the deficit incurred through the building of new houses, when it waged its "war against slums." Circumstances were ripe to establish a more ambitious policy.[42] The difference between the 1908 proposal of De Arbeiderswoning and that of 1911 was only a matter of scale, which could only be another indication of the seriousness of the housing shortage.

The SDAP confronted the political consequences of this enormous problem with a plan for 2,000 housing units, submitted to the municipal council in 1911, almost at the same time as the proposal of De Arbeiderswoning.[42] The difference between the two proposals was that one was submitted by politicians, while the other came from a private organization working within the framework of the housing law. This law gave a significant executive role to the municipality, but the initiative for the construction of low-income housing was left to special private corporations. The municipality had a relatively passive role: mostly the drafting of the building and health codes, statistics on housing and occupancy rate, and control of the housing corporations. They also had an active, albeit secondary, role: the notifications for housing improvements, decisions on insalubrious slums, and expropriations. The construction itself was left to private contractors and housing corporations. Therefore, it could not be said that the municipality had an active building policy. The shrewd strategy around the proposal of De Arbeiderswoning was to create a precedent and to show the municipal authorities that an active and coordinated policy for low-income housing was necessary.

The municipal council found it as difficult to decide on the proposal of De Arbeiderswoning as on the SDAP's plan for 2,000 housing units. By the end of 1913 it still had not given its answer. At the budget meetings of 1914, the SDAP insisted for the creation of a sixth council seat, to deal specifically with low-income housing. The party put forward one of its men, Wibaut, as a candidate. He was confirmed in March 1914.[43] He immediately asked Tellegen, the director of the Bureau for Construction and Housing, for a report, which he got in June 1914. Meanwhile, the municipal council granted the loan to De Arbeiderswoning; the state, however, persisted in its denial.

During this time, Keppler did not remain inactive. He wrote a book, *Gemeentelijke woningbouw*, in which he reviewed the arguments in favor and against such policy and drew up an inventory of municipal housing projects built since the housing law was promulgated.[44] According to the law, each borough can underwrite the cost of the buildings "needed to comply with the housing law." The main objection to municipal construction of housing was that it would spoil the market for private business. Others were in favor of a municipal plan, "as long as the building of new housing was due to the removal of slums." Keppler concluded that, although the law allowed for municipal

94. *Low-income project for the Algemeene Woningbouwvereeniging, south Amsterdam, 1911–13, floor plans of types F, K, L, H, and sketch plan, June 1911.*

95. *Low-income project for the Algemeene Woningbouwvereeniging, south Amsterdam, 1911–13, floor plans of types F, K, L, H, and sketch plan, March 1912.*

96. *Low-income project for the Algemeene Woningbouwvereeniging, south Amsterdam, 1911–13, elevation of the street front, June 1911.*

97. *Low-income project for the Algemeene Woningbouwvereeniging, south Amsterdam, 1911–13, elevation of the street front, March 1912.*

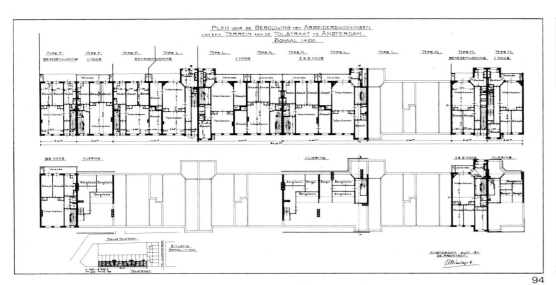

94

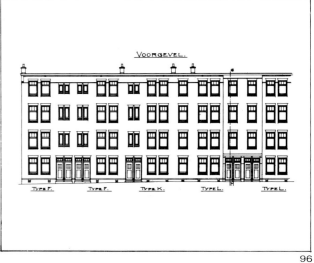

96

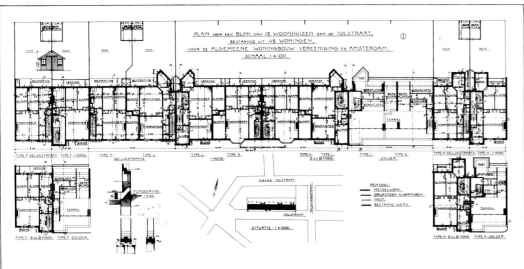

95

97

initiatives in the field of housing, the municipalities had only a marginal role in view of the great number of dwellings built by private corporations. These housing corporations, however, were regulated by the municipality and their independence was only relative. They were controlled by a trustee representing the municipality, they could not accept funds without the borough's authorization, and their plans had to be submitted to the municipality for approval. Moreover, as a rule, the municipality is the first mortgagee. The difference, Keppler concluded, between privately and publicly managed housing was only relative.

In his 1914 report to Wibaut, Tellegen repeated Keppler's observations.[45] Two other critical components of the SDAP plan were submitted for a series of evaluations: of the scale of the plan and the rents "below cost." If it were true that contractors and private corporations did not fulfill their responsibilities and alleviate the housing shortage, and if the municipal administration had to consider building apartments, then a few questions had to be asked: What were the housing requirements? What was the type of housing? And for whom? Using statistical data, Tellegen established the number of vacant dwellings of any kind in each district of the city. He came to the conclusion that there was an acute need, mostly for dwellings with a rent that would be below the management cost of newly built dwellings. Renting "below cost" in the future construction was a necessity. He then considered a delicate point: how to cover the deficit. In the cheapest housing, for which he recommended the type built by De Arbeiderswoning, a ceiling was to be established for the rents; the municipality would meet half the difference between actual management cost and rent ceiling and the state, the other half. The rent was not to not be more than one sixth of the tenants' income; whenever it was higher, the difference was to be paid by Welfare. Thus he established the difference between subsidies for low-income housing and welfare, between productive costs and social costs. Clearly, the income of the tenants had to be verified before the amount of the rent was established. This required supervision and control. Tenants had to pay their rent regularly and abide by the regulations stipulated in the lease; otherwise, they would be evicted. Tellegen proposed to special build housing for "asocial" families, which had been evicted and seemed unable to live in the same building with normal families. The settlements built in Zeeburgerdorp and Asterdorp in the 1920s had such a purpose.[46] Low-cost housing would be managed by private corporations in the same manner as by De Arbeiderswoning; their freedom of action would be limited, and they had to abide by the decisions of the municipal administration, which they represented in some manner. The number of apartments (2,000) in the SDAP proposal was ridiculously low; according to Tellegen, one should start with a minimum of 3,500. While the slums were removed, at least 800 new dwellings, or a total of 8,300, had to be built each year until 1922. Tellegen suggested the creation of a mu-

nicipal Bureau of Housing, independent of the Bureau for Inspection of Construction and Housing and of that of Public Works. The new agency would manage the whole program and be the coordinator for the municipality and the housing corporations.

Tellegen's report brought into perspective the municipality's role in confronting the problems of low-income housing. He was the first to formulate the institutional mechanism later known as public housing policy, by which the building and management of housing are regulated and a significant part of the urban infrastructure can become an instrument of social and political manipulation. The management requires the quantitative and qualitative analysis of the city's physical infrastructure and its inhabitants. It is also necessary to analyze and plan the building requirements, existing housing stock, removal of slums, upkeep of existing buildings, new buildings, and urban expansion. This implies a demographic research of the structure of the population, focused on housing needs, mobility, and commuting. It also means that the relationships between different institutions should be clearly outlined—between housing corporations and contractors, Welfare and other social agencies, as well as the Bureau of Public Works.

On April 1, 1915, the Amsterdam municipal council discussed and approved the proposal for 2,000 housing units, in a slightly modified form to include some of Tellegen's suggestions.[47] At the end of June of the same year, a municipal Bureau of Housing was created and Keppler was named its director. Meanwhile, Tellegen became mayor of the city and Van der Waerden succeeded him as director of the Bureau of Inspection of Construction and Housing. Wibaut remained councilman for low-income housing. The Bureau of Housing was responsible for preparing the construction, managing municipal housing, controlling the housing corporations, and designing detailed site plans to allocate the housing projects. Shortly after it was created, the Bureau asked Van der Pek, De Bazel, Berlage, Gratama, and Versteeg to submit designs. Van der Pek was commissioned for two-storied housing northrth of the IJ, De Bazel for housing on Spaarndammerbuurt, and Berlage and associates for the housing complex in Transvaalbuurt. Berlage, however, could not work on the designs himself; because of his contract with Wm. H. Müller & Co., he gave the work to Gratama and merely supervised the design. The Bureau of Housing prescribed the use of De Arbeiderswoning's approved types for five-story buildings. It should be noted that the plan for the housing complex on Transvaalbuurt is based on the same sort of composition of high and low masses as that which Berlage had proposed a few years earlier, when he designed buildings for the Algemeene Woningbouwvereeniging in the same neighborhood.

Although the Netherlands remained neutral during the First World War, the war had a deep influence on life and society. During the last years of the war, private business ceased completely to build low-income housing

98. Four buildings of low-income housing
for the Algemeene Woningbouwvereeniging,
east Amsterdam, Transvaalbuurt,
1911–13, floor plans of the types J, G,
E, E', and outline plan of the third
building, June 1911.

99. Four buildings of low-income housing
for the Algemeene Woningbouwvereeniging,
east Amsterdam, Transvaalbuurt,
1911–13, elevations and cross-section of
the third building, June 1911.

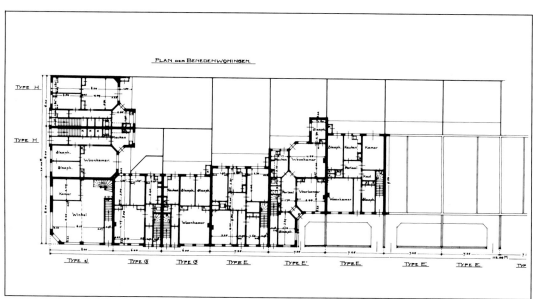

98

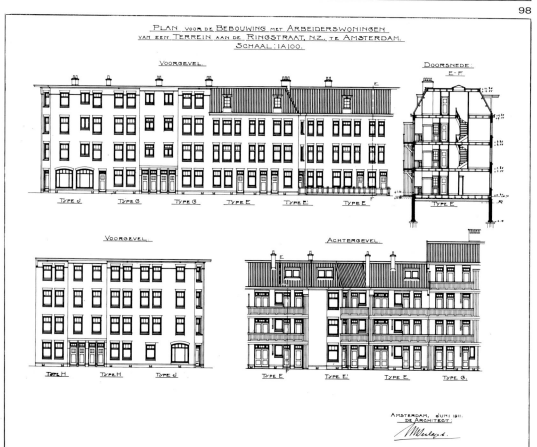

99

and the publicly funded construction provided in the housing law was reduced to a minimum.[48] Because of the resulting shortage, a conference on housing was organized in 1918, where the issue of standardization was discussed. The Minister of Labor (Housing) took note and, in July 1918 and November 1919, he announced two measures to stimulate the construction industry through subsidies.[49] The municipal authorities did not dissimulate their disappointment and regarded these state subsidies as an undermining of their own policy on housing construction, by which tenants, rather than the construction industry, were subsidized. On November 25, 1919, a proposal came before the municipal council to build 32,500 subsidized housing units in five years. The motion stated that "There are now several architectural plans that are very good from the point of view of form and present very good types of dwellings. These designs have been worked on for several years. We can hope for a good urbanization if we distribute judiciously these designs in the development plan. The preparation time should be relatively brief, since plans and designs are ready down to the last detail. We do not mind if a housing complex designed for one part of the city is duplicated in another part. We do not foresee any aesthetic objection, provided that the design of the street plan is taken in consideration. With this in mind, it would be wise to consult Dr. Berlage, at least for the development plans on which he has already worked."[50] The mayor and the council were very clear: The prerogatives of the municipality should be left alone. The manner in which the new program was conceived calls to mind Berlage's position in the face of Van der Waerden's proposal on standardization: The new program established a link between institutionalized housing policy and the realization of a development plan.

From all points of view, the work of De Arbeiderswoning was exemplary for the municipal housing policy. At the beginning, it seemed to align itself with such corporations working for the improvement of certain social groups as the construction company Jordaan and the housing corporation Oud-Amsterdam, which handled insanitary dwellings and—with the help of social workers—slum dwellers. However, De Arbeiderswoning took on a unique role because of its link with the Social-Democratic party. It introduced the most significant premise for a municipal housing policy, the rental below cost. It also brought about the definition of several types of dwellings by giving very specific assignments to its architects, and these types were subsequently adopted by the municipality. Finally, it offered a model for the management of municipal housing, including the type of administration, the social workers in charge of the tenants, the assessment of the tenants' ability to pay their rent, and also the criteria for the stabilization of the rents. Meanwhile, the corporation faced serious problems: Rents were not paid; there were many administrative scandals; there were evictions, acts of vandalism, and fights. On January 1, 1918, De Arbeiderswoning was liquidated and its assets were turned over to the municipality.[51] The task

100

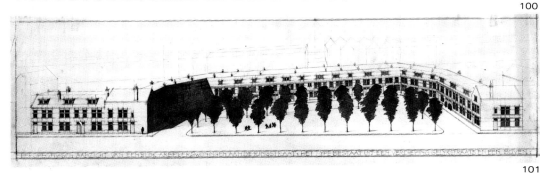

101

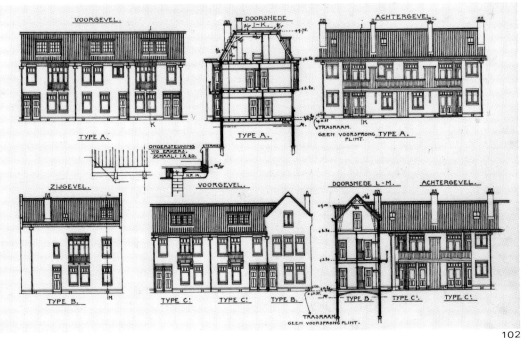

102

of the corporation was completed, and Berlage's role had been considerable. As a trustee of the corporation and as an influential and social-minded architect, he took part in the first battles of De Arbeiderswoning. As a designer, he willingly accepted the constraints that Keppler put on his work. With De Bazel, he proved that with a few types of apartments, a housing complex can become beautiful architecture.

Berlage's second development plan for the south of Amsterdam was drawn up in 1915 and approved by the municipal council in 1917. It would never have been executed had it not been for a grand program of low-income housing and the political structure to implement it. The fruitful combination of a municipal housing program and an orderly urban development had convinced Berlage more than ever that there was a new *Overheidskunst*, an "art of public authorities." The purpose of his first development plan for the south of Amsterdam, in 1904, had still been to slow down a middle-class exodus by offering a beautiful natural environment in the city's immediate vicinity. It gave more importance to the urban environment—which he designed with irregular squares and curving streets, in a style influenced by Sitte—than to housing. From the first sketches of the second development plan, housing clearly played a much more central role. In "Memorie van toelichting," Berlage explained that his development plan called for housing complexes. This would reduce construction cost and simplify the administrative procedures; combined with a right-angle street plan, it would make traffic easier; it would also have aesthetic considerations.[52] These would include the shape and the arrangement of the complexes, their orientation, and, finally, the relationship between the façade of the building and the structure of the urban plan.

Already in 1894, in his essay "Bouwkunst en impressionisme," Berlage took a positive stand on mass construction of housing.[53] He had come to the conclusion that economic development had created a kind of urban development, with its corresponding housing complexes, and that architects had not responded adequately. He further concluded that construction of housing on a large scale should lead architects to a conception of the whole mass of a housing complex and to the possibility of an overall simplification. Instead, they kept elaborating on details and individual characteristics of single houses. The 1896 design for a housing complex on Museumplein offers an excellent architectural solution to the relationship between housing construction on a large scale and a housing complex. It is a colossal complex, with stores and large apartments, covering an area 750' x 200', almost twice the area of the Rijksmuseum or the Amsterdam Stock Exchange. The design of the entrances, covered passageways, recessed corners, and roofs ensures a sculptural effect. The large scale is used to create an urban space: A street is covered; the recessed part of the building forms a square in front of the Stedelijk Museum. At first sight, the open space within the complex seems to be public space. Berlage's 1910 designs for low-income housing are more or less in the same style, but on a larger scale. In 1896 as well as later, Berlage clearly used the architectural elements of Baroque city planning. The regular shape and repetition of blocks in the Museumplein complex, with its accessible interior courtyard, evokes an Italian palazzo, while the crescent shape of his complexes for the Algemeene Woningbouwvereeniging brings the English Baroque to mind. Thus the shape and structure of the housing complex are the starting point for the shaping and structuring of the whole city.

Bird's-eye views of Berlage's development plan for the south of Amsterdam clearly show the articulation in each housing complex and the relationship between these articulations and the grouping of buildings. The division into housing units is visible. The designs for the Algemeene Woningbouwvereeniging had already shown a relationship between the articulation in housing units and the rhythmic divisions of the façade. The roof can also be seen as means of articulation that clarifies certain parts of the structure by indicating endings, continuations, and directions. In some cases, when a street meets a housing complex at a right angle, the façade and the roof are treated differently. Articulations and groupings are subservient to the aesthetic unity of the space outlined by a street or a square. With very simple means, the architecture of a housing complex becomes aesthetically significant in the whole urban plan.

Regarding the orientation of housing complexes, the 1910 report published by the Housing Council, *Rapport over de Volkshuisvesting in de nieuwe stad te Amsterdam*, was decisive.[54] It summed up the negative aspects of the apartments and buildings erected after 1870, but it judged the shape of the housing complexes to be good. The size of the complex and the relative width of the interior courtyard must ensure good air circulation within the complex and ventilation in the apartments. The greatest improvement suggested in the report was to build the complex on a north–south axis and to leave the north and south sides unbuilt, as is usually done in English terrace houses. In this manner, both the front and the back get sunlight. The report also suggested increasing the depth of the complex, allowing for the interior courtyards— which are open because the north and south sides are not built up—to be used for small individual gardens. Berlage took these recommendations to heart. His three housing complexes on Javaplein, designed for De Arbeiderswoning, were placed at a right angle from the east–west axis of the preestablished plan of the site. A quick look at his second development plan for the south of Amsterdam reveals that all the housing complexes are oriented northwest, with a few exceptions along the edges of the plan and the major streets.

On several occasions Berlage returned to Brinckmann's significant considerations on the relationship between buildings and streets. The façade, in particular, was not an easy problem to resolve. "The façades of houses and housing complexes must fill two purposes: First, they must contain the mass of the building standing behind them and indicate its structure; second, they must contain the space of the street and make it a consistent whole. In the Middle Ages, each house was a unit,[55] and the street was the sum total of these units. Since the Baroque, however, we regard the street as a unit." In this statement, Berlage did not regard the housing complex as a unit: The façade was treated as the consequence of the structure of this housing complex, its articulation of masses and the character of its enclosed spaces. Moreover, the concept of the street as a unit created high demands on the structure of the buildings on either side of the street. Berlage dwelled upon these problems in his presentation of the second development for Amsterdam, in particular upon the consequences of the street's aesthetic unity on the development of an urban plan. He claimed that the symmetry of the two main parts of the plan derived directly from his wish for a unified treatment of streets and squares. Once he recognized that the façade had a double purpose, Berlage gave it a more significant and independent role than he had done in his earlier reflections on architecture, in which the façade came second, after the arrangement of masses.[56]

In December 1920, the Ministry of Labor published an album with fifty types of housing.[57] They were to serve as directives for the housing to be built with loans from the State. This provoked a chain reaction on the part of architects, housing corporations, and municipal administrations. In 1921, they published their own album with fifty types of housing.[58] Berlage wrote the introduction and emphasized the architectural significance of the book. The ministry's album was illustrated mostly with plans and sections. The architects chose a greater variety of illustrations, giving an idea of whole housing complexes and the urban context, beside the plans themselves. The first album dealt with surfaces, with the intention of helping financial policy. The second album dealt with the core of architecture for housing and in the independence of municipal authorities and housing corporations. The conflict between State intervention and municipal autonomy was passionately followed by the Social-Democrats in Amsterdam and in the other big cities in particular, where they were the fiery proponents of a municipal housing policy. The first report of the SDAP on the progress of socialism still reflected an enthusiasm for the achievements between 1915 and 1918.[59] It claimed that the municipal management of low-income housing was a reality and that it guaranteed a more socialistic approach. The atmosphere changed in the following years, caused in part by State support of the private construction industry.

The dialectical relationship between central and local government must be kept in mind to understand correctly Berlage's lecture at La Sarraz in 1928, given on the occasion of the foundation of the CIAM.[60] The title of the lecture was "Der Staat und der Widerstreit in der modernen Architektur" (State and opposition in modern architecture). Berlage stated that the Netherlands were the single exception in the conflict between State and archi-

103. *Two buildings of low-income housing for the Algemeene Woningbouwvereeniging, with Van Epen, north Amsterdam, 1912–15, elevations and floor plans of the type A, January 1914, (October 1912).*

104. *Two buildings of low-income housing for the Algemeene Woningbouwvereeniging, with Van Epen, north Amsterdam, 1912–15, elevations and floor plans of the type B, January 1914, (October 1912).*

105. *Two buildings of low-income housing for the Algemeene Woningbouwvereeniging, with Van Epen, north Amsterdam, 1912–15, elevations and floor plans of the types C and D, January 1914, (October 1912).*

106. *Two buildings of low-income housing for the Algemeene Woningbouwvereeniging, with Van Epen, north Amsterdam, 1912–15, elevations and floor plans of the types F and F', January 1914, (October 1912).*

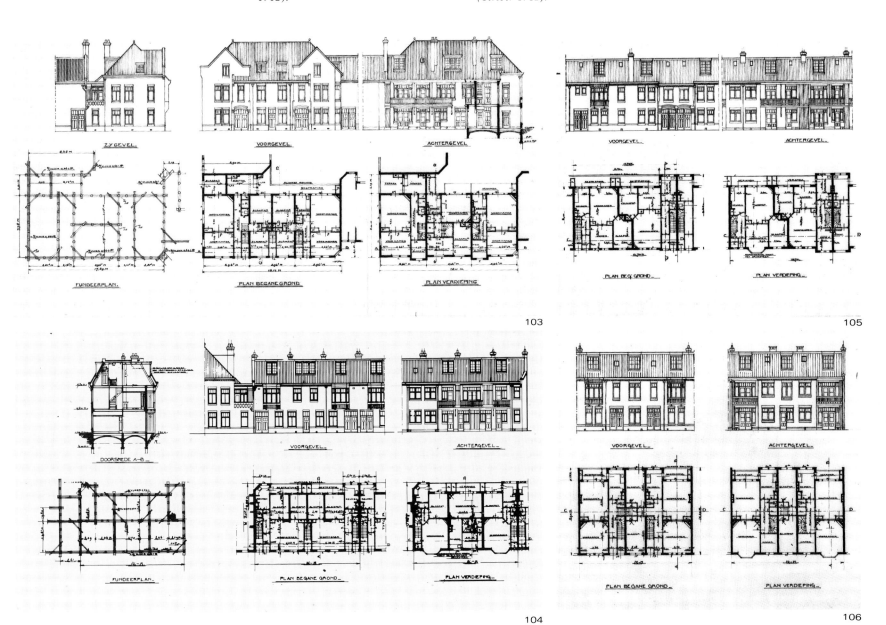

103

105

104

106

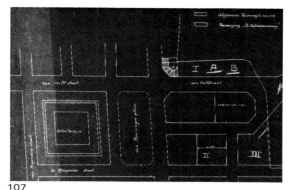

107

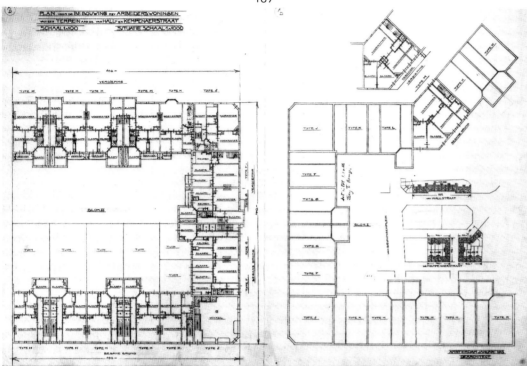

108

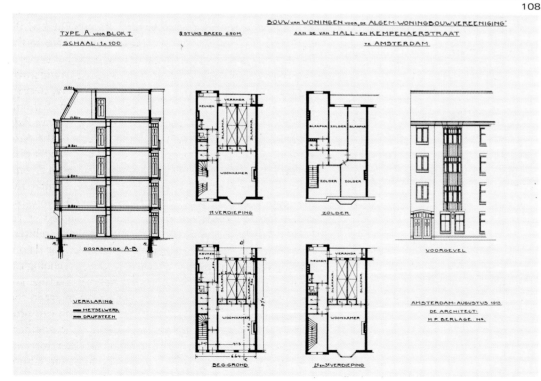

109

107. *Three buildings of low-income housing for the Algemeene Woningbouwvereeniging, with Van Epen, west Amsterdam, Staatsliedenbuurt, 1913–19, suggested location of buildings I A and B, II, and III. The square building on the left is the first of De Bazel's buildings on Van Beuningenplein.*

108. *Three buildings of low-income housing for the Algemeene Woningbouwvereeniging, with Van Epen, west Amsterdam, Staatsliedenbuurt, 1913–19, building plan with outline sketch and site of the two opposite buildings, January 1913.*

109. *Three buildings of low-income housing for the Algemeene Woningbouwvereeniging, with Van Epen, west Amsterdam, Staatsliedenbuurt, 1913–19, cross-section, floor plans and elevation on the street of the type A in the first building, August 1913.*

110. *Table of the main types in low buildings for the Algemeene Woningbouwvereeniging; from top to bottom: ground floor, second floor, cross-section; from left to right: types A, B, C, D, E (author's reconstitution).*

111. *Table of the main types in high buildings for the Algemeene Woningbouwvereeniging; from top to bottom: ground floor, second floor, third and fourth floors; from left to right: types F, G, H, K, L (author's reconstitution).*

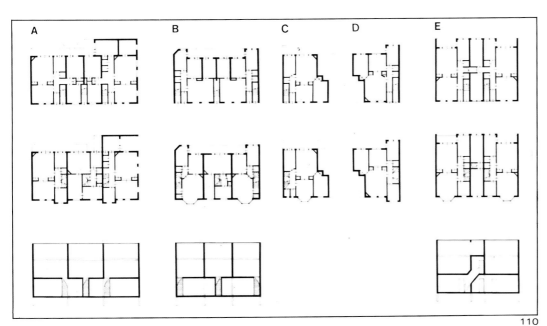

A   B   C   D   E

110

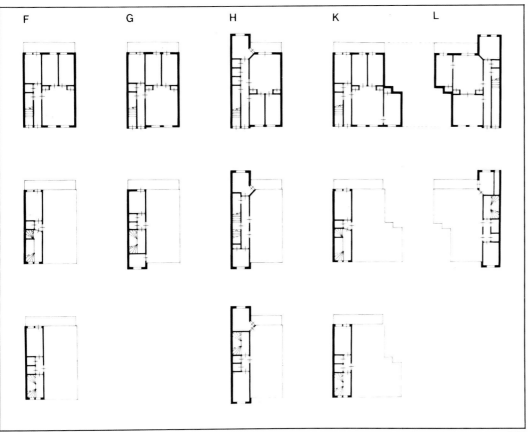

F   G   H   K   L

111

tecture. When he gave more ample explanations, however, he clearly referred mostly to Amsterdam. According to Berlage, the new Dutch architecture started with standardized housing. A modern national architecture could grow on this base, in spite of diverging trends. He was thinking mostly of the development plan for the south of Amsterdam and the architecture of the so-called Amsterdam School. Even more than in his *Schoonheid in samenleving*, Berlage celebrated at La Sarraz the artistic form as separate from the utilitarian function. In *Schoonheid in samenleving*, he championed the concept of utility as the basis of architecture, or, more concretely, championed certain forms of normalization in housing construction, from which a new spiritual artistic form could rise. At La Sarraz, he wanted the architecture of the Amsterdam School to be recognized as a new artistic form and the Dutch national architecture.

Berlage's point of view at La Sarraz was not substantially different from the one he had put forth in *Schoonheid in samenleving*, but it moved away somewhat from the rationalist position he had taken when outlining a general picture of nineteenth-century architecture. This change resulted from an expansion of his ideas on architecture, the object of which he defined as an entire city and no longer as a single building. Earlier, Berlage had regarded the façade as a secondary ornament applied to a building, a synthetic relationship between mass and building techniques. Later, he gave the façade a much more independent role by which it contributes to the whole urban character. The aesthetic dimension of architecture, whether in the design of an urban plan or in that of a façade, has a double purpose: It allows for an advanced standardization of low-income housing while avoiding monotony. For that reason, Berlage was in favor of the municipality's institutional role and against the central authorities' attempts to regulate the construction of housing. Only in the municipal framework can the coordination of the different institutional levels remain in the hands of the same person—from the selection of types of apartments to the whole urban plan—which would guarantee the development of great plans. Personally, Berlage liked the façades designed by the Amsterdam School, which he opposed to the rationalism of the *Nieuwe Zakelijkheid*, or New Objectivity. The architects of the Amsterdam School were working together at designing a plan for their city, and their spiritual unity was that of a community. Theirs was a "national architecture," unlike the internationalism of the New Objectivity. "An international mankind does not exist," Berlage claimed at La Sarraz, "therefore neither does an international architecture. The latter is only to satisfy the intellect, for whom science is also international, without any psychological basis. The creations of such universal architecture are born without an 'idea,' they are not works of art in the traditional sense, although their technical form can provoke our admiration. They also resemble one another, because they come from an international, therefore intellectually similar, spirit."[61] The artistic form can ensure a transcendental and symbolic level in an urban plan, which everybody can understand. It is precisely this level—the meeting of art and society—which can never be achieved through the rationalism of the New Objectivity, and uniformity becomes inevitable.

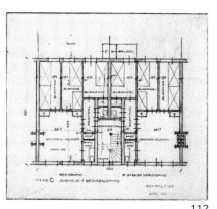

112

112. *Study for housing, plan for the type C, June 1922.*

1. M. Bock, "Woningbouw," in M. Bock, K. Broos, and P. Singelenberg, eds., 1975; H. Searing, "Berlage and Housing, 'The most significant modern building type,'" in AA.V.V. 1975, *H.P. Berlage 1856–1934. . . .*

2. H.P. Berlage 1918, "Over Normalisatie in de uitvoering van de woningbouw," in *Normalisatie in woningbouw.*

3. J. Van der Waerden, "Maatregelen waardoor bouw in massa bevordert wordt," in *Normalisatie in woningbouw*, Rotterdam 1918. The following papers were also given at the congress on housing: M.J.A. Moltzer, director of the Central Office of Social Services, "Over de woningnood en de huidige wijze van voorziening in de behoefte van volkswoningen" (The solution to the present low-income housing shortage); F.M. Wibaut, councilman of Amsterdam, "Over produktie, aanvoer en distributie van bouwmaterialen" (The production, shipping, and distribution of building materials); J. Schulte Nordholt, director of the Bureau of Inspection of Construction and Housing in Amersfoort, "Over maatregelen waardoor een snellere bouw wordt bevorderd" (Measures to shorten the time of construction); J. van der Waerden, director of the Bureau of Inspection of Construction and Housing in Amsterdam, "Maatregelen waardoor de bouw in massa wordt bevorderd. Normalisatie in uitvoering, in het bijzonder wat betreft de te verwerken onderdeelen" (Measures for mass construction. Standardization in construction, with special attention to accessory elements); H.J. Nieboer, secretary of the Health Commission in The Hague, "Over wettelijke noodvoorschriften waardoor een snelle en voeldoende bouw van volks- en middenstandswoningen wordt bevorderd" (Emergency laws to build quickly quality low- and middle-income housing). Cfr. *Bouwkundig Weekblad* 1918, p. 1.

4. H.P. Berlage, op. cit., pp. 24–25.

5. Ibid., p. 40.

6. Ibid., p. 41.

7. Ibid., p. 28.

8. Ibid., p. 34.

9. H.P. Berlage 1894, "Bouwkunst en impressionisme; see also M. Bock 1983, *Anfänge einer neuen Architektur*, p. 383 ff.

10. Stenographic proceedings of the Conference on Housing, February 11–12, 1918, p. 133 ff.

11. H.P. Berlage 1917, "Memorie van toelichting," in *Gemeenteblad van Amsterdam* I, pp. 901–14.

12. Cfr. H. Muthesius, *Die Werkbundarbeit der Zukunft*, Jena 1914, which includes a paper by Berlage, "the representative of the Dutch Werkbund" (p. 16 ff.). Several works by Berlage were also shown at the Werkbund exhibition; cfr. *Architectura* 1914, p.20298.

13. Z. Gulden, "Dr. Berlage en de normalisering der woningen," in *Bouwkundig Weekblad* 1918, p. 22 ff.

14. H.P. Berlage 1918, "Over normalisatie," p. 43.

15. H.P. Berlage, *Schoonheid in samenleving*, Rotterdam 1919.

16. T. van Doesburg 1920–1921, "De Taak der nieuwe architectuur," in *Bouwkundig Weekblad* XLI, 1920, 50, pp. 278–80; 51, pp. 281–85. Revised and amplified in "De Betekenis der mechanische esthetiek voor de architectuur en andere vakken," in *Bouwkundig Weekblad* XLII, 1921, 25, pp. 164–66; 28, pp. 179–83; 33, pp. 219–21. His views found their final precise definition in "De nieuwe architectuur," in *Bouwkundig Weekblad* XLV, 1924, 20, pp. 200–04. See also the anthology of Van Doesburg's writings, *Naar en beeldende architectuur*, Nijmegen 1983.

17. J.J.P. Oud, "Bouwkunst en normalisatie bij den massabouw," in *De Stijl* 1918, 7.

18. T. Van Doesburg, *Naar en beeldende architectuur*, op. cit., p.2035.

19. Ibid., pp. 60 ff. In *Mécano* red, 1922, and under the pseudonym of I.K. Bonset, Van Doesburg contributed a "Chronique scandaleuse des Pays-Plats," in which he made fun of Berlage and wrote of "arabesque romantique—maison avec closet hégélien, sentimentalisme infantile" (romantic arabesque—house with Hegelian toilet, childish sentimentality).

20. Cfr. H. Quitzsch, *Gottfried Semper. Praktische Aesthetik und politischer Kampf*, Braunschweig 1981.

21. H.P. Berlage 1919, *Schoonheid in samenleving*, pp. 10–11 and 39–41.

22. T. Van Doesburg, op. cit., p. 38.

23. Ibid., pp. 96–97.

24. H.P. Berlage, *Gedanken über Stil in der Baukunst*, Leipzig 1905, p. 29. See also M. Bock 1983, *Anfänge einer neuen Architektur*, p.2063 ff.

25. H.P. Berlage, ibid., p. 52.

26. See the correspondence Keppler-Wibaut in the Wibaut archives, at the Instituut voor Sociale Geschiedenis in Amsterdam.

27. Sociaal-technische Vereeniging, "Adres aan de Minister in Verband met de herziening der Woningwet," in *Architectura* 1907, p. 400. See also the corporation's brochure, *Herziening der Woningwet*, Amsterdam 1912, and Amsterdamsche Woningraad, *Het Ontwerp tot herziening der Woningwet*, by J. Kruseman, Amsterdam 1912.

28. See the Wibaut archives, letter from Keppler to Wibaut, dated June 4, 1908.

29. See the Wibaut archives, letter from Tellegen to the corporation, dated October 10, 1908.

30. Municipal Bureau for Construction and Housing, *Report on the housing built by the municipality of Amsterdam in 1909.*, Amsterdam 1910, p. 4.

31. Amsterdamsche Woningraad, *Rapport over de Volkshuisvesting in de nieuwe stad te Amsterdam*, Amsterdam 1910. See annex F, ill. 4, 5, and 6. Ill. 3 is the ground plan of the type in the 1908 proposal of De Arbeiderswoning.

32. Koninklijk Instituut van Ingenieurs, *Verslag aan den Koning over de vereisten en inrichting van arbeiderswoningen*, The Hague 1855. See also J. de Heer, "De Nederlandse arbeiderswoning uitgeschreven," in *Te Elfder Ure* 1978, p. 26.

33. Algemeene Woningbouwvereeniging, *Verslag loopende van de oprichting op 23 maart 1910–31 december 1911.*, Amsterdam, undated, p. 5 ff. See also Jan de Jong and Peter Korzelius, *Driekwart eeuw Algemeene Woningbouw Vereeniging Amsterdam*, Amsterdam 1985.

34. M.J. Meijers wrote a series of outstanding articles, "Volkshuisvesting—De Architectuur en de woningbouw," in *Bouwkundig Weekblad* 1916–17, starting with No. 27, November 24, 1916, in which he gave an excellent overview of the Dutch situation.

35. Algemeene Woningbouwvereeniging, op. cit.

36. P. Singelenberg, *H.P. Berlage, Ideas and Style*, The Hague 1972, p. 141.

37. Algemeene Woningbouwvereeniging, op. cit., pp. 8–9.

38. Ibid., pp. 9–11, which reports on the request to the municipal administration for a long-term land lease for low-income housing; and pp. 13–15, with the administration's denial of the request.

39. P. Singelenberg, "Werk 1903–1919," in M. Bock, K. Broos, and P. Singelenberg, op. cit., p. 43.

40. *Het Volk* October 18, 1915. The article gave a better review to Berlage's design, which was judged more pleasant and attractively peaceful, over De Bazel's design, judged too austere.

41. F.M. Wibaut, "Uitvoering der Woningwet," in *De Gemeente*, January 15, 1909. See also G.W.B. Borrie, *F.M. Wibaut—Mens en magistraat*, Amsterdam 1968, p. 98.

42. E. Ottens, *Ik moet naar een kleinere woning omzien want mijn gezin wordt te*

113. *Block on Mercatorplein, west Amsterdam, 1924–27, elevation of the third building, including the part with the portal which was not built.*

114. *Block on Mercatorplein, west Amsterdam, 1924–27, elevations of the eighth building, including the part with the portal and the tower.*

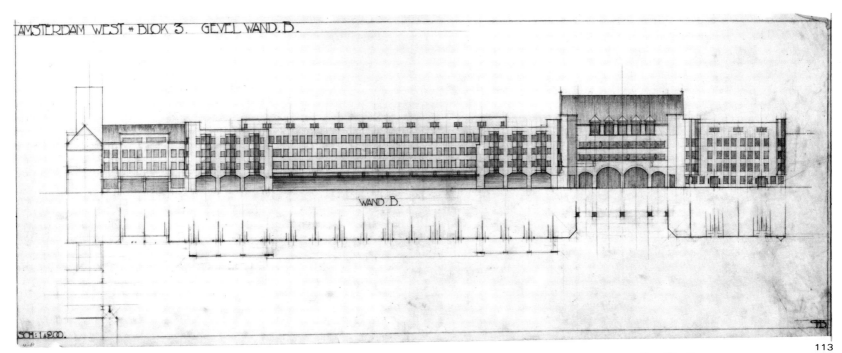

113

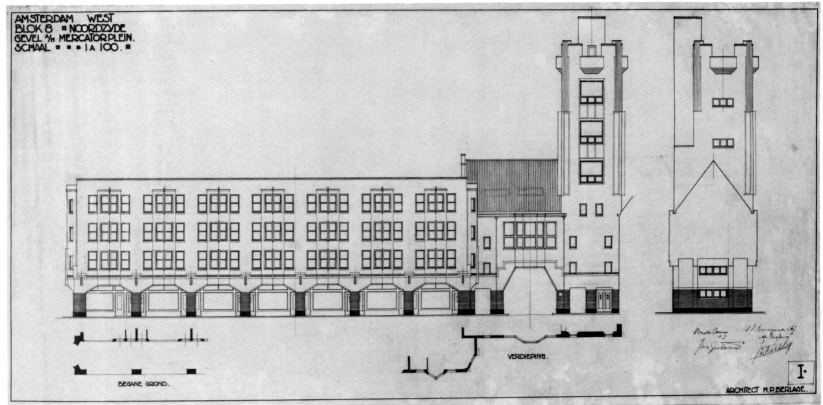

114

groot, Amsterdam 1975, p. 26 ff. The plan was presented on June 18, 1911 by several SDAP councilmen: Wollring, Wibaut, Gulden, Oudegeest, Vliegen, Pothuis, Loopuit, Van Kuijkhof, and Van den Tempel. It also had the support of the Bureau of Health, the president of which, J. Kruseman, wrote a letter to the council on December 18, 1911 and declared that notices of insanitary dwelling had been suspended because of the serious housing shortage. He recommended that a large quantity of low-cost housing be built as quickly as possible. See J.H.W. Leliman, "Volkshuisvesting te Amsterdam," in *De Bouwwereld* 1912.

43. G.W. Borrie, op. cit., fn 41, p. 105; E. Ottens, op. cit., fn2042, p. 26.

44. A. Keppler, *Gemeentelijke woningbouw*, Amsterdam 1913, published by the Amsterdam Housing Council.

45. *Woningbouw van Gemeentewege, voordracht van Burgemeester en Wethouders met bijbehorend rapport van den directeur van het gemeentelijk bouw- en woningtoezicht*, Amsterdam, October 191420(I), April 1915 (II), June 1915 (III).

46. See also A. Habets, J. de Heer, and A. Reijndorp, "Stadsontwikkeling en stadsreiniging," in *Stedebouw in Rotterdam*, Amsterdam 1981. The authors study the connection between extended low-cost housing programs and the issue of eligibility.

47. E. Ottens, op. cit., p. 29 ff.

48. J. Nycolaas, *Volkshuisvesting*, Nijmegen 1974, p. 176.

49. A.J. de Jong, "Overzicht van de steunverlening van regeringswege op grond van de koninklijke besluiten van 18 juli 1918, 6 november 1919 en van 8 november 1920 (vervolg op het overzicht van de voorschot- en bijdrage-verlening ingevolge de Woningwet van 1901 tot 1926)," excerpt from *Tijdschrift voor volkshuisvesting en stedebouw* 1928 and 1929. See also J. Kruseman, *De Woningwet*, Haarlem 1921, table B. SDAP's response to these measures was best formulated by A. Keppler and F.M. Wibaut, in *De Gemeente en de volkhuisvesting*, Amsterdam 1925.

50. "Plannen voor de eerstvolgende jaren ter voorziening in den woningnood, voordracht van Burgemeester en Wethouders," Amsterdam, November 25, 1919, in *Gemeenteblad* I, p. 3859 ff.

51. E. Ottens, op. cit., fn 42, p. 52.

52. H.P. Berlage, "Memorie van toelichting," p. 10 ff.

53. H.P. Berlage, "Bouwkunst en impressionisme," pp. 106–107.

54. Amsterdamsche Woningraad, op. cit., fn 31, pp. 16 and 41.

55. H.P. Berlage, "Het moderne stadsplan," unpublished lecture in the Berlage archives, undated, p. 28.

56. See also P. Panerai, J. Castex, and J.C. Depaule, *Formes urbaines: de l'îlot à la barre*, Paris 1980. This study emphasizes two aspects of the development plan for the south of Amsterdam: the monumental quality of the plan and the typology of the housing complex. It gave little place to the architecture of housing in its relationship to the street; nor did it consider that the façade's independent role had the purpose of alleviating the tension between monumentality and rational housing. Berlage used the *Füllwerk* of these housing complexes as a background to enhance the monumental network.

57. *Album bevattende een 50–tal woningtypen voor met rijksvoorschot te bouwen woningen*, Departement van Arbeid, The Hague, undated. See also *Kort verslag van de vergadering, gehouden op Zaterdag 26 Februari 1921 des voormiddags om 11 Uur in het Beursgebouw te Amsterdam*, Nederlandsch Instituut voor Volkshuisvesting, Haarlem, undated. The album published by the Ministry of Labor was discussed at this meeting.

58. *Arbeiderswoningen in Nederland, Vijftig met rijkssteun, onder leiding van architekten uitgevoerde plannen met de financiële gegevens*, ed. by H.P. Berlage, A. Keppler, W. Kromhout, and J.20Wils, Rotterdam 1921.

59. *Het Socialisatievraagstuk, Rapport uitgebracht door de commissie aangewezen uit de SDAP* 1920. Wibaut was the president of the commission.

60. H.P. Berlage, "Der Staat und der Widerstreit" 1928, 1979, pp. 24–25.

61. H.P. Berlage, "Het Congres van La Sarraz over de internationale architectuur," unpublished lecture held in Weimar, at the Staatliche Hochschule für Handwerk und Baukunst, the Berlage archives, undated, p. 15.

Modern Architecture

Hendrik Petrus Berlage

When I lately returned from Italy and compared the works of modern architecture in Northern Europe with those of former times, I thought of Ruskin's words: "Our architecture will languish, and that in the very dust, until the first principle of common sense be manfully obeyed, and a universal system of form and workmanship be everywhere adopted and enforced."

Even in Italy, one cannot forego a comparison between the classical and the medieval, the medieval and renascent classical, and that which characterizes the earlier as against the later Renaissance. I, for one, have acquired during my last sojourn in the South, a deeper insight into the essence of art than I did twenty-five years ago, and have only then recognized that a peculiar condition will have to be fulfilled in order to attain a great architecture. And when we speak of great architecture, we speak at once of great art in general, that is to say, of an epoch in which architecture is the style creating art—an epoch in which architecture leads, while both the other plastic arts are neither subjected to it, nor leading a life of their own, but cooperate with it in the creation of a noble entity. Such will be the result of an intellectual propelling power, a spiritual dogma, notwithstanding the fact that architecture is not in reality a liberal art. It does not originate in itself, but springs from material necessity. This does not sound very artistic, though architecture is, perhaps, just therefore the highest form of art. For by this, it is the leader of culture, of which in turn it is the reflection, since culture stands for harmony between material and spiritual necessities.

So when architecture is a growing power, it follows that there will also be general material progress, and accordingly an intellectual progressive movement. Is this really the case now, when so much is being said about a modern architecture over against that of the nineteenth century? This latter can, indeed, hardly be called a great architecture, for that it bore an electrical character, endeavoring, as it did, to instill new life, first into the classical style, and later into the medieval, but principally into the style of the Renaissance.

In this connection, it should be remembered that during the period of the Renaissance, architecture was already the weakest of the arts, as compared with painting and sculpture, which developed on their own lines.

The cause of the weakness of Renaissance architecture was that it took Rome, and not Greece, as an example.

Burckhardt even puts the question in his fine work on the Italian Renaissance: "Why did the Italian architects look back at Rome, and not at Greece?" For Roman architecture showed a weakness, when it did not apply the pilaster and the column in a purely constructive manner, as the Greeks did, but put them, cut through entirely or halfway, against the wall by way of ornamentation, without the least endeavor to find an aesthetical solution for the ornament of the capital (column head).

It was this which made Goethe exclaim: "Take care not to use the column in an improper way; its nature is to stand free; woe betide those who have riveted its slender form onto heavy walls."

And Hegel, in his "Aesthetical Considerations," analyzes this mistake even more keenly by saying that split pillars are simply repulsively ugly, because in them, two distinctly opposite intentions are put into juxtaposition without any intrinsic necessity for merging them into one another. How much weaker, therefore, was an architecture doomed to become, which after a lapse of a thousand years tried to revive an architectural scheme that itself had been so weak.

I may venture to say that the way in which the Renaissance repudiated the principles of construction has principally caused architecture to decline into a decayed art. If, for instance, on the basis of this principle, the town hall of Siena is compared with the Coliseum, the former deserves to be ranged first, notwithstanding the enormous difference in dimensions; whilst for the same reason, the Palazzo Pitti is to be put above the Coliseum.

And how powerfully does this mighty structure stand out against and above all later palaces of the Renaissance, because the scheme of pilasters or columns immediately points at a weakening of architecture. And after all this, does the nineteenth century go to learn its lessons from that same Italian Renaissance, and this not in consequence of an independent intellectual (spiritual) movement, but by reason of an arbitrary (capricious) inclination toward classical antiquity. It would, however, be unfair not to acknowledge that, notwithstanding this circumstance, the architecture of the nineteenth century has also produced beautiful works. But they all lack just that what one desires in a work of art in the highest sense, that which might be called the "inexpressible" (unutterable). We are awestruck at the sight of a Greek temple, as well as at that of a medieval cathedral, though they are, as regards the spiritual principle, diametrically opposed.

But we do not feel like this at the sight of a Renaissance structure, and most decidedly not at the sight of a similar building of the present time.

I believe that these two distinct emotions can be best explained by distinguishing between the qualities of "beautiful" and "sublime," as has been done by Schopenhauer in these words: "With the beautiful, pure recognition is supreme; with the sublime, this state of pure recognition is attained by a conscious and violent removal of the avowedly unfavorable relation of the same object to the will, by a free and conscious elevation above the will, and the recognition related thereto."

The classical and the medieval architecture attain the sublime; the Renaissance came no higher than the beautiful.

Now, to approach the sublime, the very intellectual (spiritual) propelling power, of which I spoke at the outset, is necessary. In classical times it was the spiritual dogma, exactly as in Middle Ages, whilst the Renaissance, taken as an intellectual movement, simply meant a reaction against such a conception, as is more fully explained in my work on "Art and Society."

Now, it is very remarkable to notice that, as regards architecture, it was exactly the pure principle of construction which led both the Greeks and those of medieval times to a sublime architecture, whilst the Renaissance, which abandoned this principle, could do no more than approach the beautiful.

These observations apply also to other arts.

Is not an epic poem, which even, therefore, can only originate in a period of all-pervading beauty, sublime, whilst a lyrical verse can only be beautiful? Is not a mural painting, decorating a monumental structure, sublime, whilst a picture can but approach the beautiful?

And are not the same qualities of beauty and sublimity found in nature itself?

So do the Falls of Niagara offer a sublime spectacle, so is the relation of female against male beauty as that of beauty pure and simple against beauty that is sublime; and there is even a sublimity of distances and dimensions, of the abysmal, of the night and of death.

The Renaissance means, therefore, a weakening of architecture, over against a free development of the arts of painting and sculpture in all directions. Both these arts felt themselves free from architectural fetters. They certainly developed themselves into grandiose individual expressions, but were thereby detrimental to the development of a great style.

This free utterance of mind, the making of individual thought, led at last with the French Revolution to a confusion of intellectual life as a whole, which in architecture resulted in the so-called building in style, that is to say— the eclectic school.

That was a historic necessity. For intellectual discord leads to thoughtlessness, to lack of imagination, so that one has to fall back on copying. And it is generally known what has been the consequence of this, as countless ex-

115

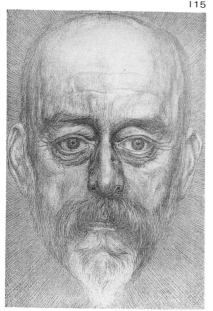

116

115. *H.P. Berlage in 1910.*

116. *Chris Lebeau, Portrait of Berlage*
     for De Wereld *April 19, 1912.*

amples of that soulless architecture exist in Europe as well as in America.

The structures, built in the modern Gothic and neoclassical styles, are either barren or overloaded, whilst those in the so-called personal styles are simply ridiculous.

This was, in general, not due to a lack of talent among the architects, because it is not true that more men of genius are born in some periods than in others. Genius requires for its development certain favorable circumstances which did not exist during the last century, so far as the development of a great architecture is concerned.

Scheffler, the well-known German thinker, speaks of a desperate struggle of men of genius on the battlefields of art, which takes place under such circumstances; and Hegel arrives at the conviction that, in consequence of the actual social relations, art, as regarded in relation to its most exalted destination, belongs to the past—that we have outgrown the possibility of adoring and worshipping works of art and that what still moves us must be able to endure a higher trial.

This philosopher had of necessity to arrive at this not very encouraging observation, because the task of philosophy is to determine and explain the phenomena, and not to express wishes or draw ideal consequences concerning them.

Numerous are the inconsistencies and foolishness in a time where industry and traffic offer architecture such great problems to solve.

A Gothic railway station, which may well be called a fundamental piece of nonsense, is not exceptional in and of itself. But when built in the style of the Renaissance, such a structure occasions all sorts of inconsistencies, the more so, where iron, as a modern building material, plays so preponderating a part in its construction. And as matters stand, it is difficult enough a problem to join iron and stone harmoniously, as these materials, the one trellis-like mobile, the other massively reposeful, show contrasting characters.

If, therefore, an old form scheme is used, it becomes almost impossible to attain a harmonious result, because traditional forms of iron do not exist.

From this most remarkable state of things it followed that iron columns were produced with classical capitals, iron rafters with Gothic window tracings, etc., whilst, in cases where the iron offered too many difficulties, the details were often made of more easily pliable materials, like zinc.

But not even when iron construction was applied in its proper character, which is in the end the best aesthetical solution, was a harmonious solution found. This is painfully evident in countless buildings, amongst them the most monumental.

It is, in fact, not easy to rid oneself of traditional forms.

And it appears also to be a human characteristic not to look for new forms, appropriate to the new demands of modern inventions, but to start by trying the old, established forms.

Thus the first railway-carriage, aye, even the locomotive engine, had the shape of an old-time coach, and the first automobile motorcar was a cab without a horse. The first steamboat was simply a sailing vessel with paddles. And to these examples could be added numberless others.

Very gradually does the purely artistic form grow from the technically constructive one, which in the end proves to be the most practical. And herewith is at once expressed the great truth, to which all architecture must respond and which has been satisfied by all good architecture—that the artistic form must be the result of practical considerations.

Viollet-le-Duc has expressed this in his formula: *"Que toute forme, qui n'est pas ordonnée par la structure, doit être rejetée."* Whilst the great Englishman Ruskin, and Semper, the great German architect, came to similar conclusions in their writings.

At last reaction was bound to come against the so-called "style" architecture of the nineteenth century, against an architecture that totally neglected this principle, for the very reason that it was itself no longer the outcome of principles. The truth does not submit to being suppressed, neither in art nor anywhere else; the fight against pretense and for reality will be waged forever anew.

Now, which are the new ideas concerning the modern movement? What is the character of modern architecture?

Professor Schumacher, of Dresden, expresses himself in an interesting article as follows: "The kernel of modern ideas concerning architecture is to replace this kind of style architecture by a quest after a "reality" style, which tries to derive its beauty from the purely realistic, as much as possible, from the manner in which one shapes and groups, and not in which one ornaments and decorates. And so it would be an intrinsic lie when one tried to cover modern buildings with an idealistic cloak; and it would not be a sign of culture when one should clothe these structures artistically in order to give them an agreeable aspect. Many an important work has doubtless originated from a kernel of practical necessity, framed in a certain style; but this means would never work with purely practical buildings, which, by the influence of social conditions, were pushed to the forefront of the building industry. In such, the meager remnants of a style, developed for other objects, became a caricature."

So this architect, too, arrives at the conviction that especially in architecture a tendency towards being "businesslike" makes its appearance, in the same way as, generally speaking, the really modern element in art is circumspection. This does not sound artistic either, and may lead the layman to believe that formerly architecture might perhaps have been counted among the arts, but that with such a tendency, this is no longer the case.

117. Jan Toorop, *Portrait of Berlage*
     for De Nieuwe Amsterdammer
     February 19, 1916.

118. *S.H. De Roos, Portrait of Berlage*
     for the 1916 Festschrift.

And yet it is just the reverse; for architecture was not businesslike when she copied the ancient forms, whilst the return to the businesslike is the very condition for its development into a great art. Moreover, does this tendency in architecture accord with the general intellectual movement of our time—that of organization?

And what else is organizing but regulating and putting into order, that is to say, simplifying? Is it not curious that in most languages the words for command are synonymous with those for order, whilst, moreover, one speaks of an order of architecture?

And, after all, this same businesslike element in the spiritual movement has loftier intentions than that simply of satisfying necessities, so that not alone is this matter-of-factness, this circumspection in art, not artistic, but represents a closely related loftier intention.

Scheffler even holds this tendency to be religious; and as, indeed, the idea therewith becomes a reality, the ideal is approached in accordance with Hegel's conception of it.

It appears, therefore, that in our time, architecture derives her forms from the kind of buildings which now represent the organized intellectual life—the office building and the shop. And as regards character, the office building cannot have another appearance than that of a massive pile, with façades that are simply large surfaces with window openings. The architect who has the courage to act on this principle, and not otherwise, thereby shows that he understands the trend of our time.

And it really requires courage to come forward with such a conception, as he surely cannot count on the sympathy of the general public. For the public ever prefers the façade of an Italian palace with the usual column scheme, or the gabled front of this or that French chateau. The public ever knows and values in a work of art simply the nice, the pretty, the handsome, which find responsive chords in their trivial souls.

In the severe style there is nothing to satisfy the casual observer, whilst the agreeable style contains the greatest subjectivity. In her the artist occupies himself with the public. But for all that does this plain pile, with its simple distribution of windows, lead to the sublime, whilst the Italian palace, which in its time also certainly approached the loftiest beauty, furnishes in its regeneration the irrefutable proof, not even of decadence, but of complete impotence? It is a question of principles, and not one of antiquated traditions, that is decisive here. For it cannot be too often repeated that the matter-of-fact not only does not exclude the beautiful, but does not approach it; whilst the immaterial has in reality led to the ugly.

Art does not, by any means, commence with the ornament, the presence of which is not a question of principle but one of more or less luxurious treatment. And when Goethe says to Eckermann, "That not everything that is useful (suitable, appropriate) is also beautiful, but that all that is beautiful is certainly useful," he expresses the same sentiment, because, after all, the artist has to see to it that the useful becomes beautiful.

Now, it appears from these observations that the object pursued by the modern architect is really not at all new

119

120

121. *On board of the "Juliana," July 1, 1923.*

122. *Venice, October 17, 1927.*

121

122

but that the same striving after matter-of-fact simplicity has been one of the very characteristics of all great style periods.

This proclaims itself most purely at the beginning of an epoch of development, so that as proof from the absurd the inference may be drawn that we now find ourselves, indeed, at the commencement of such a period. For every style has a period of rise, prime, and decline, or, as Hegel expresses it, of striving, attaining, and overreaching.

It is the succession of the severe, the ideal, and the agreeable styles, so that a style will not at the outset, but certainly at the end, have the sympathies of the public. For the products of all arts are works of the mind, and therefore not within immediate reach, ready for all, like the forms of nature.

In the first period, that of the severe style, the decorative element will be the least evident, because the fundamental form has to be looked for in the first instance.

In the period of its prime, or that of the ideal style, the harmony between form and decoration is reached, but at the same time the border of the period of decline.

This latter is that of the agreeable style, and bears, perhaps, this name, because the decorative element takes the foremost place, to the detriment of the material element, as the general public, choosing between these two prefers the ornaments.

These observations lead to the recognition that in these terms the nineteenth century has not been a great period, because antiquated style forms were used, whilst the very style forms ought to be the consequence of a generic practical pursuit. "Only that is spiritual which makes its own form; art only begins where imitation ends," is a dictum which I borrow from Oscar Wilde.

A movement in this direction is noticeable at this very moment; and this is in accord with that which formerly revealed itself at the beginning of a great period. This matter-of-factness stands for rational construction with the application not only of the old, but also of all the modern building materials, which our time has made available for this object. The question 'What is modern' is not decided by the *whether* but by the *how* of this application, whilst it is evident that the architecture of the nineteenth century did not employ the building materials so as to fit with a given style.

At the commencement of the twentieth century, we do really stand at the beginning of a modern architecture. It shows itself certainly still rather sporadically, and of course with different national characteristics, whilst reactionary tendencies are once more noticeable, with a renewed bent for the styles of Louis XVI and the Empire.

And even here, in America, where in accordance with the very peculiar problems one should expect a very forward and thoroughly principled movement in modern direction, old forms are too much adhered to.

This has gone even so far that in a building skyscrapers, column orders have been employed, which in such structures creates a highly curious impression.

They were used for decorating the nether stories, which can be seen; but also for the upper stories, which are hardly to be seen. But as the numerous intervening stories could, of course, not be decorated by piling up rows upon rows of columns, there arose a singular style conflict. Ought not, after all, the character of these Titanic buildings be that of a mass grouping, with the omission of everything that ought detract from this expression? For here we certainly have the concentration of the modern business life, and therefore also its architectural expression, so that these buildings could establish the architectural forms for the whole of modern architecture.

And yet, for the great private palaces, examples from ancient Europe are still preferred, whilst it would be in perfect harmony with modern culture if the character of these palaces also were one of matter-of-fact simplicity. This would even mean an artistic expression of a higher order, and give assurance of a new, and in this case, nobly rich form.

With this character of mass grouping, which indeed ought to be the character of modern architecture, the philosophy of architecture in general would change, which at the same time proves that we find ourselves at the beginning of a period of entirely new outlooks. For in classical architecture, support and burden were expressed in column and architrave—an expression copied by the Renaissance of the nineteenth century. This led Schopenhauer to say, "The only and permanent theme of architecture is that of support and burden," therefore its principle ought to be that there should be no burden without sufficient support and no support without appropriate burden; that, in a word, the relation between these two should be a proper one. The purest expression of this theme is formed by column and architrave, so that the column order became, in a certain sense, the keynote of architecture.

However, in my opinion, not even medieval architecture can be judged by this dictum, because in opposition to the classical horizontal line, it arrived at the vertical line through the development of the vault system, which, in a certain sense, meant a negation of the material.

Now, modern architecture would be able to express the enclosing of space through her mass grouping by way of external appearance, which would, generally speaking, also be the most ideal expression, as the art of building consists of the art of creating space. It is for this very reason that we speak of space art, an expression which is, as far as I am aware, quite new. The external appearance is, therefore, not the cause, but the result of the harmonious form given to the different spaces.

This shows at the same time that the architecture of the façade is not the principal thing, but that it should be the outcome of the internal arrangement.

This seems to be self-evident; but even this principle was completely neglected during the nineteenth century style period.

Now, as regards the mass grouping which should be supreme in modern architecture, it appears that Oriental art, in a certain way, seems to already respond to this principle, so that those who are afraid of a new direction

123

124

125. *Color proof for plate IV for the monumental edition of the* Gijsbreght van Aemstel, *1894.*

126. *Ex-libris Albert Verwey.*

125

126

may be assured that, after all, there seems to be nothing new under the sun.

The principles are always the same, that it is simply a question of whether or not they are being maintained, the external appearance becoming, relatively, a secondary matter. And now it is evident that the architecture of the nineteenth century has thought fit to abandon these principles altogether, which has called forth so fierce a reaction. For architecture, this means that we should work on purely constructive principles and follow our own creative power. This alone can assure an ideal development of architecture. This alone will be able to restore to her works what we have missed in them during the nineteenth century vigor.

What this means, I will tell you in the words of an interesting article about the Swiss painter Hodler: As regards Hodler's art, says the author, "People will never agree as long as it is reckoned with the conventional ideas of beauty; his works can, to express myself baroquely, rather be reckoned, like engines, by horse powers." This certainly sounds brutal.

But there have been at all times great works of art, not simply without beauty, but of an undoubted ugliness. What does, for instance, Wolflin, in his work "The Classical Art," say about the David of Michelangelo: "Then the disagreeable movement, hard and angular, and the abominable triangle between the legs; nowhere is there a concession to the beautiful line."

And yet the figure shows a reproduction of nature, which, on this scale, borders on the miraculous. It is admirable in every detail, and ever surprising. But honestly said, it is thoroughly ugly. Such works have always been produced, since olden times; and it is so again with Hodler. Were not the three red soldiers of the Marignano picture a work of genius? But they were certainly not beautiful; thence the general opposition against the execution; but one became afraid of them.

I do not mean that Hodler is the ultimate object, but his art is a road; and what is great is already contained in the road, not in the goal alone; only that which possesses no possibility of development is outside the pale of consideration.

When, therefore, the opponents of Hodler's art contend that his paintings are not beautiful, they are nearly right, because it is a notion which does not fit. In this way, the opposing parties are hitting the air. For Hodler's works are the expression of an extraordinary strong temperament; and in this case, "beautiful and not beautiful" are mere details.

I believe that this explanation makes perfectly clear what is necessary to the external impression of a work of art. And that it has nothing to do with proportions is evident from the fact that this impression is given to us even by paintings of Brueghel or Fragonard. But these observations certainly apply to the works of architecture in particular, because this property of vigor is the very consequence of style treatment through one's own creative power.

The works of the nineteenth century have, therefore, only been able to approach the traditional conception of beauty, because their creation was not attended by initiative. Therefore they remain vigorless; but therefore, also, they retained, notwithstanding their dimensions, the adherence of the public, because that same public only understands conventional beauty.

Artists, however, pass by these works with indifference, because these works lack the vigor necessary to rouse their interest.

And when, in these times, a vigorous work of matter-of-fact simplicity happens to be created, it is not understood, and for that reason is considered ugly. And in competitions it is the same, so that with deadly precision, the prize is awarded to an architecture of the usual, easily comprehensible beauty, whilst the project of a young architecture, bearing the possibilities of development, the only truly interesting one, is laid aside with a gesture of self-sufficient disdain.

And such a modern structure finds the severest opposition in the midst of ancient city quarters, as must naturally repeatedly be the case in the European towns, because there is then, moreover, talk of the spoiling of the surroundings. Nobody thinks, then, of the fact that in their time, the medieval masters placed their works next to the classical, the masters of the Renaissance, theirs, next to the Gothic ones. But in those times people were not yet so sensitive as nowadays.

In conclusion, these considerations lead to the conviction that now, indeed, a modern architecture is by way of developing itself, in consequence of intellectual currents and requirements. This movement, though originating in Europe, is general. Its character is that of matter-of-fact simplicity, equally in construction as in ornamentation, whilst as regards form in a general sense, geometrical arrangement is to be perceived.

In the composition of this work, use is indeed again being made of geometrical and arithmetical proportions, even in the spirit of Plato, who has already called measure and proportions of measure the essence of beauty. And as this character really reflects the intellectual movement of our time, this method of treatment alone will be of value for the development of modern architecture.

The art of the nineteenth century possessed no possibility of development, owing to its eclectic and subjectivistic tendencies, whilst, on the other hand, the work of the architects, who are now working in the spirit here described, and are thus in touch with the coming era, surely possesses this possibility.

"I am full of hope," says William Morris, the great English pioneer, "that from the very necessary and unpretentious buildings will spring the new and true architecture, at any rate, more likely than from experimenting the the methods of some popular styles."

On these principles, it is that a great style may be expected in coming times—a style which shall not simply be beautiful, but will once more be able to attain sublimity.

For that style will prove to possess the vigor to lift the works of architecture to that elevation, which is necessary to have them be once again the ideal expression of a great culture.

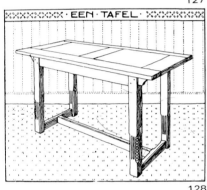

127–130. Furniture by Berlage, drawings by Johan Briedié for Studies over bouwkunst, stijl en samenleving, *Rotterdam 1910.*

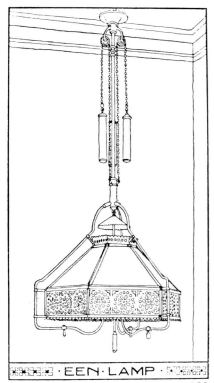

· EEN · LAMP ·

129

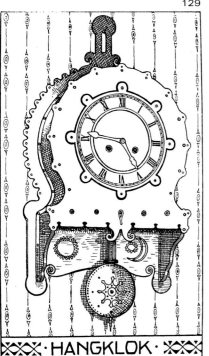

✕✕✕ · HANGKLOK · ✕✕✕

130

Hendrik Petrus Berlage was born on February 21, 1856, in Amsterdam, the son of Nicolaas Willem Berlage, chief municipal registrar, and Anna Catharina Bosscha. He was the eldest of four children: Henrietta Jacoba was born in 1857, Joannes in 1861, and Nicolaas Willem Jr. in 1863. His mother died of tuberculosis in 1868, and his father married Gesina Catherina Keer in 1870.

After he finished secondary school in 1874, Berlage passed the entrance examination to study painting at the Academy of Fine Arts in Amsterdam, but he left before the academic year ended. In October 1875, he enrolled at the Bauschule, the architecture school at the Zürich Institute of Technology. Created in 1855, the college had over one thousand matriculated and nonmatriculated students (half of them foreigners) in the academic year 1875–76. The architecture school was strongly influenced by Gottfried Semper, who had taught there from 1855 to 1871. It had around thirty students, and only twenty in the year Berlage received his degree. His teachers in architecture were G. Lasius and J.J. Stadler, who had been called to Zürich as Semper's assistant (he succeeded him in 1872 and taught there until 1893); in art history, G. Kinkel; and in building techniques, L. Tetmajer.

The Berlage Archives contain many exercises in design and architecture dating from these three years at the college: from the first year, 1875–76, drawings of a villa, a châlet, and a waiting room in a small public building; from the second year, 1876–77, drawings of a chapel in the Ionic style, an elegant mansion in the style of Mansart, the façade of a two–apartment house, and studies for an *Anatomiegebäude* and an exhibition hall; and from the third year, 1877–78, drawings for a bathing establishment, a country house, and a façade on a court. There is no precise date for the designs of a casino, a summer theater (on the philosophical theme "Know thyself"), a clubhouse, and a merchants' house. There are also many decorative and architectural tracings, tables of descriptive geometry, graphic exercises, and drawings from life. In August 1878 Berlage received his degree in architecture with honors (except in geology). The theme and idiom of his final qualifying design was inspired by Semper: a school and museum of arts and crafts (*Gewerbeschule mit Gewerbemuseum*).

These three years of study were followed by three years of traveling, in the tradition of the *Grand Tour*. In the spring and summer of 1879, Berlage went to Germany. We know that he spent the fall working on the building of the *Panoptikum* in Frankfurt. He returned to Holland and was briefly employed by an architectural studio in Arnhem. From September 1880 to August 1881, he toured Italy, visiting Turin, Genoa, Pisa, Rome, Naples, Sicily, Naples again, Rome, Orvieto, Perugia, Siena, Florence, Verona, and Venice, from where he went to Trieste.

This catalogue of Berlage's works features entries with a short narrative; they are arranged in chronological order and follow the same format. Beside the title, each entry indicates:

— Berlage's associates
— the city and the address of the work
— who commissioned the work
— the dates of beginning and completion of the work.

It also contains a short description, as well as historical and critical notes. I have established the narratives with the help of Marco Mulazzani, except for some ten entries written by Herman van Bergeijk and signed "H.v.B." Besides researching archives and documents, we studied many works on location and made use of information from the literature. We are particularly indebted to the seminal books by P. Singelenberg 1972; G. Fanelli 1978; and M. Bock 1983. Among the designs examined in over 140 entries, about a hundred were actually built and about fifty are extant.

The bibliography at the end of each entry reviews specific titles, in chronological order, to the exclusion of a number of standard texts. References to the catalogue of Berlage's writings and the general bibliography are succinct: author and date (with the most significant part of the title to avoid possible confusion). It seemed convenient to indicate—preceded by "cfr."—the essential data of titles that are relevant to the work under examination but not included in the general bibliography for one reason or another. For a useful study of sources, iconographic sources in particular, see G. Fanelli 1968, especially pages 236–39 in the second Dutch edition. We used a few convenient abbreviations: "Berlage Archives," for the largest collection, kept at the Nederlands Documentatiecentrum voor Bouwkunst in Amsterdam; "Festschrift," for a basic collective book published in 1916 by Brusse, *Dr. H.P. Berlage en zijn werk*; "M.B.B.," for Maatschappij tot Bevordering der Bouwkunst, the omnipresent association for the promotion of architecture; and "general plan," for an elaborate graphic representation of the whole design, which is usually meant to be distributed for the registration or the execution. Each work is presented in a separate entry. Within a general chronological order, designs are featured before buildings, and major works before lesser ones. Some entries, however, vary in format or chronological sequence. For example, the first two entries cover Berlage's education and training and his association with Theodore Sanders. A few biographical allusions will also be found in other entries. A large series of individual houses is preceded by a text divided into a few entries, presenting a more informative comparative perspective. Trademark designs such as the Amsterdam Stock Exchange or the development of the south of Amsterdam needed a longer narrative and a more detailed approach. For the architecture of multiple dwellings, it seemed preferable to refer to the essay by J. de Heer featured in this book. A few entries give no description for lack of data. Finally, some departure from straight chronological order is intended to highlight differences or resemblances between designs.

Apart from those described in the catalogue, the archives contain few other architectural studies; their dates and attributions are uncertain, and they are of minor importance—such as a fountain, a monumental tombstone, and a draft plan for a library. The wide field of Berlage's work as a designer still remains to be explored and is often difficult to separate from his work as an architect, since interior designs and furniture form an integral part of his most significant commissions. The scope of this book did not permit a census and description of this versatile activity, which would have made the catalogue too heterogeneous. Moreover, while his work as a designer is fascinating, it should be mentioned that actual industrial production was limited to a few objects.

As for possible errors and inevitable omissions, I hope that they will be corrected in future studies that will have used this book as a basis.

131. *Still Life, 1874.*

132. *Diplomarbeit, final qualifying design, 1878, perspective drawing.*

131

132

Berlage returned to Holland at the end of his Grand Tour. At the end of 1881 he found work with the firm of the engineer Theodore Sanders.

Sanders offset his mediocre artistic stature with frenetic self-promotion and entrepreneurial activity, with which he associated Berlage, albeit with limited success. From the beginning of the 1880s on, he tried in particular to develop the local infrastructure and the railway public transportation system and waged a constant battle against the monopoly of the bus company, the Amsterdamsche Omnibus Maatschappij. He was also an active member of the most important professional association of architects, the Maatschappij tot Bevordering der Bouwkunst (M.B.B.). To put it succinctly, Sanders was a typical representative of late nineteenth-century liberalism, who successfully combined a search for profits (even from speculation) with a desire for progress (even social progress).

In the first half of 1881, Sanders built the orientalizing *Panorama* in Copenhagen for a company financed by public and private funds. He also designed the *Panopticum* in Amsterdam for a company in which he probably held shares. Construction work for the *Panopticum* started in July 1881 and lasted a year. The reason Berlage was hired by Sanders's firm may have been that, beside being a skillful draftsman, he had had experience with a similar project in Germany. Because of the inevitable competition of the cinema, the *Panopticum* was partially converted in 1912 into a theater. In 1919 the building was purchased by the Amsterdamsche Bank, and it was torn down in 1965–66 to make room for an extension of the bank's headquarters. The latter had been built between 1926 and 1932; Ouëndag had designed it, with Berlage's collaboration. In 1884 Berlage, who executed almost all the designs produced by the studio, was promoted to full partnership. His association with Sanders lasted until 1889.

Bibliography: cfr. *Bouwkundig Weekblad* 1881, pp. 4 and 12–13; *Bouwkundig Weekblad* 1881, pp. 36 and 153; *Bouwkundig Weekblad* 1882, pp. 319–20 and 346.

133. Theodor Sanders, Panopticum, Amsterdam, 1881–82, elevation.

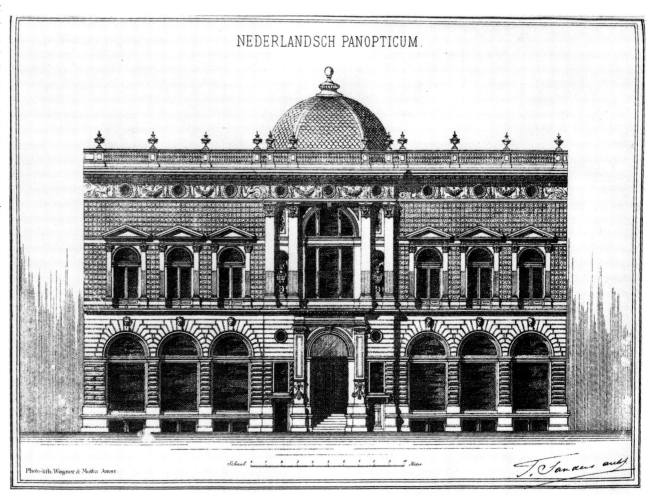

133

With Theodor Sanders
75 De Ruyterdake, Amsterdam
Commissioned by the Maatschappij
vor Volkskoffiehuizen

In a brief presentation in *Bouwkundig Weekblad*, Sanders and Berlage described the coffee house as a "building for workers." The presentation featured a perspective sketch by Berlage dated May 1884, while Sanders's drawings for the building permit dated back to July 1883. The "De Hoop" coffee house was inaugurated in June 1884. It was built on an isolated plot near the new central railway station. Construction work on the station had started shortly before, and the extension of the station caused the coffee house to be torn down in the early 1920s. The coffee house was built for a corporation—Sanders was a member of its board of directors—recently created to promote "shelters" for the working class.

The coffee house and a dining room are on the ground floor. The three floors above feature around sixty single rooms. The mansard roof is steeply pitched with narrow dormers. On the façade, the stonework alternates with bricks to strengthen the base and outline a simple design. The composite structure creates an asymmetrical front: The entrance, the balcony above, and the seventeenth-century-style vertical structure at the right of the dormers form a part separate from the rest. The idiom chosen for this tall building has a civic-bourgeois tone meant for the uplifting of its customers; it oscillates between references to the Dutch late Renaissance and Berlage's own Italian memories. Its rich mixture of cultural allusions was to be found—albeit on another scale—in the competition design for the Stock Exchange.

Bibliography: H.P. Berlage 1884, "Het Volkskoffiehuis."

134. Contemporary photograph.

134

With Theodor Sanders
Damrak, Amsterdam
Commissioned by
the City of Amsterdam
1884–85

The complex set of events and stormy affairs of the new Stock Exchange in Amsterdam—which lasted several decades and was justly dubbed "a saga" by contemporaries, because of its length, plot, and cast of characters—started with the almost immediate observation that the existing Stock Exchange was inadequate. The Italian traveler-writer of the end of the nineteenth-century, De Amicis, noted that, "since it contained nothing remarkable aside from a peristyle made of seventeen columns, it was called a door without a house." It had been built between 1840 and 1845 by J.D. Zocher on the very central Dam, a better location than that of the old Exchange built in the seventeenth century by Hendrik de Keyser.

There were several plans during the 1860s for the extension and improvement of Zocher's building. In 1879 the municipal council announced a competition for a concept, leaving open the choice of the site. The 123 designs submitted were representative of the whole range in the contemporary debate in Dutch architecture: Beside the controversy about a suitable "style" for the building and the city (Dutch Renaissance or Classicism?), there were supporters of the opinion that the architectural and urban composition of Amsterdam should remained untouched, as well as inevitable speculators who saw in the building of a new Exchange an opportunity for the lucrative development of wide areas of the city. Problematical designs continued to be submitted after the municipality decided in May 1882 on the choice of a site: an area filled in on the Damrak in 1883, on a water-and-street axis that runs near Zocher's Exchange and connects the Dam to the new central railway station built between 1882 and 1898 by P.J.H. Cuypers. At the same time, preparations were made for the design of an international

competition to be announced at the end of June 1884, with a deadline set for the beginning of November of that year.

There were many candidates: 199 submissions had to be evaluated in a fortnight by a commission made of three Dutch architects (among whom the prominent Cuypers), five foreigners, and three representatives of the categories involved. A chronicler maliciously figured out that the members of the commission—each of whom was paid thirty florins a day—devoted no more than two minutes and twelve seconds to each design. No wonder that the jury's report stirred a strong controversy. It had chosen ten designs after two votes, and each was awarded a prize of 1000 florins. Critics argued that the notice for the competition was vague, and that height, interior design, and construction materials were not specified. They also remarked on the jury's bias against neoclassical designs, to the point that eight of the ten designs selected were neo-Gothic and neo-Renaissance in style. For this reason, even Otto Wagner's design had been rejected. Finally, the composition of the jury was also criticized, albeit casually. The violent reactions provoked by the exhibition of the designs near Cuypers's recently built Rijksmuseum revived the polemics.

In June 1885 the five finalists of the second phase of the competition were announced. Their designs remained on view for a year at the headquarters of "Arti et Amicitiae" in Amsterdam, a cultural society for which Berlage worked in 1893–94. L.M. Cordonnier, the architect of Lille, won first prize with a design decorated with the motto "Y"; the second prize went to Amsterdam's J. Groll and Vienna's F. Ohmann, who had joined forces for the second phase, with the motto "In hoc signo floresco." They were followed by Berlage and Sanders, with "Mercaturae," Berlin's J. Völlmer, with "La Bourse ou la vie," and L. Klinkenberger with Bremen's F. Tauschenberg, with "Ammerack."

The commission judged the façades in Berlage's design for the first phase of the competition as "pictur-

esque and artistic," and "commendable" for the treatment of decorative themes. The tripartite design was criticized, however, as an obstacle to the inner flow and lighting, leaving out the consideration that this separation of the three different Ex-

135. J.D. Zocher, Stock Exchange, Amsterdam, 1840–45, front view.

136. First level competition, 1884, south view.

137. Second level competition, 1885, south view.

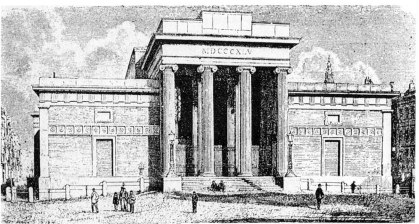

135

136

137

changes—stock, commodities, and grain—was functional. The façade on the Damrak features an Italianate colonnade, two set back towers, and roofs in the French Second Empire style. Grand steps lead to the main entrance on the projecting part of the southern façade. The interior design clearly shows Berlage's direct knowledge of Italian architecture: The cupola resembles that of the Pantheon; the wide arches are reminiscent of the Pazzi Chapel; the Palladian angular exedrae and the decoration in the style of Donatello are combined in a varied splendor.

The design for the second phase of the competition, while more innovative, met with less approbation: It was found less pleasing because the cement rendering had been eliminated—for reasons of economy—and the metallic structure in the roof was visible. The fronts were made simpler to limit costs, but this brought about more criticism: In particular, the jury minded the fact that the colonnade on the Damrak had disappeared, and it did not regard the projecting towers as sufficient compensation.

The jury's decision was based on "aesthetic" criteria only. Witness the fact that, although the cost ceiling was set at two million florins, the winning design was estimated around three million—moreover, it came without the required cost estimate. Therefore there were many scandals and sensational turns of events. Cordonnier was publicly accused by a group of thirty architects of having copied the façade on the inner courtyard of the town hall in La Rochelle. In order to justify himself, he had to document his case with photographs. Ohmann, who was omitted from the award to Groll, accused the latter of having been improperly helped by an engineer and a painter. As a revenge, he improvised the drawing of a façade to demonstrate his skill.

The critical problem was that of costs: In November 1885, the cost estimates of the first two designs were reviewed and trimmed, especially in the choice of building materials for the roof. Finally, in January 1886, a decision was made to award the prizes—10,000 florins for the first prize, 6,000 florins for the second, and respectively 5,000, 4,000, and 3,000 for the others—without committing the administration to a definitive choice.

In May 1887 the new commissioner for public works proposed a design by A.W. Weissman—who was promoted city architect from 1891 to 1894—which combined and simplified further the two winning designs of the competition. This plan had the open support of an anonymous contributor to the journal *De Opmerker*, and there was an uproar when it was discovered several years later that the contributor was none other than Weissman himself. In spite of this support, the design met with such opposition that the municipal council resolved in April 1888 to plant trees in the area filled in on the Damrak and previously planned for the new Stock Exchange. The inhabitants of the area were very satisfied with this seemingly final decision.

In 1891, the association of stockbrokers, exasperated by these continuous postponements, proposed three private plans to the municipal authorities. The plan promoted by Werker, the owner of the Bible Hotel, was selected, and Weissman was told to produce a new design. In 1894, however, the municipality put forward its lack of funds and a new consensus around the reclamation of the old Exchange, and it considered the possibility of extending Zocher's building. A committee was formed; in April 1894, Weissman's proposed design was examined and approved with some "aesthetic" reservations, especially for the façade along the Damrak.

In the fall of 1895, M.W.F. Treub, the new commissioner for public works, became president of the committee for the Exchange, in which the categories involved were well represented. Treub suggested that Berlage, whom he knew from the Breero Club, be appointed artistic consultant. The suggestion was accepted in February 1896, and Berlage's consultantship assumed the unofficial task of designing a new Exchange. When Berlage was finally commissioned for the design by the municipal assembly in October 1896, he was able to announce that he had already started on a concept costing less than the projected cost for the renovation of Zocher's building. In November 1896, the municipal authorities approved the construction of a new Exchange, in a secret meeting that gave rise to protests and caused a flow of criticisms. They had been swayed by Berlage's preliminary drawings, which were to be greatly modified in the years to come, and by Treub's impassionate speech, which had concluded with these words: "You can be confident, from now on the Stock Exchange will be a monument reflecting the resolution and practical spirit of Amsterdam's merchants."

138

139

138. First level competition, 1884, interior view.

139. Second level competition, 1885, interior view.

Bibliography: J. Kok 1884; editorial 1884, "Prijsvragen"; editorial 1884, "Prijsvraag voor den bouw"; J.R. de Kruijff 1885, editorials.

With Theodor Sanders
Amsterdam, 152 Kalverstraat/7 Spui
Commissioned by the company
Focke & Meltzer
1884–86

The building for Focke & Meltzer was the first of Berlage's works to be recognized by the *Festschrift* in 1916. It was done in two phases, with Sanders, between 1884 and 1886. The store on the ground floor and a few offices were opened to the public in November 1885. Another twenty offices, a photographic studio, and the janitor's apartment in the attic were completed in March 1886.

It is a typical commercial edifice of the late nineteenth-century city, with oriels on the corner, above the entrance; a roof in the style of the French Second Empire; classical orders freely used; and a rusticated base. A sort of little round temple, with a Gothic roof, stands above the oriel windows. The façade is of cement, except for string courses made of the same sandstone as the base of the building. Decorations abound: Since the store sold glass, fine china, and refined household objects, the lunettes above the windows on the second floor feature medallions with portraits of artists working with glass or ceramics. Ornamental sculptures were carved by Bart van Hove, who was to collaborate again with Berlage.

The wide windows on the ground floor are recessed in order to display, and give more relief to, columns in Swedish granite carrying bronze capitals. The rich decoration of the cement pilasters and the corbels supporting the corner balcony were executed under Berlage's direction at the Quellinus School, the school of arts and crafts created in 1879 by P.J.H. Cuypers. Berlage also designed the furnishings in an idiom reminiscent of the Dutch Renaissance and in harmony with the interior architecture. The chromatic contrast of the showcases is particularly effective: The color black ensures that the objects exhibited stand out against a background painted dark red.

Bibliography: H.P. Berlage 1885, "Bij de plaat"; editorial 1885, "Het Winkelhuis."

141

140. *Perspective view.*

141. *Contemporary photograph.*

WINKELHUIS
met
KANTOREN.
Sanders Berlage Archt.

140

With Theodor Sanders
Amsterdam, between the Dam and Westermarkt
1885

Sanders was an active proponent of plans to develop and restructure the street network of Amsterdam—not without some personal interests. He conceived of a connection between the center of the city and the west side. In February 1883, he designed the Raadhuisstraat: a grandiose demolition plan to make room for the tramway, which was an old dream for this architect-engineer. In February 1885 he presented the municipal council with a more elaborate design of a "Passageway for pedestrians and tram," dated January 1885 and bearing Berlage's signature. It features a glazed gallery made of three separate but consecutive sections. The section between the Dam and Spuistraat contains twelve stores, while eleven more stores are planned in the section between Spuitstraat and Singel. The entrance of the gallery on the Dam is a monumental arch. The major section between Heerengracht and Keizeesgracht is more complex in structure: Two dozen stores are distributed at either end of the passageway; on each canal, the beginning of the passageway is marked by a similar structure, a central building flanked by two towers, in the style of a sixteenth-century palace. The center of this section crosses a park, where a veranda outlines a sort of courtyard and a beer hall. Of course, the plan was too expensive. The Raadhuisstraat, however, was to be built in the 1890s, in a modified form. In 1896 the Van Gendt architectural firm designed the commercial gallery on the south side, and Berlage's contribution to the character of the street was his 1897 façade of a building on the opposite side, designed with Bonda.

Bibliography: cfr. *Amsterdammer* 1885, February 14 and 15; *Nieuwe Rotterdamsche Courant* 1885, February 15.

142. General design.

Amsterdam, Sophiaplein (today Muntplein)
1885

In May 1885 demolition work was started on buildings surrounding the Munt Tower. The tower had been constructed in 1490 as a gate to the city; it was redesigned by De Keyser in 1620, and after 1670 it had been used for minting. Because it was a historic building, the municipal council appointed an architects' commission for the redevelopment of the site. P.J.H. Cuypers, A.N. Godefroy, I. Gosschalk, and C. Muysken sat on this commission. In July 1885, a design was proposed, for which a full-scale wooden model was built. W. Springer, the assistant to the city architect, was put in charge of the construction of the Munt Building between 1885 and 1887. The building was partially demolished in 1938–39 to make place for the extension of a bridge nearby.

Berlage was inspired by the theme and created on his own four studies, which were exhibited in September at a show. The studies were well received; he elaborated on two of the proposals and added perspective views. In 1886 he was awarded a silver medal at the annual architecture show organized by the M.B.B.

Berlage started from the same assumption in each study: He refused to isolate the monument and created several variations on the same theme. The two more extreme designs are the ones he later elaborated on. In the first one, the building is two stories high, with a long sloping roof and dormers; it is connected to the tower by a common base. In the second design, it is a sort of gate next to the tower, connected to the latter by an entrance only. All the studies show a search for stylistic harmony and environmental unity.

Bibliography: cfr. J.R. de Kruijff, in *Bouwkundig Weekblad* 1885, pp. 222–23; *Bouwkundig Weekblad* 1886, p. 41.

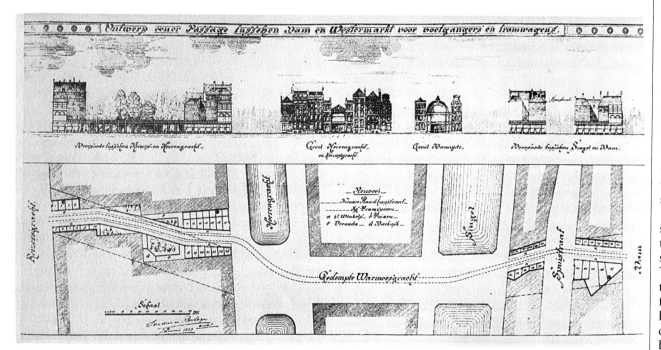

142

143

144

109

143. *Four studies.*

144. *Second version and perspective view of the first proposal.*

1885

In April 1885 the association "Architectura et Amicitia" announced an open competition, customary in the nineteenth century, for an ideal "royal palace in the country's capital."

Berlage must have thought of submitting a design, because he showed in 1886, at the annual architecture exhibition organized by the M.B.B., a colored perspective drawing entitled

"Hall of a royal palace." This drawing is reminiscent of a similar one executed for the first level in the competition for the Stock Exchange: Berlage combines allusions to Roman architecture with sumptuous decorations. The vast central hall features a skylight; it is circled by tiers of structured openings connected by majestic stairs.

Bibliography: cfr. *De Opmerker* 1885, pp. 138–139; *Bouwkundig Weekblad* 1886, p. 90.

145. Interior view.

Lochem, 50–52–54 Nieuweweg
Commissioned by Nairac
1886

Three simple brick villas, still extant, with a châlet-like roof and balconies covered with a wooden structure, were built in Lochem, between Arnhem and Enschede.

146. Present state of a villa.

146

With Theodor Sanders
Baarn
1885–88

In 1885 Sanders & Berlage designed a sanatorium for the town of Baarn, east of Hilversum. It was built in three phases between June 1886 and fall of 1888.

The first phase was finished in the summer of 1887: a central hall and stairs, with two asymmetrical wings at right angles from each other. In October, work started on the dining room at the end of one wing and on the completion of the other. A bathing establishment behind the building was constructed last. The whole sanatorium cost around 100,000 florins.

The layout shows great clarity and a remarkable spatial distribution. The rooms run along the two façades, with a central corridor intersecting the axis formed by the entrance, hall, and stairs. In the main portion of the building, the right-angle shape, matching that of the hall, and the different treatment of entrances establish a hierarchy in the composition, which is reinforced by the smaller mass of the construction in the back. The latter portion of the building contains offices, a kitchen, and bathrooms; it is L-shaped and forms a sort of inner courtyard, and it is connected to the bathing establishment.

The façade is reminiscent of Swiss architecture and more in keeping with contemporary taste. Smooth, cement-rendered walls highlight the decorative patterns created by the verandas' wooden architraves and the colonnade circling the main portion of the building. The corner with the entrance is designed as an octagonal tower, with diagonal axes; its distinct upper structure is emphasized by a panoramic balcony and a narrow spire.

Bibliography: H.P. Berlage 1888, "Het Sanatorium"; editorial 1978, "Baarnse."

147. Perspective view.

147

With Theodor Sanders
Berlin, Friedrichstrasse
Commissioned by
the Erven Lucas Bols Company
1886

In 1886 Berlage traveled to Berlin. There he visited the Jubilee exhibition, which he reviewed in *Bouwkundig Weekblad*. The trip was probably related to a commission received that year by Sanders & Berlage: the interior of a drinking hall on Friedrichstrasse, at the very center of town, for the Bols Company, a famous producer of Dutch spirits. The drawings for the design were shown in April 1887 at the annual architecture exhibition organized by the M.B.B.

From 1891–92 on, after he left Sanders's firm, Berlage designed several other interiors for Bols.

Bibliography: cfr. *Bouwkundig Weekblad* 1887, p. 109.

With Theodor Sanders
Weesp
Commissioned by Scheffer
1886

In 1886 Berlage designed with Sanders a mansion for the Scheffer family in Weesp, a small town east of Amsterdam. Built on a plot measuring 120 feet x 75 feet, the mansion has two stories and attics: on the ground floor, five rooms, and a pool room, sitting room, kitchen, pantry, and bathrooms; and on the second floor, six master bedrooms. The main entrance is slightly projecting, flanked by a high spire with a weathervane; it is highlighted by a decorated gable rising above a polygonal oriel window. The corner of the two faces is chamfered on the ground floor, with an opening echoing the oriel window above and its spire. The side is made of two symmetrical portions of building, connected on the second floor by a balustrated veranda. The exterior is marked by ornamental architectural elements: The walls are of cement rhythmically decorated by horizontal bands of tufa, the thickness of which is proportionate to the height of the base and the string course.

Small ancillary portions of the building stand on the left side of the main entrance.

The villa became the property of the confectionery industrialist Van Houten, on the grounds of the factory. It was recently demolished.

Bibliography: H.P. Berlage 1886, "Bij de plaat."

148. Perspective view.

VILLA VOOR DEN HEER SCHEFFER TE WEESP

148

Milan, Piazza Duomo
Commissioned by the administrators
of the construction works
of the cathedral
1886–87

On March 1, 1886, the Board of Trustees of the Milan cathedral announced "a two-level competition for the design of new façade, open to Italian and foreign artists." The announcement gave "the competitors a free hand in the choice of artistic and historic criteria." Fifteen designs would be considered at the second level. The deadline for submission was between April 1 and 15, 1887. Each proposal had to be presented by a resident of Milan representing the competitor. The jury was composed of twelve Italians and three foreigners: a French architect, Fernand de Dartein; a prominent German neo-Gothic architect, Friedrich von Schmidt; and a British architect, Alfred Waterhouse.

In the lecture he gave in April 1886 in Vienna, which he repeated in Frankfurt am Main and which was translated into Italian, Von Schmidt claimed that "the competition was based on the idea that traces of the interruption (due to an outbreak of bubonic plague in 1524) must be cleared away; only then could the unity of the building be reestablished." With these words, he expressed the jury's intention.

Berlage probably decided to compete immediately after the announcement. He regarded this competition—and the many others in which he took part during these years—as a good promotional vehicle. Only two other Dutch firms submitted designs, H. Evers and G. & C. Krook. They were, however, listed as German architects.

On May 14, 1886, Berlage gave a lecture in Amsterdam—published the same year in *Bouwkundig Weekblad*—in which he analyzed the problems created by the theme of the competition. Unlike Von Schmidt, he gave pride of place to redesigning the square, making the issue of style

subordinate to that of urban planning. His façade is both a great screen, which covers and alludes to the architecture behind it, and a decorative wing, which defines the square. This accounts for the creation of a bell tower with a clock, and its placement clearly was inspired by Giotto's campanile in Florence. The attention to a comprehensive approach, however, was to the detriment of the façade, which is a disorganized mixture of Gothic and Nordic elements.

G. Mongeri published in his *Il Politecnico* a repertory of the 126 designs for the first level of the competition that were examined by the jury. Berlage's presentation bears the number two, with the motto "Et Domus quam aedificabo magna erit, Deus enim noster omnibus Deis major est." Mongeri judged the four drawings to be of "an uncertain hand."

Berlage's design, done with a proportional layout based on the shape of the equilateral triangle, was not selected for the second level. Aside from Dutch reviews, the wide literature on the competition referred to him only once, in an article by L. Chirtani in the *Corriere della Sera*, translated shortly thereafter in *Bouwkundig Weekblad*. Chirtani was Berlage's representative in Milan, but who really knew that the "submission No. 2" mentioned in the article was that of a Dutch participant? From a professional point of view, Berlage did not achieve much recognition in a competition which had strong nationalist overtones. The only acknowledgment was a request from the museum in Brera for a photograph of the design. It may be on the occasion of this competition, however, that Berlage met Bernhard Sehring, a German architect who had some influence on him. Sehring's design was executed with Peters, with the motto "Noli me tangere," and was admired by all for its splendid draftsmanship. (H.v.B.)

Bibliography: H.P. Berlage 1886, "De Dom"; editorial 1887, "Prijsvragen"; C.T.J.L. Rieber 1889; see

also *Bouwkundig Tijdschrift* 1887, p. 80, pl. XIX; C. Boito, *Il Duomo di Milano e i disegni per la sua facciata*, Milan 1889.

149. Elevation.

With L.J. Eijmer and H.W. Veth
Dordrecht, Toulonschelaan,
and surroundings
Commissioned by the municipality
of Dordrecht
1887

The directors of the M.B.B. gave Berlage his first commission for an urban plan, in partnership with the architects L.J. Eijmer in Amsterdam and H.W. Weth in Dordrecht. This was in response to a request in January 1887 from the municipal council of Dordrecht, a town southwest of Rotterdam, for advice on a limited development plan.

The planning team designed a sinuous plan in the English style, in an area between Toulonschelaan and Vrieseweg, in the so-called Karremansweide southeast of the fortified town. It featured a great tree-lined boulevard running north/south and a residential area with eight villas and around forty attached houses. The plan was clearly reminiscent of the Agneta Park in Delft, built in 1885 by the industrialist Van Marken. It was adopted by the municipal council with only minor changes.

Bibliography: cfr. *Bouwkundig Weekblad* 1888, p. 50.

With Theodor Sanders
Amsterdam, Stationsplein
Commissioned by the Public
Transportation Company Noord-
Hollandsche Tramwegmaatschappij
1888

Sanders made many proposals to modernize the local infrastructure and public transportation system in Amsterdam, against the excessive power of the A.O.M. bus company. Finally, in 1887 his plan for a tram connection with Edam, the center for the production of cheese, northeast of Amsterdam, became operational. The tram line was run by the NHTM, in which Sanders held a major position; a second track was laid in the early 1890s to link up with Alkmaar, another center for the production of cheese, northwest of Amsterdam.

Sanders & Berlage executed a series of buildings for the first track of the line: two depots with offices, respectively on the north side of Amsterdam and in Edam; a series of bridges; and the tram terminus in Amsterdam. This small building was moved and then demolished long ago. It features a waiting room, measuring 18 feet x 14 feet, and a small store, measuring 6 feet x 9 feet. The style, clearly Nordic, is highlighted by the colors of the materials: American pine, glazed bricks, colored glass, and ceramic tiles, contrasting with the zinc and iron used for the angular roofing.

Berlage also drew some advertisement for the NHTM.

Bibliography: H.P. Berlage 1888, "Bij de Plaat"; for the advertisement work, cfr. *De Opmerker* 1889, pp. 183–85, and *Bouwkundig Weekblad* 1895, p. 216.

150. Development plan.

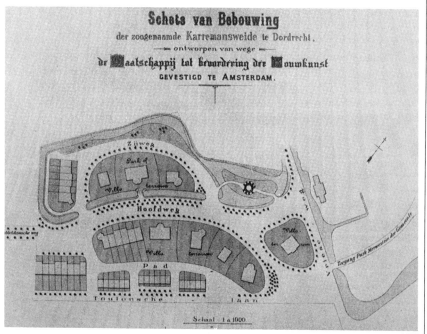

150

151. Perspective view.

151

Design for a Competition for the Concept of a Studio

1888

In 1888 Berlage won first prize at the annual competition for ideas organized by the M.B.B. He submitted a design for an artist's studio and house. P.H.J. Cuypers, H. Evers, and J. Verheul sat on the jury. Berlage's design was selected from among 22 submissions for its masterful draftsmanship, compliance with the program, and its remarkable matching and use of different styles.

The layout is centered on a circular stair leading to the studio and bedrooms on the second floor. The ground floor features a vestibule with Pompeiian wall decorations, a Renaissance dining room, a Louis XV boudoir, and a Louis XVI sitting room. The exterior design combines a rich Italianate decoration with a structure appealing to contemporary taste. A portico unfolds into the garden, leading to a small pavilion.

His success at this competition may have encouraged Berlage, who had married Marie Bienfait, to leave Sanders's studio and create his own. Their collaboration had met with little success in spite—or perhaps because—of Sanders's grandiose plans.

The design's motto was indicative of the critical assessment Berlage was making of his own work and his future plans: a quotation from Goethe's *Torquato Tasso*, "Es bildet ein Talent in der Stille/Sich ein Charakter in dem Strom der Welt" (Talent develops in quiet places/Character in the full current of human life).

Bibliography: editorial 1891, "Tafel 51"; also cfr. *Bouwkundig Tijdschrift* 1888, and *Bouwkundig Weekblad* 1889, 49.

152. Floor plan.

153. Perspective view.

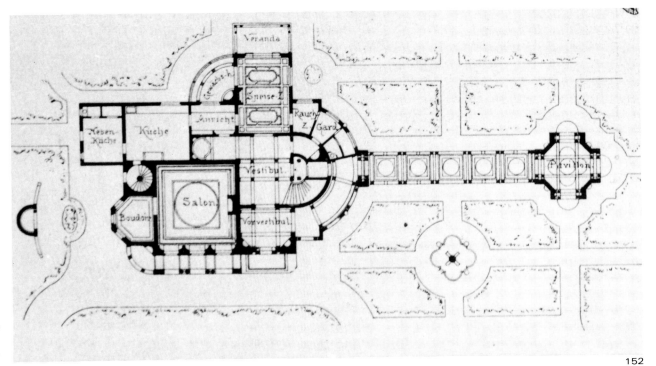

152

153

1889

In 1889 France celebrated the centennial of the French Revolution with a world fair under the symbolic shadow of the Eiffel Tower. The Dutch participation was strong: Eighteen architects—among them Berlage, Evers, Leliman, and Verheul—presented drawings of designs and buildings. The *Bouwkundig Weekblad* published reviews and reports for a whole year, an indication of the attention given to the event.

Berlage sent his design of the Milan cathedral and his *Monument historique*, *Projet d'un Mausolée*, *Monument crématoire*. He did not receive any award because prizes were given only to buildings. The critic Rieber protested in the *Bouwkundig Weekblad*, and pointed to the quality of the work produced by Berlage's studio.

The Monument hints at his future Pantheon of Humanity of 1915, including its location on hills surrounding the capital. A sequence of impressive rooms is inscribed in a central plan. The high points of the design are a triumphal arch at the entrance, a central chapel which rises into an immense cupola, and a Gothic chapel leading to the crematorium, while the very long wings contain a pantheon of illustrious men. Past styles are not used for a paraphrase but for a complex composition, and a section through the design shows many references: the temple of Horus at Edfu, the Choragic Monument of Lysicrates, the temple of Amon at Karnak, the temple of Jupiter in Rome, the cupola of the Baptistery of Constantine in Rome, the façade of the Parthenon, the Pazzi Chapel in Florence, the cupola of the temple of Minerva Medica in Rome, the door of the Redentore in Venice, the tower of the Strasburg cathedral, the rose-window and tower of the Reims cathedral, the tower of the Antwerp cathedral, the cupola of Saint Peter

154. Sketch of an interior view.

154

116

in Rome, the tower of the Vienna cathedral, and a small tower of Saint Paul in London and another of Santa Agnese in Rome, in a paradoxical collage befitting "the great international commercial fair." In a lecture given in 1890 on the theme of "man's housing" (*De menschelijke woning*), Berlage described his time as "a time of chaos and confusion. . . . We perceive an improvement for the last twenty-five years of the nineteenth century. We are witness to a renewed study of the best works of the past, while now, at the end of the nineteenth century . . . well, what will happen?"

Bibliography: M. (H.C. Muller) 1890; P. Singelenberg 1963, "Berlage's"; also cfr. *Bouwkundig Weekblad* 1889, 10, p. 55; 11, pp. 61–2; 23, pp. 133–35; 40, pp. 235–36; *De Architect* I, 1890, pl. 7–9; for a brief account of Berlage's lecture on the architecture of the World Fair, cfr. *Bouwkundig Weekblad* 1889, p.20273.

155–157. Sketches of interior views.

158. Elevation.

155

156

157

158

Utrecht, Runnebaan
Commissioned by the association "Sic Semper"
1889

In July 1889, the association "Sic Semper" in Utrecht announced a competition for its headquarter building, with a deadline set in September of the same year. Berlage's design, bearing the number 61 and presented with the motto "Trans," ranked among the eleven best designs of the almost seventy that were submitted. The jury, however, which included C. Muysken and Theodor Sanders, did not give him any prize or mention.

Berlage designed the building at the corner of two streets, following closely—and making the best possible use of—the trapezoidal shape of the site. The entrance is on the longer side; it leads to a central stair, around which the main rooms are organized. The ground floor features a coat room, a reading room, a hall for recreational activities, bathrooms, a kitchen, and a large community room in the corner of the building, probably for public meetings. The second floor features a smaller meeting room, also in the corner of the building, administrative offices, and more bathrooms. The layout is a mere variation on that of contemporary buildings for associations, without any outstanding innovation.

The jury praised the design of the façade but found it more suitable for an administrative building. The façade combines a classicist structure with ornamental motifs drawn from the Dutch Renaissance. A small tower jutting out on the corner and symmetrical gables over three following spans reflect the spatial hierarchy ruling the interior layout. In the same manner, the openings highlight the spatial organization on two levels for work and three levels for services. Finally, the unity of the exterior contrasts with the strong functional differentiation of the interior.

Bibliography: cfr. *Bouwkundig Weekblad* 1889, pp. 176–78, 255–58; *De Opmerker* 1889, 426–28.

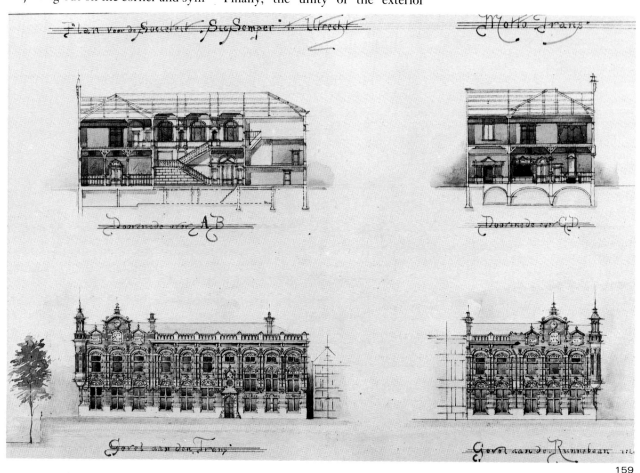

159. Sections and elevations.

159

Zutphen, Gravenhof
Commissioned by the municipality
of Zutphen
1889–90

In October 1889, a competition was announced for the design of a town hall in Zutphen, an old city on the Ijssel river, in the eastern Netherlands and midway between Arnhem and Hengelo. Berlage, W. Kromhout, and the team K. Muller-J. Ingenhol were among the 55 participants in the competition.

This time again, the jury, which included C. Muysken, did not award any prize or mention to Berlage. It first selected Kromhout, and then, in the second phase, Muller-Ingenhol. Finally, the whole project was abandoned by the municipal administration.

Berlage's design was quite similar to that of Muller-Ingenhol. It was criticized for a lack of consistency between the exterior and the interior. The building follows closely the trapezoidal shape of the site, which is located on the historic Gravenhof. As a result, there is no clear relationship between main and ancillary space. The flow between the main entrance on the square and the two lateral stairs inside is also problematic, and the vast council hall is almost hidden in the back.

The façade is a repertory of northern Dutch Renaissance architecture around 1600. The corner on the square is set off by two symmetrical stepped gables and a pinnacled tower with a panoramic balcony. A section at an angle of 45 degrees conceals the opposite end of the building from the main public part. Berlage was to explore again the possibilities of such a device, but he did not seem to treat it with sufficient rigor in this design.

Bibliography: cfr. *Bouwkundig Weekblad* 1889, pp. 262–63, and 1890, pp. 81–85; *De Opmerker* 1890, pp. 120–22; *De Architect* I, 1890, pl. 32.

160

160. Façade.

Amsterdam, 115 Heerengracht
Commissioned by the brokerage firm
Kerkhoven & Co.
1889–90 and 1906–07

In 1889 the brokerage firm Kerkhoven & Co. commissioned Berlage for the renovation of its headquarters on the Heerengracht, in Amsterdam's historic center. The commission was probably secured thanks to Berlage's cousin, also named H.P. Berlage, who was married to a Kerkhoven and employed by the firm. Construction work began in the summer of 1889 and was completed in March 1890. Berlage entirely redesigned the building and reduced the decorative elements to a minimum. The asymmetrical façade is made of exposed bricks. Ornaments are limited to the rusticated ashlar surrounding the doorway and the lunettes above the windows. Ashlars mark the keystones and imposts of the small arches around the windows. Narrow horizontal courses of stone run across the façade; they divide the glazed surface and design a fret around the basement windows, which strengthens the connection to the ground.

As he often did, between 1906 and 1907 Berlage worked on the building again.

161. Elevation.

VERBOUWING van het KANTOOR KERKHOVEN en Cº. AMSTERDAM.

VOORGEVEL. 1:50

161

Apeldoorn
Commissioned by the administrators
of the construction works on the
Reformed Church in Apeldoorn
1890

In August 1890, a competition was
announced for a new church in Apeldoorn, a city in the eastern Netherlands, halfway between Amsterdam
and the German border, to replace
the old church which had been destroyed by fire.

Berlage approached the competition's theme with special attention to
the problem of religious buildings—
referring in particular to a classic text
published in 1857 by J.A. Alberking
Thijm, *De heilige linie*, on the symbolic orientation of churches before
the Reformation—and to Gothic
tradition.

The main entrance is designed as
a portico leading to a long nave; the
interior features a barrel vault with
exposed beams. The intersection with
a short central transept is marked by
the wide span of arches interrupting
the nave's sequence of rounded arches.
A bell tower with spire stands at the
end of the transept. The women's
galleries are in the aisles. The
congregation and altar are placed
transversally, along the axis of the
transept.

The design was submitted with the
motto "Het Haantje van den toren"
(The cock of the tower, visible in the
exterior view on top of the spire). The
jury deemed it "fairly rational and
simple." A controversy arose in the
press after the competition and
P.J.H. Cuypers wrote an article in
favor of Berlage's design.

Bibliography: *Bouwkundig Weekblad*
1890, pp. 220, 292, 298–300, and
317–19 (P.J.H. Cuypers); *De Opmerker* 1890, pp. 220 and 411; *Bouwkundig
Tijdschrift* 1891, pl. 7–15; K.E.O.
Fritsch, ed., *Der Kirchenbau des Pro-
testantismus von der Reformation bis zur
Gegenwart*, Berlin 1893, pl. 281–82.

162. Perspective view.

162

Enge (Zürich), Burgliterrasse
1890–91

At the end of 1890, a competition was announced for a church in Enge, on the outskirts of Zürich, with a February 1891 deadline. Berlage had learned from his recent experience in Apeldoorn, and while his design was not awarded any prize, he won a silver medal in 1891 at the annual architecture show organized by the M.B.B. Here, the layout is more traditional than that of the Apeldoorn design. The altar and the congregation are placed along the axis of the main nave. The pointed arches of the nave rest on short columns. The

Gothic vault features exposed, decorated metallic beams supporting the reduced section of the roof.

The bell tower is placed off center with the façade, at the end of the transept. The rich decoration includes rose-windows on the main sides. The visual importance of the roof is accentuated. The main entrance is designed as a portico flanked by two small towers with spires. In other words, Berlage introduced some careful modifications to his Apeldoorn design, which were suggested by observations and polemics caused by the competition. The church at Enge is a variation of the Apeldoorn one, in which Berlage has strengthened the "rational" accents *à la* Cuypers. The drawings in the Berlage archives include a technically interesting presentation: The perspective view is integrated in a photomontage.

Bibliography: cfr. *Deutsche Bauzeitung* 1890, p. 584, and 1891, pp. 108 and 140; *Bouwkundig Weekblad* 1891, p. 118.

163. *Photomontage.*

164. *Façade.*

163

164

Design of the Façade of a House

Amsterdam, 17 Egelantiersgracht
1891

In 1891, Berlage proposed two variations of a new façade for the renovation of a traditional house in the center of Amsterdam, not far from the Westerkerk Bank.

The first version features a rusticated base under a decorated horizontal band, a façade framed by a depressed arch, and a triangular gable. It obviously refers to Dutch houses of the first half of the sixteenth century, eclectically combined with elements of other idioms.

The second final version is reminiscent of Dutch Renaissance architecture of the second half of the sixteenth century, especially in the design of the gable. This version and the previous one have in common the rusticated base, exposed brick front, horizontal strips of stone at the level of the window sills, and decorated lunettes.

165. Elevation of the final version.

Amsterdam, 72 Van Baerlestraat
Commissioned by E.D. Pijzel
1891–92

In the early 1890s Berlage built a
house for E.D. Pijzel in the vicinity
of the Stedelijk Museum in Amsterdam, which was erected between
1892 and 1895. Pijzel was editor-in-
chief of the monthly *Mannen en Vrouwen van Betekenis*, in which Landré
published an essay on Berlage in
1916, and a member of the music society "Toonkunst," for which Berlage
executed some drawings. The two
men knew each other from the Breero
Club, where artists, intellectuals, and
politicians of a progressive stripe
could meet. Berlage made many such
useful acquaintances among prominent members of the club. Suffice it
to mention M.W.F. Treub, the liberal politician who played a role in
the commission of the new Stock Exchange; the Social Democrats who
introduced Berlage to H. Polak, the
leader of the A.N.D.B.; and F. van
der Goes and P.L. Tak, whose review, *De Kroniek*, enlisted Berlage as a
contributor. The architects J. Springer and A.W. Weissman were also
members of the club, as were artists
and critics G.H. Breitner and J.
Veth, and journalists and editors E.D.
Pijzel and H. Binger—the promoter
of the *Feestgids* of 1887, for which
Berlage produced several illustrations.

The design of the house was presented in April 1892. In spite of the
elaborately drawn frame, the design
itself has a careful sobriety befitting
Pijzel's status and circumstances. The
building is set on a traditional lot,
deep and narrow. It has a simple layout, with minor variations on Berlage's previous spatial distribution
and decoration: The rooms all face
two fronts, from the basement to the
attic, and the stairs run along the side
walls.

The façade is in keeping with that
of the two adjacent buildings, like
Berlage's other designs in the city's
historic center. The lines formed by
the vertical and horizontal edges reg-

ulate the asymmetrical partitions and
irregular openings. A horizontal strip
of stone marks the basement level and
strengthens discreetly the connection
between the house and the ground.
The salient feature of the ground
floor is a deep opening for the stairs
at the entrance and its mullioned

window with two lights and an ocu-
lus. Brick cornices form a pattern of
courselines with right-angle shapes.
The structure of the archivolts above
the slightly recessed windows is
highlighted by yellowish brown
glazed bricks. There are a few purely
decorative elements, such as the lu-

nette on the dormer and the typically
Dutch iron hoist above.

Bibliography: cfr. *Bouwkundig Weekblad* 1892, pp. 147–48.

166. Elevation of the final version.

166

Berlin, Friedrichstrasse
Commissioned by the Erven Lucas
Bols Co.
1891–92

In 1891 Berlage was commissioned for the interior renovation of the "'t Lootsje" in Berlin, which was part of an international chain of drinking halls managed by the Bols Company and which he had designed with Sanders in 1886. Between 1891 and 1892 Berlage drew a series of new furniture pieces—buffet, tables, stools, even the fireplace. These designs were shown with that of the Pijzel house in June 1892 at the annual architecture exhibition organized by the M.B.B.

This work was wrongly dated 1887 in the *Festschrift* published in 1916. Between 1892 and 1897, Berlage renovated several "'t Lootsje," in Amsterdam, Hamburg, Bremen, Antwerp, and Paris.

Bibliography: cfr. *Arti et Industriae* 1892, p. 39, pl. III and V; *Bouwkundig Weekblad* 1892, pp. 147–48, and 1893, p. 127.

167. Complete design.

168. Contemporary photograph.

167

168

125

Lochem, 3 Dr. Rivestraat
Commissioned by the Lochem
Savings Bank
1891–92

Between 1891 and 1892 Berlage built a Volkshuis with a bank annex in Lochem, a small town in the eastern Netherlands, near Zutphen and the German border. The building was commissioned by the local savings bank and inaugurated in April 1892. It was located near the fortifications of the old city and has been demolished since.

Berlage made at least two variations on the design, which were shown in 1892 at the annual architecture exhibition organized by the M.B.B. The final version had greater clarity in the spatial distribution, with a change in the placement of the stairs, the bank, and the ancillary rooms. There were several functional requirements: a public hall on two levels, a lending library, a school for drawing and household management, a public bath, and a bank. In the layout, each function corresponds to an almost autonomous building mass, forming a sort of swastika around a small tower. The latter features a three-light Gothic blind window facing the street, under which there are openings for the lighting of the stairs. Only certain portions of the exterior are designed symmetrically, such as the long side of the meeting hall featuring a modest portico. The openings are arranged freely on smooth walls, without the decorative pinchbeck present in the first version of the design.

Bibliography: cfr. *Bouwkundig Weekblad* 1891, p. 98, and 1892, pp. 147–48.

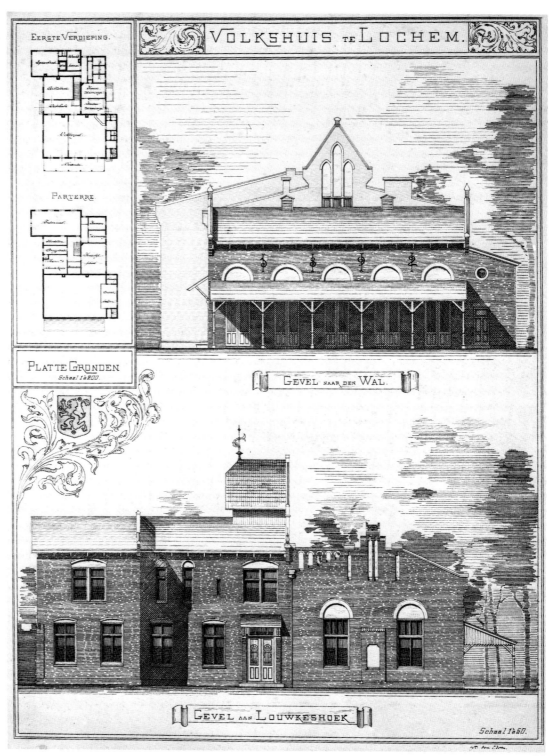

169. Complete design.

1892

At the end of 1891, the M.B.B. announced a competition to celebrate the fiftieth anniversary of its foundation. The theme was "a royal residence in the vicinity of a great city," a theme similar to that proposed in 1885 by "Architectura et Amicitia."

Berlage made several drawings, which were shown with other works of his at the 1892 exhibition organized by the M.B.B. Their caption was significant, "Sketches of architectural fantasies."

These drawings were wrongly dated 1888 in the *Festschrift* of 1916. They illustrate three variations on period forms of a grand façade: eclectic pastiches, set off by architectural elements and ornaments drawn from the German and Dutch Renaissance.

Bibliography: cfr. *Bouwkundig Weekblad* 1891, pp. 259–60, and 1892, pp. 147–48.

170. Sketch of a perspective view.

170

Bussum,
24 Nieuwen 's-Gravenlandscheweg
Commissioned by E. van Eeden
1892–93 and 1902

In October 1892 the municipality of Bussum, a small town near Amsterdam, issued a construction permit for a one-family house commissioned by Frederik van Eeden, the neurologist, writer, and poet. In August of the same year, Van Eeden went to Britain. His correspondence with his friend, the man of letters Lodewijk van Deyssel, indicates that he was able to see much English domestic architecture and appreciate the functional comfort of country houses.

For several years, interest had been growing on the continent, and in Germany in particular, for English houses and domestic architecture. In 1888, Robert Dohme published *Das Englische Haus*, in which English houses are chosen over the best German ones, because they are sunny, "comfortable," "convenient," and "cheerful."

Other architects, among them Cornelius Gurlitt and Karl Henrici (one of whose articles was translated by Berlage in 1892), proposed to spread a new German domestic architecture (*Wohnkultur*) similar to the English one. They were the forerunners of Hermann Muthesius. They claimed that a house must be practical and well suited rather than have "style": The dwellers must feel comfortable.

In the Netherlands, such ideas were championed by Van Deyssel. In his 1894 essay "Over impressionisme en architectuur," he introduced in the debate on "Architecture and Impressionism" the notion that a house should not be "foreign, new, or with a style," but above all should be "comfortable." The client's needs must prevail over the architect's ideas about form.

Upon his return in 1892 from England, Van Eeden clearly wished for a cottage according to a new ideal concept of housing, in spite of the fact that he had modest financial means.

Berlage designed a simple but spacious house. He limited costs to a minimum and created a prototype that was to be quickly imitated but that he himself was to criticize later. Construction work was completed very quickly, within five months. The house was ready in April 1893 and Van Eeden moved from Amsterdam.

Berlage set aside preoccupations of style and gave pride of place to his client's program and needs. The result, however, is not fully convincing. The layout is somewhat rigid and the spatial arrangement awkward. On the ground floor, the rooms are arranged around a large vestibule, according to rules of English design. On the second floor, there are three bedrooms—a master bedroom, a guest room, and a children's room—and a large bathroom, which was a rarity in a Dutch house. The third floor features an attic and two maid's rooms. It should be noted that traditional ornamentation was eliminated, although some structural elements such as archivolts and architraves take on a decorative function, forming a design of brick arches against the white cement-rendered walls. There are also a few references to medieval architecture: a battlement with a horizontal brick cornice, and exposed timber under the roof. The villa achieves a pictorial effect with a simple chromatic contrast between the red roof tiles, the green shutters, and the dominant white of the cement-rendering (an unusual finish in Holland, but justified by the poor quality of the bricks used). This chromatic effect is strengthened by the asymmetry of the exterior.

It may be a consequence of Van Eeden's appreciation that Louise Gorter, the wife of the poet Herman Gorter, asked Berlage to design a small villa. The relationship between Van Eeden—who was satisfied with his villa—and Berlage ended with this one experiment. Several years later, when he decided to create "Walden," an agricultural community inspired by Thoreau's ideas, Van Eeden called on W.C. Bauer, who was then able to turn down the designer's position Berlage had offered him for the construction of the Stock Exchange. In

March 1902, however, Berlage designed a small extension to the house, which in the meantime had become Villa Momma De Dennenhof. (H.v.B.)

Bibliography: cfr. *De Architect* VIII, 1897, pl. 259; O. Haenel, *Einfache Villen und Landhäuser*, Dresden, undated, pl. 5; for W.C. Bauer's case and his relationship with the group "Architectura," of which he was a member along with W. Kromhout, H.J.M. Walenkamp, K.P.C. de Bazel, and J.L.M. Lauweriks, cfr. M. Bock, ed., *Architectura*, exhibition catalogue, Architectuur Museum, Amsterdam, 1975[1], and the monograph in the issue of *Museumjournaal* 1976, 5, February, an abridged English version of the abovementioned catalogue.

171

172

171. Perspective study.

172. Contemporary photograph.

173. Perspective view of the first design, 1894.

174. Contemporary photograph.

De Algemeene Building

Amsterdam, 74–76 Damrak and later
71–79/1–5 Baafjessteeg
Commissioned by the insurance
company De Algemeene
1892–94 and 1901–05

In the 1880s Dutch insurance companies entered a time of economic growth, and they invested in real estate, commissioning works from architects. De Utrecht Company called on J. Verheul, then J.E. Staal and A.J. Kropholler, to design its headquarters (cfr. J. Roding, *De Utrecht een Nederlands voorbeeld van Art Nouveau-architectuur*, Het Spectrum, Utrecht-Antwerp 1977[I], 1978[II]). De Nederlanden van 1845 and De Algemeene, respectively specialized in fire and life insurance, turned to Berlage for architectural designs and advice in real estate, entrusting him with the creation of their "corporate image." Founded in 1880, De Algemeene had become by 1890 the most important Dutch insurance company. For years it was able to challenge strong foreign competition and attempt to expand abroad, in Germany in particular. In March 1891, the opportunity arose to build headquarters on the Dam, across the street from Zocher's Stock Exchange. In April 1891, the board of directors—including E.W. Scott, for whom Berlage built a villa in Bussum—commissioned him for a preliminary design. His friendship with Albert Verwey may have been instrumental in this commission. He was a man of letters and the brother of Chris Verwey, who became the company's chief accountant in 1896 and Berlage's brother-in-law in 1898. The sketches came with a cost projection around 50,000 florins, but the negotiations for the acquisition of the land failed.

In the meantime, De Algemeene acquired several buildings between Damrak and Baafjessteeg, almost facing the site of the future Stock Exchange, for 150,000 florins. In December 1891, Berlage submitted a new general study, with a cost assessment no higher than 45,000 florins to ensure the best return on the investment. He was immediately

173

174

asked to execute a final design, and building was projected for the following year. A second version of the design was presented in 1893. The contract was ready in March 1893, with an estimate of 120,000 florins, equipment included. The building permit was issued in April and demolition works were begun. In January 1894 Berlage started work on the furnishings, and in April the company moved into its new headquarters.

The building site is 44 feet wide on Damrak and 108 feet deep on Baafjessteeg, without reaching the Nieuwendijk behind it, and it covers around 4,700 square feet. In order to align with the Damrak, the façade is at a slight slant, which makes it a little wider. The ground floor on the Damrak features stores and the entrance hall closed by a sliding gate. The second floor has the company's offices, while the third and fourth floors have rental offices. The whole back of the building is designed as one fireproof strong vault for the archives. The interior stairs are lit from the side by an inner courtyard. The windows of the stores are on Baafjessteeg; the light for the rooms on that street—in particular, the showroom for samples on the third floor—also comes from a side court closed by a wall. The technical equipment, which represents 18 percent of the estimate, includes an elevator, electrical lighting, and central heating.

The two versions differed only slightly in the façade. The first version was executed at the same time as the stage designs made for the monumental edition of Joost van den Vondel's *Gijsbreght van Aemstel*, and it is not a coincidence that the architectural drawing should be framed by the same decorative border (cfr. H.P. Berlage, 1893–01, *Gijsbreght*; E. Braches, 1971, and L. Rebel-Benschop, 1981). The fronts in sandstone from the Oberkirchen give a general impression of smoothness. The reliefs and sculptures are part of a very careful iconographic program; the animal and symbolic motifs were carved by L. Zijl, while the more traditional statue of J. de Witt on the corner was executed by B. van Hove.

The frontispiece is divided asymmetrically. On the corner, a block rises like a large pinnacle and features on the Damrak side a rose-window and a promotional mullioned window with two lights. On the angle of this block, a turret is poised above the statue of De Witt. A pelican in bas-relief crowns the block: As a symbol of family solidarity, it has become the emblem of De Algemeene. On the right of the block, between two acroteria, the coping of the façade is perforated with the sign of the company, its lettering designed by Berlage. An even more stentorian "Algemeene" reads clearly on the ridge and pitches of the block's

roof. Through a sober and sparse interpretation of period architecture, Berlage achieved his goal and created an expressive and monumental effect, strengthened by the imposing scale of the building when compared to the rest of the Damrak.

It was decided in 1895 to decorate the interior with murals. At the end of the year Berlage contacted A. Derkinderen, with whom he had worked on the publication of

Gijsbreght. He had the first sketches for the mural decoration of the stairs at the beginning of 1896. It was not until 1900, however, that the eight allegoric murals were shown to the press.

Extension work on the headquarters of De Algemeene was done in two successive phases. In 1901–02, two spans were added toward the Dam, each enclosed by turrets; on the top, the coping lined up with the

175

176

177

perforated one of the original building. In 1903–05, the building was extended in the direction of the central railway station, following the inauguration of the new Stock Exchange. The original triangular gable was demolished to be rebuilt on the next span, with proportions better adapted to the size of the renovated building. The free rhythm of the frontispiece is closed by another span, flanked by a turret similar to that on the opposite corner. A gallery is opened between Damrak and Nieuwendijk, the Beurspassage; it is lit from above and lined with shop windows. At either end of the gallery, a stone arch is supported by pilasters in polished granite, grayish with black and white veins. Inside the gallery, the low vault features a glazed cream-colored covering, with strips of blue and yellow; the ceiling is made of concrete-framed glass bricks (patent Falconnier), with strips of color to allow in the light from inner courtyards.

The building extends as far as the Nieuwendijk, where the façade is at a slight slant in order to follow the street's alignment. After the extension and renovation work were completed, the building covered a site measuring around 20,000 square feet. The stores have a waterproof basement built in reinforced concrete. The entire second floor is occupied by the offices of De Algemeene—including the boardroom designed by Berlage, with reliefs by M. da Costa—and the janitor's apartment. The offices on the third and fourth floor are rented, and there are more service lodgings in the attic. Eight inner courts ensure the lighting and hygiene of the building. Two new stairwells with elevators serve, respectively, the extension on the right of the gallery, on Damrak, and the entrance on Nieuwendijk; because of the mural paintings, the stairs of the original building remained untouched in spite of earlier criticism.

The great covered courtyard near the original stairs becomes the building's architectural center. It has a complex design: On the ground floor,

it has the shape of a square, outlined by wide arches supported by granite pilasters; on the second floor and upward, the square develops into an octagon. The balconies' arches are supported by eight columns, connected by an openwork balustrade in greenish sandstone, with a slab of granite as a handrail. The columns are made of the same sandstone. The skylight above is formed by eight elliptical pendentives, made of the same concrete-framed glass bricks as the gallery's ceiling, with similar chromatic variations. The walls of this monumental volume are textured by bricks and stones (alternatively cream-colored and dark), with inserts of colored glazed tiles. The floors are made of stone and marble mosaics. An extraordinary biomorphic light fixture descends like an intricate illuminating crown from the skylight to the ground floor; its geometric adaptation of natural forms was inspired by Haeckel's *Kunstformen der Natur*, as were the designs for the furniture, ironwork, and lighting of the Stock Exchange.

Later the department store C. & A. took over almost the whole building (see the study of the 1903 renovation) and added more floors. In February 1963 it was destroyed in a fire. After it was demolished, it was replaced by an anonymous building.

Bibliography: H.P. Berlage 1893, "Het Kantoorgebouw"; M.K. 1894; J. Kok 1894; R. 1894; J. Veth 1900; W.N. van Vliet 1905; editorial 1906, "Wahrheit"; P. Singelenberg 1963, "Het Bizondere"; M. Bock 1983, p. 42, pl. f.t., and 1984, p. 55; *Bouwkundig Weekblad* 1893, pp. 127, 159; *De Kunstwereld* 1894, 16, 17, and 18; *De Opmerker* 1894, pp. 114, 138–139; *Haarlemmer Courant* 1894, April 23; *Nieuwe Rotterdamsche Courant* 1894, May 30; *Academy Architecture and Annual Architecture Review* II, 1895, pp. 119, 144; *Architectura* 1905, 31, pl. f.t.; *Bouwkundig Weekblad* 1905, pp. 667–68; *De Architect* XVI, 1905, pl. 571–76.

Interior design for the establishments of the Bols

Amsterdam (99 Rozengracht),
Hamburg, Bremen
Commissioned by
De Erven Lucas Bols Co.
1892–93

In 1892–93, Berlage did the interior design of the "'t Lootsje" in three cities: Amsterdam, Hamburg, and Bremen. Whether in Amsterdam or in the other cities, the establishments were designed with a reference to the Dutch Renaissance tradition, which was the company's required trademark. It is not a coincidence that the extension work of another establishment in Amsterdam on Rozengracht—the westward continuation, beyond the Westerkerk, of the Raadhuisstraat—was commissioned in 1900 from Eduard Cuypers, an architect less openly modernist than Berlage.

178. Design sketches, Bremen.

Interior design for the establishments of the Bols

178

179. *Interior view, Amsterdam.*

180. *Contemporary photograph, Amsterdam.*

181. *Ornamental detail, Hamburg.*

179

With A.C. Bleys
Amsterdam, 112 Rokin/Spui
Commissioned by the association
"Arti et Amicitiae"
1893–94

In March 1893, the cultural association "Arti et Amicitiae" commissioned A.C. Bleys and Berlage to design the interior renovation and fixtures of its headquarters in Amsterdam, a neoclassical building dating from 1855 and designed by J.H. Leliman. Construction work was completed in May 1894, and the building was inaugurated with great pomp. The only major change in the exterior was the removal of the main entrance from the side facing the Rokin—a main thoroughfare between Dam and Muntplein, in the heart of Amsterdam—to the side facing the Spui, which had recently been filled in.

The new entrance leads to a wide corridor, which in turn leads to the administrative offices on the right and, on the left, a reading room attached to the library, a coat room, and a pool room. The latter opens onto the central corridor, where stairs lead to the exhibition rooms. The staircase is lit by stained-glass windows at the level of the second-floor landing. The corridor is covered with wainscoting and marble. The rooms of the ground floor, with the exception of the pool room, are clad with oak wainscoting and "modern" wallpaper; they have parquet floors and decorated wooden ceilings. The great wooden beams in the ceiling rest on marble columns. In the exhibition rooms of the second floor, the design is more sober and big skylights provide an even light. Berlage also designed the tables, benches, chairs, and stools.

Bibliography: Berlage 1894, *Verbouwing . . .* ; L. 1896.

182. *J.H. Leliman, headquarters of "Arti et Amicitiae," photograph, ca 1875.*

183. *Interior view of the staircase in the renovation design.*

182

183

133

Groningen, 108 Ubbo Emiussingel
Commissioned by G. Heymans
1893–95

Berlage designed and built the Villa Heymans in 1893–95. This is the first work he did in northeast Holland.

The work was commissioned by Gerard Heymans, a philosophy scholar and psychology professor at the University of Groningen. Although he did not take part personally in the cultural debates raging in the Netherlands at the end of the nineteenth century, Heymans was generally regarded as an authority. He certainly was one of the deepest and most original Dutch thinkers of the time. His wide culture was oriented toward Germany, and he published several books and articles in German. It is unclear how he met Heymans, but Berlage was certainly influenced by their acquaintance since he was very interested in philosophy. In 1886, he had published an article, *De Plaats die de bouwkunst in de moderne aesthetica bekleedt*, in which he reviewed the ideas on architecture of several nineteenth-century German philosophers, among them Gustav Theodor Fechner. Heymans's theories on metaphysics and "psychological monism" derived from Fechner's theories and were close to the ideas of Theodor Lipps. In *Aesthetik von Unten*, Heymans took a different stand from the Romantics and Idealists; his aestheticism was based on an inductive method by which the empirical study of the relationship between aesthetic impressions and subjective reactions leads to definition of constant psychological and aesthetic factors. There are several key words in Heymans's writings, especially in *Die Gesetze und Elemente des Wissenschaftlichen Denken*, published in 1894 and clearly influenced by Fechner: truth, utility, and unity. These words often recur in Berlage's own writings, with the same symbolic significance. Berlage's discussions with Heymans were probably not limited to the design of the villa

but covered also many problems of philosophy and aesthetics. In his momentous lecture *Bouwkunst en impressionisme*, published in 1894, Berlage used arguments inspired by Fechner and Lipps and proposed that the architect consider the material components of a design, the client's financial situation and functional requirement, and his own aesthetic considerations as opposed to the engineer's more technical approach. Berlage believed that the architect should achieve aesthetic effects and thet his building could be understood more easily and enjoyed by the public while he still abides by the client's wish "to limit costs." Therefore, architecture must become "impressionistic," concentrate on the composition of masses, and "restrict the decoration to crucial points in the design."

In his 1925 monograph on Berlage, Jan Gratama argued that the Villa Heymans was not regarded as an achievement in forms, although it was one of the first buildings for which Berlage used the "principle of rationality," one of the first examples of his "simple and realistic work." The villa features such elements of Berlage's architectural idiom as the three-light window and wide expanses of brickwork, but the design lacks the balance and compositional clarity to be found in later works. It is more "picturesque" than "monumental."

The villa is located in a neighborhood south of the old city, a residential area for the upper-middle class, and it faces the Eemsgracht. The blind wall on the west side of the

building suggests that Berlage foresaw a possible extension. The uneven height of different portions of the façade reflects the irregular floor plan, according to a principle of "truth." Gratama noted, "If, for practical reasons, the windows are not lined up, the architect does not try to contrive a symmetry." To give a material shape to Heymans's ideas, Berlage must avoid designing a façade with stately proportions; the small entrance is anything but majestic.

The house must be comfortable—Fechner's word is *behaglich*—and its is designed from the interior outward. The chimney is the symbolic feature of the design, but the rooms are grouped around a large hall, a trait borrowed from the English house and recurrent in Berlage's work. The

Villa Heymans could be regarded as a meditation on the themes he had tackled in the Villa Van Eeden, in 1892–93. It is a sort of architectural expression of the saying, "My home is my castle." (H.v.B.)

Bibliography: cfr. *Dekorative Kunst* 1898, p. 23.

184. Layout of the ground floor.

185. Contemporary photograph.

184

185

Hilversum Trompenberg,
Ceintuurbaan
Commissioned by Cruys
1894

In less than twenty years, between 1892 and 1914, Berlage designed around twenty villas apparently commissioned by very different people—painters, poets, critics, philosophers, businessmen, and trade-unionists—who in reality belonged to the same cultural elite and were often related. Until 1910 he designed a villa every year, with the exception of the years 1902 and 1905, during which most of the villas of the century's first five years were built. His own house in The Hague, in 1913–14, marks the end of this cycle, as at the time of its design he started work on ambitious designs of villa-museums, Ellenwoude (1912) and Fransche Berg (1917–18), as well as the St. Hubertus hunting lodge (1914–19), commissioned by the Kröller-Müllers.

The Villa Scheffer, executed with Sanders in 1886, the contemporary three small villas at Lochem, and the academic design for a villa with an artist's studio in 1888 offer little resemblance to Berlage's later work. The Villa Scheffer is still fraught with quotations from the Dutch Renaissance, while the 1888 villa is noteworthy mostly for its use of different styles in a masterful design.

Starting in 1892, Berlage's designs revolved around ideas that were emerging at the time and growing gradually more articulate and complex. His first series of villas, executed between 1892 and 1898, is characterized by a central hall, and he explored the relationship of that hall with the rooms both around and above it.

The Villas Van Eeden (1892–93), Cruys (1894), Heymans (1893–95), and Hubrecht (1895–96) start from the same matrix. The entrance to the house is in the middle of a side elevation; it leads immediately to a central hall and a kitchen, without a corridor. The living area features a clear separation between sitting and dining room, and they often face onto the street.

The Villa Van Eeden has a fairly rigid layout, which Berlage criticized shortly after it was built. It features two flights of stairs, which are off-center and at a right angle from the outer wall. In the Villa Cruys, the stairwell stands against the façade while the other elements of the floor plan are shifted to face the four cardinal points; consequently, the hall takes the shape of an asymmetrical trapezium to connect the different rooms. In the Villa Heymans, as in the Villa Hubrecht, the three flights of stairs lean against the walls of the hall, which has the shape of a square on the second floor, and that of a rectangle on the third floor. Although it is two stories high, the hall does not rise to a skylight, perhaps because its position off-center allows for light coming from the side. The Villa Henny (1898) presents a skillful synthesis of Berlage's different experiments. The porticoed entrance on a corner leads to a hallway hidden in the center of the building. The hall is designed independently from the position of the stairs; it forms the house's geometric core which determines the composition of the space around it, including the shape of the skylight on top of the roof. The diagonal shift in the Villa Henny is not an innovation, however. In the Villa Liesbet (1896), built in Noordwijk aan Zee, the main rooms are shifted at an angle of 45 degrees from the ancillary rooms behind them, although in this case such a choice in design may be related to the configuration of the site in the dunes of a small coastal town.

The search for a different layout started in the years following the building of the villa for Carel Henny. Berlage did not abandon completely the basic composition he had experimented with earlier. In the Villas Parkwijck (1900–01), Roland Holst (1902–13), and Polak (1905), he proceeded to simplify progressively the spatial components until he found the essential definition of space achieved in the design of his own house. The absence of separation between sitting and dining room (which he had already tried in the Villas Roland Holst and Polak) and the significant contraction of the hall are echoed in Berlage's own villa by a flowing layout, characterized by a simple arrangement and an explicit honesty of purpose.

Berlage's attention to the design of the façade and the treatment of the materials call for further comparisons. In such cases as the Villas Van Eeden and Hubrechts, he took into account the requirements and financial limitations of his clients and used cement rendering, probably to hide the mediocre quality of the brick. He also took into account particular local traditions, such as thatched roofs for the Villas Roland Holst and Polak, both in Laren. Combining these different factors, he reached a clear *Zakelijkheid* (objectivity), expressed in the arrangement of domestic spaces developing outward from a center and the rejection of academic symmetry

186. Perspective view.

186

and pre-established location of the openings. The shift in the ground plan of his early designs is combined with a complex arrangement of masses and an interplay of bay windows, verandas, and loggias. In the Villa Heymans, as in the Villa Hubrecht, the ever-present reference to history is made through small balconies, galleries, buttresses, and embrasures, as if to invert the English aphorism and claim that "My castle is my home." The Villa Henny is a turning point. Its references to the past are more subtle—the minuscule tower on the chimney-top and the pointed skylight on the roof—and they are clearly overshadowed by the intrinsic volumetric complexity. One cannot but note that the later designs—whether the Villa Parkwijck or his own house—are comparable in size to the earlier ones, but they are stripped of any suggestion of a manor. In the Villa Parkwijck, this is replaced by a play around the theme of the chimney, and in his house, by a discreet expression of the essential concepts of dwelling, in keeping with a work that stands as both a conclusion and a summary in his series of villas.

Interior design for an establishment of the Bols Co.

Antwerp
Commissioned by De Erven Lucas Bols Co.
1895

Executed in 1895, the interior design of the "'t Lootsje" in Antwerp was done in a fairly irregular space and presents the characteristics required by the company: tiles, wainscoting, and wallpaper, the motifs of which clearly referred to the Dutch Renaissance.

187. Study for an interior view.

188. Perspective view of the first design.

Building of De Nederlanden van 1845

Amsterdam, Kalverstraat/ Sophiaplein (today Muntplein)/Rokin
Commissioned by the insurance company De Nederlanden van 1845
1894–96 and 1910–11

In December 1894, Carel Henny commissioned Berlage for the design of the company's new headquarters in Amsterdam, in the center of town, on Sophiaplein (today Muntplein), on the site where E. Breman had built the company's first headquarters in 1889–90. Carel Henny had succeeded his father as the director of De Nederlanden and had introduced significant innovations in operation and personnel management, such as continuous working hours until 5:00 pm, which were still unusual in the Netherlands.

This marked the beginning of Berlage's happy collaboration with Henny and his company, which lasted almost forty years. During that time, he executed seven office buildings and two private houses, and he enjoyed Henny's complete trust.

The headquarters built in Amsterdam in 1894–96, on the corner of the block between Rokin and Kalverstraat, are characterized by a dynamic relationship between the clean walls, the treatment of the corners, and the irregular skyline rising on top of the building. Several elements in the composition express Berlage's quest for a relationship between the general and the particular, leading to an exceptional objectivity and a cultured re-invention of the past: the small balconies hollowed out of the rounded corner on Kalverstraat, which is capped by a small pointed tower with small balconies on both sides facing the street; the cylindrical staircase projecting on the façade, slightly off-center, and bearing on top a pointed tower with a clock and narrow chamfers.

Berlage still rejected the use of metallic structures, but the shallow depth of the building and the wide glazed surface ensure a good light in the offices. Two small courtyards in the back, on either side of the vertical block created by the stairs, help the ventilation of the bathrooms.

Berlage called, as he often did, on the sculptor Lambertus Zijl to execute five bas-reliefs placed on the façade, from among which the woman's figure on the corner of Kalverstraat was chosen as the company's emblem.

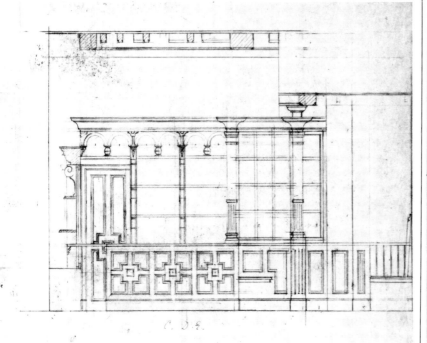

187

188

Berlage himself did the renovation and extension of the building in 1910–11. The building doubled in depth and a floor was added throughout. The vertical effect and complexity of the coping were lost, therefore—as they were after the extension work done on the company's building in The Hague—to be replaced by a more discreet pierced parapet, made of brick and stone.

Bibliography: D. Minderman 1956; also cfr. *Architectura* 1895, 20; *De Architect* VIII, 1897, ill. 277; *Ons Amsterdam* 1977, 10, p. 313.

189. *Contemporary photograph.*

190. *Contemporary photograph after the extension.*

189

190

With H. Wesstra, Jr.
The Hague, Kerkplein/Prinsestraat
Commissioned by the insurance company De Nederlanden van 1845
1895–96, 1901–02, and 1908–09

In November 1894, the board of directors of De Nederlanden commissioned the architect H. Wesstra, Jr. to design the company's office building in The Hague, on a square in the city's historic center, facing the Grote Kerk and the old municipal building.

In March 1895, immediately after his design for the company's building in Amsterdam was approved, Berlage was put in charge of of the building in The Hague and Wesstra accepted an offer to work with him on the company's request. The design was approved in August 1895 and construction work lasted throughout 1896. In January 1897, the installation of the board of directors in the building on Kerkplein officially established the move of the company's head office from Zutphen to The Hague, the political capital of the country.

There are resemblances between the composition of the buildings in The Hague and Amsterdam, which are reinforced by the sites being similar as well. The façade features a projection—polygonal in the first version, and rectangular in the final one—marking the main entrance. A loggia and a stepped buttress emphasize the coping between the small tower created by the projection and the corner of the building. The corner is first chamfered at an angle of 45 degrees, then becomes sharp when it reaches the level of the extrados decorating the coping on both sides facing the street. The first drawing features a strong stone base and a gallery facing the square, which were eliminated in the final version. The ground floor is used for stores: The entrance to the smaller one is on the right side of the projecting part and the other is on the corner, facing Prinsestraat.

The plan of the building was finally drawn by Berlage alone. It is

wider on Prinsestraat than on Kerkplein. It puts the stairs well inside the building, linked by a short flight of steps to the vestibule. The grand staircase is designed around a central empty space and lit from above. It is a skillful combination of simple materials—exposed brick and hewn stone—and masterly architecture. The rise is scanned by a strong sequence of solid planes and arched openings echoed by side rooms. Basreliefs by L. Zijl stand out against the carefully smoothed elevations made of red brick with stone inserted at structural points and small references to "classical art." Zijl's sculptures illustrate different activities of man—trade, agriculture, industry, education. The elevations also bear the coat of arms of the cities where branches of the company are located and have strips of mosaics between the second and third floors.

Berlage brought modifications to the building in 1901–02 and again in 1908–09, in particular the façade on Kerkplein, which is doubled in size and made slightly asymmetrical. He added a floor, making the whole building into a parallelepiped at the loss of the vertical effect. He reworked and unified the elevations by extending the divisions of the lower floor. The coping above the attic is used to carry advertisements for the company; it features a series of small square windows at the level of connection with the lower floor and a crenellation lined with hewn stone. The three acroteria are repeated on the corners. A high tower—an echo of the design of the Stock Exchange—rises behind the facade; it features a clock, a terrace, and a cylindrical chimney. The small tower on Kerkplein loses it pinnacled crowning bearing the name "De Nederlanden" on the side, which was a variation of the design for the building of De Algemeene.

Bibliography: D. Minderman 1956; also cfr. *De Architect* VIII, 1897, ill. 257–58.

191. *Perspective view of the first version.*

192. *Elevations and floor plans of the final version.*

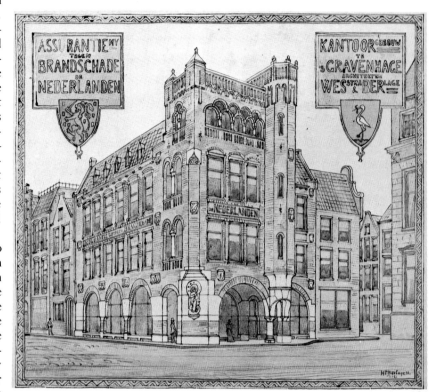

191

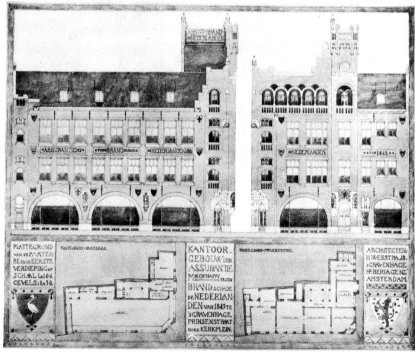

192

193. Contemporary photograph.

194. Contemporary photograph after
extension work was completed.

195. Meeting room, photograph ca 1909.

193

194

195

Amsterdam, Museumterreinen
1895–96

Berlage executed this plan for the area around museums in the mid–90s. It had a precedent as early as in 1883, when Sanders and Berlage planned to form a corporation to raise funds to invest in the building of a public bath south of the Rijksmuseum. They had made a few sketches, which included a public swimming pool and "Russian and Roman" baths.

In 1884, the M.B.B. announced a competition for a building plan in the same area. J.B. Kam and C.H. Verhulst won the competition in 1885 with a design combining a checkered grid with a radial street plan centered on the Rijksmuseum and featuring a university, a royal palace (which was the theme of other competitions), and

a public bath. Between 1889 and 1891, E. Gugel drew a plan with three great boulevards converging on the Rijksmuseum; this plan was reworked by the municipal authorities and approved in 1891. Between 1891 and 1895, A.W. Weissmann, the city architect and one of the protagonists in the events around the Stock Exchange, executed his masterpiece, the Neo-Renaissance Stedelijk Museum, at the southwest of the area.

Berlage drew a building plan for the area to raise capital for real estate investment—and perhaps for De Algemeene. In front of the museum he placed a gigantic apartment complex, with 139 luxury apartments, 13 stores, and a café-restaurant. He designed a block made of two housing complexes with a courtyard, connected by a street underpass, a theme he used again for the Mercatorplein. The block is designed on a site 195'

x 750' (60 x 270 meters), double the size of the Rijksmuseum. The side of the building facing the Stedelijk Museum (named "Museum Lopez Suasso" in the plan) has a recessed and porticoed portion with the same axis of symmetry as that of the museum. A square is thus formed, at the center of which stands a monument. The uniform long façades are enlivened by projections and small pointed towers, which add to the skyline. The corners are reinforced by angular bastions with buttresses and battlement. The triple arcade of the building rising above the underpasses, the complex design of which is brightened up by plays of light and shade, lead to the right-angle pathways and geometric green parterres in the courtyards. The building plan also indicates, albeit with little conviction, the other functions of the neighborhood. A royal villa stands on the southern part

of the area, in the axis of the Rijksmuseum and surrounded by a winding garden. The villa is separated from the museum by a stretch of land earmarked for villas and a public garden. Finally, on the east side of the area, there is what it defined in the brief caption as a zone of "specific purposes." Other drawings—a sheet with a plan outline, façades, and perspective sketches—show that Berlage intended to put the terminal station for the Haarlem line there, flanked by a playing field and a site for a circus. It can be easily guessed that the concept of a "south station" was inspired by Berlage's old colleague Sanders, who promoted such a plan in 1895 in the framework of

196. Development plan.

197. Sketches for a railway station.

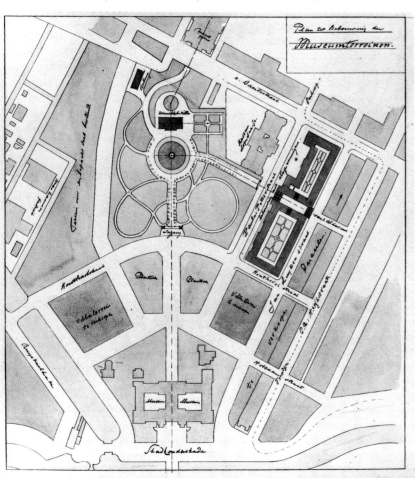

196

197

his steadfast attempt to create a new transportation network for the capital. It was featured again, with a different purpose, in Berlage's development plan for the south of Amsterdam.

Bibliography: AA.VV. 1976; for the dating, see M. Bock 1983, pp. 194–95, fn 128.

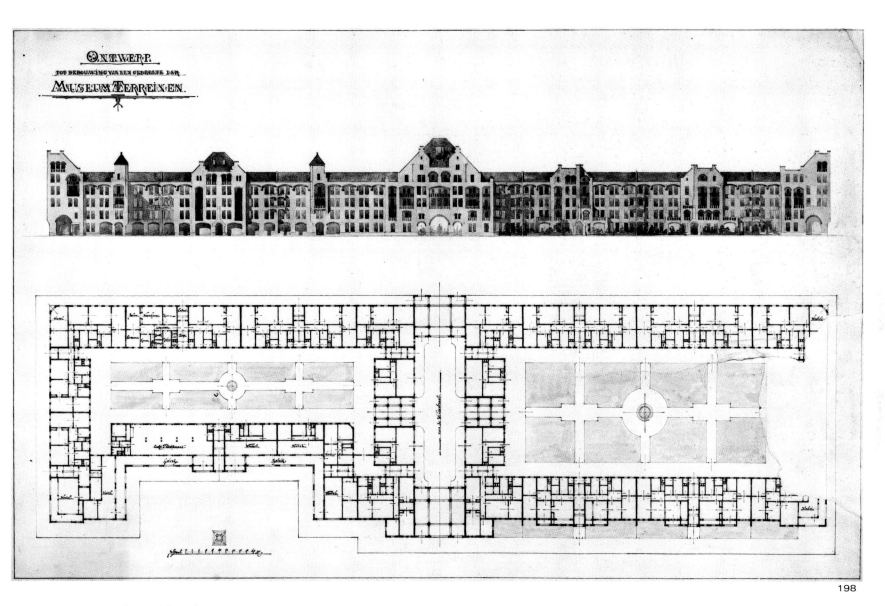

198

198. Main elevation and ground floor plan of a housing complex.

Villa Hubrecht

Hilversum Trompenberg,
Ceintuurban
Commissioned by Mrs. Hubrecht
1895–96

Villa Liesbet

Noordwijk aan Zee
Commissioned by Mrs. Van Vloten
1896

Bibliography: cfr. M. Verwey, *1 uit 7*, Uitgeverij Tor, Amsterdam, 1968

199. Contemporary photograph.

200. Contemporary photograph.

199

200

Villa Hubrecht

Villa Liesbet

Amsterdam
Damrak/Beursplein/Beursstraat/
Brugstraat
Commissioned by the municipality
of Amsterdam
1896–03

The extraordinary significance and intrinsic complexity of the Amsterdam Stock Exchange force us to limit this essay to the essentials. The building is extraordinary in the context of the time as well as that of Berlage's own production, in which it found few equivalents. The reference to a very large bibliography does not compensate for the lack of an exhaustive critical monograph.

After 1896, the frequent contacts between Berlage and the committee that commissioned him for the new Stock Exchange dealt mostly with a list of functions that the building had to fulfill: three great halls for the commodities, stock, and grain exchange; a smaller shipping exchange; offices for the stockbrokers and the chamber of commerce; a post office, state and municipal telephones, a telegraph, a café-restaurant, and a strongroom in the basement. The commodities exchange was to be used also for political events and celebrations, and the hall of the chamber of commerce was to double as town hall for official ceremonies. In reality, however, an intent that went beyond purely utilitarian requirements permeated the discussions of the program: The committee wanted the Stock Exchange to be a palace of commerce and finance, or, as Treub put it, "a monument reflecting the resolute and practical spirit of Amsterdam's merchant class"; as for Berlage, he intended to turn this palace representing the bourgeoisie into a building testifying to a newly rediscovered urban community. He was free to choose any style. Not surprisingly, he asked a friend, the poet Albert Verwey, to help him draw up a program of symbolic art equal to this task. Verwey became his official adviser and, in 1898, published in *Het Tweemaandelijksch Tijdschrift* his own thoughts on the themes illustrated in the Stock Ex-

change by the sculptors L. Zijl and J. Mendes da Costa and the painters J. Toorop, R.N. Roland Holst, and A.J. Derkinderen. Thus the most significant among contemporary Dutch artists were associated in an effort toward a *Gemeenschapskunst*, an art of the community.

At the end of March 1898, the issue of Berlage's exclusive commission was resolved and he was finally authorized by the municipal council to hold a conference and present his design; at almost the same time, the contract was allocated after many revisions. During the public debate, he ac-

201. *West and south views. first version, before April 1896.*

202. *Perspective view from the southwest, first version, after April 1896.*

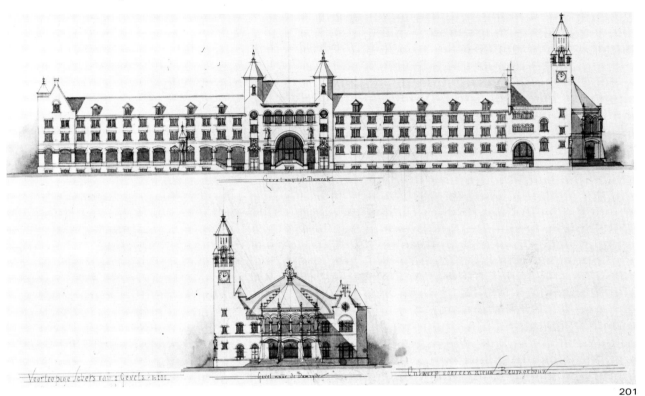

201

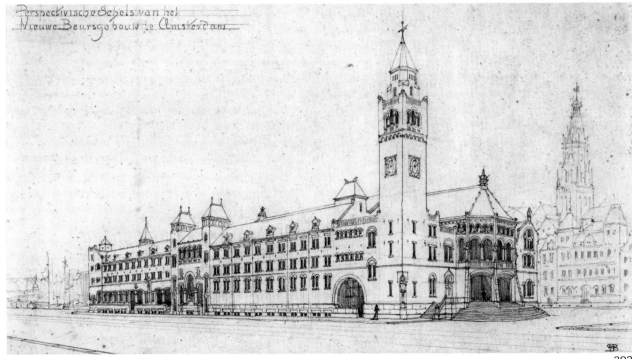

202

203

204

205

206

207

DE·GOEDERENBEURS·IN·DE·NIEUWE·BEURS·TE·AMSTERDAM·

208

knowledged his debts toward ancient and modern architecture. After a long period of work, however, the ideas on which he based his Stock Exchange were solid—more so than the substrata of the chosen site. A wide range of works dated from the same period: the office building of De Algemeene in Amsterdam, facing the future Stock Exchange (1892–94), the buildings for De Nederlanden van 1845 in The Hague (1894–95) and Amsterdam (1895–96), the headquarters of the Diamond Workers' Union in Amsterdam (1897–1900), and the Villa Henny in The Hague (1898). They all constituted relevant experiments that, combined with a deep theoretical reflection, lead Berlage to conceive this extraordinary Stock Exchange. During the two years between the time he received the commission and the contract, he executed several series of designs. Three different versions emerge, with intermediate variations in details. They show a quest for a logical simplification and growing economy of means, an "honest synthesis" of building and reasoning. This process can be easily followed in the steady modifications brought to the tower, a part of the building rich in symbolic significance as well as a distinctive feature rising in the urban landscape.

The first drawing made for the committee for the Stock Exchange was probably executed before April 1896, as is suggested by the generic caption reading "Design for a new building of the Stock Exchange." The tower rises on the south corner, on the left side of the main entrance, which is a sort of multifoiled, buttressed apse. The tower is a simple, tall parallelepiped; it features clocks and small rectangular windows, and pinnacles make the transition with the octagonal belfry and spire on top. In the perspective sketch for "The new Stock Exchange building in Amsterdam"—by then, Berlage had received the official commission, hence the change in the caption—the openings at the base are stretched vertically, as if the tower had become taller. The belfry forms a slight overhang crowned by a baluster and resting on a cornice made of small projecting arches. A small recessed tower with spire and chamfered buttresses stands on top of the belfry. A few studies, also dated 1896, try to restructure the relationship between the main portion of the tower and the top: Conical pinnacles of varying slenderness are connected to the belfry's ogival crowning by cylindrical and sometimes splayed blocks.

The second version of the design dates between the end of 1896 and the beginning of 1897. The tower is treated as a monolithic block furrowed by tall three-mullioned embrasures; its edges are chamfered at an angle of 45 degrees to make the transition with the crowning. The complex composition of the flat surfaces and the unusual shape of the spire, decorated with small arches, form a contrast with the newly designed main entrance, which is noticeably simplified but not yet flush with the south elevation. The 1897 perspective view of the second version of the design features an incongruous octagonal spire that is raised on small pillars connected by a baluster, above a visible belfry. Shortly thereafter, he drew a different version, just before designs were executed at the end of 1897 for the contract allocated in 1898. This new version establishes the main elements of the final design. The main entrance is now flush with the wall of the façade and marked by a range of three big arches. The tower loses its problematic spire; it is tapered at the level of the clock and crowned by a simple loggia, with a pitched roof, on top of the belfry. In the 1898 design made for the contract allocation this is replaced by a slender and chamfered short tower, standing on the corner toward the main entrance, and the arches of the loggia are placed between the clock and the belfry. In the main trunk of the tower, small coupled windows replace the tall embrasures.

Construction work finally started in 1898 on the basis of 200 pages of specifications and around fifteen drawings. The refined perspective views published in *De Architect* in 1901 show the design modifications made during the construction. They are minor but not negligible. The design of the tower becomes sparser. The loggia is eliminated, as well as all hints of a pitched roof. Above the clock, a light vertical line puts a dynamic emphasis on the belfry, which is crowned by a pierced baluster. A later series of drawings, dated around two years after the inauguration of the Stock Exchange in 1903, shows the last decorative changes and illustrates the actual state of the building.

Only an aerial view of the finished work shows how the articulation of the skyline responds to the many functions of the building, while the attention given to the view from the street results in a unified volumetric arrangement. The building occupies an irregularly shaped site and measures 465 feet (143 meters) on Damrak, 117 feet (36 meters) on the main façade, and 179 feet (55 meters) on the north side. In spite of their size, the elevations are quite modest in scale, to fit into the environment and stay in proportion with the tower of the Ouderkerk nearby. The designs exhibited for the presentation of the plans in 1898 are regulated by a modular grid, the definition of which is different in the floor plan and the elevations. The vertical grid is based on a rectangular module calculated on the "Egyptian triangle," a proportion derived from the study of Gothic architecture and much discussed among contemporary Dutch architects. It is defined as a 4:5 relationship between the base and the height of the rectangle. The square module regulating the ground plan is based on the shorter side of the vertical module, measuring 12'5 5/8" (380 centimeters).

Three major halls are arranged along the longitudinal axis of the building and occupy its full height. On the south side, the commodities exchange was designed on 12 x 6 modules and bordered on the sides by arcades of 2 x 6 modules; it is located immediately behind the main entrance, which features a vestibule, a coat room, and an information office. On the north side, the widening of the site allows for two parallel rooms, the stock exchange and the grain exchange, both designed on 10 x 5 modules. These two exchanges have independent entrances on the northern corner. Communication between the stock exchange and the two other exchanges is ensured by a central passageway designed on 5 x 3 modules, which runs along the whole building and serves also the postal, telegraphic, and telephone services as well as the small shipping exchange facing Damrak. By virtue of this passageway, a visitor to the building has a sense of the spatial structure and, standing in the commodities room, is able to have an interior view of the whole building. Also on Damrak, a coffee house stands next to the grain exchange, the northern corner of which is designed as a court for the traditional open-air trading of samples. The long walls of the stock exchange are grooved by three orders of arches: Six wide openings—each designed on two modules—mark the lower floor and develop into a less spacious structure in the side galleries and double tiers, where the arches are reduced to the size of one module. Six oculi are pierced in the wide strip at the top of each wall, and their spacing is regulated by the beams. They create air circulation through special pipes. The top of the walls is bordered by the fret of a slightly projecting strip of brick resembling the fringe of a banner. The balcony on the third floor is extended as a projection along the two shorter sides of the room; that on the second floor is extended only on the south side of the room, above a small central open gallery pierced with a tight series of small arches. A big clock on the northern short side of the room faces a geometrical window on the opposite side. Both are design elements used also for the

DE·NIEUWE·BEURS·OP·HET·DAMRAK·TE·AMSTERDAM·GEZIEN·KOMENDE·VAN·DEN·DAM·

209

209. *Perspective view from the south, drawing published in* De Architect, *in 1901.*

210. *Aerial photograph, late 1950s; one can recognize in the lower part the building of* De Algemeene, *which has since been destroyed by fire in 1963.*

tower and the façade. The wide sky-lights, made of two transparent layers of glass, are set into both slopes of the roof and supported by five parabolic iron trusses. The rest on the edges of brackets that are progressively tapered until they meet the space above the flush capital of the pilasters on the ground floor. Brick pillars, featuring hewn stones inserted to mark structural points, penetrate edgeways into the balconies, displaying their autonomy from the walls and uncovering the structure around which the outer shell of the building is constructed. Texture and color of the different materials are skillfully combined. The dominant vibration of the brick is balanced by a discreet web of decorative marks created in darker bricks. Also, strips of glazed bricks, colored yellow and blue, run along the walls at about 6'6" (2 meters) above the floors, developing into wall decorations in some places. The pilasters are in polished granite, and chiseled strips ring their shaft at top and bottom; the shaft's edges between these two decorative bands are rounded. By contrast, roughly cut granite and sandstone are used for the base, the flat capital which hints at a volute, and all other stone components with a structural function. Another strip of granite connects the base of the pilasters to the floor, so as not to create the impression that the pilasters rest on the wood. For the floor, Berlage found all other materials inadequate and chose different-sized strips of teakwood from Java, using the longer strips to make a border around the room. The bright yellow trusses, with their riveting visible in blue, complete the chromatic composition of the commodities exchange.

The solutions tested in the building's major room are developed more simply in the grain exchange and the stock exchange. The latter is separated from the passageway by a gate. On the ground floor, the center of the east wall features only one arcade, while the north wall has a double arcade. Blue metal trusses with yellow riveting support the skylights; they lean on brackets similar to those of the commodities exchange, but these brackets continue to the floor in order to buttress the thin partition between the stock exchange and the grain exchange.

The grain exchange faces north through a wide strip of openings onto the outer courtyard. Two tiers of balconies form the upper part of the west wall, toward Damrak. Brick pillars similar to that of the commodities exchange support the reticulated beams of a covering designed as a series of pent roofs, which are oriented in such a manner as to catch the best light for the examination of samples.

Slightly recessed strips of decorative glazed tiles, with opera sectilia designed by Jan Toorop, run along the walls at the level of the balcony of the second floor. The tiles' design refers to the activity taking place in the two rooms: bundles of grain in one, and in the other an imaginary coat of arms— a royal crown on a round yellow ground—that places the stockbrokers under the emblem of the Gulden.

This playful warning is repeated in the office of the stockbrokers' association, a room of 2.5 x 2.5 modules on the second floor of the northern corner: The office's gilded decorations are variations on the theme of the circle. The warning is even clearer in the bronze bas-relief by Mendes da Costa, illustrating honesty in a gigantic fireplace, and in the ironic quatrains by Albert Verwey incised in the walls. The stockbrokers countered by complaining almost immediately about having inadequate space, and they commissioned J. Th. J. Cuypers to design a separate stock exchange on Beursplein. The stockbrokers moved to their separate building in 1914.

More or less at the same time, between 1911 and 1913, the fate of the site that had triggered the whole saga of the new Stock Exchange was concluded: J.A. van Straaten built the department store De Bijenkorf on the corner between Dam and Damrak, after Zocher's Exchange was torn down. Drawings found in the Berlage archives reveal that, in 1903, he had designed a study for a book exchange, with marketing departments and stores and a layout resembling that of the new Stock Exchange.

The realization of the visual ideas imagined by Verwey and Berlage is a fundamental chapter in the program of an "art of the community" for the whole building, and it deserves to be studied with more depth than is possible in these notes. We can only mention the unfailing control in the design, including minor details and fixtures for the whole building.

211

212

148

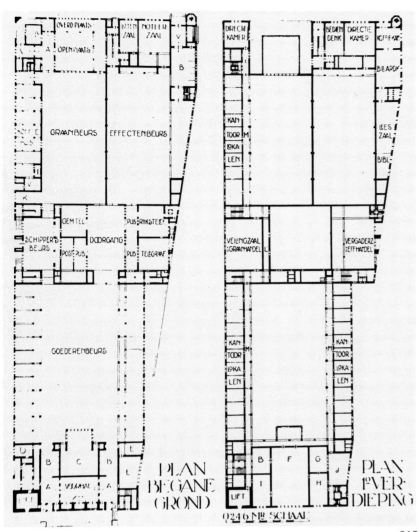

213

214

215

Verwey's quatrains are incised over the main entrance and surmounted by a three-part bas-relief by Lambertus Zijl, Jan Pz. Coen, and Hugo de Groot. Zijl also carved the bas-relief of the Gijsbreght van Aemstel on the south corner of the tower, and other sculptures by Coen and Groot decorate the east and west sides of the Exchange's north corner. These sculptures are part of Berlage's effort to create an architectural *Gesamstkunstwerk* (total artwork). In the interior, Jan Toorop designed more opera sectilia for the entrance hall; they illustrate the theme of the past, present, and future. Richard N. Roland Holst painted a mural on the theme of commerce and industry for the northwest staircase. Finally, Zijl created some other significant sculptures for the interior.

The interior design of the chamber of commerce was conceived as a visual high point. It is formed by 4 x 3 modules on the second floor of the south façade. Its walls were to be decorated by A.J. Derkinderen.

They form a surface of over 1,300 square feet, including the wide windows on the façade and the lunette of the gallery, which is framed by a majestic arch. After the walls were primed and the surfaces to be decorated were determined, the architect and the artist strongly disagreed on the themes of the paintings. The disagreement was resolved in 1901 through the mediation of an arbitration committee. Berlage's efforts to

complete the work, even at the cost of some compromise, were frustrated by the urgent necessity to improve the acoustics of the hall. The hanging of curtains and tapestries in 1904 could not resolve the problem. This brought about a completely new design of the interior in 1909, which made it impossible for Derkinderen to complete his task, apart from the windows. The whole base of the room is clad with wainscoting; the ceiling is made of wood, and the long walls are draped with heavy tapestries. During the period between the two "acoustic designs," the arched opening of the gallery was modified into a three-mullioned arch because a dangerous recent settling of the substratum made works of reinforcement necessary. Berlage was exonerated of all responsibility in the matter by the report of the municipal commission of inquiry, the members of which were P.J.H. Cuypers, J. Th. Cuypers, A. van Hemert, J.F. Klinkhamer, and D.A.N. Margadant. The report was published in 1906 and

concluded that the site was not solid. In the following years, Berlage had to carry out a series of modifications of which he clearly disapproved. In the commodities exchange, the span of the arches on the ground floor is reduced by the insertion of a more slender and slightly recessed pilaster, which holds up two new small arches. The side arches on the second

211. *Contemporary photograph.*

212. *Contemporary photograph; in the foreground, the demolition work on the site on which J.Th.J. Cuypers's Stock Exchange was to stand.*

213. *Floor plan of the first and second floor.*

214. *The commodities exchange, view from the south; contemporary photograph, which, like the other following pictures, was taken after the consolidation work.*

215. *The commodities exchange, west side gallery.*

149

floor of the south gallery are filled and tie-rods strengthen the metal trusses. The great barrel vault preceding the glassed passageway between the northern and southern part of the building had to be redesigned and reduced to the size of the arched openings. Similar modifications were done throughout the building to strengthen the structure.

The Stock Exchange was inaugurated by the Queen in 1903 and fullfilled its purpose for more than fifty years. The threat of demolition at the end of the 1950s provoked an immediate reaction in the press and among the public, which lead to a new study of Berlage's work. This masterpiece now stands almost empty, waiting to find again a role other than that of a simple monument, a role that would befit its stature.

Bibliography: H.P. Berlage 1898; J. Cuypers 1898; W. Kromhout 1898; J.B.L. 1898; editorial 1898, "De nieuwe . . ."; editorial 1898, "Verslag . . ."; J.E. van der Pek 1898; A. Verwey 1898; H.J. Walle 1898; A.W. Weissman 1899; H.P.Berlage 1901, "De nieuwe Beurs . . ."; J.H. Schorer 1902; H. von Poellnitz 1902–03; H. Walenkamp 1902–03; P.J.H. Cuypers 1903; K.P.C. de Bazel 1903; L. 1903; J.L.M. Lauwericks 1903; R. Neter 1903; editorial 1903, "De nieuwe . . ."; E. Redelé 1903; L. Simons 1903; W. Vogelsang 1903, "H.P. Berlage . . ."; J.H.W. Walenkamp 1904; A.W. Weissman 1904; J.H.W. Leliman 1906; K. van Leeuwen 1906; W. van der Pluijm 1913; Hahn 1914; AA.VV. 1928; J. Duiker 1928; P. Zwart 1928, "De Betekenis . . ."; editorial 1934, "Dr. H.P. Berlage . . ."; A. Verwey 1934, "H.P. Berlage ter . . ."; J.P.M. 1946; J.J. Vriend 1953; J.M.P. 1953; editorial 1959, "Een Discussie . . ."; P. Singelenberg 1959; A.J. Kropholler 1960; J.J.P. Oud 1960; J.J. Terwen 1963; A.W. Reinink 1975, with a basic bibliography of about 500 titles; also cfr. De Architect XII, 1901, ill. 397–99.

216

216. *Passageway between the exchanges, view from the north.*

217. *The grain exchange, view from the north; standing at the center: Berlage.*

217

Design of the façade of a building

With H. Bonda
Amsterdam, 30–32 Raadhuisstraat/
184 Herengracht
1897

In 1897, H. Bonda designed with Berlage a building with commercial, office, and residential space at the corner of Herengracht and the new Raadhuisstraat, the street where Sanders and Berlage had foreseen a portion of their passageway for trams and pedestrians in 1885. The clients were worried that the façade might not be approved and they called on Berlage, who, since he was the architect of the new Stock Exchange, was obviously on good terms with the municipal authorities.

The building has five floors and an attic. It bends along the Raadhuis-straat and takes on the irregular shape of the site. It features oriel windows at the points of change in the curve, above the entrances to the building. Small towers with different crownings mark the continuity with the beautiful historic façades on Herengracht as well as the edges of the façade on Raadhuisstraat. The corner is designed with a symmetrical loggia on three floors, and the pointed gables are shifted to either side. The infilling is of stones varying in kind and shape, creating a rough structural decoration.

Bibliography: Editorial 1897, "Het in aanbouw . . ."; also cfr. *Die Architektur des Jahrhunderts* 1901, 3, p. 43, and ill. 63.

Interior design for an establishment of the Bols Co.

Paris, 32 Boulevard des Italiens
Commissioned by De Erven Lucas Bols Co.
1897

In 1897, Berlage received his last commission for a " 't Lootsje" bar, in the center of Paris, on the Boulevard des Italiens. Wainscoting and tapestries bearing the monogram "ELB" cover the walls of the establishment.

The dominant feature on the ground floor is a big fireplace clad with tiles. Exposed beams rest on decorated wooden brackets. The entrance is recessed and protected by an awning. It freely mixes different materials: brick base, stone, wood, and colored glass; an elaborate wrought-iron bracket holds up the sign of the establishment.

Bibliography: cfr. *De Architect* VIII, 1897, ill. 268–70.

218. Perspective view.

219. Drawings.

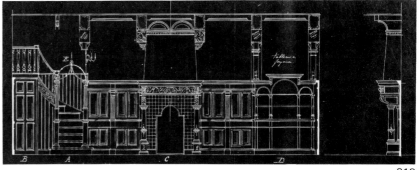

219

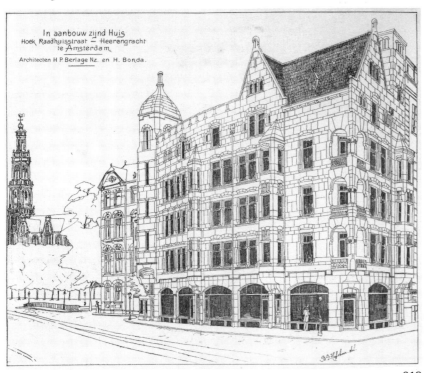

218

Headquarters of the Algemeene Nederlandsche Diamantbewerkersbond

Amsterdam, Plantage Franschelaan (today 3–9 Henri Polaklaan) Commissioned by the Algemeene Nederlandsche Diamantbewerkersbond
1897–1900

In December 1897, the brotherhood of diamond workers—a truly Dutch federation, which was in the lead of the country's trade-union movement, with close ties with the Social-Democratic Party—decided to commission Berlage for its headquarters in Amsterdam. Berlage had already designed the logo of the union's weekly in 1895. J. van Zutphen and H. Polak were among the members of the union's executive board. Polak was the president, and he must have met Berlage through his fellow party member P.L. Tak, who was the editor of *De Kroniek*. The building was to have several purposes: It had to respond to the union's needs in matters of promotion and management, express its desire for democracy, and stand as a symbol of organized labor. The building was erected near the Waterlooplein, which had the city's greatest Jewish population until the Second World War and was the neighborhood of the diamond workers in particular. Berlage drew two versions of the building. The first version was completed in February 1898; it featured a two-story meeting hall, with a capacity of 1,200 seats and marked on the façade by a double balcony fitted with a fire escape. The municipal authorities used various pretexts to reject this version.

Perhaps thanks to Berlage's intervention, the disagreement with the municipality was resolved in August 1898. The building was completed in June 1900, after a design executed in March 1899. In this second version, the building is smaller and the proportions of the façade are modified. Berlage returned to a solution he had tested in his design for the Stock Exchange: The series of triple openings in the first three floors is inscribed in an ideal rectangle; a strip of exposed bricks creates a pause, above which smaller windows are grouped in threes and connected on top by an inserted strip of stone. The ternary rhythm is thus maintained. In place of the first version's range of small blind arches under a pitched roof, Berlage designed four embedded stones with the initials of the union, ANDB, and multifoiled acroteria in the Venetian style as a finishing touch to the façade. On the left side of the façade, a small tower rises above the coping of the building, balancing the dramatically projecting stairs and the strong arch framing the entrance door. The tower is crowned by a layered and rounded pyramid. It features a two-mullioned window on the level of the fourth floor, below which a serrated stone bearing the association's monogram, masterfully designed by Berlage, is inserted flush with the wall. In place of the usual clock, Berlage put a faceted window within the outlined circle of an oculos, as a symbol—perhaps too obvious—for diamonds.

The back elevation reinforces the design of the street front, with the strengthened rhythm of the openings and the elimination of all decorations, however spare. The spatial interior arrangement takes advantage of a rational double façade. The janitor's lodge, printing works, and technical offices are placed in the half basement. Their entrances are under the steps on the street and at the other end of the façade; they involve a redesigning of the sidewalk and hence play a role in the definition of the building's connection to the ground. The meeting hall and the offices on the elevated first floor face the front and the back, respectively. The second floor features more offices, and the third floor is reserved for the library and archives. Guest rooms are nested in the attic floor. The furniture was designed by Berlage.

220. *Study of floor plan for the final version.*

221. *Perspective view of the vestibule, drawing published in* Studies over bouwkunst, stijl en samenleving, *Rotterdam 1910.*

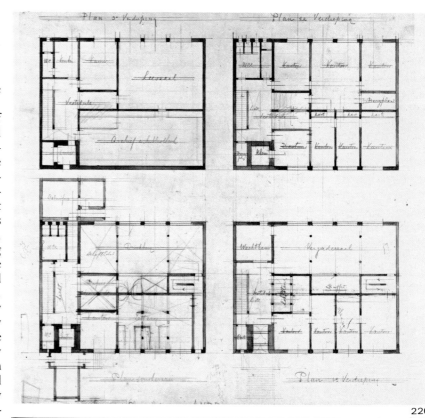

220

221

The vestibule is the core of the interior design. It occupies the full height of the building, adjoining the stairs leaning against the outer walls, and it is lit from above by a skylight. The graceful chamfer of the stone-clad articulations plays with the beautiful texture of yellow and white bricks on the walls. Alternate bricks of different colors outline the soffits of the gallery's rounded arches; the latter rest on stone capitals in the shape of flattened volutes. The stone parapets feature decorative incisions and a rhythmic order of geometric pillars bearing similar decorations. On the elevated first floor, the opus sectile on the wall calls "Workers of the world unite!"

The meeting hall combines traditional and modern materials: Stones inserted in the brick wall serve as brackets holding up the iron main beams; the secondary metal frame is emphasized by banners under the plastered ceiling. Allegorical murals by R.N. Roland Holst decorate the room. They were redone on asbestos panels in 1934 because of the saponification of the paint's alkaline casein base.

In 1912, Berlage redesigned the boardroom on the third floor. It was completely clad with wainscoting, as a gift from the young members of the union and in celebration of the recent law on the eight-hour workday. Holst executed the paintings illustrating the hours of work, leisure, and sleep.

Bibliography: Editorial 1899, "Vereenigingsbouw . . ."; H. van der Velde 1925; J. Kroes 1979; also cfr. *Weekblad van den A.N.D.B.* May 20, 1898; *De Architect* XIV, 1903, ill. 499–501; *Bouwkunst* 1910, p. 102.

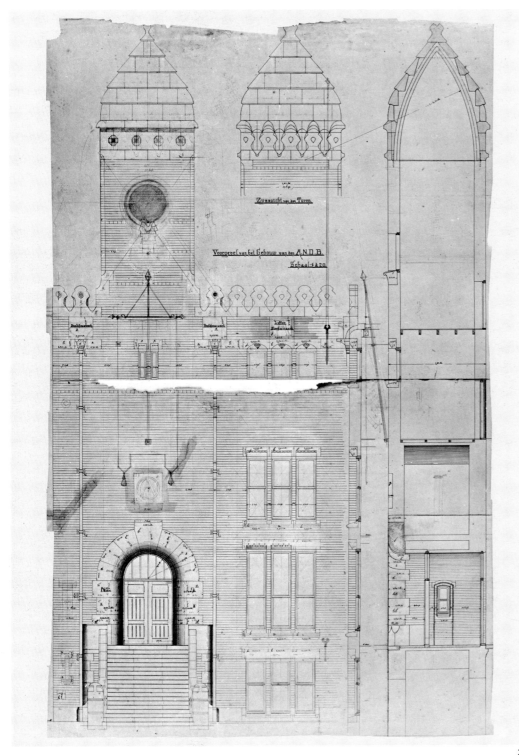

223

222. Building plan of the façade.

223. Letterhead for the ANDB.

224. Contemporary photograph.

222

224

153

Study of an apartment building

1898

This is probably a reworking, on a smaller scale, of the gigantic apartment complex designed in 1895–96 for the "museum area" in Amsterdam. The plan in the Berlage archives was signed and dated later. It was drawn on paper ruled to form a module—rectangular for the elevation and square for the ground plan—similar to the one used in the design for the Hobbemastraat in 1903–04.

225. Typical floor plan and main elevation.

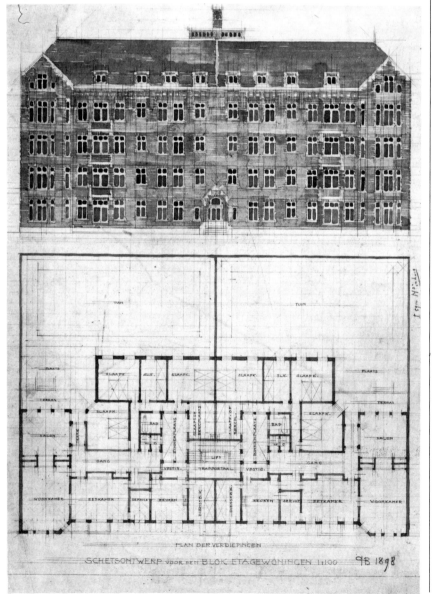

Villa Henny

The Hague,
Oude Scheveningscheweg/
Stadhouderslaan
Commissioned by Carel Henny
1898

In 1898, Berlage designed a villa for Carel Henny, the director of the De Nederlanden and one of his best clients. It was built on the corner of Oude Scheveningscheweg and Stadhouderslaan, in the north of The Hague and on the road to the seaside suburb of Scheveningen. The house immediately became the target of mockery and controversy because of its innovative spatial arrangement, materials, and furniture. W. Kromhout wrote of the "yellow peril" in a 1900 article for *Architectura*, alluding to the bright yellow roofing tiles. Conservative citizens called it the "mad house." They were particularly scandalized by the immodest exhibition of bare brick walls inside, visible through the screenless windows.

The plan is ruled by a modular grid based on a 63 inch (160 centimeters) square. Following the diagonals on the grid, Berlage shifted the plan on a northeast/southwest axis, creating a flowing spatial arrangement around a central vestibule shaped on a Greek-cross plan. The first floor features the following rooms around the hall, starting counterclockwise from a porticoed entrance on the north side: a two-story staircase at a right angle from the outer wall; a studio on the east end of the house; a boudoir with a small terrace connected to the garden; a parlor in the shape of a trapezium, with a conservatory and veranda on the southeast side; the dining and adjacent smoking room; and finally, on the northwest side, the whole area for the kitchen and connected facilities, from where one goes down to the cellar and boiler room. On the second floor, six bedrooms and a single bathroom are arranged around the empty space above the hall, the two master bedrooms sharing a closet. The third floor, with its sloping ceiling, features a guest room with a small terrace facing southeast.

The arrangement of masses is a rational expression of the complex plan, which is emphasized in the elevation by the different types of roofs—flat,

pitched, and glazed; the miniature tower with its chimney top on the east; and the constant variation in the modulations of openings.

The plans are dated 1898 and were barely modified during construction. The spatial distribution is strengthened by a central, two-story vestibule serving as the core of the villa's architecture, in which structural innovations successfully uphold an intuition in forms. On the ground floor, the central square of the Greek cross is enclosed by four lowered arches connected by a keystone made of angular spandrels. The use of stone inserts for the keystone, imposts, and corbels illustrates the static engagement of the structure The empty space on the second floor has the shape of a square inscribed in the basic square at a 45–degree angle; it is enclosed by a wrought-iron rail connecting four columns standing on the center line of the arches on the pointed floor. A double range of pointed arches rests on each column. The frame of the interior skylight is shifted at an angle of 45 degrees from the square formed by the columns. The interior skylight is a richly decorated pyramidal prism. Placed on the vertical line of the hall to close an interior empty space, the exterior skyline is made of transparent sloping panels that are cut into the pitch of the roof, the complexity of which is a tridimensional reflection of the vestibule's Greek-cross plan.

For the first time, Berlage did not plaster the interior walls of a villa: The soft red of the natural brick is combined with the primary colors of yellow, blue, and white glazed bricks. The floors and exposed beams are made of wood. Some drawings of the furniture, dated June 1898, are in the Berlage archives. Refined and spare, they consist of tables, chairs covered in pigskin, cabinets mostly fitted into the wall, to be arranged with a few paintings—such as the three portraits of Henny's children by Jan Toorop—and big rugs. This concept of living was not entirely shared by the inhabitants of the house, a fact we can assume from a few episodes of intransigence on the part of Berlage. This accounts for the few concessions in comfort made in the boudoir: plastered walls, upholstered chairs, and

225

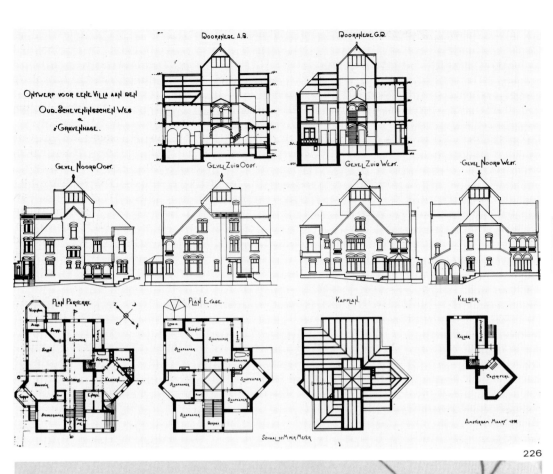

226. Design plan.

227. Exterior, contemporary photograph.

228. View of the hall on the ground floor, contemporary photograph.

229. View of the hall on the upper floor, contemporary photograph.

226

227

228

229

parquet floors. It was Toorop, presumably, who chose the colors of the house in harmony with his paintings, but a colleague from the "'t Binnenhuis" arts and crafts workshop promoted by Henny also contributed to the color scheme: J. van den Bosch is supposed to have designed the tiles in the kitchen.

The villa was used as a dwelling until the First World War. It was later sold and used for other purposes. In the process, it lost the unity of Berlage's concept of *Binnenhuisarchitectuur*, which had made it one of his better examples of good housing.

Bibliography: M. Boot in AA.VV. 1975, "H.P. Berlage . . . "; also cfr. *De Architect* X, 1899, ill. 355–56; *Bouwkundig Tijdschrift* 1901.

Villa Scott

Bussum, Eslaan
Commissioned by E.W. Scott
1898

The plan in the Berlage archives is dated September 1898.

Design of a villa with a studio

The Hague, Stadhouderslaan
1898

230. Design plan.

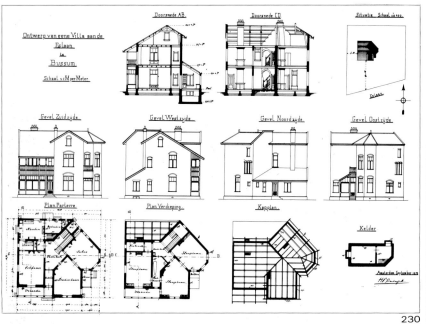

230

231. Design plan.

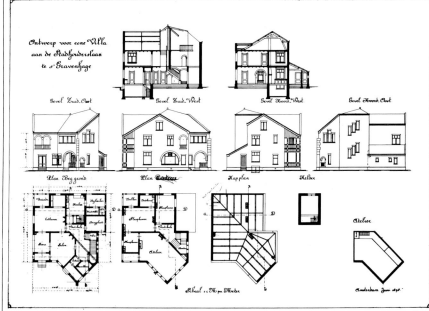

231

Katwijk aan Zee, Van der Plaskade (north side of the present boulevard), at the corner of today's
J. Tooropstraat
Commissioned by Jan Toorop
1899

Between 1898 and 1899, Berlage drew two designs of a villa that offer resemblances suggesting that they were executed for the same client: They feature similar spatial arrangements and elevations, and they both include a studio.

The first design, dated June 1898, sets the villa on Stadhouderslaan in The Hague, the same avenue where Carel Henny's villa was built at the time.

The second design was done for the artist Jan Toorop in 1899, at Katwijk aan Zee, a small seaside town nine miles north of The Hague. Toorop moved from The Hague and lived in this villa with his family until 1904. Already in 1902, however, he commissioned another villa, *Ons Prinsesje* from the Leiden architect H.J. Jesse. Berlage had called on Jesse in 1896 to work on his ambitious decorative program for the Stock Exchange, and Henny had consulted him in 1898 for the color scheme of his own villa. Toorop was one of the most interesting Dutch Symbolist painters. He was born in Java, the son of a Norwegian father and a Chinese mother, and he lived there until the age of ten. His Eastern origins play a subtle role in the element of the fantastic present in such early work as *De Venus der Zee*, painted at Katwijk aan Zee around 1890. His was a versatile talent and he was a man passionately curious of everything, and of literature and music in particular. In 1895 he became close to James Ensor and Henry van de Velde, whom he had met through the group "Les XX." He was fascinated by Javanese puppets, Edvard Munch's expressionist symbolism, Audrey Beardsley's perverse linearity, and Maurice de Maeterlinck's visionary poetry. After 1894, the music of Richard Wagner and César Franck, as well as William Blake's lyricism, pervaded Toorop's work until 1905,

when his conversion to Catholicism brought about a certain peace of mind.

In a first version of the design for the villa in Katwijk aan Zee, Berlage widened the simple interior geometry by cutting corners at an angle of 45 degrees and shifting the ground plan. Starting on the left side of an off-center vestibule, the ground floor features the following rooms, clockwise: a parlor with a conservatory, a veranda, and French windows leading to the entrance portico; a dining room facing two sides of the house, with a small veranda on the corner; the kitchen and other facilities, facing the garden; the stairs to the upper floor; and an office. On the second floor, a short corridor leads to two bedrooms, one a master bedroom with a bathroom and a corner balcony; and a studio with a loggia, lit from above through a skylight facing northeast and connected to a small bedroom. A spiral staircase leads from the ground floor to the rooms under the mansard. The volumetric composition is crowned by asymmetrical pitched roofs, juxtaposed in the shape of a T, and it is rendered more complex by its combination with the flat-roofed portion that contains the staircase. The varied distribution of openings—arched in the case of the loggias, the verandas, and the porticoed entrance—responds to the logic of the interior layout. This is particularly evident on the façade, where a continuous strip of windows was designed for the studio. On the corner, between the portico and the studio, a projecting strip supports a winged bas-relief, a hinted homage to the figure obsessively recurring in Toorop's paintings.

The final version used to build the house was drawn in January-February 1899. Berlage made many changes, limiting the size—and the costs. The diagonal connection of the side elevation ensures the transition from the ground floor to a smaller second floor with a flat roof. The elevations are characterized by a large number of openings, placed according to the house's interior needs. The villa was demolished for tactical reasons by the German occupation forces during the Second World War,

as were most buildings on the road along the sea. We have, however, a description of its bright primary colors. Ludwig Hevesi wrote about the house of his hosts in 1902: "Then the white house opens its blue and yellow shutters on the distant dunes. The blond former Miss Hall sits in a chair of her beloved parlor, and the master of the house tinkers diligently

at a copper ornament for the fireplace or at some stone object that is to stand over the door one day."

Bibliography: cfr. L. Hevesi, "Jan Toorop," in *Ver Sacrum* February 15, 1902; *Jan Toorop in Katwijk aan Zee*, exhibition catalogue, introduction by R. Siebelhoff, Stichting Katwijks Museum, Katwijk aan Zee, 1985.

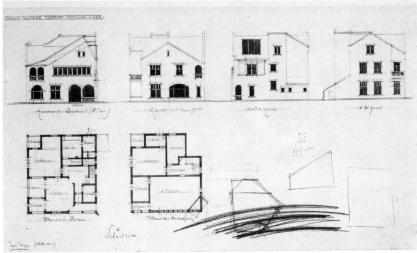

232

233

232. Plan studies and elevations of the first version.

233. Contemporary photograph of the final version; left in the background, a glimpse of the future Villa Allegonda by J.J.P. Oud.

Partial renovation of the Boissevain house

Building for the De Algemeene

Groningen
Commissioned by Boissevain
1899

Soerabaja, Dutch Indies
Commissioned by the insurance
company De Algemeene
1899–1900

This renovation was limited essentially to a modification of the interior flow, with the substitution of a winding staircase and the designing of the living area.

At the time when he was working on the first extension of the De Algemeene building in Amsterdam, Berlage designed buildings for two foreign branches of the company, one in Soerabaja, Dutch Indies, and the other in Leipzig, Germany.

For the building in Soerabaja, in 1899–1900 Berlage reworked a design that had been done by J. Hulswitt in 1898. The building was erected 1900. Berlage himself did not go to the Dutch Indies until much later.

The building was constructed on a warped plot of land. While it presents characteristics of contemporary Dutch architecture, they are weakened by a "colonial style." The façade features a portico and loggias on the second floor. An oriel window that rests on small stone corbels serving as a portal draws the attention to the main entrance of the building and the stairs behind it. A dormer juts out of the long slanting roof, above the oriel window; its wooden cornice is decorated with native motifs, and it holds a flagpole. The side and back elevations are blind walls: An inner courtyard brings light and air to the offices in the back, which are connected to the front by two short side corridors. The façade is cement-rendered, except for the archivolts in exposed brick. Two narrow strips of tiles form a colored frieze at the level of the second floor and immediately below the decorated molding of the cornice. A mosaic with the company's emblem and the date of its foundation is set in the wall above the main entrance. The blind walls on the side are real slabs, the thickness of which is visible, and they serve as a separation from the disorderly architecture surrounding the building. A tall metal sign on the ridge of the roof puts a finishing touch on the building.

Bibliography: *De Architect* XIII, 1902, ill. 464.

234

234. Contemporary photograph.

235. Plan of the ground floor and the first floor.

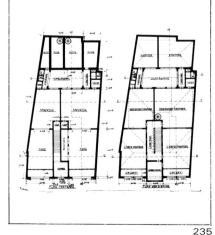

235

Amsterdam, 104 Da Costakade
Commissioned by the company
Koning & Bienfait
1899–1900 and 1908

At the close of the century, Berlage built a laboratory to test construction materials for the company Koning & Bienfait. It was located in the west of Amsterdam, on a street beyond the Singel, the furthest of the concentric canals surrounding the city.

The building is on a narrow site and has two main elevations. It is divided in two parts: The main entrance and the offices face Da Costakade; the testing laboratories are in the back, directly connected to the exterior garden. The two parts of the building are separated by a covered, one-story-high inner courtyard. The two side corridors connecting the two parts of the building on the upper floors have flights of stairs because of the differences in level between the testing laboratories.

In 1908 Berlage designed the single-floor extension of the building, and he drew his first sketch on the building plan of 1899. The size of the building in the 1899–1900 version, compared to that of the adjacent ones, and the flat roof reveal that the client intended to extend the building in the future.

The simple façade on the street is made of exposed brick. The windows of the second and third floors mark a binary and ternary rhythm. The entrance is off-center, on the axis of the vestibule and the main staircase. A strip of mosaics above the entrance bears the name of the company. The extension is characterized by a long bay, with a central panel stretched out horizontally, and a pitched roof with a simple dormer.

Bibliography: cfr. *De Architect* XXI, 1914, ill. 721.

236

238

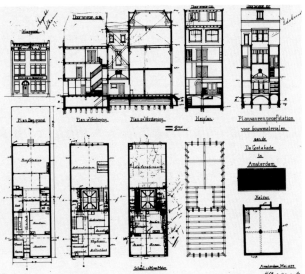

237

236. *First building, contemporary photograph.*

237. *Design plan of the first building, with elements for the extension.*

238. *Contemporary photograph, after 1908.*

East Amsterdam, 3rd Conradstraat
Commissioned by the De Eenheid association
1899–1900

Berlage designed the school for De Eenheid between 1899 and 1900, to be built in the dock area, on the east side of Amsterdam. The wooden building has a simple rectangular plan. The only entrance, at the end of one of the longer sides of the rec-tangle, leads to a vestibule with coat room, which in turn leads to a hall on the right and the janitor's lodge on the left. The latter also includes two rooms on the second floor. The elevations are very simple, with paired windows along the long wall of the hall and a single large rectangular window on the short side. At the other end of the building, the symmetry of the sloping roof, with the projecting shed for the heating unit in the center, is slightly modified by the flat roof of the staircase leading to the janitor's rooms.

239. Design plan.

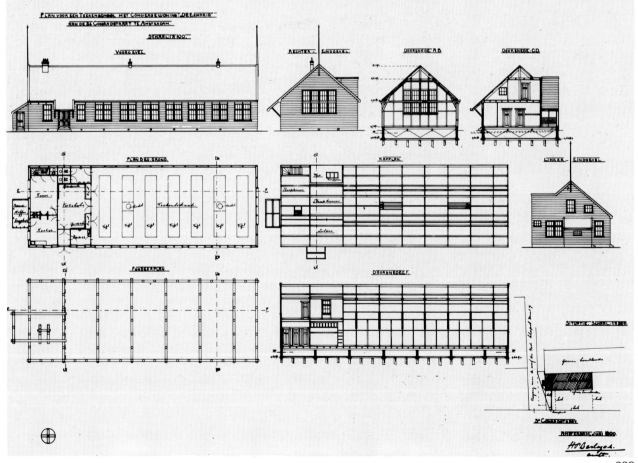

239

Amsterdam, 95–96 Damrak/Damraksteeg
Commissioned by the Amsterdamsche Bank
1899–1901

Berlage drew two versions of a double-purpose building for the Amsterdamsche Bank, to be built near the Stock Exchange on the other side of Damrak. The first version, dated December 1899, is limited to the foreign exchange department. Between 1899 and 1901 he executed the final design, which also included a lunchroom.

The building was designed with a steel frame and brick infilling. The structure of the façade on the street is in harmony with the first design for the De Algemeene Building near-by. The foreign exchange building features an asymmetrical gable flanked by the sloping roof of the "De Beursbengel" lunchroom. A small projecting tower marks the corner at Damraksteeg; it rests on small stone corbels, which also support the balcony and wrought-iron rail on the second floor. The layout of the openings, grouped according to a skillful rhythm, maintains a strong orthagonal bias, except for the gable. The smoothness of the façade is hardly affected by the stone string courses, segmented at times, the brown brick, and the mosaics in the architrave of the windows.

In 1913, Berlage made a study for interior changes. In 1985–86, a good part of the site was redesigned, and the right half of Berlage's building was preserved and the façades cleaned.

Bibliography: cfr. *De Architect* XIII, 1902, ill. 439.

240. Study for the first version.

241. Exterior, contemporary photograph.

242. Design plan for the final version.

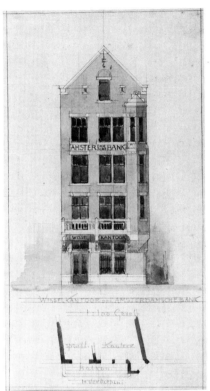

240

241

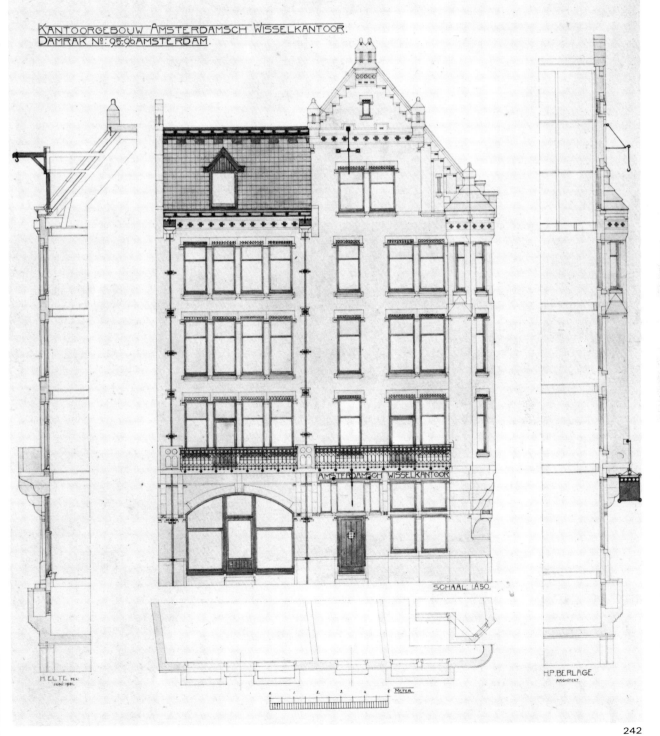

KANTOORGEBOUW AMSTERDAMSCH WISSELKANTOOR.
DAMRAK No: 95:96 AMSTERDAM.

SCHAAL 1:50

H. ELTE DEL.
JUNI 1901.

H.P. BERLAGE.
ARCHITECT.

242

Amsterdam, between Amsteldijk (Ceintuurbaan) and Weesperzijde (Ruyschstraat)
Commissioned by the municipality of Amsterdam
1899–1903

Since 1898, Amsterdam municipal authorities were considering the construction of a new bridge on the portion of the Amstel—the city's original waterway—outside of the historic center. In November 1899, the bridge division of the Bureau of Public Works proposed three designs. Before the end of the year, Berlage was consulted for the "aesthetic" aspect. He made a few notes on the formal definition of the bridge, which did not win everyone's agreement, and redesigned the electrified pylons for the streetcars and the street lamps. The final design was approved in March 1900 and construction was begun. When the bridge was inaugurated in July 1903, only the electrified poles were not yet in working order; they were realized in 1906.

Bibliography: cfr. W. de Boer and P. Evers 1983; also cfr. *De Bouwwereld* 1903, p. 214.

Paris, World's Fair
Commissioned by J.B. Hillen
1900

Berlage designed architectural fittings on a proportional grid based on the "Egyptian triangle."

243. Contemporary photograph.

244. Study plan with grid.

243

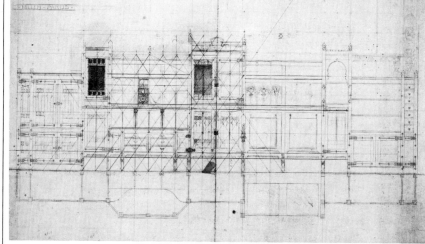

244

Amsterdam, 90 Van Eeghenstraat
Commissioned by L. Simons
1900–01

245. Design of details, published in De Architect, *1903.*

At the turn of the century, Berlage designed the Villa Parkwijk on the southern edge of the Vondelpark in Amsterdam. The clients were Leo Simons, the historian of the theater, and his wife, the writer Josine Simons-Mees. Simons's esteem for Berlage went back to the early 1890s, when they were both working on the monumental edition of *Gijsbreght van Aemstel* by Joost van den Vondel, the "Bard from Amsterdam" in the Dutch Golden Age. Simons wrote the introduction and Berlage designed the illustrations. Later, both contributed to *De Kroniek.* Simons was a partisan of the "socialist progressive realism" put forth by moderate socialists. He was among the first to write about contemporary Dutch architecture in a foreign journal when, in 1899, he published an essay in *Dekorative Kunst.* In 1902 he became director of the "'t Binnenhuis," the arts-and-crafts workshop financed by Carel Henny, where objects designed by Berlage, J. van den Bosch, W. Hoecker, K. van Leeuwen, and C. Lebeau were produced and sold. He then took part in the heated debate over the Stock Exchange and supported Berlage. In 1903 he published an article on the Stock Exchange, "De Bouwkunst als toekomst-kunst," one of the most beautiful and most interesting to this day, in the influential journal *De Gids.* Three years later he founded the Maatschappij voor goede en goedkoope lectuur, an association for "quality and inexpensive reading" which published a very wide range of texts. Berlage was among the authors published.

For the Villa Parkwijk, Berlage designed the kitchen and laundry room in a low annex with a pyramidal roof. This annex is attached to the main part of the building on the narrow side facing the street. He combined masses varying in scale and used the slight differences in the

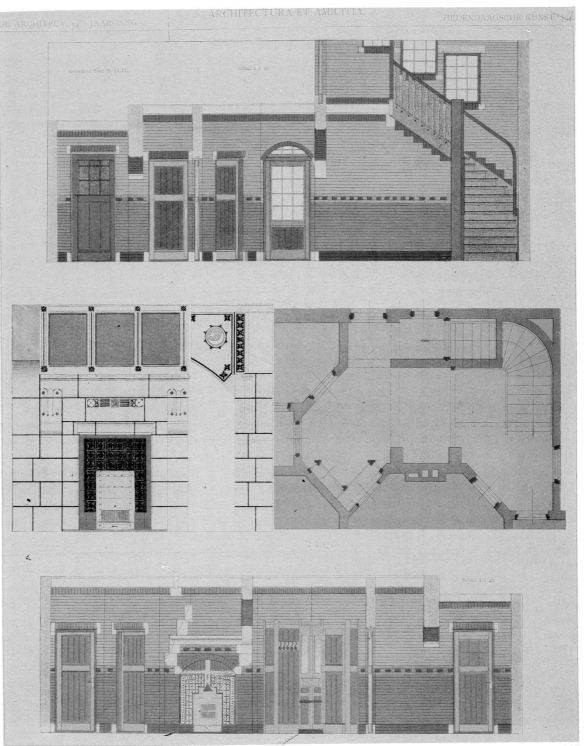

ground level to create a stepped composition. The long elevations on the east and west sides of the house are inscribed in an imaginary isosceles triangle. The regular spacing of chimney pots ensures a certain unity.

The ground plan also reflects this articulation of masses. The entrance leads to the kitchen on one side and the hall on the other. The hall is slightly off-center; it turns twice at an angle of 45 degrees and forms the shape of a "C." The rooms are laid out around the hall, counterclockwise: the dining-room, study, sitting room with a triangular veranda, toilet, and an isolated parlor. The second floor features two guest rooms sharing a bathroom, the master bedroom with its own bathroom, a boudoir, and closets. There are more closets, an attic, and two other bedrooms under the mansard roof. The eaves, rainwater heads, and exterior wooden structure are painted white, with archaic motifs in red and green. Inserted stones mark the quick rhythm of the openings. These are recessed to emphasize the smooth surface of exposed brick, which is broken at three levels by the eaves. The house was widely nicknamed the "teapot" because of the unusual shape of the kitchen's chimney.

In 1903, Van der Pek wrote in *Onze Kunst* that the villas's interior owed a lot to the domestic tradition of P.J.H. Cuypers. In his essay for the 1916 *Festschrift*, however, W. Vogelsang noted that all references to medieval castles had disappeared.

In 1913 Simons moved to The Hague, settling in another house designed by Berlage. The land was sold for 35,000 florins. The villa in Amsterdam, assessed for the equivalent of 42,000 German marks at the time, was dismantled and rebuilt in Zeisterbosch-De Bilt (319 Soestdijkweg, Bilthoven), near Utrecht. The modifications then made provoked protests and polemics. (H.v.B)

Bibliography: A. Moen 1913; J. de Meijer 1916; H.P.L. Wiessing 1960; also cfr. *De Architect* XIV, 1903, ills. 493–94; *Bouwkundig Weekblad* 1913, 6, ill.

246. *Drawings for the presentation, executed in 1903.*

247. *Contemporary photograph.*

246

247

Commissioned by the Municipality of
Amsterdam
1900–05 and 1914–17

Amsterdam boomed during the last
quarter of the nineteenth century and
quickly reached the edges of the
pragmatic plan that J. Kalff, then director of the municipal bureau of
Public Works, had designed in 1876
to contain the development of the
built-up area. The trends in demographic growth and construction of
housing revealed, however, that the
housing shortage had become chron-
ic. It had become necessary to extend the municipality's territory. The
municipal administration had attempted since the early 1880s to
expand beyond its boundaries established in the seventeenth century.
These efforts were finally rewarded
in May 1896 by an extension to the
south of 8,027 to 11,436 acres. Also
in 1896, a law was passed and land
belonging to the municipality could
not be sold but had to be granted on
a long-term lease. At the end of the
century, therefore, the administration
embarked on a real-estate policy that
led to its direct involvement in the
issue of housing, and it launched
an innovative action in favor of low-
income housing.

Several surveys and studies on the
housing conditions among the working class had drawn a dramatic
picture that was alarming to the
administration. In the wake of such
studies, the report *Nut* was published
in 1896, suggesting a number of urgent measures and proposing specific
regulations on expropriation, building permits, and public subsidies.

At the end of the nineteenth century the Netherlands were undergoing symptomatic political and economic changes, which were echoed
in many newspapers. The government was directly influenced by such
changes when it drew up the *Woningwet*, the new housing law. But the
situation did not simply change at the
end of the century. Amsterdam grew
by another half-million inhabitants,

and insistent reports on the "misery,
filth, and immorality" described the
struggle for survival by the gigantic population crowding the urban
ghettos. This situation was becoming
unbearable in the face of social rationalism, control, and appeasement
adopted by the ruling political and
economic forces of the time.

It was in an atmosphere of profound changes, therefore, that the
municipal administration asked the
Bureau of Public Works for a study
of a partial development plan for the
recently acquired land to the south.
In 1899, C.L.M. Lambrechtsen van
Ritthem, an engineer and the director
of Public Works from 1895 to 1900,
submitted a proposal in which he attempted to maintain the city's existing concentric plan. In March 1900,
a closed meeting of the municipal
council rejected the plan, on the
grounds that it was lacking in hygiene
and beauty. The same month, Berlage was commissioned to "design a
development plan that would satisfy
superior aesthetic requirements." He
was to work with J. van Hasselt, the
director of Public Works until 1907.
Despite the fact that Berlage was
working on many other assignments
at the time, he finished the plan in
six months, by September 1900. In
October, Van Hasselt received the
presentation, two plans, and three
perspective views, which may have
been influenced by the views Karl
Henrici designed for Munich in 1893.
Lambrechtsen's slavish design had
been radically modified. Berlage
wished to achieve a synthesis of the
picturesque and the monumental—
the concepts he had used in the
1880s, when comparing Amsterdam
and Venice—in order to avoid monotony. He again took up the idea of
a significant canal link between the
Amstel and the Schinkel, the water-
ways east and west of the city, and
he designed a network of new canals,
the winding flow of which structure
the plan. The street plan was designed on a similar pattern. A tree-
lined boulevard bordered by villas is
the dominant element, running in the
same direction as that of the main

canal. Two squares, featuring precisely defined monumental buildings,
are the focal points of the street plan.
One square contains the Volkshuis,
the people's hall—with a theater,

concert hall, and meeting hall—and
union and cooperative buildings, as
well as stores. The other square features municipal offices, public baths,
the firehouse and police precinct, and

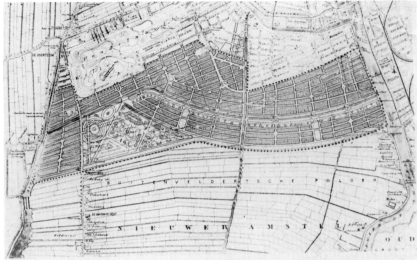

248

249

*248. C.L.M. Lambrechtsen van Ritthem,
study plan for the south of
Amsterdam, 1899.*

249. Design plan, 1900.

stores. Because of still-confused expectations, the new area was also to have an industrial area, a great park next to a parade ground designed for sporting events and exhibitions, a garden-village for workers, a market area, two hospitals, and a sumptuous villa as a new royal residence.

The resulting urban panorama is dominated by a complex combination of high- and low-density housing areas. Housing becomes progressively less dense as it nears the edges of the plan, so as to ensure a transition between city and countryside. The areas of high-density housing form lines around the city, their broken radial geometry converging on squares of varying shapes. They reveal how difficult it is to coordinate a centripetal plan with a general design of "unity within diversity." The areas of low-density building are juxtaposed in complex curving strips in a free arrangement that betrays insufficient control. The relationship between the different areas of low-density buildings expresses, in a manner not yet quite sure, a wish to reshape the city without trauma around some points of community assembly. To use Berlage's terminology, however, one could say that the "picturesque" prevails over the "monumental."

The municipal council reviewed the plan only in October 1904. It was approved by a prudent resolution in January 1905, provided that it not be regarded as binding and the content not be immediately executed.

With the turn of the century, the long political debate on the issue of housing came to a head. In June 1901, the Dutch Parliament passed a law on low-income housing proposed in 1899 by the liberal Borgesius government. After a debate and a difficult ratification, the Woningwet came into effect as Law 158 by a royal decree of 1902. This law had a significant impact on the country's cities because it established on a national scale the municipality's right to expropriate for the purpose of building, and it forced the communities undergoing sustained demographic growth to design a development plan. It had an all-important effect on the quality and quantity of housing to be built. During the first forty years of the twentieth century—before the problems of reconstruction widened in scope—20 percent of the residential complexes

were subsidized through the Woningwet. During the second and third decades, the proportion was extremely high, revealing the role of the housing law as a steadying force in the housing cycle.

In fact, most of the municipalities ignored for several years the obligation they were under to design a development plan, as well as the possibility offered them to reach into the state's coffers to build low-income housing. Significantly, for many years and at least through the 1920s, the larger cities experiencing the most acute housing problem—such as Amsterdam and Rotterdam—preferred partial plans to general ones such as those for The Hague and Utrecht. It is also remarkable that Berlage was instrumental in the designing of urban plans for the four largest cities in the Netherlands. In other words, he is the main point of reference in the Dutch tradition of urban planning, from the turn of the century to at least the mid-1920s. Coherent urban growth, which characterizes Dutch urban planning, is an essential part of Berlage's approach to planning—whether in the variety of technical approaches or in his working solutions—and is directly con-

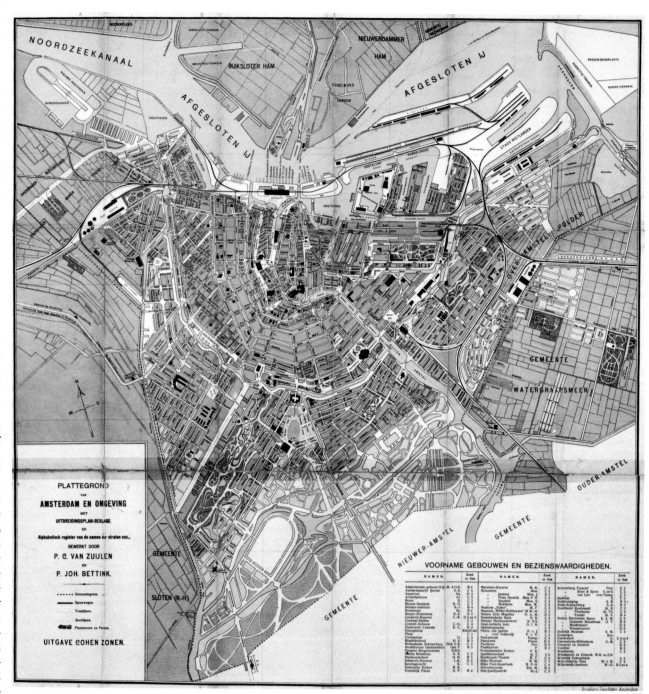

250

250. The first plan for the south of Amsterdam in the general city plan, map dated 1909.

nected to his logical acceptance of the modern city.

The municipal council of Amsterdam had solid reasons to be cautious about Berlage's plan as well as the passage of the Woningwet through Parliament and political assessments of its administration. Structural conditions were inadequate and the municipality did not own enough land to the south. Other questions were raised, on the left as well as on the right, relative to the low rate of building on the land—around 40 percent—which resulted in very high public expenditure to build "a luxury neighborhood." The plan was ratified by the royal decree of January 1906, which confirmed that the stipulations regarding the allotments had no legal effect since they were not included in the housing law. It stated, however, that "there was no reason to refuse the requested authorization, but only for the stipulations relative to streets, canals, and squares."

The discussion of the plan gave rise to little reaction among architects, who were still uninterested in issues of planning, and in the press in general, unlike the extraordinary repercussions of the debate around the Stock Exchange.

In the following years, Berlage worked intermittently on the plan. He was consulted in 1903 for the revision of a development plan for the east of Amsterdam, and he was also a consultant between 1907 and 1911 for the wider plan of The Hague. After some direct contacts with A.W. Bos, who succeeded Van Hasselt at the Bureau of Public Works, he was finally commissioned in October 1914 for a new version of the development plan, for a fee of 5,000 florins. He was given a few suggestions, such as the placement of a new railway station. By March 1915, he had finished the plan and the presentation. In the same year, J.W.C. Tellegen was appointed mayor of Amsterdam. He was an engineer who had been director of the Bureau of Inspection and Construction at the turn of the century and who had promoted innovative building regulations in 1905. It was a sign of the change in climate that Tellegen submitted a construction program for 3,500 housing units at the first meeting of the municipal council. With the help of such personalities as Wibaut and Keppler, he set in motion the policy of municipal involvement in mass construction which characterized Amsterdam during the 1920s. It was also Tellegen who presented the second development plan for the south of Amsterdam. The debate lasted from July to October 1917, and the plan was approved.

Two squares are still the focal points of the whole layout: the square of the railway station on the southwest, and the square lined up with the bridge on the Amstel. They are tightly connected with nine access routes to the city that impose an arrangement opposite that of the first version of the plan. Berlage drew masterful bird's-eye views to illustrate the whole plan, improving on the fragmented presentation he had designed for The Hague.

The varied structure is organized by a hierarchic superimposition of two networks: A monumental out-

251. *Second plan for the south of Amsterdam, map of the property and allotments inside the municipal limits, 1915.*

252. *Design plan, 1915.*

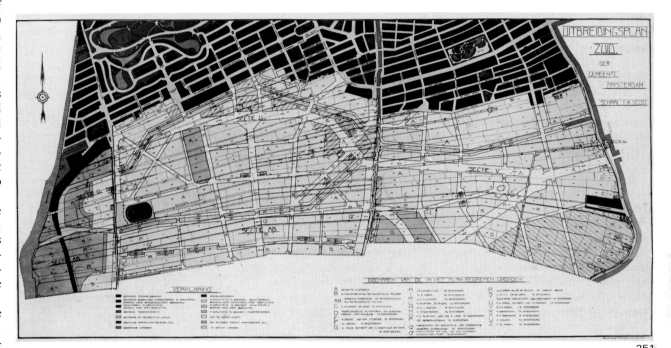

251

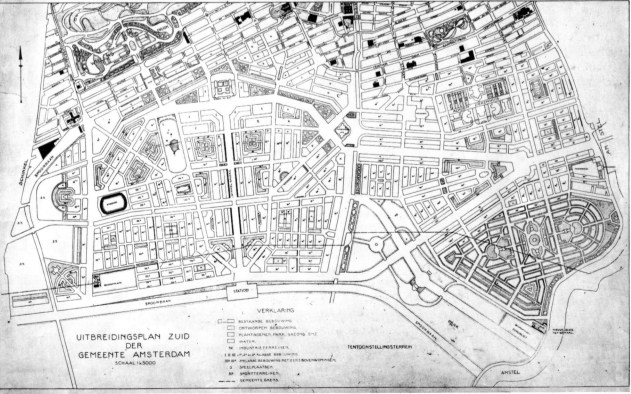

252

167

line, based on simple geometric figures and symmetry, is defined by fairly wide arteries; a secondary network linking the main thoroughfares ensures a continuity while breaking the perspective views. This secondary network is connected in the north to the old urban fabric.

Structural diversity pervades the whole plan. More than the street plan, the network of canals clearly divides the plan into two zones: west and east. The canal linking the Amstel to the Schinkel marks the northeast boundary of the partially constructed suburban area, where a series of connections strings together new and old urban fabrics. It crosses the north-south waterway—the axis of the dividing line between the two zones—in a monumental basin, after which it forks into the west zone. The two arms of the canal "isolate" a large section of the city and merge again to flow into the Schinkel.

In the east, the street plan is marked transversally by three monumental avenues joining to form the shape of a "Y"—like a great crow's foot—centered on the square that is lined up with the bridge on the Amstel. In the west, an outer ring is connected to the branches of the "Y" and crossed by two arteries. The largest of these two arteries forms a trident, the summit of which is the square with the railway station.

Using his now solid experience in urban planning, Berlage turned to the details after having situated a structure with the help, perhaps, of regulating geometrical figures. In the west, he placed an industrial zone, a cemetery, stores, the railway station, the Academy of Fine Arts, and the Kunstenaarshuis (which he had designed in 1912). In the east, he placed a university hospital, the Amstelpark, and a "quote" integrated in a manner similar to that in the plan for The Hague: the design by J.F. Repko that was selected in a 1915 competition for a garden-neighborhood, built on 141 acres, which bears some resemblances to the design in the first version of the plan. Once the relationship between the major components is made clear and the public elements are provided for, the plan establishes a division of the fundamental residential component according to three types of housing. The first part is made of one-family houses, built on an area around 50 acres, with a den-

sity varying from 50 to 100 people per acre; most of these houses stand around the academy. The second part is made of two-family houses, built on 171 acres, with a density of 300 people per acre; these houses stand along the railway track and the "Y" of the avenues. The second part features multi-family low-income housing with common rooms, built with a uniform distribution on 467 acres—almost 75 percent of the residential area—with a density of 600 to 800 people per acre, according to the height of the building (three to four floors and an attic). The type of low-income housing chosen is clear: the *Blokbouw*, big housing complexes with a courtyard, as can be seen from the perspective views of the design and the presentation.

A political decision to expropriate—and not only in the south of the city—had been made after deliberation in 1906, which was important for the future urban development of Amsterdam: When Berlage's plan was approved, a great part of the area south of the city already belonged to the municipality. This did not mean, however, that the plan was faithfully executed. It was only after 1921, when the municipality had grown from 11,436 to 43,114 acres, that the southernmost part—that with the railway station, the Amstelpark, and a part of the Tuindorp, which could not fit within the abstract geometry of the old boundaries—was included in the city's boundaries. The execution of the plan, filled in by the Amsterdam School and, mostly, by the extraordinary De Klerk, was done in separate phases, with varying intensity and progressive modifications, until the Second World War.

Unlike the bridge on the Amstel—the Berlage Bridge, for which he lovingly oversaw the construction until 1926—the railway station and the majority of the public buildings were never built. In the mid-1920s, private enterprise recovered a certain initiative in the field of construction; the building of low-income housing never reached the proportions foreseen in the plan, and another essential political component was thus diluted. What remained—and took root—was the concept of a design for large housing complexes, which was true to the unity required in Berlage's presentation: "In the past each house was regarded as an aesthetic whole;

today the whole includes the street, the square, the urban sector."

Composite and interconnected theoretical foundations, combined with an exceptional ability for self-promotion, opened the way to Berlage's rich career as an urban planner: The Hague (1907–11), Purmerend (1911), the Vreewijk in Rotterdam (1913–16), the Transvalbuurt in Amsterdam (1916–19), Utrecht (1920–24), the Hofplein in Rotterdam (1921 and 1926), the Mercatorplein in the west of Amsterdam (1925–27), and Groningen (1927–28), not to mention minor consulting assignments.

Bibliography: H.P. Berlage 1904, "Memorie . . ."; J.H.W. Leliman 1904; editorial 1904, "Het Uitbreidingsplan . . ."; H. Walenkamp 1904; H.P. Berlage 1915, " Bij de . . ."; A.W. Bos 1916; M. Eisler 1916; editorial 1916, "Het Uitbreidingsplan . . ."; H.P. Berlage 1917, "Memorie . . ."; J.H.W.L. 1917; editorial 1917, "Amsterdam . . ."; J. Stübben 1918; H. Cleyndert 1923; F.F. Fraenkel, in AA.VV. 1975, *H.P. Berlage . . .* (and in F.F. Fraenkel 1976); P. Panerai, J. Castex, and J.C. Depaule 1980; N. de Boer 1983.

Building of De Algemeene

With Hetzer
Leipzig, Augustus Platz/
Johannes Gasse
Commissioned by the insurance company De Algemeene
1901–02

In 1901, Berlage designed the building for the branch of the insurance company De Algemeene in Leipzig. It was to be the company's German main office. Construction work started in 1902, with the assistance of Hetzer, a Leipzig architect.

From the point of view of the company, these building were erected also as a real estate investment. As a

253

254

consequence, only half of the second floor in the big building is used by the company (director's offices, administration, archives, and related space). The rest of the building was for the rental of offices, apartments, and stores.

The building stands on a square site facing the central Augustus Platz. It is laid out in the shape of an "L" around a small interior courtyard. The staircase is placed near the corner, against the inner elevation, allowing for the most efficient usage of the space, especially in the apartments. There are four luxury apartments, on the third and fourth floors. The apartments on the third floor have five rooms with kitchen and bathroom; those on the fourth floor have six rooms, a parlor, a kitchen, and a bathroom. The main rooms face the square or the street; kitchens and bathrooms are connected to the front by a corridor and face the interior courtyard. The elevations are designed with rational simplicity. The corner is chamfered at an angle of 45 degrees and enlivened by a vertical sequence of solid masses and voids. It is emphasized by the symmetrical gable over the windows on either side of the corner and by the recessed tower with spire and clock, which rises on the line bisecting the corner. The stores on the ground floor feature wide windows, four-centered arches, and pilasters in polished granite. Berlage used a grayish sandstone for the imposts of the arches, the corbels of the oriel windows, the architraves of the windows, and the coping of the gables and small flat-roofed towers on either end of the building.

Bas-reliefs by L. Zijl decorate either side of the main entrance, facing the square, as well as the vestibule inside, where an opus sectile features the company's headquarters in Amsterdam. For the walls of the staircase, the red brick of the façade is combined with glazed bricks colored off-white, yellow, green, and blue. This arrangement of colors is heightened by the granite and sandstone of

253. *Exterior, contemporary photograph.*

254. *View of the vestibule on the ground floor, contemporary photograph.*

255. *Cross-section of the staircase, drawing published in* De Architect, *in 1905.*

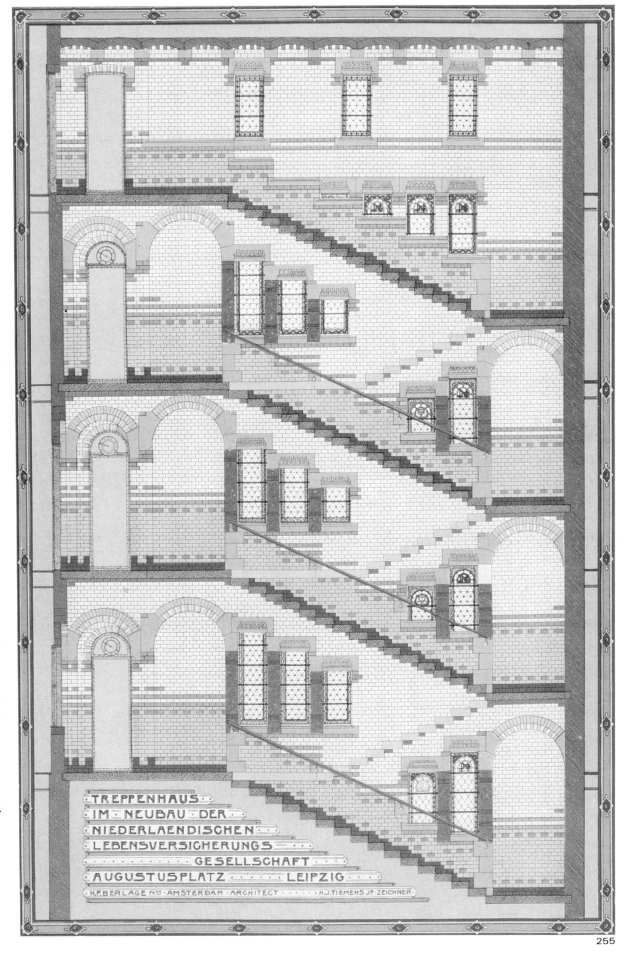

TREPPENHAUS
IM NEUBAU DER
NIEDERLAENDISCHEN
LEBENSVERSICHERUNGS
GESELLSCHAFT
AUGUSTUSPLATZ LEIPZIG
H.P.BERLAGE Nzn AMSTERDAM ARCHITECT · · · · · H.J.TIEMENS Jr ZEICHNER

255

the pilasters and imposts and the ceramic mosaics framing the windows on the courtyard.

In keeping with his unified concept of architecture, Berlage also designed the furniture for the director's offices and the wainscoting for the waiting room.

Bibliography: Editorial 1903, "Der Neubau . . ."; editorial 1903, "Het Leipziger . . ."; H.P. Berlage 1904, "Het Gebouw . . ."; also see cfr. *Leipziger Neueste Nachrichten* January 22, 1903; *Onze Kunst* 1903, 3; *Die Architektur des XX. Jahrhunderts* 1903, 3, pp. 38–39 and plate 55; *De Architect* XVI, 1905, plates 561–62.

Design of an apartment house for the Eigen Haard

Amsterdam, Frans van Mierisstraat
Commissioned by the building cooperative Eigen Haard
1902

256. Design plan.

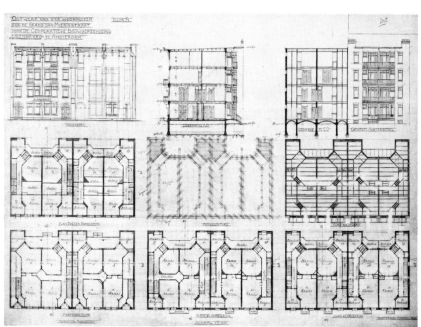

256

Villa Roland Holst

Laren
Commissioned by
R.N. Roland Holst
1902 and 1913

At the turn of the century, Richard Nicolaus Roland Holst was commissioned to do the murals in the meeting room of the ANDB building and in the southwest stairway of the Stock Exchange. At the same time, he asked Berlage to design a country house for himself and his wife, the socialist writer Henriëtte Roland Holst-van der Schalk. It was she who, in 1915, was to write the postscript in verse to the small volume of the *Pantheon der Menschheid*. They chose a site in Laren, a small residential town near Hilversum that was a favorite among painters. A.J. van Derkinderen lived there, and Piet Mondrian and Van der Leck stayed there between 1910 and 1920.

In the 1890s, Derkinderen worked on the modern edition of the seventeenth-century drama *Gijsbreght van Aemstel*, and he had a noticeable influence on Berlage, who was illustrating the play. Roland Holst surely knew Berlage at that time, since they belonged to the same circles. Jan Toorop, Thorn Prikker, Derkinder-

en, and his friend Roland Holst were part of the Dutch Symbolist group pursuing an ideal of *Gemeenschapskunst*, "the art of the community." For Derkinderen, this was an attempt to combine monumentality and symbolism and it took on an almost religious value. Roland Holst, however, regarded it as a necessary means for the construction of socialism.

Roland Holst was a champion of English aesthetic theories, from Ruskin to Morris, and he wrote regularly in *De Kroniek* as did Berlage, whom he admired and supported. In 1916, he contributed to the *Festschrift* edited by Mrs. Kröller-Müller and H.P. Bremmer, and his essay on architectural unity in the arts was influenced by the tension of the war years. While he appreciated the Stock Exchange, he disapproved of artists employed by industrialists of modern capitalism, whereby he implicitly criticized Berlage, who was then working for the Kröller-Müllers. Nevertheless, he felt that Berlage had achieved great results "thanks to his childish optimism, seriousness, and naïve trust, a quality sadly lacking in our time." On the occasion of the twenty-fifth anniversary of the Stock Exchange, Roland Holst praised the building again in a column for the *Bouwkundig Weekblad*.

In 1902, Berlage designed a villa for him that in a way repeats the model of the English country house, laid out around its central vestibule. The house also fits into the local

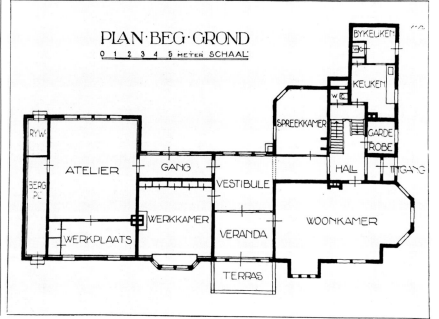

257

170

countryside tradition and features a sloping thatched roof, the edges of which are curved over the windows. This roof ensures the unity of the house built in exposed brick, in spite of the volumetric discontinuity created—as in the Villa Parkwijk of 1900–01—by the lower and projecting parts containing the kitchen and toilet.

Berlage did the extension work in 1913. He added a studio, a workshop, a storeroom, and the usual bicycle shed, connected to the old house by a corridor leading to a new vestibule-veranda with terrace. (H. v. B.)

Bibliography: cfr. *De Architect* XVIII, 1906, ill. 580; H. Roland Holst-van der Schalk, *Het vuur brandde voort*, Van Ditmar, Amsterdam, and Antwerp, 1949.

258

257. *Plan of the ground floor in the design for the extension.*

258. *Original building, contemporary photograph.*

259. *Contemporary photograph after the extension work.*

259

Villa Wiggers　　　　**Summer house Hesseling**

Beek
Commissioned by D. Wiggers
1902

Noordwijk aan Zee
Commissioned by D.C. Hesseling
1902

The plan in the Berlage archives is
dated February 1902.

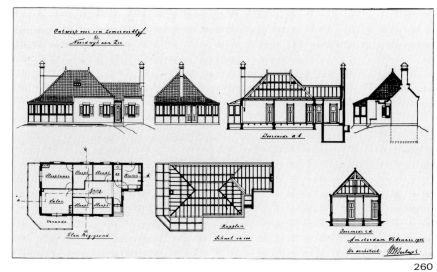

260

260. *Design plan.*

261. *Contemporary photograph.*

261

Villa Wiggers　　　　Summer house Hesseling

Turin, International Exhibition
Commissioned by J.B. Hillen
1902

Leiden, Zoeterwoudschensingel
Commissioned by D.C. Hesseling
1903

A small part with a terraced roof was added for the library, next to the studio on the ground floor and on the left side of the frontispiece. On the right hand side, two rooms were added on the ground floor, connected by a narrow staircase to a small landing on the second floor and two low-ceilinged bedrooms.

262. Study plan.

263. Design plan.

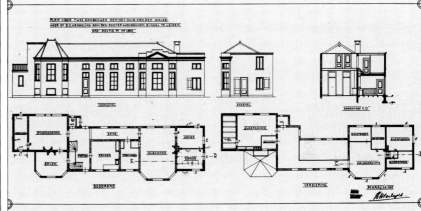

263

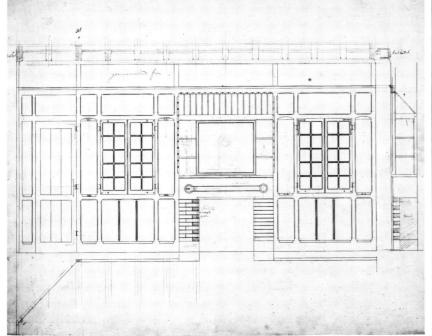

262

East Amsterdam, the area between the curve of the railway/Ringvaart/Linnaeusstraat
Commissioned by the municipality of Amsterdam
1903

In June 1903, the municipal council considered the plan developed by two building associations wishing to develop an area of about 62 acres. Since the turn of the century, Berlage had been responsible for the development of the area south of Amsterdam. In December 1903, the municipality decided to consult him on the "aesthetic" aspect of the Transvaalbuurt plan and commissioned him to rework the rigid geometry of the street plan.

During the following ten years, Berlage worked several times in the area. He designed two housing complexes and a more limited construction plan.

Bibliography: cfr. *De Amsterdammer* 1904, December 4.

264. *General plan of the city of Amsterdam in 1909; on the right, the area being developed.*

265. *New layout suggested by Berlage.*

266. *Street pattern.*

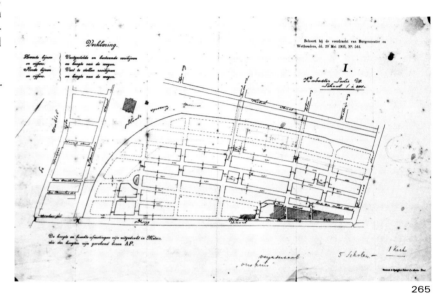

265

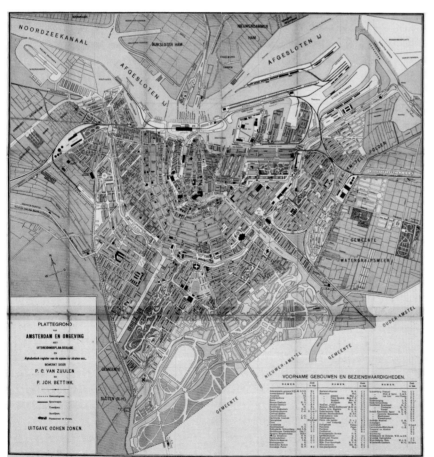

264

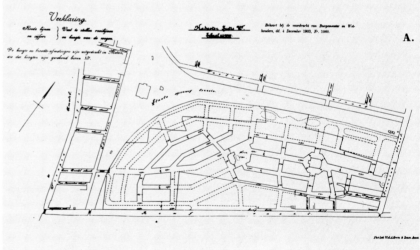

266

Study for an interior design

Amsterdam, Nieuwendijk
Commissioned by
C. & A. Brenninkmeijer
1903

This is the interior layout and wainscoting of the C. & A. department store, located in the wing of De Algemeene building near the Dam. This wing was designed for stores in the first extension of the building.

267. Study plan.

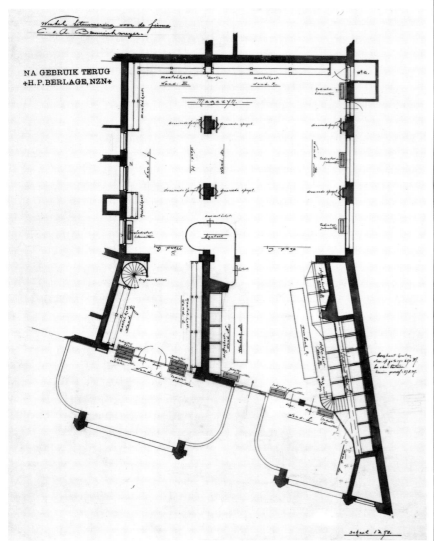

Building with residential and commercial space

Amsterdam, 4–8 Hobbemastraat
Commissioned by the insurance company De Algemeene
1904–05

Between 1904 and 1905, Berlage designed two buildings with residential and commercial space in Amsterdam.

For a careful discussion of the Hobbemastraat design, see the essay by Jan de Heer in this book, in which the author analyzes the whole range of Berlage's work in the field of housing. The building may have a distant precedent in a study dating from the early 1890s, for town houses on a site nearby, on the corner of Hobbemastraat and Jan Luykenstraat.

The drawings in the Berlage archives are dated from April to September 1904. This was the last commission Berlage received from De Algemeene, at the same time as he was doing the second extension work on the building on Damrak.

Bibliography:: cfr. *De Bouwwereld* 1905, 10, pp. 77 and 80.

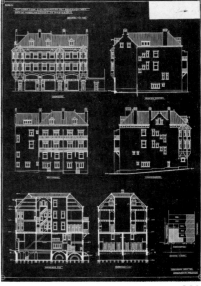

268

268. Drawings, elevations and cross-sections.

269. Contemporary photograph.

267

269

East Amsterdam,
74–96 Linnaeusstraat/
1–2 Praetoriusstraat
Commissioned by Brouwer
1905

Berlage was always guided by a sensitivity to the crucial points of the urban structure. This was again the case, when he designed buildings on the northeast end of a cross-street in the Transvaalbuurt, a neighborhood in Amsterdam that he had been planning since 1903.

These twin buildings were constructed for renting middle-class apartments of the worst type. They stand symmetrically on the funnel-shaped edge of the junction between Praetoriusstraat and Linnaeusstraat. The skyline recalls the building of De Algemeene in Leipzig, dated 1901–02. The corbels supporting the oriel windows on the corners, however, seem more informal and playful: Columns stand on either side of the entrance to the stores on the ground floor, and their shaft is surmounted by an ample curvy capital. The rhythm in the tight sequence of paired windows is marked by the oriels and the round towers containing the staircases, amplifying the vertical effect in the façades of the curved complex.

The final drawings in the Berlage archives are dated February 1905.

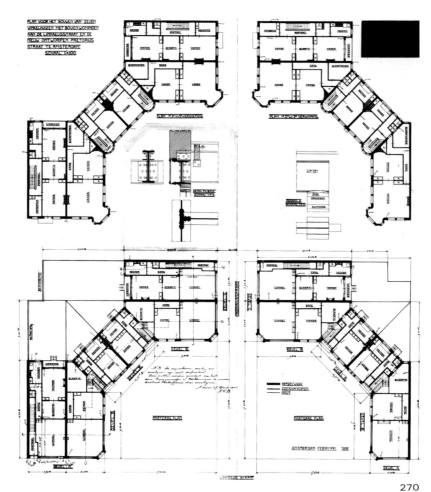

272

270. *Design plan, plan of the ground floor and typical floor.*

271. *Exterior, contemporary photograph.*

272. *Entrance to a store on the ground floor, present state.*

270

271

Amsterdam Jordaan, 6–8 Rozenstraat
Commissioned by
the association Ons Huis
1904–05

In the wake of the emancipation movement of the working class, which brought about the construction of the Toynbee Hall and the People's Palace in London, another "people's hall," the Ons Huis, was inaugurated in Amsterdam, almost at the same time as the Lochem Volkshuis designed by Berlage in 1891–92. The building was designed by C.B. Posthumus Meyes, a neo-Renaissance architect of some fame. It stands on Rozenstraat, the same street as that of the "'t Lootsje" of the Bols Company, the interior of which was done by Berlage in 1893. The people's hall features a coffee house, a library, and several rooms for educational activities on the second floor and, on the top floor, a theater with a capacity of 500 people, lit from the skylight

273. Exterior, present state.

274. Study of the plan for the ground floor.

above. Extension work became necessary, within the limitations of the site, because of the high usage of the building. In 1904–05 Berlage designed the extension on the right-hand side of the main part of the building.

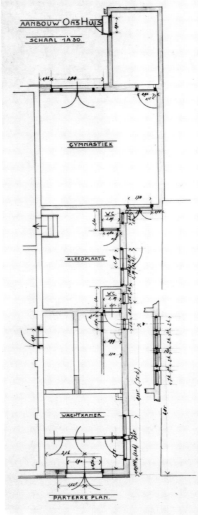

274

East Amsterdam, Czaar Peterstraat
Commissioned by the association
Oosterspeeltuin
1905

In 1905, Berlage designed a small reading room for the health association Oosterspeeltuin, established in 1902, in an almost triangular open space at the beginning of the Czaar Peterstraat. This was in the dock area east of Amsterdam, not far from the site where he had built a school of design in 1899–1900. Both buildings have since been demolished.

The plan features a central reading room with spare wainscoting and, as three side annexes, the entrance with toilets, a storeroom, and a veranda. The helm roof is crowned by a ventilation shaft. Below the roof, in the middle of the wall between the room and the veranda, a sort of reinforced chimney rises on the opposite side of the dividing wall from where the fireplace stands.

Berlage designed other "people's recreational buildings" for the same association, mainly public baths and a gymnasium (1911). He produced a sheltered playground in 1908 for a similar association, the Westerspeeltuin.

275. Design plan.

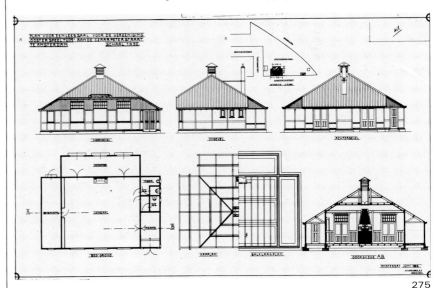

275

273

The Hague, 21–23 Kettingstraat
Commissioned by De Veije
1905

276. Design plan.

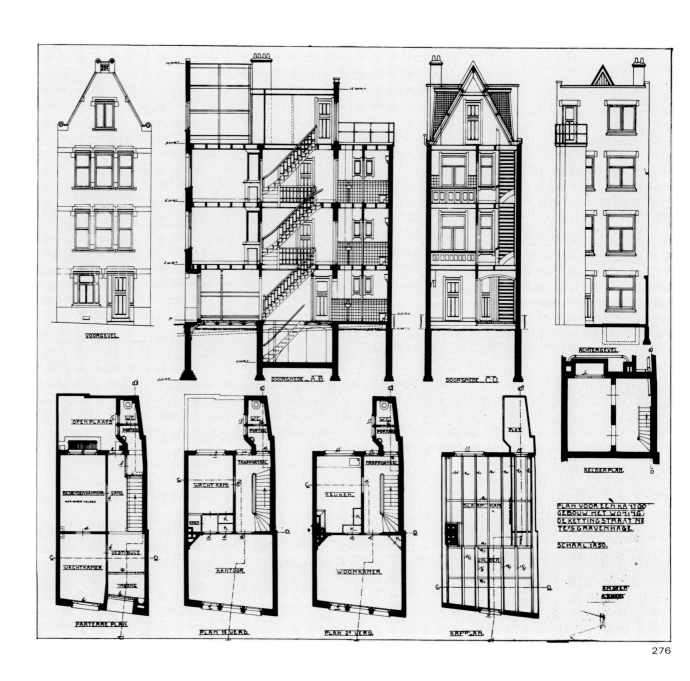

276

Laren
Commissioned by H. Polak
1905

Henri Polak was a Jewish diamond cutter who, in the early 1890s, became involved in the union struggle shaking his trade in the "city of diamonds" as Amsterdam was known at the end of the nineteenth century. He played a fundamental role in organizing and centralizing the various unions of elite workers. The Algemeene Nederlandsche Diamantbewerksbond, the association of the diamond workers' unions, was formed in 1894, and he was elected president. The ANDB commissioned Berlage in 1897 for the design of its headquarters in Amsterdam.

In his youth, Polak went to Great Britain, where he became acquainted with the theories of William Morris, the work of British unions, and the political strategy of the Fabian Society. He then set out to spread these ideas in the Netherlands: He translated two volumes on the British trade unions by Sidney and Beatrice Webb (with a cover design by Berlage) and wrote a brief biography for a collection of lectures by Morris, entitled *Kunst en Maatschappij* and published in 1903.

Polak was president of the SDAP, the major Dutch social-democratic party, from 1901 to 1905. In 1902 he became the first municipal councilman to represent his party in Amsterdam. With P.J. Troelstra, another charismatic leader of the SDAP, he became the editor in 1902 of the series "Sociale Bibliotheek" published in Amsterdam by A.B. Soep. Berlage published his first book, *Over stijl in bouw- en meubelkunst*, in this series in 1904.

Berlage had known Polak since 1893–94. He was commissioned to design his house in Laren, where he had built the Villa Roland Holst in 1902. The Villa Polak is a modest building, but its layout is very clear. The rooms are arranged around a vestibule, the shape of which is cut diagonally on one corner. The ground floor features the kitchen, which is also connected directly to the entrance, a study, a living room, the staircase, a closet, and a toilet. The second floor features a children's room, a guest room, a master bedroom, and a maid's room, with a bathroom between the master bedroom and the guest-room. The main rooms face south, while the north elevation has no openings on the second floor.

To limit construction costs, cavity walls were built: two thin leaves separated by a continuous gap, which ensure good insulation. The traditional thatched roof, in keeping with the local architectural style, also contributes to the house's insulation.

The simple mass is enlivened by a free arrangement of the openings. The projecting veranda topped by the balcony of the master bedroom on the second floor and the roof's curve on the edge of the eaves articulate the south elevation. The tall chimney of the living room is secured by a tie-beam and its vertical thrust balances the horizontal projection of the veranda, rising above the dormers' half-open eye. Built in 1905, the villa cost the equivalent of 10,000 German marks at the time, according to the notice in the 1910 publication *Das Einzelwohnhaus der Neuzeit* by Haenel and Tscharmann, which gave it as the least expensive in its category, incurring less than a third of the cost of the Villa Parkwijk. (H.v.B.)

277. Design plan.

278. Perspective sketch published in Beschouwingen over bouwkunst en hare ontwikkeling, Rotterdam, 1911.

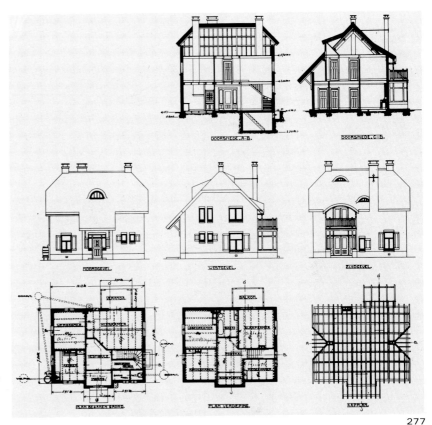

277

278

Wassenaar, Rijksstraatweg
Commissioned by De Veije
1905

The plan in the Berlage archives is
dated May 1905.

279. Design plan.

280. Exterior, contemporary photograph.

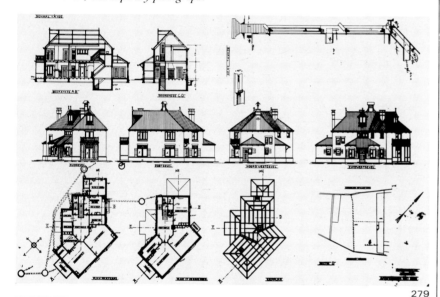

279

280

Wapenvelde
Commissioned by H.J. de Lang
1905–06

The extension work was done in the
basement, where Berlage added a
cellar and a storage room for the
heating, and in an addition between
the two major parts of the building.
This resulted in a more rational volumetric arrangement. The consistent
increase in usable areas led to a complete modification of the layout, with
a new dining room and veranda on
the ground floor and more bedrooms
on the upper floors. Berlage redesigned the entrance on the west side,
adding a projecting vestibule, which
is connected to the hall by an oriel.

281. Design plan.

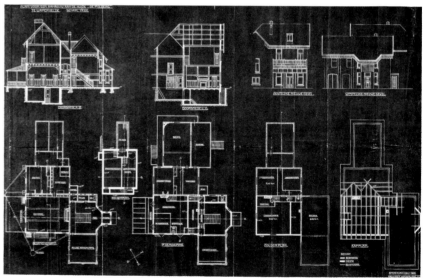

281

The Hague, area between
Van Meerdervoortlaan
and Scheveningscheweg
1906

In 1899, the Netherlands hosted the
first international peace conference
called by Czar Nicholas II. In 1903,
as a token of the pacifist and neutral
aspirations of the Netherlands, the
Carnegie Foundation offered a million and a half dollars for the construction of a Palais de la Paix in The
Hague. The problem of the choice of
a site was resolved when the Dutch
State offered a vast area at the beginning of the Scheveningscheweg,
north of the historic center and near
Park Zorgvliet. An international
competition was then announced.

The jury for the competition was
presided over by A.P.C. van Karnebeek, and P.J.H. Cuypers was a
member. In May 1906, the jury announced the winner among 216 designs. They selected the design by
L.M. Cordonnier, who had been an
unsuccessful competitor for the Amsterdam Stock Exchange in 1884–85.
No Dutch architect ranked among
the first six selected designs. Otto
Wagner ranked fourth. Besides Berlage, Eero Saarinen, Eduard Cuypers, Willem Kromhout, Josep Puig
i Cadalfach, Wilhelm Kreis, Ignacs
Alpar, and the Italians G. Mancini
and G. Magni were among the many
participants.

In 1906 a large volume was published with 74 loose plates, some in
color; 100 more drawings; the six designs selected by the jury; and some
40 others selected by the MBB.

Berlage's design is featured on plate
29 (perspective view in color), 30 (elevation), and 31 (plan and section). It
is characterized by a direct link between plan and masses. The complex
is made of three connected buildings.
The palace of justice is the main
building, on the east side of the area;
it is laid out around a monumental
square vestibule, surrounded by an
articulated system of passageways.
The vestibule's regulating grid is extended in all four directions and pro-

vides the basic structure for the rooms
around it: north and south are the
large and small courtrooms; in the
back, on the west side, and beside the
technical units marked by tall chimneys, the passageways converge on a
sort of peristyle, closed on one side
by wide stairs and surrounded by library rooms. South of the library, the
book reserve forms a separate building connected to the offices of the
library by a gallery.

The section reveals the vertiginous
rise of the central hall; circles of balconies on the second and third floors,
under monumental arches connected
by pendentives; a drum; and a cupola.

282. Plan of the ground floor.

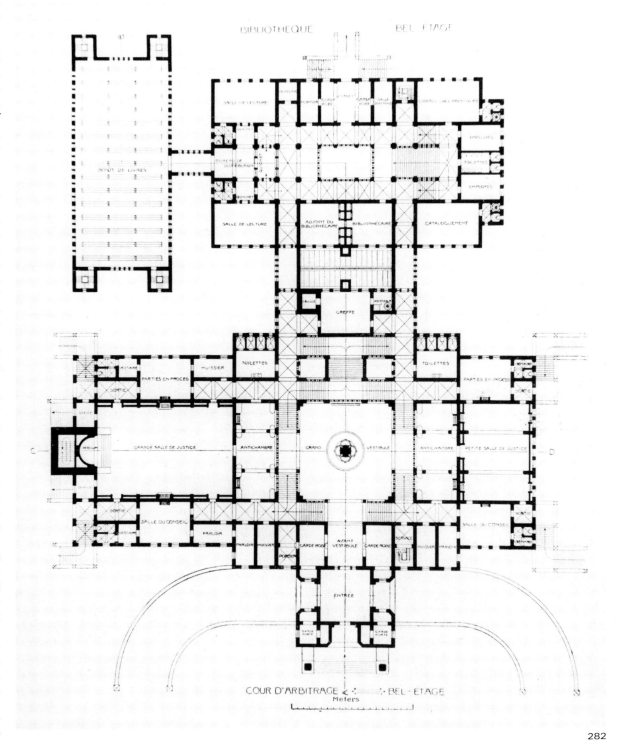

Allegorical mosaics decorate the recesses divided by raking arches at the meeting point between the archivolts of the pendentives and the main arches. Light enters the vestibule through three ranges of decorated windows, illuminating the gigantic monument standing at the center of the main floor as a symbol of the uniting of the people of the world.

In the exterior design, the mass of the vestibule dominates the concentric structure around it, confirming once again that Berlage conceived of architecture as designed from the interior outward, starting from a symbolic core. The fortress of peace rises at the center, bastioned by a small tower on the corners and capped by a spherical vault reminiscent of the Orient. It is balanced on the south edge by a tower tapering into an octagonal baptistery crowned with a solar sphere. Significantly, the motto of the design was a quote from Goethe's *Wanderers Nachtlied*, "Über allen Gipfeln ist Ruh" (Over all the mountaintops is peace). The solemn monumentality of the whole design is reinforced by the noble architectural and building idiom: the stone base defining the connection to the ground; the stairs on the sides of the courtrooms; the projecting part made of a triple portal with winged obelisks; the strong architectural presence of the stone finishing. The library and the book reserve are consistent with the vestibule, albeit less important: a parallelepiped featuring small corner towers with a pitched top and a tight range of openings.

Construction work of Cordonnier's design started on July 1907—with significant modifications—with the collaboration of Van der Steur. The Vredespalais was inaugurated in August 1913. It has been the seat of the World Court of Justice since 1922.

Bibliography: AA.VV. 1906; J.H.W. Leliman 1906; R. Blijstra 1975.

283

283. East view of the model, contemporary picture.

284. Southwest view of the model, contemporary picture.

284

Villa Stadwijck

Watergraafsmeer, 148 Middenweg
Commissioned by S. Walewijk
1906

The plan in the Berlage archives is dated March 1906, but there are several preliminary drawings. The villa was built in Watergraafsmeer. This community on the southeast edge of Amsterdam officially became part of the city on January 1, 1921; shortly thereafter, the experimental neighborhood of Betondorp was built there.

285. *Design plan.*

286. *Perspective sketch published in* Beschouwingen over bouwkunst en hare ontwikkeling, *Rotterdam, 1911.*

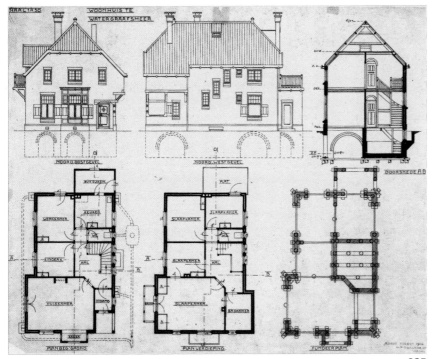

285

286

Rotterdam, Gedempte Slaak and Schoutenstraat
Commissioned by the Voorwaarts workers' cooperative
1906–07

The workers' cooperative needed rooms for different activities: production of bread, sale of food, storage, typesetting, and officework. Berlage requested permission to build in November 1906. Taking the shape and size of the site into account—56 feet wide (17 meters) and 245 feet long. (75 meters)—he proposed to construct two buildings separated by a garden.

Production activities and storage are put in an elongated building in the back. The bakery, fitted with four ovens that can be widened, faces the garden. A middle section behind the bakery contains the stairs leading to storage space, changing rooms, and a room for the supervisor. Facing the Schoutenstraat, in the back, are warehouses, a stable, a garage to load cars, and the side entrance to the meeting hall on the second floor.

The building on Gedempte Slaak is four stories high, including the attic. It features a tower on the side, above the entrance to offices on the upper floors. On the ground floor, the entrance leads to a coffee house, the rooms of which face either the street or the garden. Another entrance serves two retail food stores, with storage space behind and in the basement. Administrative and editorial offices of the *Voorwaarts* the union's newspaper, are on the second floor, and the printing is done on the third floor. Storage and technical services for the paper are on the attic floor.

The building is clearly reminiscent of the ANDB headquarters building, which Berlage built between 1897 and 1900. It is a more spartan version, however, especially in the choice of construction materials—brick and inexpensive stone—more in keeping with the client's resources. The sparseness is reinforced by the careful structuring of the façade, left of a solid tower with few openings. On the ground floor, the arched openings

are spaced irregularly to balance the splayed arch of the entrance under the tower. On the upper floors, the openings are set in a progressively tighter sequence, until they fill the whole width of the façade. The attic floor is marked by a course of stepped corbels; bricks jut out of the wall sur-

face to hold up dormers standing out against the recessed pitched roof, and they frame metopes spelling out the name "Voorwaarts." On the front of the tower, the square panel under the roof bears the cooperative's monogram, designed by Berlage. The 1916 *Festschrift* recounts how the side

panels were not fitted with the clocks featured in the design but with transparent bull's-eyes instead, gigantic telescopic lenses looking out toward the harbor, Rotterdam's labor center.

Bibliography: H.P. Berlage 1906, "Gebouw . . . ."

287

287. Exterior, contemporary photograph.

288. Perspective view and plan of the ground floor.

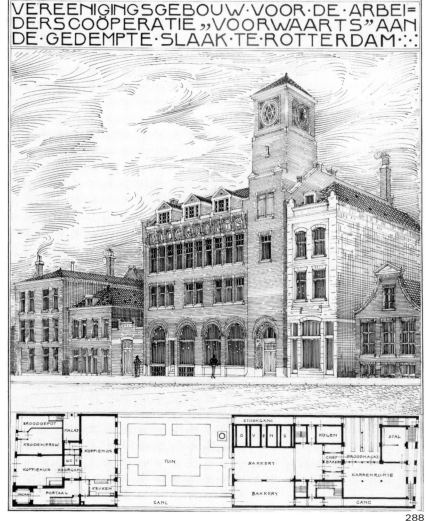

288

Design for an apartment house for the De Dageraad

with Hartkamp
Amsterdam, Nieuwe Tolstraat/
Toldwarstraat/Tolstraat
Commissioned by the building co-
operative of De Dageraad
1907

289. Study of the elevations.

289

Hingst House

Amsterdam, Koninginneweg 18
Commissioned by A. Hingst
1907

Bibliography: cfr. *De Bouwwereld*,
1908, 15, ill. p. 115.

*290. Exterior view, contemporary
photograph.*

290

Commissioned by the Municipality
of The Hague
1907–11

In 1902 engineer I. A. Lindo, director
of the public works office of The
Hague since its inception in 1890,
was asked to prepare a "general development plan" of the city according
to the town-planning guidelines contained in the recently approved
Woningwet law. His conception was
the polar opposite of the one Berlage
prepared for Amsterdam South.
Lindo designed a schematic plan in
the French style to define the principal road network along already existing lines. The absence of specific
zoning uses and public parks necessarily meant the area would be used
by private enterprise. Submitted in
1903, the plan was strongly criticized,
making formulation of a more detailed plan for the Laakwijk area necessary. This plan was completed in
1906 but was not deemed wholly sat-
isfactory. After heated comparison
between Lindo's and Berlage's plans,
at the proposal of Liberal-Democratic
city councillor J. Jurriaan Kok, a
friend of Berlage's and public works
commissioner from 1913 until 1919,
the municipal council decided that a
new general town plan was to be
drawn up "in agreement with the director of the public works office."
The plan was to be entrusted to an
expert in town planning, in other
words, to Berlage. He was officially
appointed to the task in March-April
1907, and he worked swiftly. The
new plan was presented in December
1908 and approved by the municipal
council in 1911. It was ratified by
Parliament in 1913. The plan partially exceeded the town's boundaries
and could be considered quite complex. As Van Eesteren shrewdly recognized, Berlage's was not a "general"
plan but a well-conceived chain of
partial plans. "The modern town plan
will be, therefore, the sum of sectorial
plans, in other words, a system of
regularly structured cells," noted
Berlage, as he associated the problem

with the criteria of "harmonic
assembly."

A continuous band of neighborhoods circles the city from west to
east, around the public park located
to the south. In the growing northern
sector, the sparse construction left
room for the large city park. On plots
of land largely outside the city's
boundaries to the east, Berlage made
a rather unconvincing and, perhaps,
opportunistic citation. He reinterpreted K.P.C. de Bazel's design for
a "world capital" sponsored by the
Foundation for Internationalism,
which is an octagonally shaped "ideal
city," as a garden city (cfr. A.W.
Reinink, *K.P.C. de Bazel*, Leyden,
1965; G. Gresleri and D. Matteoni,
La città mondiale, Venezia, 1982).

"The modern city," Berlage declared, "will be the plastic expression
of the democratic idea. This idea entails regular and broad streets . . . but
it also entails blocks with the most
favorable layout and siting for their
inhabitants. The streets meet in the
squares, which are the junctions and
nerve centers of traffic. But the
squares must also continue to perform
their age-old function of assuring a
proper site for public buildings."
Even more than in his plan for Amsterdam, in the Hague plan the traffic
and road patterns played a fundamental role. The major crossing axes
met in rings. In the neighborhoods
diagonal axes converged in the
squares, emphasizing the orthogonal
fabric of the buildings, which were
aligned in a variety of ways. Berlage
stated, "It is a misconception to hold
that the town planner's task is limited
to defining the street system . . . The
town planner must have a mental
picture of the different types of cities,
squares, streets and parks that will
grow out of his designs. But the town
planner will not limit himself to this
because, in the majority of cases, he
will commit to paper his architectural
ideas to make the builder take them
into consideration." The systematic
use of perspective views revealed the
continuous scale of Berlage's design
methods. He was always careful to
interpret the cityscape in precise architectural dimensions. The art of the
town planner consisted, he believed,

"in the creation of images of the city."
Brinckman's opening statement in the
1909 publication of the plan in
Bouwkunst is even more explicit:
"Stadte bauen heisst mit dem Hausmaterial Raum gestalten." The exposition of the plan described the
areas destined to be used as parks,
exhibition space, cemeteries, rail-
ways, barracks, and, with veiled
skepticism, it referred to de Bazel's
design. It lingered on the epicenters
of the city, the squares: for bathing,
for the theater, for the people, for the
museums, for the city government.
Extraordinary perspective views were
drawn for each of these squares.
They were the fruit of Berlage's
imagination of "urban places" jotted
down in a number of fascinating
sketches.

After working on the town plan of
The Hague, Berlage committed himself to spreading the results of his research in this sector through lessons
and lectures. Associated with this was
his augmented professional and financial status. To quell the polemical
concluding remark in his exposition
of the plan ("I never thought they
would treat my plan purely in bud-
getary terms"), the municipal government of The Hague awarded him
an honorarium of 12,000 florins,
while he received 2,500 florins for the
first draft of his plan for Amsterdam
South.

Berlage's plan kept in step with
The Hague's urban development until the 1940's. While it was not realized to the letter, it certainly was in
its structural principles. But the ar-

291

chitectural fantasies suggested in his perspective views were left in the limbo of the designs. The municipal government called on Berlage repeatedly in subsequent years. He resided in his own home in The Hague from 1914 on, and he was given a number of prestigious commissions including the museum and the town hall. He was also called upon as a consultant on sensitive issues such as the redesigning of the western area of the city in 1921, around which controversy swirled until the end of the decade, and the design of the Gevangenpoort in 1924–25. Thus, Berlage's enduring role in defining the urban image was recognized by the city.

Bibliography: Berlage 1909, *Het uitbreidingsplan . . .*; P.H.S. 1909; Berlage 1910, *Der Haagsche . . .*; Bakker Schut 1927; Blijstra 1970; Smit 1983; also cfr. *De Nieuwe Courant* April 1905; *De Bouwwereld* 1907, pp. 99 and 132; *Het Vaterland* March 25, 1907.

291. *Perspective sketch published in* Studies over bouwkunst, stijl stijl en samenleving, *Rotterdam, 1910.*

Project for the Beethovenhuis

Bloemendaal
Commissioned by
the Het Beethovenhuis Music
Foundation
1907–08

In 1902 music critic Paul Marsop began his battle in Germany on behalf of the reform of concert halls with the publication of "Der Musiksaal der Zukunft" in *Die Musik*. His crusade was parallel to the fight being waged by Georg Fuchs for a revolution in the theater. Marsop proposed a typology more concerned with the ear than the eye: The audience should be able to concentrate on the music without being disturbed by a view of the orchestra. The architecture must be simple and tranquil to strengthen the effect of the music. In particular, the musicologist prescribed that the hall should be oval and have no galleries, balconies, or boxes, and the orchestra should remain invisible to allow the audience to feel part of a spiritual unity. Marsop also called for construction of a "Beethovenhalle." His ideas were widely discussed in *Die Musik*. In 1907 the periodical published "Der Tempel, das apollinische Kunstwerk der Zukunft" by Ernst Haiger, in which the author explained his design for a "Symphoniehaus." The Munich architect believed that the fusion between the symphony and the Greek temple would translate into a celestial "Gesamtkunstwerk." As he conceived his design, the architect was inspired by Beethoven. He would use the text of the chorus of the Ninth Symphony, drawn from Schiller's "Ode to Joy," to decorate the interior of the "Symphoniehaus." The "characters" in Beethoven's various symphonies would be represented on the beams of the trusses.

The widespread admiration of Beethoven and his music was also at the heart of "Temple à la pensée, dedié à Beethoven," which F. Garas published in a brochure of the same year, 1907, *Mes Temples*. This was an attempt to translate the rhythm of Beethoven's music into an architectural entity, although not a concert hall. Such veneration for the German composer could be explained in a 1909 article published in *Die Musik*, "Beethoven als Kulturmacht" by Paul Bekker, which represented Beethoven as a Promothean figure.

In the Netherlands Willem Hutschenruyter, editor of the periodical *Toonkunst*, led the drive to found Het Beethovenhuis and to build it on the dunes of Bloemendaal, west of Haarlem. In 1906–1907, *Die Musik* reported Hutschenruyter's initiative and published a preliminary study by Berlage. Haiger, who for some time had been attempting to translate Marsop's ideas into an architectural design, probably learned of it and traveled to Amsterdam to offer Hutschenruyter his solution. From a letter Haiger wrote to Hutschenruyter in August 1907 it can be inferred that the latter invited him to visit Berlage, who had been entrusted with the commission. In any case, it seems improbable that Berlage would have warmed to the idea of collaboration. After their meeting Haiger decided to publish his design, dated 1906, with a lengthy commentary. This furnished Berlage with topics for debate at the conference on German concert halls held in 1908 at the Delft student association. As might have been expected, Berlage expressed a negative opinion of Haiger's eclectic

292. *Study of the plan and façade of the first version.*

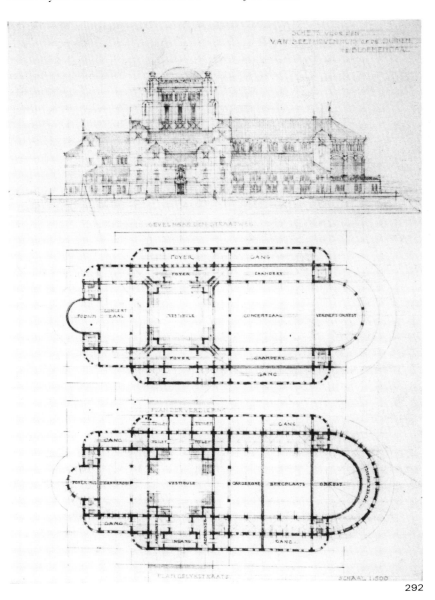

292

bent, on his use of Classicism, and
on the heaviness of mystical symbolism in his presentation. In turn,
Berlage's ideas were criticized by Jan
de Meijer, who felt that by giving
pride of place to the formal problems,
Berlage overlooked the laws of
acoustics. Berlage made no direct reply. Only in 1911, when he repeated
the same lecture, did he defend himself, declaring he expressly refused
"to involve himself in questions of
acoustics" because he was unquali-
fied. Haiger had revived the controversy a year earlier with publication
of *Tempel und Symphonie*, which presented a simplified version of his design. In it, he abandoned the "Greek
style" and recognized the merits of
the site proposed by Hutschenruyter.

294

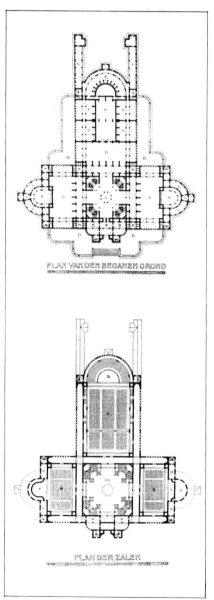

PLAN VAN DEN BEGANEN GROND

PLAN DER ZALEN

293

HET BEETHOVENHUIS

295

In the Netherlands, Berlage's definitive design of 1907 was published the following year by the specialized journals and by *Het Beethovenhuis*, edited by Hutschenruyter. Like many of Berlage's monumental designs, the imposing structure of Bloemendaal could be considered a Volkshuis where both intellectuals and workers could fraternize, thanks to music, amidst the harmony of architecture. A place for reflection and pacification, far from the noise of the city, the Beethovenhuis became a cultural edifice immersed in the purifying action of the sandy dunes. It could be considered a sort of Byzantine mosque of music, where culture and nature met and merged in a harmonic ideal unity. By no coincidence, the options in the different designs made it, in certain respects, a "variation" on the Vredespaleis. The metaphor of an edifice destined to illuminate the world, indicating with its shining light the road to the future, was made explicit by the four immense braziers at the corners of the dome, as well as by adoption of Haiger's idea of a frieze with the "Ode to Joy" from Beethoven's Ninth Symphony in the majestic basilical auditorium. Equally significant was the citation of Tolstoy's motto for the brochure edited by Hutschenruyter: "As long as the merchants are not expelled, the temple of art will not be a temple. But the art of the future will not drive them out." The critics were divided over the design. Some admired it; others condemned it for trivial reasons. A certain J.G. (presumably Jan Gratama, who wrote an important monograph on Berlage in 1925) expressed the most interesting opinion. In a typological analysis of the building he decried the scarcely functional solution of the atrium stairway, comparing the architecture, steeped in "truth, monumentality and severity," to a tree with an imposing trunk but no leaves. (H.v.B.)

Bibliography: J.G. 1908; Hutschenruyter 1908; red. 1908, *Het Beethovenhuis*; C.J.S. 1908; Huszar 1922; also cfr. *De Architect* XVII, 1910, plates 637–42.

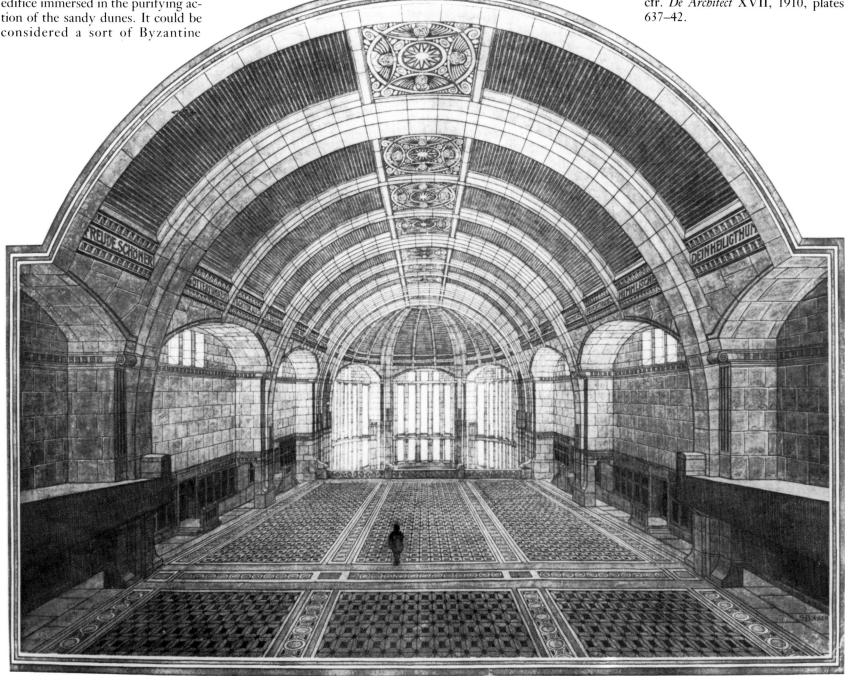

296

293. *Plan of the ground floor and of the rooms of the final project; drawing published in* De Architect, *in 1910.*

294. *Perspective view.*

295. *Model, contemporary photograph.*

296. *Main auditorium, perspective view.*

Amsterdam, 16 Gabriël Metsustraat
Commissioned by the Association
Dagteeken- en Kunstambachtsschool
voor meisjes, with public funds
1908

In 1908 Berlage designed the girls' vocational school, situated near the Concertgebouw in the "museum zone." Construction began in March of the same year and ended in August, so the day courses in drawing and the applied arts could begin on schedule in September.

It is a three-story building. The top floor is a mansard. The building also has a mezzanine between the ground and first floors. The rectangular layout was conceived to correspond to the requirements for classrooms and workshops. The entrance is placed asymmetrically on the street façade and is aligned with the interior by a large arched niche recessed in the façade. The thermal window of the storeroom faces out of the lunette on the mezzanine and is reached by a stairway inside the janitor's lodge at the side of the ground-floor vestibule. The double-height classrooms for the drawing and applied arts courses are located on the ground floor in the front. The classrooms for carving and clay modeling are located in the rear of the building, near the parlor and the janitor's apartment. The latter is directly connected from within to a room on the mezzanine. In the rear of the vestibule, next to the bathrooms, a double-ramp stairway leads to the floor above. At the first landing there is, to one side, a living room on the mezzanine reserved for the headmistress. Next to it is a darkroom.

The school office is situated on the first floor, on the vertical axis of the main entrance. There are also classrooms for drawing and painting. A teachers' room and two classrooms for lectures are located in the rear.

The second floor is used for applied arts courses. There are classrooms for geometric and style drawing, lithography, and bookbinding, as well as space for workshops. In the attic, the atelier is lit by a skylight.

The building is inserted into a continuous curtain of edifices facing the street. The main façade is done in exposed brick. Stone inserts highlight the parapets of the windows, the archivolts, and the imposts of the entrance niche. A thin band of stone runs around the base of the building. A mosaic bearing the school's name runs beneath the eaves.

The asymmetrical placement of the entrance marks the pause between the binary and tertiary modules to either side. Each module groups four windows of the double-height classrooms. This vertical rhythm is highlighted by the alignment of the front classrooms on the second floor with the dormers. The dormers have large windows and a flat roof. Their tight sequential arrangement borders the sloping surface of the roof on the second floor.

Bibliography: red. 1908, *Dagteeken-
. . .* ; red. 1909, *Dagteeken-. . . .*

DAGTEEKEN- EN KUNSTAMBACHTSSCHOOL VOOR MEISJES
TE AMSTERDAM, GABRIËL METSUSTRAAT 14. ♣ ARCH. H. P. BERLAGE N.ZN.
GEOPEND 18 SEPTEMBER 1908.

297

297. *Perspective view.*

298. *Entrance, contemporary photograph.*

298

Design of the Façades of a Residential Complex

With A.J. Tymensen
Amsterdam, 163–213 Sarphatistraat/
Valckenierstraat/Pancrasstraat 1908

Temporary Exhibition Pavilions for the "Huis Industrie" Show

With J. van Straaten
Amsterdam, 26 Hobbemakade/
Hobbemastraat/Vermeerstraat/
Honthorstraat
1909

The drawings show a covered exhibition area and a series of large circular benches in the open spread over a vast area of ground. In particular, there is a horse-shoe-shaped auditorium with an octagonal gazebo in the center for an orchestra, along with a series of perimetral exposition spaces.

299. Study of the main elevation.

300. Present state.

301. Drawing of the project.

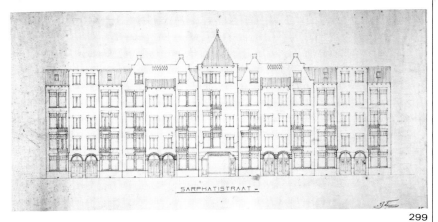

299

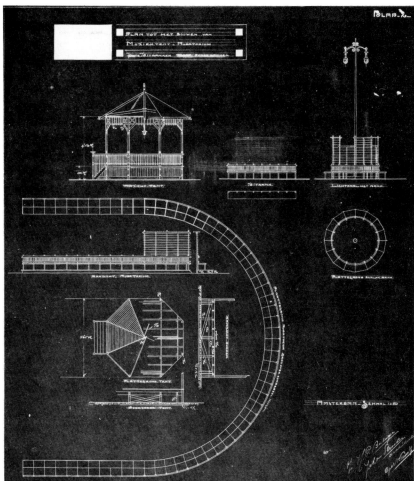

301

300

With J. van Epen
Bergen aan Zee
Commissioned by the Nassau-Bergen
N.V. Company
1908–09 and 1912–13

Thanks to the entrepreneurial activity of Jacob van Reenen, president of the committee for the development of Bergen aan Zee and mayor of the town since 1908, this out-of-the-way place situated amidst the North Sea dunes became the most prestigious bathing resort in the Netherlands in the years preceding the war.

An initial plan was commissioned from garden architect L.A. Springer between 1906 and 1907. His design of 140 villas set in two large parks was rejected, and Van Reenen called on Berlage early in 1908 to plan the complex in the context of the town. Berlage was also asked to supervise the "aesthetics" of the new constructions. Documents in the architect's archives regarding Bergen aan Zee also refer to his work on two boarding-houses, the Juliana and the Wilhelmina, and on the railway station.

At the same time, Berlage was involved with enlarging the Nassau-Bergen Hotel, in a not coincidental association with Van Epen. Designed by Van Epen, the original nucleus consisted of a café-restaurant with a room. It had been inaugurated in July 1907. Work to enlarge the building began in late March 1909 and ended in late June, coinciding with inauguration of the Bergen-Bergen aan Zee railway.

In a preliminary study, the hotel was divided into three floors with a broad, pitched roof. The long linear layout had a central hallway around which the rooms were arranged. On the western façade facing the sea, the recessed rooms were fitted with balconies. These balconies were supported by small, forked pilasters which ran uninterruptedly between the small towers housing the service stairs and the block housing the hall and main stairway. On the ground floor, a semicircular oriel window with a conical roof was used as a common room.

The executed design was essentially identical to the earlier one in terms of the typological conception of the principal portion of the structure. The horizontal extension was reduced, but this was offset by the addition of another story above the roofing that covered the balconies. The addition of a broad panoramic terrace required the almost total elimination of the pitched roof. Concomitantly, the diversity of the lateral annex housing the common rooms, kitchen, and bathrooms was highlighted. In both versions, the option to enlarge the building was implicit. In fact, in 1912–13 Berlage and Van Epen doubled the hotel's volume along the symmetrical axis of the structure housing the principal stairway, increasing the number of rooms from 39 to 77. The only asymmetrical element was the small bell tower at the end of the block containing the service stairway of the first enlargement. In 1927, P. Elders enlarged the café-restaurant to include a dance hall.

In 1909 Berlage presented Van Reenen with a color aerial view of the town from the east, facing the sea, at the conclusion of his consultantship for the town. It shows the principal nucleus of buildings grouped around a square marked by a church bell tower. In the background, the small railway station and the Nassau-Bergen Hotel can be recognized in a rendition that heralded the 1912–13 enlargement, although it lacks the lower annex at the end of the north side.

A closer perspective design shows the double residence Berlage constructed on the Kerkstraat in 1909. The building has since undergone substantial renovation, but in Berlage's rendering the typology was simple and traditional. Entrances and stairways were situated on the eastern and western façades, with living rooms and kitchens to the south and north on the ground floor. Two bedrooms were located on the upper floor. On the façade facing the street, the linked gables gave the entire con-

struction a segmented profile. The central chimneys, leaning against the party wall running east–west, rise obliquely to reconcile the position at the top of the roof with the requirements of interior circulation.

In the 1909 design the reference to the Sterkenhuis, a historic building in nearby Bergen, is evident. In that same year, Berlage designed a post office in the vicinity of the Sterkenhuis. The building had two floors and an attic with a pitched roof. The principal façade was done in exposed brick and divided into two parts. One echoes the dentellated profile of the

302. Study of the plan and façade of the first version.

303. Exterior, contemporary photograph after enlargement.

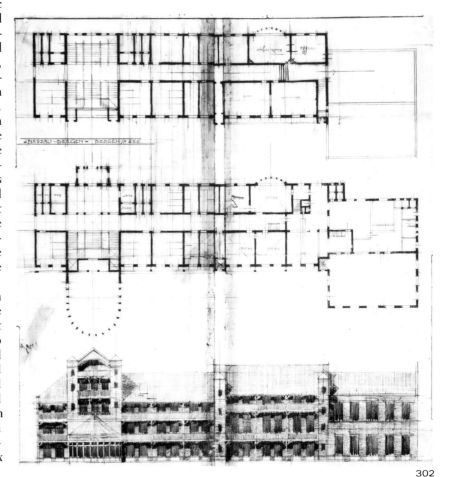

302

303

Double Residence

Concert Hall

Sterkenhuis; in the other, the alignment of the rectangular openings was interrupted by the entrance arch.

The town plan of Bergen aan Zee was completed in the late 1930s. In August 1943, a Raumungkommissar of the occupying German army blew up the Nassau-Bergen Hotel along with other buildings creating an obstacle to the defense of the "Atlantic wall". Post-war reconstruction and the elimination of the railway in the mid-1950s (and the consequent demolition of the station) definitely perverted the urban plan Berlage had envisioned.

Bibliography: Jellema 1981.

Bergen aan Zee, Kerkstraat
1909

The drawing from the Berlage archives is dated 1909.

Bibliography: Jellema 1981.

Venlo, Prinsenstraat/
55 Kaldenkerkweg
Commissioned by
the Prins van Oranje Company
1909–10

In February 1910, the municipality of Venlo was asked to issue a construction license for a concert hall with a café and adjoining custodian's residence based on a design by Berlage. Venlo was an ancient stronghold on the right bank of the Meuse River near the German border. The building consisted of a long structure for the concert hall, a small entry tower—a visual articulation of the layout—and a smaller structure for the café. The café turned at a right angle and had windows on the first floor. The building, today clumsily modified, was constructed after the demolition of a rather similar structure on the site. The designs preserved in the Berlage archives are dated January–May 1910.

304. Design plan.

305. Perspective sketch.

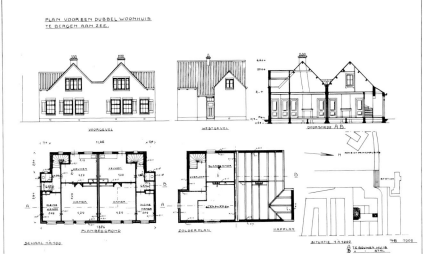

304

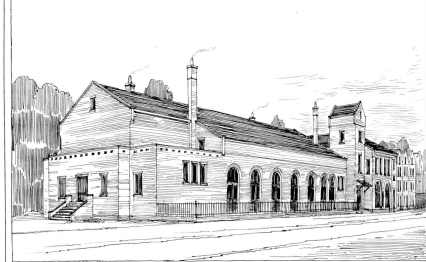

305

Bergen
1909

The drawings preserved in the Berlage archives are dated January–June
1909.

Bibliography: Jellema 1981.

306

306. Perspective view.

307. Exterior, contemporary photograph.

307

Baarn, 1 De Beaufortlaan/
Kroningslaan
Commissioned by H. Salomonson
1909–10

The drawing preserved in the Berlage
archives is dated March 1910. The
villa no longer exists.

Bibliography: Berlage 1913, Landhuis. . . .

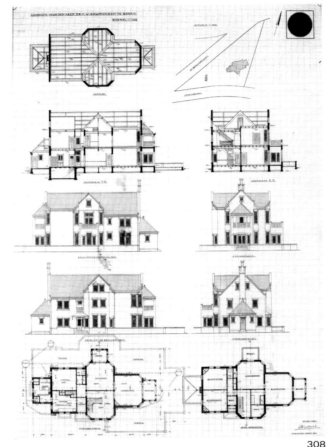

308

310

308. *Design plan.*

309. *Exterior, contemporary photograph.*

310. *Exterior, contemporary photograph.*

309

The Hague, Scheveningen
Commissioned by the Committee
for the Theater of the Hague
1910

Berlage's abiding interest in the theater, also expressed in his unpublished drawings, was integral to a conception of the place as a fundamental element in urban life. According to a very popular opinion among exponents of the Deutsche Werkbund, the theater had to contribute to the diffusion of a sense of solidarity among citizens. This sense of solidarity was the outgrowth of "Gemeenschapskunst," the art of the community. For Berlage, then, the theater fulfilled a function of spiritual education.

In this respect, Berlage's proposal in the town plan of The Hague for a theater situated either on the Raamweg, northeast of the residential area, or to the east, was perfectly coherent. He illustrated the Raamweg proposal with a significant aerial view, but both versions remained on paper. In those same years the Dutch government was debating the issue of the Schouwburg, which preeminently concerned the demolition of the old royal theater on the Voorhout and a successor to it on the same site. But even the design presented in 1912 by the Viennese architects Fellner and Helmer, who specialized in theaters, aroused little enthusiasm.

Berlage did not participate in the debate directly. His design for a Wagnertheater in The Hague, presumably commissioned by members of the theater committee, could, however, be considered an indirect reply. Its intent was to circumvent demolition of the old theater. He situated his theater in Scheveningen, The Hague's seaside suburb resort, so the building could be surrounded by a park. The two terraces placed between the foyer, entrance, and restaurant afforded a lovely view of the undulating dunes.

For his Wagnertheater, Berlage predictably adopted the typology of the Bayreuth theater. It had been de-signed by Otto Bruckwald with Richard Wagner and echoed the features of the Wagnerian Festspielhaus in Munich, which Gottfried Semper had conceived with an immense stage and an amphitheater-shaped auditorium with neither galleries nor loggias. In a 1907 lecture, Max Littmann spoke of the motives behind the design of a circular hall. "From the very outset," he declared, "we realized that if the auditorium was to provide a meaningful expression of the 'Volkstheater' even in architectural terms, it could only have had the form of an amphitheater, a form in which all differences of rank and class are abolished, while the principle of democracy is, it can be said, symbolized by equal seating rights."

One of the most praiseworthy aspects of the Wagnertheater was its seating capacity of 1,500, in addition to the guests in the royal box, while allowing the stage to be fully visible. There is no evidence that Berlage was aware of the most recent developments in German theaters, promoted, above all, by Fuchs, Littmann, and Endell. One of these developments involved, for example, locating the wardrobe next to the auditorium. Still, Berlage could have been familiar with Littmann's design, which had been published by Fuchs in *Die Schaubühne der Zukunft*. The interior design also revealed the adoption of decorative elements borrowed from Littmann, who was known especially for two Munich theaters, the Prinzregententheater (1901) and the Kunstlertheater (1908).

The linguistic elements of the front elevations, with elements from Bramante, call to mind the theater sketched in the perspective of the Hague town plan, although the volumes differ. Conversely the plan of the Wagnertheater was adopted by Berlage two years later in Amsterdam's Kunstenaarshuis. (H.v.B.)

Bibliography: red. 1911, Bayreuth . . . ; red. 1911, Het Wagner-. . . .

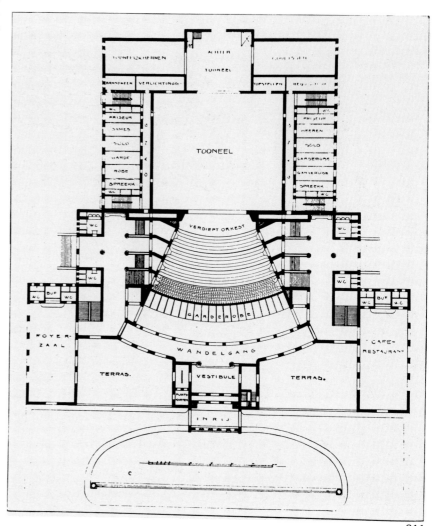

311

311. *Plan.*

312. *Perspective view.*

313. *View of the auditorium.*

Brussels, World Fair
1910

Berlage designed a small meeting
room, accurately illustrated in the
color drawing in his archives.

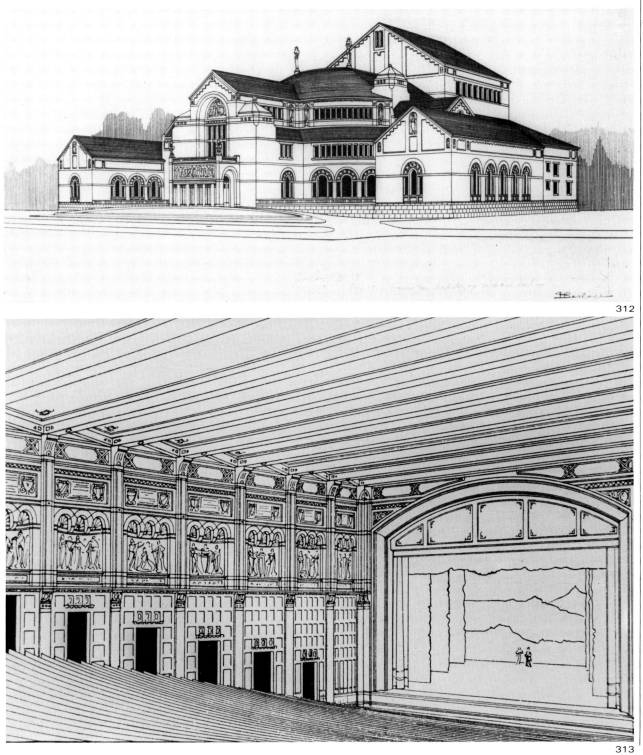

312

313

Ede
1911

Commissioned by the Municipality
of Purmerend
1911

In 1911 Berlage designed a partial
development plan on a square plot
south of the historic center for the
municipality of Purmerend, a small
town north of Amsterdam.

The north side of the plot was
closed off by a canal, whose bends
follow the ancient layout of the bastions. The remaining sides were
ringed by broad lanes with trees. The
area was arranged with a herringbone
road system. The main road ran on
a diagonal axis and routed the traffic
heading from the historic center toward the projected station square at
the southern tip. Sliced into two offset segments, this axis created a "pin-
wheel"-shaped square which Berlage
frequently employed at traffic junctions. It became the pivot around
which the whole layout rotated and
simultaneously introduced a variation
in the street alignments. The lanceo-
late shape of the entire plan thus har-
monized with the morphology of the
town walls.

314. Design plan.

315. Drawing of the development plan.

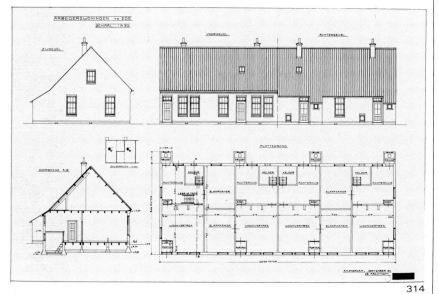

314

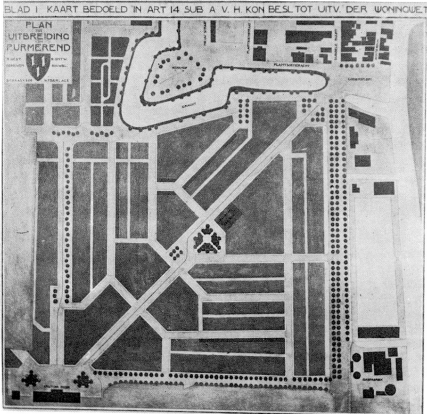

315

Rotterdam, Zuidblaak/Molsteeg
Commissioned by
the De Nederlanden van 1845
Insurance Company
1911

Berlage designed the third building for the insurance company in Rotterdam simultaneously with the enlargement of the company's building in Amsterdam, in the vicinity of Beursplein. The company utilized only a part of the building; the rest was rented out.

The building was erected on a trapezoidal plot. In the back, a small appendix of the same shape, slightly off axis to it, faces Molsteeg, a lane running orthogonally to Zuidblaak. The building had five floors. On the ground floor were a shop and a storeroom. Three floors were used for offices and were crowned by an attic. The entrance to the ground-floor shop was to the left of the two large windows, which were tapered to give the shop layout a regular shape. The shop was lit in the rear by a skylight in the inner courtyard. The entrance hall to the offices was on the opposite end of the main façade, toward Molsteeg. It penetrated the building parallel to the shop, with a single ramp stairway leading to the janitor's lodging. The stairway was lit by another skylight from above. The vestibule of the stairway was situated at this point, in the rear appendix of the building, and had an elevator. There were two types of offices on the middle three floors. One type measured some 180 square meters and had two views, one on the main façade, the other on the inner courtyard. The other type measured some 50 square meters and had a single, terraced view toward Molsteeg.

The building had an ashlar base of light Bavarian granite. Figures inspired by the company's activity, such as the phoenix rising from the ashes, were sculpted on the entrance pilasters and architraves. Similar decorations adorned the entrance hall and the stairways. L. Zijl, Berlage's long-time associate, created the sculptures; W. Brouwer created the

tiles. Series of rectangular openings gave the façade rhythm. The façade was done in exposed red brick with granite inserts for the window sills and marking the static joints. The two columns of oriel windows at either end were the outstanding feature of the Zuidblaak façade. Bent like the prows of a ship, the oriels were crowned by triangular gables edged in granite, which supported two bas-reliefs. One represented death, the other the evil spirit of fires. This choice of images probably grew out of a superstitious reconsideration of the emblem with a crowned lion grasping a sword in its fist described in the color perspective drawing of the building.

A sketch preserved in the Berlage archives suggests there was a prior conception of the building. The elements in the perspective view are analogous, but the treatment is more traditional. There is a base with closed arched windows, a single side entrance, three floors of offices, attics with four triangular dormers, and acroteria with friezes and winged sculptures. After the fire caused by

316

316. Preliminary study for the coping.

317. Exterior, contemporary photograph.

the German aerial bombardment of the center of Rotterdam in 1940, the building was demolished.

In 1911–12, immediately after the Rotterdam building was completed, Berlage constructed another building for the company in Nijmegen, the oldest city in the Netherlands, near the German border. In this building, he returned to frequently tested architectural solutions. They were clearly more reminiscent of the De Algemeene company's building in Leipzig (1901–1902), also because of the layout, than of the almost contemporary Rotterdam edifice. The

Nijmegen building was characterized by the original vertical rhythms of the very high blades of the chimneys and by the recessed angular tower. In the treatment of the surfaces, Berlage controlled the fusion of the elements with particular skill, and brick and stone were amalgamated in a very measured decorative arrangement. The building was destroyed in 1944, during the war.

Bibliography: Berlage 1911, Kantoorgebouw . . . ; also cfr. De Bouwwereld 1911, 42, p. 333.

317

199

Nijmegen, Mariënburgplein
Commissioned by
the De Nederlanden van 1845
Insurance Company
1911–12

Santpoort
Commissioned by the Consortium
for the Monogram Construction
Company
1911

In 1909 an American–Dutch joint venture company was formed in New York by G.E. Small, H.J. Harms, Jr., and H. Hana to promote the construction of homes in poured concrete based on a patent by Edison.

Berlage had been interested in the possibilities of this new building material since the beginning of the century, as his remarks at the 1904 Madrid congress demonstrate. The Dutch consortium financing the venture hired him as the "aesthetic" consultant, a role to which he was accustomed. In 1911 the first experimental home was built in Santpoort, just north of Haarlem.

The Monogram company's construction system called for the erec-

tion of the entire building in castiron molds, with spaces left for openings. The forms were filled with poured concrete material and subsequently dismantled, freeing a monolithic covering. When the work was completed, the walls were marked by the thin lines of the mold joints. The international nature of the venture was ratified in the official photographs by the American and Dutch flags waving from the roof of the workshop on the construction site.

The results of the experiment did not prove wholly reliable. The undertaking also encountered other adverse conditions that prevented it from continuing. The necessary equipment was costly, and the brick industry, producer of the traditional Dutch building material, opposed it.

Bibliography: red. 1911, Het gegoten . . . ; Van Doesburg 1918.

318. Exterior, contemporary photograph.

318

319

319. Photograph of the construction site; Berlage is in the center of the group of three.

320. Contemporary photograph at the conclusion of the work.

320

Amsterdam West, Staatsliedenbuurt.
Hugo de Groot I straat
(today Rombout Hoogerbeetstraat)/
7–13 Zaagmolenstraat/
Hugo de Groot II straat
(today Gillis van Ledenberchstraat)
Commissioned by
the De Arbeiderswoning
Construction Company
1911–15

Between 1911 and 1913, before signing an exclusive contract with the Kröller-Müller family, Berlage designed a number of low-income residences in Amsterdam. He designated this type of building a "necessity of our times." These buildings were all characterized by the grand scale of the structure. They were a key feature of the aerial perspectives of the second town plan of Amsterdam South. The five entries that follow are also part of this series. The commissioners were two of the largest building societies in the sector. They were recognized and approved by the Woningwet, the innovative housing law passed at the turn of the century but active only from the second decade, as more favorable economic conditions changed the fortunes of the construction industry. Today, the Algemeene Woningbouwvereeniging is still the principal Social Democratic building society in the Netherlands. Berlage designed some 400 residences for the society in three different complexes. For the De Arbeiderswoning, he designed some 200 in two different complexes.

De Heer's essay in this volume gives the best analytical examination of Berlage's mass-housing concepts. The topic has also been explored by Bock in Bock, Broos, and Singelenberg 1975; Searing in AA.VV. 1975, H.P. Berlage . . . ; Singelenberg in AA.VV. 1979–v. Berlage, 1921, Een . . . ; also cfr. Wendingen 1920, 3–4, and Tijdschrift voor Volkshuisversting en Stedebouw 1926, 3.

The drawings of Berlage's first project for the De Arbeiderswoning preserved in his archives are dated November 1912. An undated study, presumably from 1911, with the notations "Plan Arbeiderswoningbouw" and "Sophiaplein," is related to it. The complex was inaugurated in October 1915 and originally was made up of 70 apartments. It was renovated in 1972 by Kelder as part of the city's urban renewal program.

321. Exterior, contemporary photograph.

Amsterdam East, Indischebuurt
Java-/Molukken-/Balistraat
Commissioned by
the De Arbeiderswoning
Building Society
1911–15

The working designs preserved in the Berlage archives are dated July 1912. As in his previous work for the De Arbeiderswoning, Berlage subsequently made a sepia India-ink drawing to illustrate the building.

Because of financial difficulties, the building was constructed only in 1915. It was made up of 169 apartments. In 1972 Kelder completed renovation.

322. Corner, contemporary photograph.

321

322

Low-Income Apartment Complex for the Algemeene Woningbouwvereeniging Building Society

Amsterdam South, 21–53 Tolstraat
Commissioned by the Algemeene Woningbouwvereeniging Building Society
1911–13

There are two versions of the final design in the Berlage archives, one dated June 1911, the other March–April 1912, but the first sketches go back to the end of 1910. The complex was finished May 1, 1913 and is made up of 48 apartments. The average cost of each was 2,187 florins.

Berlage worked on the complex again to complete the section between Tolstraat and Nieuwe Tolstraat (today Pieter Aertszstraat), but it was built only in 1918 under the supervision of J.C. van Epen, who had become the AWV's architect around that time. There are no drawings of this complex in the Berlage archives.

323. *Exterior, contemporary photograph.*

324. *J. van Epen, completion of the plot in 1918, corner, contemporary photograph.*

323

324

Four Low-Income Apartment Complexes for the Algemeen Woningbouwvereeniging Building Society

Amsterdam East, Transvaalbuurt
Ringkade (today Transvaalkade), Complex I; Transvaalstraat (today Transvaalplein), Complex II; Smitstraat/Transvaalstraat/Laing's Nekstraat, Complex III; Transvaalstraat/Smitstraat/Majubastraat, Complex IV
Commissioned by the Algemeene Woningbouwvereeniging Building Society
1911–13

There are two final versions of the design in the Berlage archives, dated June 1911 and April–May 1912, respectively. Berlage also made a sepia India-ink drawing later, for exhibition purposes, as he did for his designs for the De Arbeiderswoning. The complex was completed in 1913 and is composed of 178 apartments. The average cost of each was 2,444 florins, more than that of the Tolstraat complex because of the decision to build part of the complex on a low scale. In 1930, Heineke and Kuipers expanded the complex to 218 apartments. It was renovated again in 1983 by De Kat and Peek.

325. *Exterior, contemporary photograph.*

326. *Drawing of the layout, May 1912.*

With J.C. van Epen
Amsterdam West, Staatslieden-
buurt./Van Hallstraat/
De Kempenaerstraat/
Dr. Schaepmanstraat
Commissioned by the Algemeene
Woningbouwvereeniging Building
Society
1913–19

There are various drafts of the complexes because of modifications in the
street system of the construction
plan. The earliest is dated January
1913, the second August 1913 and a
third was done after further street
variations in 1914. Construction began in 1917. As in the previous projects, modifications were made during
construction by Van Epen, who had
become the official supervisor of the
project. Completed in 1919, the 157
apartments were renovated by the
Geo Company in 1976.

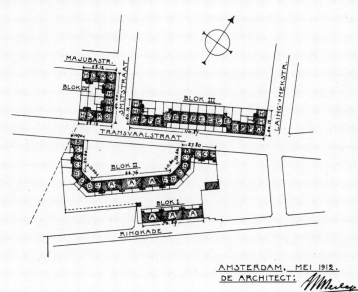

325

326

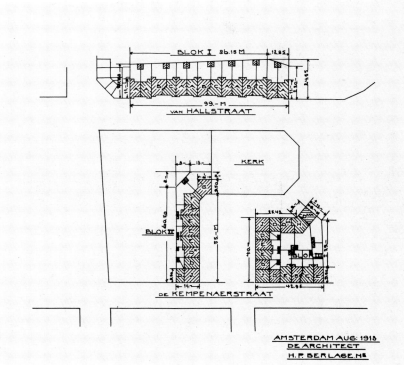

327. Drawing of the layout, August 1913.

327

Two Low-Income Apartment Complexes for the Algemeene Woningbouwvereeniging Building Society

With J.C. van Epen
Amsterdam North, Spreeuwenpark/
Sperweerlaan/
Havikslaan, Leeuwerikstraat/
Nachtegaalstraat
Commissioned by the Algemeene
Woningbouwvereeniging Building
Society
1913–15

The executive designs preserved in the Berlage archives are dated January 1914 and signed by both Berlage and Van Epen, under the notation "architects." This is a correction written over the date October 1912 and the original notation "architect," signed, prior to his contract with the Kröller-Müller family, by Berlage alone. After Berlage moved to The Hague, the project was supervised by Van Epen in a collaborative association that dated back to the building of the Nassau Hotel in Bergen aan Zee. Built in 1915, the complex was enlarged in 1920 to hold 303 apartments. It was renovated in 1984 by the Inbo Company.

Bibliography: Berlage 1918, Over. . . .

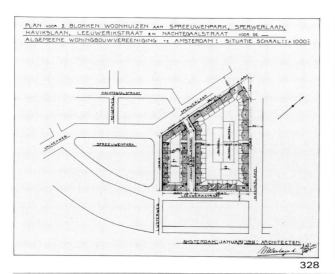

328

329

328. *Drawing of the layout, January 1914 (October 1912).*

329. *Exterior, contemporary photograph.*

330. *Exterior, contemporary photograph.*

330

Project for the Kunstenaarshuis

Amsterdam, Museumplein
and Roelof Hartstraat
Commissioned by
the Verbond van Nederlandsche
Kunstenaarvereenigingen
1911–12

In July 1911, the League of Dutch Art Associations was founded in Amsterdam. The body aimed to unite the various groups of artists—musicians, composers, painters, sculptors, writers, craftsmen, and architects—in order to form a united front to negotiate artists' rights with the Dutch government, to provide cultural consultation to the municipalities and to the state, to promote the exchange of ideas among artists of various disciplines, to organize congresses and conferences, to promote exhibitions and celebrations, to publish a journal, and, finally, to

build a headquarters for the various activities the League was to carry out.

The organizing committee was formed in the spring of 1911 and conducted a survey among the associations to choose an architect to design the headquarters. Berlage and de Bazel (at that time president of the Bond von Nederlandsche Architecten, the main professional association), received a like number of votes. The six members of the committee—J. Van den Bosch, C. Breitenstein, A.D. Loman, H. Robbers, H.L. de Beaufort, and the architect J. Gratama (replaced by W. van Boven because Gratama's association, the Maatschappij tot Bevordering der Bouwkumst, withdrew from the initiative)—finally decided on Berlage.

In agreement with the municipality, a plot in the vicinity of the Rijksmuseum (Honthorststraat/Vermeerstraat/Hobbemastraat) was originally chosen. Berlage's first design refers

to it. After the city reconsidered the choice, the committee decided on a site near the Concertgebouw, which required Berlage to make another draft. The functional requirements of the Kunstenaarshuis entailed at least five rooms for the different artists' groups; a like number of rooms for Amsterdam's art associations needing a headquarters; offices for the copyright association; a large space for theatrical performances that could also be used for congresses and assemblies; rooms for art exhibits; a small concert hall; and a conference room. This variety of requirements, considered a guarantee of success for the initiative, made the architect's task difficult. Berlage's first design suggests he may have drawn some of his ideas from the works of the German architect Martin Dulfer, who had built theaters and cultural centers. In particular, the rounded end bays—an unusual element in Ber-

lage's work—seem to reveal Berlage's German source, although the design of the main façade is, on the whole, reminiscent of the theater depicted in the Hague town plan.

In the version for Roelof Hartstraat, Berlage modified his initial design, although the structure containing the theater remained virtually unchanged. It echoed, in fact, the layout of the Wagnertheater, with the addition of a floor above the auditorium for exhibition rooms. Elevators would lead to these rooms to compensate for their unusual location. To the right of the theater entrance was another rounded structure, which held the large vestibule. This could be considered a sort of covered courtyard and the architectural pivot around which the different functions to be fulfilled by the building could be laid out. Moreover, Berlage was able to add a circular ballroom in an inner corner between the theater and

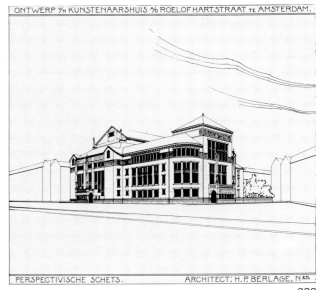

ONTWERP V/H KUNSTENAARSHUIS % ROELOF HARTSTRAAT TE AMSTERDAM.

PERSPECTIVISCHE SCHETS.   ARCHITECT: H.P. BERLAGE, N.B.

332

PERSPEKTIVISCHE SCHETS VAN HET KUNSTENAARSHUIS TE AMSTERDAM

331

331. Perspective study, first version.

332. Perspective sketch, second version.

the annex. The shape of the ballroom is visible on one side of the outer perimeter of the building, reinforcing the mixed line composition of the building. Situated in an open space at the intersection of two important streets of the city's museum quarter, the complex is the focal point of a number of perspectives. The intent was to organize the site in accordance with guidelines found in Camillo Sitte's town-planning theories. In the second version of his plan for the southern area of the city, Berlage conceived a different typology for the Kunstenaarshuis at a junction between the eastern and western sectors. The building would have been facing a basin of water but, like the previous design, it was never realized.

Bibliography: Robbers 1912.

The Henny House

The Hague, Kerkhoflaan/
146 Koninginnegracht
Commissioned by C. Henny
1912

Berlage designed the "house on the canal" for the president of the De Nederlanden insurance company, Carel Henny. It is located to the north of the city's historic center, in the vicinity of the Scheveningen parks. Berlage designed two versions, documented, respectively, by executive drawings dated February 1912 and May 1912. The differences be-

333

tween the two are most marked in the façade and roof designs because of the unusual choice of reinforced concrete in the first version, which would have entailed a flat roof.

The second version had the same layout as the first. Two independent residences (the smaller on the ground floor) use the same entrance at one end of the main façade. A single ramp stairway leads to the residence on the upper floors. On the first floor, the kitchen and living room face the front of the building and the dining room faces the rear. The second floor and the attic are reached by semi-elliptical stairs illuminated laterally by a well. The bedrooms and bathrooms are located there. The executed drawing contains jottings on the various pavement materials—marble, tile, linoleum, and parquet.

Although the conception of the façades is in the tradition of Dutch residential buildings, Berlage reinterpreted certain elements freely, such as the corner oriel window supported by a monolithic butterfly corbel. The granite base tapers to follow variations in the street level. The surface work of the exposed brick façades is majestically woven. The first and second floors are visually contained between two courses of dark brick, separated by a lighter-colored row. This light horizontal marking is repeated on the traditional polygonal façades of the attic gables, marking the boundary of the interior inhabited space.

Bibliography: Blijstra 1971; Boot in AA.VV. 1975, H.P. Berlage. . . .

333. *Present state.*

334. *Design for a reinforced concrete residence, February 1912.*

335. *Drawing of the project as built, May 1912.*

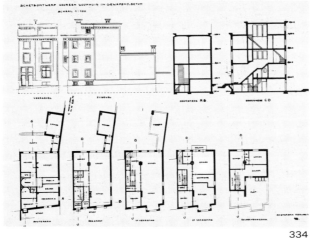

334

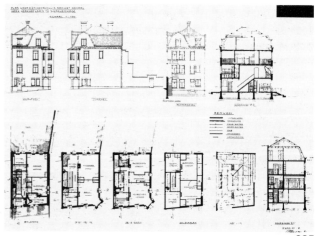

335

Wassenaar, the Ellenwoude Estate
Commissioned by the Kröller-Müller
Family
1912–13

The singular case of the project for a
villa-museum that would involve four
masters of contemporary architecture
over a ten-year period is linked to the
activities of the Kröller-Müller family—magnates, industrialists, and
patrons of the arts. Wm. H. Müller
& Co. was founded in Düsseldorf in
1876 by the German industrialist
Wilhelm Heinrich Müller. Initially,
the company dealt in the sale of fer-
rous materials. The raw material was
purchased in Spain, processed in the
factories of the Ruhr, and shipped on
the Rhine to Rotterdam, where in
1881 the branch in charge of sales and
shipping was opened. Anthony
George Kröller, the younger brother
of Kröller's Dutch partner, worked
as an apprentice in the German
headquarters before returning to
work in the Rotterdam branch in
1883, where he helped his brother,
whose health was failing. In 1888
A.G. Kröller and Hélène E.L.J.
Müller married and took up residence
in Rotterdam. After the death of his
father-in-law in 1889 and his brother's retirement from business, A.G.
Kröller found himself at the head of
a powerful multinational concern.
This economic empire had holdings
in minerals and grain. It owned
mines, a fleet of freight steamships,
docking companies, and an international shipping company.

In 1900 the headquarters of Wm.
H. Müller & Co. was moved to 3
Lange Voorhout, in the center of The
Hague, while the family moved to
Scheveningen, the capital's residential
suburb. Since the turn of the
century, Hélène E.L.J. Kröller-
Müller had enthusiastically devoted
herself to the task of cultural self-
promotion. An assiduous reader of
Kunst und Kunstler, she was familiar
with and admired the Leury and
Henny villas in The Hague, built,
respectively, by Van de Velde and
Berlage. After engaging the "Kun-
stpedagoog" and critic H.P. Bremmer
as her private tutor, she hired him as
a consultant to help her build an ex-

traordinary art collection. Bremmer
was a key figure in the history of
modern art in the Netherlands.

In 1910, after returning from a trip
to Italy, the family decided to build
a modern villa-museum, which
would be a concrete expression of a
"lifestyle" devoted to artistic values.

The site would be on the Ellenwoude
estate, at Wassenaar, just north of
The Hague, which had been bought
expressly for that purpose. Peter
Behrens was the first architect contacted, in February 1911. Behrens
accepted the commission but soon
found himself at odds with the de-

336. P. Behrens, perspective view, 1911.

*337. P. Behrens, perspective study of the
rear of the building, 1911.*

*338. L. Mies van der Rohe, general
perspective view, 1912.*

336

337

338

manding character of his patroness. Mrs. Kröller-Müller expressed more than a few reservations about Behrens' design and felt it clashed with her intentions.

Behrens organized the severe volume of his flat-roofed edifice through the use of two double-height asymmetrical wings of simple geometric shape. One wing was to be reserved for the art collection, the other for the family. The structure connecting the two wings was partially screened by a loggia supported by Doric pilasters. It faced a basin of water.

Because his wife continued to waver, in January 1912 Mr. Kröller proposed solving the matter by building a full-scale mock-up in canvas and wood that would be moved on tracks and examined on site. Mrs. Kröller-Müller's indecision grew, however, and she decided to dismiss Behrens, giving the commission to Ludwig Mies van der Rohe. Perhaps the frequent contacts between Mrs. Kröller-Müller and the young Ludwig Mies van der Rohe, Behrens' chief assistant in designing the villa-museum since mid-1911, played a role in her decision.

Between the spring and fall of 1912, Mies van der Rohe, who had resigned from Behrens' studio, worked in an office, filled with paintings by Van Gogh, of the Wm. H. Müller & Co. in The Hague. His patroness paid him frequent visits.

Although in many respects his design was similar to Behrens', Mies van der Rohe was able to better articulate the long, low profile of the villa-museum. He compressed the central structure and lowered the lateral volumes so they would come into harmony with the natural surroundings gradually. The plan was organized from the north, where the hall and reception room led to the first (west) wing, housing the art collection. The upper floor of the central structure was reserved for the family, while on the ground floor the porcelain gallery led to the south wing. The south wing also housed a hall and a series of exhibition spaces, including the large gallery, which was illuminated by the ribbon of openings in the coping. This area also housed the print collection. Further to the south was an L-shaped courtyard with an arbor, which led to a small storehouse. A second arbor with Doric pilasters connected the two wings of the villa-

museum in the rear, toward the garden. The arbor separated two ponds. The inner pond was smaller than the outer one, in proportion to the outer dimensions of the exhibition wings.

While Mies van der Rohe was working on his design, Berlage was waiting in the wings. With the backing of Bremmer, he was drafting a design of his own for the villa-museum in his Amsterdam studio.

In September 1912 the two proposals were brought together for a confrontation. According to the testimony of Van Deventer, the episode assumed the tones of a verdict. After examining both designs at length, Bremmer pronounced his sentence. Of Berlage's design he declared: "This is art." Of Mies': "This is not art." He then supported his pronouncements with a torrent of reasons. The resistance of Mrs. Kröller-Müller, by then disappointed and exhausted, was overcome by her patient husband, who again suggested employing a full-scale canvas and wood mock-up. Finally, in January 1913, Mrs. Kröller-Müller told her husband she felt Bremmer's opinion was the right one. Far removed from the abstract classicism and citations from Schinkel adopted by the two German architects, Berlage's design for the villa-museum evoked the architectural climate of an abbey. An imposing volume with broad, sloping roofs was molded into a C-shaped layout around a central courtyard. It terminated in the end bays of two asymmetrical structures. Two parallel porticoes connected these structures and closed off the courtyard. The courtyard was laid out in a cruciform module with regular geometric shapes, a motif Berlage frequently adopted to emphasize differences in heights. At the sides of the edifice, two more porticoes bent around themselves in a semi-circle to form a walk that was partially screened toward the outside. At the center of the villa-museum, a small bell tower marked the existence of a rear apse with a projecting veranda above the entrance. In the rear, in the wing reserved for the family (the two edifices with the end bays were designed primarily as exposition spaces), the intense rhythm of the façade was interrupted by the openings of the arches of the loggia, then by the central apse.

Although he defeated Mies van der

Rohe, Berlage himself was defeated by destiny. A license for a tramway with a route prejudicial to Ellenwoude was approved by the Hague town council in 1913, prompting the Kröller-Müller family to abandon the entire initiative.

In any case, the family renewed its contacts with Berlage in the same year. The scandal provoked by Berlage's exclusion from the invitational competition for the new town hall of

339. *Study of the plan with regulating grid.*

340. *Model of the project.*

341. *L. Mies van der Rohe, model of the project, 1912.*

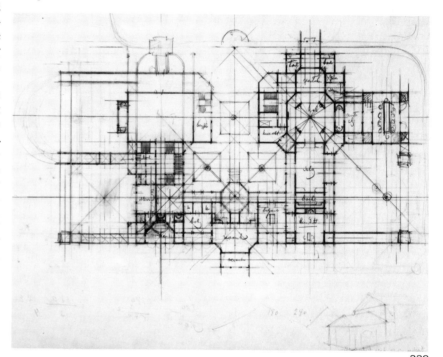

339

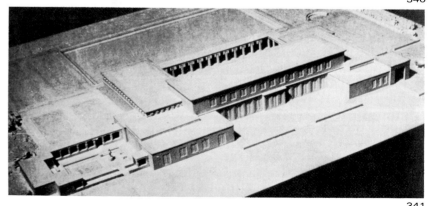

340

341

Rotterdam inspired a generous gesture to compensate him. On September 1, 1913, Berlage became head of the architecture department of the Wm. H. Müller & Co. in Lange Voorhout 1, The Hague, and entered the family service. He was given a ten-year exclusive contract with an annual appanage of 14,000 florins and the obligation to reside in The Hague.

Bibliography: Van Deventer 1956; Oxenaar and Quist 1976; Gunnink 1985; Schulze 1985.

Building for the De Nederlanden van 1845 Insurance Company

Batavia (today Djakarta),
Binnennieuwpoortstraat
Commissioned by
the De Nederlanden van 1845
Insurance Company
1912–13

Between 1912 and 1913 Berlage built the second of his "colonial" edifices in Batavia, capital of the Dutch Indies. His most reliable client, the De Nederlanden van 1845 Insurance Company, commissioned the building. The executive design was ready in March 1913.

The building, with two floors and an attic, was built on a slightly inclined rectangular plot. It leans against another building on one side.

The layout is arranged in depth around the sequence of spaces composed of the entrance, the vestibule, which leads orthogonally to the two offices, and the stairwell, which faces a small inner courtyard. A peculiar feature of the offices is their serial arrangement. They are laid out in the plan like the letter *P*. Each office is independent of the others. The director's office faces the street. There is also a work space that extends to the back of the building and a strong room. The layout is the same on the floor above. The director's office gains the space that belonged to the corridor on the main floor, to balance the corridor used as a loggia. The elevated clear height (over five meters), was designed for the tropical climate. The principal façade is plaster. The

base, pilasters, and shoulders of the arches of the loggia are in stone. Above the entrance, the projecting overhang is decorated with a mosaic frieze bearing the company's name. There is a small tower at either end of the façade, each with a massive stone coping with convex decoration. The towers stand out from the considerably projecting roof, designed to promote the circulation of air in the attic.

The other two façades are even simpler in design. On the lateral façade, the sequence of double-height windows grouped together in the center is protected by the overhangs of the two floors and isolated from the small openings on the sides. On the rear façade, the continuous rhythm of the openings under the overhangs is interrupted in the center because of the smaller size of the bathroom window.

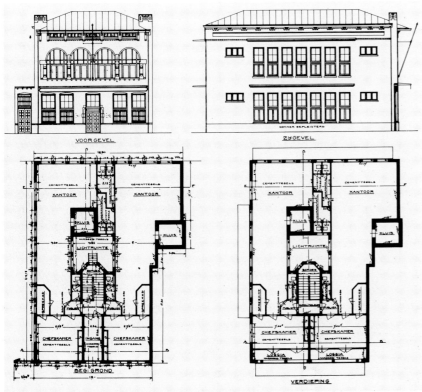

342

343

342. *Plans and façades.*

343. *Exterior, contemporary photograph.*

Amsterdam
1913

Leipzig, International Fair
1913

The Hague, Prinsevinkenpark 42
Commissioned by L. Simons
1913

For the fair, Berlage designed a study. Among the drawings in the Berlage archives, a sketch by J. Wils, Berlage's associate until 1916 and among the founders of De Stijl, illustrates his design.

Bibliography: Berlage 1913, *Reisindruk*.

The balance between orthogonal grid and diagonal inflections that Berlage had achieved in the Villa Henny (1898) marked the high point of a trend that simultaneously led him to a new process in the composition of villas, a process different from the one described in the entry for the Villa Cruys (1894). In 1898, in his design for the villa with atelier in The Hague, probably for Toorop, and in the Villa Scott in Bussum, Berlage partially rotated the geometry of the plans 45 degrees in respect to the car-

344. Study of a section.

345. Contemporary photograph.

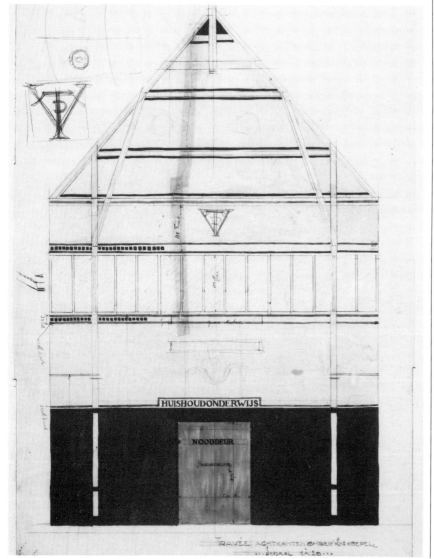

344

345

dinal axes. This is reflected in the irregular shape of the halls of these edifices. In the villa with atelier the vestibule loses its peculiar unity, in part because of a double archway that acts as an inner diaphragm. In the Villa Scott the vestibule has a curiously splayed plan. Although the vestibule maintained its strategic role, it was no longer the center of the house. Instead, it became a sort of quoin able to break up the geometry. In his 1899 design for the Toorop residence at Katwijk aan Zee, Berlage peremptorily recomposed this dismemberment in a controlled system of offset axes and chamfered edges played out within an orthogonal grid. But Toorop was a demanding and, perhaps, penny-pinching client, and the Katwijk aan Zee villa was further simplified during construction. For this reason, very little of the complex intersection of volumes and the bold symmetries of the two previous projects remains.

In 1902 Berlage constructed a small, graceful vacation home for the Hesseling family at Noordwijk aan zee, the same seaside resort in which he had built the Villa Liesbet (1896). In 1903 he enlarged the Hesseling home in Leyden and the Villa De Polberg at Wapenvelde. Different studies of enlargements and restructuring reveal that Berlage did not hesitate to make significant changes in existing houses. Besides the buildings mentioned in the entries, there are other undated drawings scattered throughout the architect's archives. These include the restructuring of the Villa Van Vlissingen in Helmond, the enlargement of a home on Van Meerdervoortlaan in The Hague, the restructuring of the Mees house in Rotterdam, and the new design for the façade of the Touw house.

The novel elements in the designs of 1898–99 reemerged only a few years later. In the Villa Stadwijck (1906), not only the position of the entrance (angled and protected by a small portico) but the entire plan substantially refers to the villa at Katwijk aan zee. Simultaneously, in an early and little-known version (spring 1905) of the Villa Polak at Laren, he reattempted a composition with a corner entrance with greater decisiveness. One of the diagonals of the square plan became the symmetrical axis of the entrance-vestibule unit. The directional nature was emphasized by the cut corner on

the plan and the chamfered 45–degree roof angle above the entrance. The entrance-vestibule axis as the bisection of an angle was, moreover, the dominant feature of the Villa De Dennen of the same date. In this building the disarticulation of the plan took two directions, both hinging on the vestibule and forming a strong obtuse angle. Reduced in volume, the entrance appeared to be gently nestled in a river-bed formed by the two wings of the building.

But even in buildings in which the geometrical composition seemed on the verge of exploding, a regulating grid checked any transgression. In the final group of villas Berlage designed just before he built his own home in The Hague, the recognizable presence of this grid in the studies of plans and façades is, nevertheless, the only unifying element in design experiences that had been concluded.

In the Hingst Home in Amsterdam (1907), the strictly urban siting conditioned the development of the layout in terms of depth and the relationship between the building and the street, which was resolved by linking the projecting entrance to the raised living room.

In the Villa Salomonson at Baarn (1909–10), instead, an unusual telescopic plan characterized by the sharp, longitudinally symmetrical axis unfolded on a large site in relationship to the surrounding environment.

Berlage had built a first villa for Simons at Parkwijck. The second villa, in The Hague, has echoes of Frank Lloyd Wright in the horizontal roof, which translated into the fluid perimetral line of the roof projection. The drawing in the Berlage archives is dated June 1913. This solution was also present in the preliminary version, in reinforced concrete, of the house on the Koninginnegracht in The Hague (1912). This shrewd device, together with the projecting and curved oriel window of the living room in the central portion of the façade of the Villa Simons, softens the potential rigidity of a layout whose apparent symmetry was negated by the shifting of one of the lateral façades of the entrance and by the consequent decentralization of the hall and the stairwell.

Bibliography: for Villa Simons, cfr. *Bouwkundig Weekblad* 1917, 38.

346. Plans and façades.

347. Exterior, contemporary photograph.

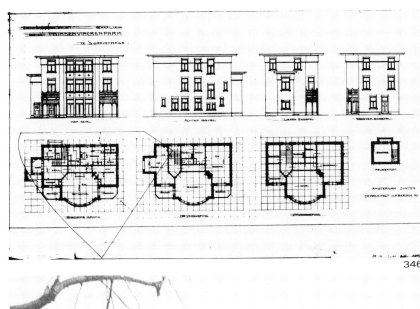

346

347

211

The Berlage Home

The Hague, Violenweg 14
1913–14

The drawing in the Berlage archives
is dated February 1914 and refers to
the architect's home.

348. Design plan.

349. Exterior, contemporary photograph.

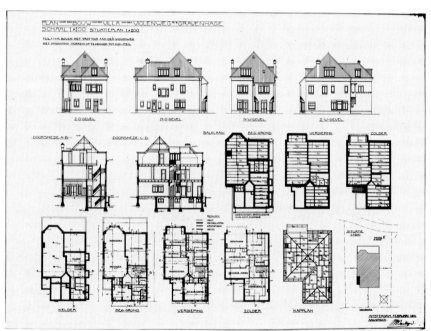

348

349

Study for the Girobank

The Hague, Korte Vijverberg
1913–15 (?)

350. Study of the plan and façade.

350

212

The Hague, Hofweg
Commissioned by the Meddens
en Zoon Company
1913–15

Between 1913 and 1915, Berlage designed a department store in The Hague for Meddens en Zoon, a clothing company. The store is located on Hofweg, a key route between Spui and Buitenhof.

The plot is a rough triangle covering some 1,000 square meters. Part of the area has an irregular perimeter along the side that abuts against the adjacent buildings, especially in the rear. The longest side of the triangle, on Hofweg, is the only real façade.

The layout of the building is governed by a grid. It is based on a 1.65–meter square module that regulates the interior despite the exterior irregularities. Toward Buitenhof, a covered passageway assures only a partial connection to Achterom. The sector of the plan bearing that name (just under 20 percent of the entire surface area) was occupied by the R.S. Stokvis en Zonen stores. Between 1914 and 1915 Berlage did the interior designs for these stores. Several drawings are preserved in his archives. Toward Spui, to the east of the passageway, the building is occupied by the Medden en Zoon stores. The ground-floor layout on the south side was made regular by the layout of small rooms lit directly from above by a skylight. These small rooms were used as fitting rooms. The adjacent departments, which had higher ceilings, were lit from the side by a small, irregular source and also by electrical outlets in the ceiling, since the building is graded toward the interior. The entrances to the department store and, in the center, those to the stairways to the offices on the upper floors were located among the display windows of the main façade on Hofweg. Other entrances to offices and apartments were located in the rear, at the beginning of Achterom.

The elaboration of the plans, dated between May 1913 and February 1914, shows the process Berlage went through in defining the layout. While the principal elements remained unvaried, Berlage did reconsider certain aspects, especially the form and the position of the space housing the main stairwell. Similarly, the study of the façades between June 1913 and June 1914 reveals a progressive refinement. This also holds true for the decoration. In the façade, Berlage defined his original intention to create an interaction between serial forms that enlarge the street façade horizontally and the vertical rhythms of the three monumental pilastered gables standing out from the sloping roof with dormers.

The passage between the refined dark granite base and the light natural stone façade is highlighted by the architrave, in this case a band with lettering bearing the names of the stores. This architrave is supported by the small pilasters of the show windows. The pilasters are supported by a scaled base. The chromatic contrasts were carefully executed.

The bas-reliefs were the work of Lambertus Zijl, Berlage's inseparable comrade in the service of the unity of the arts under the wings of architecture. He created the rams' heads (which are maned in the passageway) which interrupt the festoons under the row of the eaves in the triangular gables and the representation in the rectangular attic decoration.

351. Plan of the ground floor.

352. Exterior, contemporary photograph.

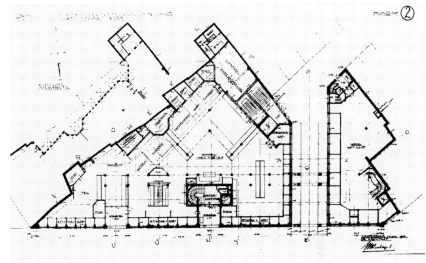

351

352

Rotterdam South
Commissioned by
the Eerste Rotterdamsche Tuindorp
N.V. Company 1913–16

In the Netherlands the idea of the garden-city was conceived on a smaller scale than in other countries, and numerous "Tuindorp," or 'garden-villages," were built. The garden-village of Vreewijk is exemplary in all respects, including its size. Situated beyond the Maas of Rotterdam, it is composed of 4,100 residences for some 17,000 inhabitants. It was built between 1916 and 1936.

The banker and philanthropist K.P. van der Mandele promoted the Vreewijk through a company founded in April 1913. He commissioned Berlage to design a plan for the first 16 hectares, which would hold 500 residences (with variations ranging from 466 to 482), a school, a community building, and a sports field. Berlage submitted his plan in November of the same year to the municipal authorities, and it was approved. A drawing of the road network with street profiles, dated October 1914, answered technical questions posed by the municipality. The war slowed down completion of the project.

Since Berlage was bound by his exclusive contract with the Kröller-

Müller family, in May 1916 he suggested that the architectural planning of the Tuindorp be turned over to the architectural firms of Granpré Molière, Verhagen & Kok, and De Roos & Overeynder. The presence of Granpré Molière among the designers was decisive. He influenced the outcome of the entire complex and expanded Berlage's plan. He also defined the term "Tuindorp": low-density construction of single-family homes. In any case, urban continuity was not denied. For Granpré Molière, "the neighborhood offers the possibility of conforming harmonically in the sector of expansion. A garden-city would have always remained an element extraneous" to the city. By no coincidence, the ambiguous possibilities of the Vreewijk stirred considerable debate over the Dutch idea of the garden-city in the 1920's and 1930's.

353. Study of the layout.

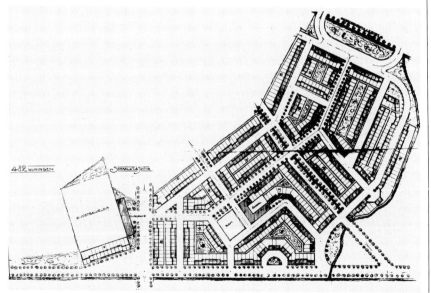

353

Nijmegen, Kiezer Karelsplein
Commissioned by the Municipality of
Nijmegen
1914

In 1914 J.J. Weve, director of the public works of Nijmegen, commissioned Berlage to provide consultation on the design of the Kiezer Karelsplein, a star-shaped square in the vicinity of the railway station at which the city's boulevards converge.

Berlage came to terms with the site, which was surrounded but not completely closed off by shoddy architecture, by working on distinct levels. A double row of trees, just next to the buildings facing the square, forms a first exterior barrier. The central space was dug up and redesigned. A "picturesque" English garden was replaced by a geometric design of concentric circular sections, fitted out with benches, arbors, and a fountain in the center.

354. Study of the intervention.

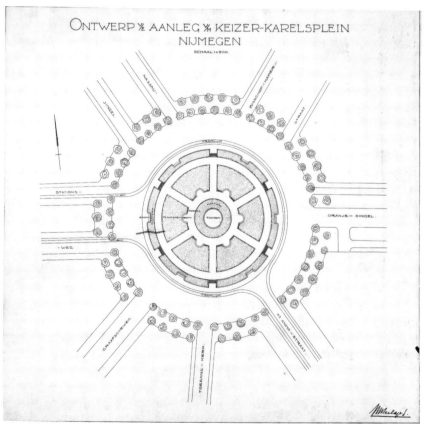

354

Between Arno and Westlaren
(Drenthe)
Commissioned by the
Kröller-Müller Family
1914

In 1914 Berlage moved into his new home in The Hague, where he was head of the architecture department of Wm. H. Müller & Co. In September 1913 he had been asked to design a model farm some 20 kilometers southeast of Groningen for the Kröller-Müller's oldest son, who was the administrator of the family's landholdings in Drenthe, one of the country's northern regions.

Completed in 1914, the farm complex occupies three sides of a square area. On the fourth side, the entrance gate of the boundary wall frames the two-story residence of the owners in the distance. The optical cone, framed by the arch of the portal, is guided to the focal point by paired pilasters with lanterns placed at each end of the four arms of a cruciform horse trough at the center of the brick-paved courtyard.

The volumes of the structure vary freely, in relation to the different functions of the complex. On the plan they form a C-shape. The walls of the storerooms and the lower-profiled stables form a smooth curtain and flank the residence, then extend orthogonally toward the entrance. The chimneys and ventilation shafts mark the changed functions as they rise from the double sloping slate roof at each end of the structure. The rustic sobriety of the exposed brickwork of the façades is tempered in the interior design of the residence, which is entered through a covered portal. The severe nudity of the inner wall surfaces, which are also in brick, is animated by cunning inserts of stone and ceramic tile.

Berlage's artistic collaboration with the painter Bart van der Leck began at the De Schipborg farm and lasted until 1919. After an abortive commission for the De Nederlanden van 1845 Insurance Company, Van der Leck met, through Bremmer—to whom he had been under contract since 1912—Hélène E.L.J. Müller.

In March 1914 he was commissioned to create a glass window for the principal headquarters of Wm. H. Müller & Co. on the Hague's historic Lange Voorhout. The subject of the window was mining, the company's key activity. To learn more about his subject, the painter was invited to visit the company's mines in Spain and Algeria, which he did between April and June 1914. The visual impressions of his trip, collected in over 100 sketches and drawings, had a profound influence on his pictorial quest. They became manifest in 1916 in his emblematic painting *Triptych of the Mine*. From 1914 to 1916 Van der Leck was the color consultant to the architecture department of the company. With scarce satisfaction, he was in charge of the interior color scheme of the Huize ten Vijer, the elegant residence in the woods of Scheveningen adopted by the Kröller-Müllers

355

356

355. Aerial perspective view.

356. Interior, contemporary photograph.

215

when they moved to the Hague from Rotterdam. For this residence, Berlage sketched a study for the gardener's residence and some furnishings (carpets, chairs, a fireplace, and a wash basin).

A clear example of the difficult working relationship between Berlage and Van der Leck occurred over the interior design of the Kunstakamer, where Bremer held his classes, in the Groot Haesebroek. This was another of the Kröller-Müllers' villas, acquired in 1916, in Wassenaar. Berlage was commissioned to do the furnishings and architectural details. Van der Leck studied the color scheme of the walls and designed the carpet and wallpaper. In a whining letter to his patron, Van der Leck complained that it was impossible to work efficaciously with an architect who insisted on subordinating everything to his own discipline. He staked his own claim to the title of "monumental" painter of great promise through the future developments of "De Stijl."

Van der Leck's participation in Berlage's projects for the Kröller-Müllers was, in effect, obstructed by the unitary conception of the architect's design methods. At the De Schipborg farm, Van der Leck's role was limited to designing the tile surfaces.

Bibliography: Van Deventer 1956; also cfr. *De Architekt*, XXII, 1915, plates 760–762; for Van der Leck, cfr. R.W.D. Oxenaar, *the Birth of De Stijl: Bart Van der Leck*, in *Artforum* 1973, pp. 36–43; P. Hefting and A. van der Woud (eds.), *Bart Van der Leck, 1876–1958*, Catalogue of the Exhibit, Rijksmuseum Kröller-Müller, Otterlo, 1976; N.J. Troy, *The De Stijl Environment*, The MIT Press, Cambridge, Mass. and London, 1983.

357

357. *Detail of the entrance, contemporary photograph.*

358. *Aerial view, present state.*

358

216

London, 1–4 and 32 Bury Street
Commissioned by
Wm. H. Müller & Co.
1914–16

The second building Berlage designed for the Kröller-Müllers was the London headquarters of Wm. H. Müller & Co. Berlage's shrewd structural use of decoration is exemplary in this building, also known as Holland House. Inserted between existing buildings, the building faces Bury Street (a lane with a right-angle turn) and St. James Court. Its plan is irregular and resembles two opposing and offset *C*s. The inner courtyard echoes this form in the opposite direction. The interior division of the typical floor is limited to the definition of several offices and bathrooms, which are grouped around two main stairwells. Most of the work space has been left free and can be adapted as needs change.

The steel frame is externally sheathed in glazed grey-green terracotta especially manufactured to meet fire codes and to withstand corrosion of smog. In the vertical ribbons between the large ribs, simplified metal window frames are attached to terracotta spandrels of geometric design. The very shortened perspective, dictated by the narrow width of the lane, gives the façade a vibrant image. The repeated pattern of the pilasters rises to the coping, hiding a recessed attic. The pilasters also weave an overall orthogonal pattern, with the voids predominating over the solids.

The slightly projecting base is formed by a continuous band of black granite approximately one meter high, from which the pilaster strips emerge like masts of a ship. J. Mendes da Costa sculpted the prow of a ship in granite at the foot of the building at the corner of Bury Street and St. James Court. Two black bands rise from this allegorical reference to the company's activities and vertically lock the chamfered end of the façade. Similar bands of granite frame the entrances and mark the vertical attachments to the adjoining buildings, giving Holland House a suave and elegant frame. Bart van der Leck designed the color scheme for the glazed tile sheathing and the ceiling decorations for the sumptuous interiors, which are open to the public. Henri van de Velde completed the interior decoration, in particular the furnishings not yet finished in 1919, when the contract between Berlage and the Kröller-Müller family was rescinded. In the eighties the exterior of the building was restored.

Bibliography: Van Loghem 1915; Kropholler 1918; red. 1921, *Dr. Berlage* . . . ; Langejan in AA. VV. 1934, *H.P. Berlage ter* . . . ; Van Deventer 1956; Singelenberg 1984.

359. Exterior, contemporary photograph.

360. Interior, contemporary photograph.

359

360

The Environs of Hoenderloo
(Gelderland)
Commissioned by
the Kröller-Müller Family
1914–20

The Kröller-Müller family built up the De Hoge Veluwe estate, today a national park, through a series of land acquisitions between Otterloo and Hoenderloo between 1909 and 1921. It covered a surface area of some 6,800 hectares and was initially reserved for hunting. In 1914 Berlage was commissioned to design a "hunting lodge," which was actually a sort of castle for the family of magnates. The fairy-tale residence was used for vacations set amidst natural surroundings, but also to welcome prominent guests from the political, financial, and art world. It was named after Hubertus, patron saint of hunting. According to legend, Hubertus lost his way in a forest during a hunt but was saved by a stag bearing a cross between his antlers, which appeared to show him the way.

The design was conceived between August and December 1915. The executive plans were ready in May 1916 and the municipality of Ede approved them in July of that year. The contract to build the lodge was assigned to the construction company that had built the full-scale mock-ups of the villa museum at Wassenaar and of Holland House. The contractors began their work between the end of 1916 and the start of 1917. During construction, modifications to simplify the complex were made.

The composition of the building implicitly refers to the legend of Hubertus. The layout has the shape of two horns, and the tower rising between the horns refers to the cross, which is explicitly represented in the cusped gable facing the basin. The legend of the hunter-saint is also represented in J. Mendes da Costa's two reliefs in the courtyard and in the glass window above the entrance. The main structure faces the body of water to the south through the long terrace with the verandas of the

living room. In the main structure the entrance hall intersects, forming a cross with the living room and the connected spaces, the small, semi-circular tea room and fumoir. The passage between the hall and the living room houses an elevator, which leads to the sixth-floor of the tower. On the west side of the hall, a stairway also leads to the upper floors. The bedrooms and bathrooms are situated on the first floor and the billiards room on the second floor. The kitchen and pantry are situated on the ground floor adjacent to the stairs. The eastern portion of the ground floor was reserved for Mrs. Kröller-Müller. The master of the house lodged in the eastern horn, the guests in the western horn. The horns extended diagonally at the back of the main structure, symmetrically surrounding the entrance courtyard. To the sides of a small edifice used as a kennel and bicycle storeroom, two small gates close off the pararhomboidal paved courtyard, designed with the same painstaking attention to detail that went into the residence itself. Berlage molded two colored, crystalline peepholes in the main door. The image of the crystal was a significant representation in contemporary architectural culture and in Berlage's own work. Important examples are found in the headquarters of the ANDB, in Lenin's Mausoleum, and in the skylights of many halls. It was reiterated at St. Hubertus in the exteriors (e.g., in the lanterns at the sides of the gates) and in the interiors (e.g., in the chandelier designs). The façades are done in red brick. The small stone pilasters supporting the large lights of the architraves in the bands of openings counterpoint the brick. The interplay of the low volumes, balanced by the vertical thrust of the tower-observatory, is heightened by the slate roofing, which follows the compositional flow with the changing design of the slopes. The slopes vary in angle and are sometimes, coherently, semi-conical. Berlage studied the relationship of the building with its surroundings as carefully as he designed the complex. The tower, whose vertical thrust was more accentuated in the executive plans than in the prelimi-

nary drawings of 1915, dominates the panorama and is characteristic of Berlage's work. Like the tower, the layout was also simplified during construction. Berlage also designed the road system, the geometric layout of the garden and the fluid figure-eight patterns of the artificial basin

of water where, at the heads of the promenade, the conical domes of the small tea and recreation pavilions are situated. Construction was completed at the end of 1918. Between 1918 and 1919 Berlage supervised the interior design, with its splendid finishings and furnishings. He was assisted by

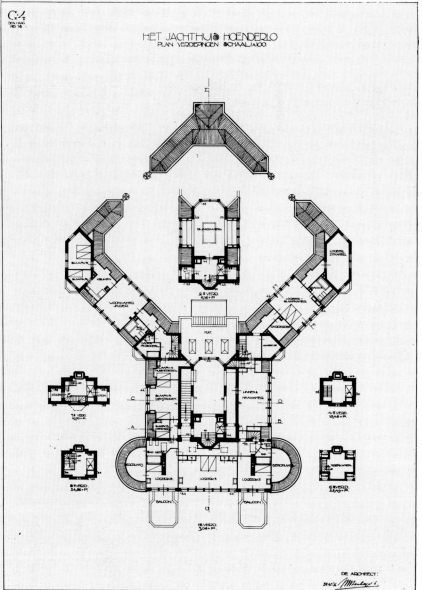

361. *Plan of the first floor, May 1916*

Bart van der Leck for the color and decorative schemes. But Van de Velde, Berlage's successor in the service of the Kröller-Müller family, completed the interior design in 1920.

Between 1917 and 1920 the separate service building for the staff, with garages and stables, was built according to Berlage's design. Its substantial references to Frank Lloyd Wright strengthen, by contrast, the affinities of the hunting lodge with developments in the English Domestic style, reinterpreted in a monumental key.

Bibliography: Van Deventer 1956; Gunnink 1985.

362. *Aerial perspective view from the north.*

363. *Perspective view of the first version.*

364. *Aerial photograph.*

365. *Present state.*

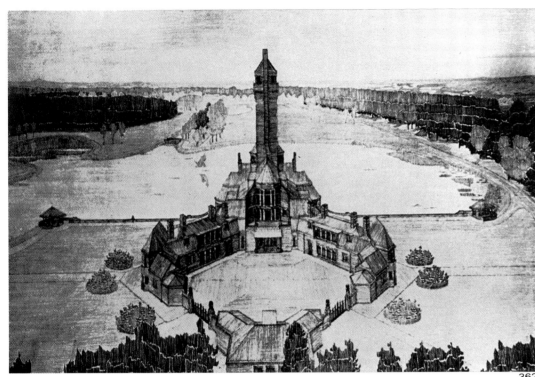

362

364

363

365

1915

In 1915 the association "Architecture et Amicitia" organized an important exhibition of architecture at the Stedelijk Museum of Amsterdam. Among the numerous architects represented in the show were De Bazel, De Klerk, Lauweriks, Landsorp, Wijdeveld, and Van Anroy. That year Berlage was almost 60. In 1916 the "Festschrift" consecrating his myth was published. At this exhibition he was represented by Holland House and his new plan for Amsterdam South. Most significantly, the hall of honor was reserved for his Pantheon of Mankind, an ideal contribution to the pacifist and internationalist cause aimed toward utopia. The demonstrative power of the project was keenly felt by Van Loghem. In his review, the critic and architect wrote: "Berlage the idealist has overtaken [Berlage] the artist." The building was to be sited on an unspecified hill in a country in the center of Europe, a location which immediately calls to mind the siting of the Monument Historique.

In a letter dated November 1916 to his American correspondent, William Gray Purcell, Berlage wrote about the monument. Referring to the presentation booklet published by Brusse, Berlage wrote: "I do not remember whether I sent you a booklet about a peace monument and whether the remark in your letter about the book of the great memorial refers to this, but therefore I send it to you once more in order to make sure. During the first part of the war I made a project for the Pantheon of Mankind, a very ideal project for the future and at the same time a peace monument which should be built after the war is over. It is dedicated in the first place to the future when, as we may hope, there will be a new spiritual understanding among the people, a new religious contemplation of life, for which a peace monument is built up in the large hall. Besides, it is a peace monument to remind us of the war and, for this purpose, gal-

leries have been built up which contain the names of the dead and other victims of the war. It was my idea that this monument should be placed in the center of Europe and there was much to be said in favor of this location because the war was a European war. But now that the United States have joined, and as we believe with ideal purposes, the monument might as well be built in the United States."

Berlage wanted the entrance to the wandering secular temple of mankind to be entirely built of reinforced concrete. The entrance would be guided by eight roads connected by a network of tree-lined avenues forming an octagon. Ascending a series of ramps, the paths would lead to high encircling ramparts. The eight trapezoidal sectors enclosed by these ramparts would be dedicated to meditation and to the commemoration of the soldiers of all the nations who died in the war: Germany, Serbia and Montenegro, Russia, Bulgaria and Belgium, Aus-

tria, Turkey and Italy, France, Japan, and England. The eight areas would communicate with one another by means of a like number of tower-beacons situated at the points of the octagons. Berlage dedicated them to liberty, love, life, strength, peace, courage, prudence, and knowledge. Once the visitors had crossed the monumental gateways of the ramparts, which were adorned with anthropomorphic sculpture, their purifying walk would continue amidst high walls decorated with archaic-style reliefs reminiscent of Egyptian sculpture. The interminable steps would penetrate the gigantic octagonal structure and continue to the base of the monument to the "unity of mankind." It was crowned by a globe exalting the renewed flourishing of the earth. The section of the project outlines an immense atrium covered by a ribbed spherical cap with an opening that allows one to see "the sun from the height of a slice of blue sky, in a circular space, and

this also allows thoughts to be concentrated," to quote Berlage's description of the Pantheon in Rome in 1880. The series of lateral galleries was arranged sequentially at progressively higher levels. The virtually subterranean gallery of remembrance was followed by the galleries dedicated to gratitude, solidarity, edification, and, last but not least, the gallery of universality, which faced the atrium under the roof impost. The pure quest of design Berlage pursued in this project was charged with a contemplative tension that led him to interpret the abstraction of the historic forms of architecture with a peculiar combination of orientalizing elements and Imperial Roman repertory in the colossal tone that pervades the complex. The colossal scale systematically adopted for the various parts (walls, towers, entrances, sculptural decoration, balconies, loggias, porticoes, and openings) and for the empty representational forms accentuated the vertical dynamics, as if it sought to exalt the spiritual ideas of the program. At the same time, this scale imposed on the perception of the building a particularly expressive charge.

So, a quarter of a century after the redundant and, perhaps, disenchanted accumulation of the Monument Historique, which sought to be a reflection on the uncertain destiny of architecture, the path through Goethe's *Storm der Welt* (then barely evoked) seemed to have led to a monument that piously meditated on the destiny of mankind.

Bibliography: Berlage 1915, *Het Pantheon* . . . ; Van Loghem 1915; Berlage 1919, *Schoonheid* . . . ; also cfr. *Deutsche Bauzeitung* 1916, 29, pp. 153–156, and 32, pp. 169–170.

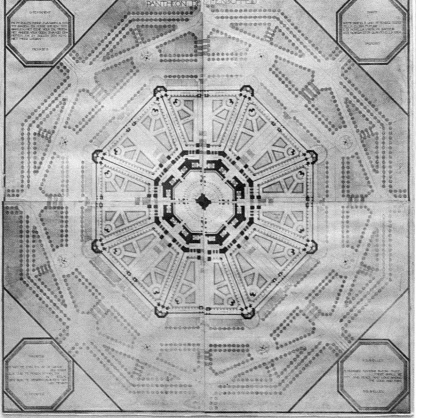

366

366. Plan.

220

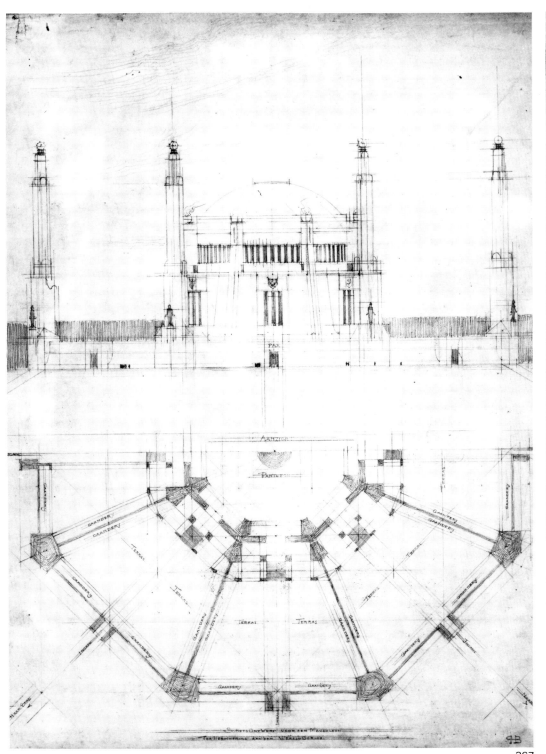

367. *Study of the plan and façade.*

368. *Perspective sketch of the tower lighthouse.*

With J. Gratama and G. Versteeg
Amsterdam East, Transvaalkade/
Jouberstraat (today Hofmeyrstraat)/
Krugerstraat/Bothastraat/
Transvaalstraat/Cronjestraat
Commissioned by the Municipality
of Amsterdam
1916–1919

In 1914, not long after the appointment of Arie Keppler as head of the municipal service for low-income construction in Amsterdam, an ambitious plan for 3,500 workers' residences was drafted.

The architects close to the workers' movement were asked to prepare the executive plan. Van der Pek was in charge of the area north of the IJ. De Bazel was given the Spaarndammerbuurt in the east; Berlage supervised the Transvaalbuurt, with a program for 800 residences in an area he had redesigned in 1903.

Since September 1913 Berlage had been bound by an exclusive contract with the Kröller-Müller family, but town planning was permitted under this contract. However, his change of residence from Amsterdam to the Hague, also stipulated in this con-

tract, obliged Berlage to work with J. Gratama and G. Versteeg on the project. A first study in June 1916 provisionally designed the siting of the area and was based on previous experiences.

The Woningwet funds were delayed because of the war, so the program was also delayed. A drawing from April 1918 signed by all three architects outlines the overall layout. There were two belts of residences in the area—high ones to defend the boundaries and low ones around the inner perimeters. The executive designs were refined by the municipal Woningdienst before the construction contact was signed. The public works commission was in charge of construction in the 1920's. Gratama was the supervisor, and he is credited with the architectural definition of the plan.

Bibliography: cfr. *Bouwkundig Weekblad* 1920, 4; *Wendingen*, 1920, 3–4; *Het Bouwbedrijf*, 1924, pp. 98–103.

369. Drawing of the plan, April 1919.

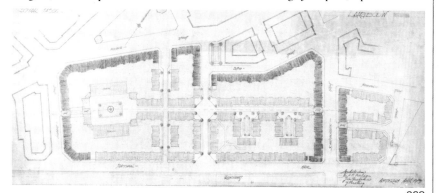

369

De Hoge Veluwe, Fransche Berg
Commissioned by the Kröller-Müller
Family
1917–18

In 1916 the Kröller-Müllers sold their Wassenaar estate and their Huize ten Vijver residence in the Hague. At the same time, they added almost 4,000 hectares of land to the over 2,000 they already possessed at De Hoge Veluwe, in the sandy heart of Gelderland, where Berlage had already begun to construct their fabled hunting lodge. Perhaps Hélène E.L.J. Müller would finally be able to realize her long-desired project in the setting of the vast natural park. At the foot of the modest summit of the Fransche Berg, she would construct a residence that could also adequately house her by-then very rich art collection.

Commissioned to design a new villa-museum, Berlage made preliminary studies in May 1917 and presented a final plan between December 1917 and January 1918.

The complex was designed like a fortress. It rose on a platform protected by broad ramparts extending southward. The ramparts were partially covered by arbors. The principal nucleus of the complex was a compact quadrangular edifice, with a sunken interior and segmented perimetral bands. The hall occupied the central space. Around it, Berlage shrewdly grouped spaces and courtyards of widely varying dimensions and with rotated axes. These spaces and courtyards were supported by a structure of paths whose geometric matrix had surprising affinities with certain medieval Christian emblems of the "quaternity" of universal elements. The decision to place the hall at the center, with stairways on the projections of the diagonal axes, was declared on the exterior of the building. It was even more pronounced in the final plan, where this solution was enhanced by the sloping roofs and by the gables on the coping of the façades.

The volume of the villa-museum, an authentic telescopic structure, as-

cended in tight increments. It culminated in a complex prismatic structure counterpointed by four minarets tightly placed between the jutting prows at the points of the plan.

The main entrance was on the west side and preceded the rotunda that marked the end of the driveway. Balconied gateways led to the octagonal vestibule, which in turn led to the central hall. On the opposing eastern side, a majestic stairway led to the garden level. The garden surrounded the edifice and covered the entire surface area of the ramparts. The entrance to the hall from this side was screened by a small patio, onto which the library faced. On the north side, the symmetrical ramps of a great staircase led to the exhibition halls and to a Kunstzaal with apse. The other nucleus of the complex began at this point. It was composed of the wings of the sculpture galleries, which were flanked by lanes connecting with the auditorium. These lanes faced a green inner courtyard.

The perspective studies of the hall fully reveal the importance Berlage attributed to the architectural fulcrum of the complex. In the May 1917 version, the hall was imbued with greater horizontal tension in part because of the smooth extension of the walls, interrupted by balconies only on the vertical axes of the entrances. In the January 1918 version the hall had a predominantly vertical thrust, which carried it across the entire complex. The invention of a second level re-established the three-dimensional balance. The advancement of the balconies of the first level to the external row of pilasters above the entrances, almost as if to design portals, organized the architectural elements of the base into a hierarchy. In the upper part of the hall, the rhythm of the free-standing pilasters, crowned by geometric capitals, gave the column a vertical thrust. The constant alignment of the second-level balcony with the inner row of pilasters gave the marked girdling of the string course and the railings the task of horizontally connecting the design of the inner façades. The emerald cut of the roof was the base of the impost for a complex colored-glass skylight with an octagonal base, which rested on a tall square tie beam. The four monumental suspended chandeliers, the eight statues resting on parallelepiped bases and crowned by urns, the eight lions facing each other in pairs at the portals, and the symbolic rams serially arranged on the balustrade set the tone for the grandiose interior design of this space. The last in a long series of disappointments, the rejection of the design by the Kröller-Müllers induced Berlage to dissolve his exclusive contract with the family in 1919, four years before it was to expire.

Henri van de Velde was Berlage's successor as the "in-house architect" of the Kröller-Müllers. In 1920 he designed another museum for the same site, which met with the family's approval. Construction commenced in 1921, but the recession that began the following year affected the family's resources so drastically that work was halted when the foundations were almost completed. In 1928 the Kröller-Müller Stichting was created. The task of this foundation was to oversee the family's artistic patrimony. In 1935, however, the natural park was deeded to the state for the sum of 800,000 florins through a new foundation, the Het Nationale Park De Hoge Veluwe, along with the entire art collection. The agreement stipulated that the museum was to be completed within five years and that the estate was to be adequately maintained. Because of the financial dimensions of the undertaking and the lasting economic crisis, Madame Hélène's lofty aspirations as a patroness of the arts could not be achieved even by the state. In 1938, one year before her death, the "temporary pavillion" was built to Van de Velde's design not far from the original site of the villa-museum. This was a very small version of his last design. Today it is the Kröller-Müller Museum, one of the most important modern art collections. It was completed in 1953 and finally enlarged by W.G. Quist in the 1970's.

Bibliography: Van Deventer 1956; Oxenaar and Quist 1978.

370. *Perspective study of the central hall, first version, May 1917.*

371. *Interior perspective view of the library, January 1918.*

372. *H. van der Velde, project of the villa-museum, 1920, perspective view.*

373. *Perspective view of the central hall, January 1918.*

370

371

373

372

The Hague, 41 Stadhouderslaan
Commissioned by the Municipality of
The Hague
1919–20 and 1928–35

In 1912, H.E. van Gelder, archivist,
then director of civic collections, advanced the idea for a new museum
that would reunite in a single building
The Hague's various art collections.
In 1918, at the behest of J. Juriaan
Kok, an influential member of the
city council, and of the mayor, H.A.
van Karnebeek, a municipal organization for the arts and sciences were
founded. Van Gelder was appointed
head of this body, whose purpose was
to make a feasibility study for the new
museum. In 1919 their final report
proposed a site on the Stadhouderslaan, near Zorgvliet Park, the site for
a museum forseen in the town plan.
Berlage conceived three plans, which
were attached to the report when it
was submitted.

The architect received the commission in August 1919. In the spring
of 1920, the designs and the large
plaster model were ready. Although
in an earlier phase Van Gelder perhaps had favored another architect,
he worked profitably with Berlage on
both versions of the project in terms
of the designs and the layout and of
resolving museum-related problems.
Berlage designed a larger museum
than the one the civic administrators
requested. In the first version the
complex included the decorative and
modern art collections, rooms for
temporary exhibitions, a large auditorium for concerts, congress halls,
workshops, and other spaces for museum srvices. The structures were arranged in an irregular trapezoidal
plan. The pavilions fronting on the
Stadhouderslaan, with the visitors'
reception hall, were joined by a low
profiled portico with no direct access
from the street. The large inner
courtyard held a basin of water in
which the structures were reflected.
The courtyard was surrounded by
the promenade. The promenade was
situated below ground level and could
be reached by means of the stairs
leading from the portico. The wings
surrounding the basin join in the large

and small inner courtyards (three on
each of the long sides). They were
connected by continuous passages
through the museums. Temporary
exhibition spaces and some of the
museum services (The library, small
conference rooms, and workshops)
were located on the ground floor. The
rooms housing the permanent collection were located on the upper floors.
In his treatment of the structures,
Berlage seemed to want to experiment
with the expressive possibilities of
reinforced concrete, following in the
direction that led from the Pantheon
of Mankind to the second building for
the De Nederlanden van 1845 in The
Hague. This was evinced, for example, in the perspective of the large
hall by the design of the progressive
projections in the upper connection
between horizontal and vertical
planes. Approved by the municipal
administration in June 1920, the
project was exhibited between the
end of the year and the start of 1921
at the "Pulchri Studio" in The Hague, provoking a wave of contrasting
reactions. In October 1921 the museum consulting-committee objected
to the size, which it deemed excessive, and requested a review of the
construction plan. After a paralyzing
evaluation of the project requested of
the museum directors of Hamburg
(favorable) and of Frankfurt (contrary) in November 1922, the decision
to build was shelved *sine die* in 1923
after the city budget for the following
year had been examined.

In 1927 Van Gelder threatened to
resign unless the city reconsidered the
matter. Berlage received a new commision in December. The scale was
reduced, and Berlage worked to meet
the request for a flexible edifice that
would permit future expansion of the
exhibition area. The general plans
were submitted and approved in
February 1928. The working plan
was ready in June 1929, and the construction contract was awarded at the
end of the year. Construction began
in May 1931 and was completed exactly four years later, in May 1935.
During construction, the plan
underwent several modifications.
The principles guiding Berlage and
Van Gelder in the first project stood
out even more clearly in the second
and final version, despite the changes

made. The architect and the organizer took numerous hints from the
innovative *Museum Ideals of Purpose and
Method* by Benjamin Ives Gilman,
published by the Boston Museum of
Fine Arts in 1918. They reiterated a
concept of the museum as a multivalent cultural center set in a park and
organized in such a way as to prevent
"museum fatigue." The layout resulted in a museum building with a
central courtyard and a peripheral
structure for the conference rooms,
offices, and other museum services.

374. Plan of the ground floor, first design.

375. Plan of the first floor, first design.

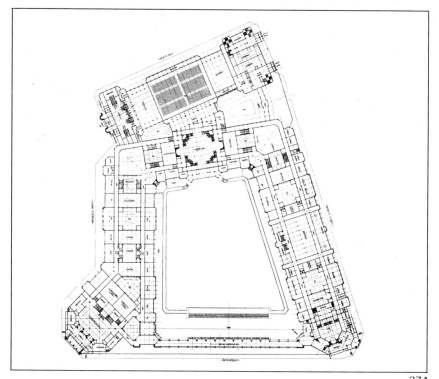

374

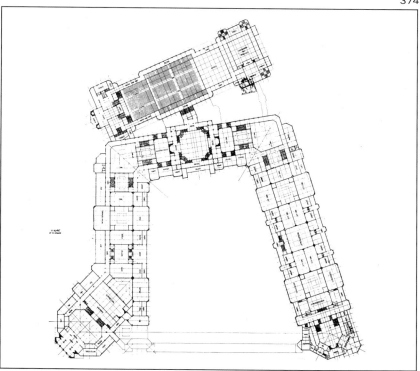

375

376. Model, view of the central hall from the water courtyard, contemporary photograph.

377. Perspective sketch of the entrance hall.

378. Plan of the ground floor, second design.

379. Plan of the first floor with indication of the itineraries, second design.

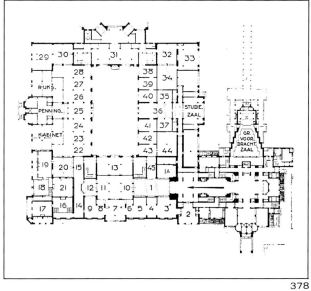

378

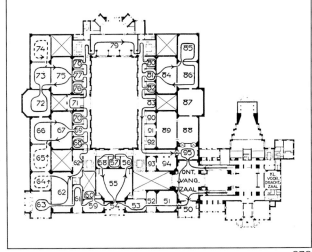

379

377

The complex is located at the virtual center of the site. An elongated basin of water (an obvious echo of the first design) asymmetrically starting from the entrance gallery separates the museum from the main street, while a long arbor connects it to the small refreshment building in the rear. The grid that regulates the proportions of the structure is created from a module measuring 110 square centimeters, a measure dictated by the size of each of the 4,000,000 bricks used to face the reinforced concrete curtain wall. The museum itineraries were designed to continually reinforce the museum experience. The carefully studied and diversified lighting system also contributes to this experience. The exhibition spaces are revised in this version. On the ground floor, the applied arts collections are located in the wings to the west and north of the inner courtyard, taking a hint from Semper in regard to aesthetic education. Also on the ground floor are the musical instruments collection and the print collection, located, respectively, in the rooms to the east and south of the inner courtyard. On the upper floors are the section regarding the history of the city of The Hague, the modern art collection, and sculpture gallery. Each of these sections can be entered independently by means of the four stairways arranged at each of the points of the rectangular inner courtyard, which measures 20 x 40 meters. The distinction between serving and served spaces has been carried over from the first project. The inner ring is composed of three hallways that face outward only in their middle section. It follows the perimeter of the courtyard and laterally serves intimate exhibition areas arranged in series and screened by low walls. These areas lead to the larger rooms arranged in a median ring, which alternate with the wells of light on the ground floor. These larger rooms lead to the outermost ring, made up of spaces illuminated from above and generally lacking views outward. The pronounced hierarchical structure with courtyard is exalted in the treatment of elevations. This is achieved through the movement of the volumes of the central section of each side and the juxtaposition of prismatic skylight roofs. At the same time, there are a number of elements typical of a compositional process

BOUW VAN HET NIEUWE GEMEENTE MUSEUM TE 'S-GRAVENHAGE. GEVEL AAN DE STADHOUDERSLAAN

380

380. *Main frontage, perspective study.*

381. *Contemporary aerial photograph.*

382. *Corner solution, present state.*

383. *Detail of the main frontage, present state.*

384. *View from the east of the conference room, present state.*

381

226

founded on, among other things, the virtual transparency of the architectural organization, evidenced by the accentuated central locations of the museum's service spaces. These elements include the majestic prow-shaped volumes rising from the rear of the structure, a clear reference to the design of the villa-museum at the Fransche-Berg; the smokestacks of the nearby heating plant, arranged in pairs; and the telescopic structure of the conferencerooms, a device designed to counterweight the articulated box of the entrance block. The play of the volumes is rigorously counterpointed by the various solutions: the precious texture of the facades created by the yellow brickwork facing; the sunken frames in the openings; the reverse inversion of the corners of the buildings; and the primary color schemes of the interiors. In several projects dating roughly between 1916 and 1920, such as the Pantheon of Mankind and the villa-museum at the Fransche-Berg, reinforced concrete was molded into complex shapes. In this museum edifice, it is utilized with mature mastery. A fruitful dialectic has been established between tectonic and stereometric elements. This can be seen in the construction details visible in the structure, especially in some of the larger spaces. By no coincidence, the deep meaning of the "Zakelijkheid" that the aging architect continued to pursue in the 1920s, particularly in the Christian Science Church, the De Nederlanden van 1845 building, and Lenin's Mausoleum—often in silent opposition to the "Nieuwe Zakelijkheid"—found its highest expression in the Hague museum. In 1935 the Italian critic Persico divined that Berlage's work "must not be judged by the yardstick of rationalism but with a subtle understanding of its role as a mediator between the ancients and moderns" that enabled us to comprehend the complex roots of the design. In this regard, the sequence of spaces in the entrance hall is exemplary. The entrance to the museum is a sort of novice's itinerary, with subtle symbolic aims. The covered gallery, closed by a low wall and large glass windows, crosses the basin of water on the principle frontage. This arrangement underscores the separation from the "mundane" and alludes to the need for purification—a necessary

complement to the renunciation of the things of this world before entry into the temple of art. The vestibule is cloaked in shadow, signifying a state immediately preceding consciousness.

With a deliberate rotation of the axis, the vestinule leads to the large and luminous hall, whose rhythm of solids and voids is accentuated by the light entering directly from above. The hall is situated at the crossroads of all the museum itineraries, but its role goes beyond that of merely providing a junction. In fact, it constitutes an entrance to the museum that provides an interpretive key to it. By no coincidence, the inscription initialing W. van Konijnenburg's delicate wall composition invites the spectator to become aware of the value of "divine light in the revelation of art." Berlage explores the significance of "divine light" by adopting a complex system of illumination that satisfies his own predilection for a chiaroscuro and the museum specification for a homogenous diffusion of light, both natural and artificial, to promote the viewing and the conservation on the works displayed. The rooms on the ground floor are illuminated by the large glass windows on the inner courtyard and by the high slits around the perimeter. The sequence of more intimate exhibiton spaces is perceived from the shadow in which the inner ring of the

hallway is kept, through the rhythm of the perforations. The system of illumination on the first floor was tested in situ with mock-ups. It is composed of a Venetian-blind mechanism that permits the diffusion of the natural light to be reflected. In some of the rooms, a velarium of glass panels embedded in the ceiling spreads a soft light. In many of the others, the velarium is doubled by suspended opaline glass panels, al-

lowing the complexity of the design of the interior roofs to be perceived. Opened in 1935, The Hagues's Municiple Museum is a capital work in Berlage's oeuvre, comparable only to the Stock Exchange, and represents a summation of his design experience. The old master never saw it completed, since he died in August 1934. Until the inauguration, the work site was supervised by his son-in-law and associate, E.E. Strasser.

382

383

384

In 1961 an ineffective pavillion for temporary exhibits designed by S. Schamhart was added to the left of the main facade. In the 1980s Berlage's edifice was flanked by an educational museum designed by Quist, who gave a better demonstration of his design skills.

Bibiliography: Berlage 1920, *Het ontwerp* . . . ; Boeken 1921; Hoogenboom 1921; Van Gelder 1921; Bonset 1922; red. 1922, *Nieuwe* . . . ; Bercklaers 1923; Zwart 1928, *De Haagsche* . . . ; Zwart 1929; red. 1929, *Het nieuwe* . . . ; Van Loghem 1929; Van Moorsel 1929–30; Jansen 1935; Persico 1935; De Gelder 1935; Strasser 1935; Van Gelder 1935; Van Zuiden 1935; J.W. 1935–36; Zadoks 1935; Zwartendijk 1935; Slagter 1936; Singelenberg in AA. VV. 1975, *H.P. Berlage* . . . ; Meijers 1978; Van Velzen 1982; also cfr. *The Architect and Building News* 1935, 3484 and 3485; *De Ingenieur* 1935, 24, June 14.

Project for an Invitational Competition for the Transformation and Enlargement of the Chamber of Deputies

The Hague, Hofweg/Hofsingel (today Hofstraat)
Commissioned by the Government of the Ntherlands
1920

In the national budget for the year 1915, Minister Lely, the main proponent of reclamation of the Zuiderzee and head of the characteristically Dutch Department of the Waterstaat, allocated the conspicuous sum of 50,000 florins for an invitational competition for the enlargement of the Chamber of Deputees in The Hague. Postponed because of the economic crisis brought on by the war, the project was reintroduced in 1920, with similar terms. But this time the competition was worth 60,000 florins. In January 1920, five architects were invited to submit sketches and designs on a scale of 1:200 by the end of the year. Besides Berlage, E. Cuypers, K.P.C. de Bazel, J. Limburg, and J. Stuyt were invited to participate, along with a sixth competitor, Knuttel, in his capacity as architect of the state. A heated debate was touched off in the press, which called for public judgement of the projects. Concomitant with the exhibition mounted in The Hague in July 1921, a special issue devoted to the projects was published by the *Bouwkundig Weekblad*. Because of a lack of available funds, the Dutch government shelved the entire operation in October 1921, causing a further outcry. The competition announcement called for the restructuring of the layout of the Tweede Kamer der Staaten General in the Hague facing Binnenhof and for enlargement of the building on a trapezoidal plot between Hofweg and Hofsingel. A new assembly hall and the related parliamentary services were to be constructed.

Berlage proposed a compact structure with "urban" characteristics. The itineraries would delimit different islands of activity. The entrance vestibule, the inner garden, and the assembly hall, surrounded by a continuous path, formed a sort of wedge inserted to connect the wings facing Hofweg and Hofsingel. A series of studies testifies to the habitual care Berlage employed to define the tower, placed to one side of the entrance vestibule and crowned by a large polyhedron, an explicit image of a crystal frequently found in Berlage's architectural images. The competition to enlarge the Chamber on an immediately adjacent site was announced again in 1978. P. de Bruijn was the winner and created the definitive design in 1981.

Bibliography: J.P.M. 1920; AA. VV. 1920; also cfr. *De Telegraaf* August 27, 1921; *Wonen TA/BK 1982, 12, pp. 18–19*.

385. Study of the façade.

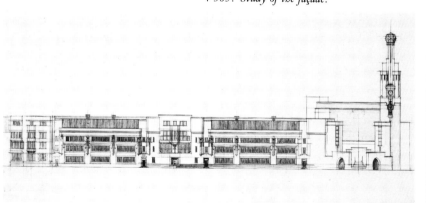

385

Siting of the Spiekman Monument

Rotterdam Spangen, P.C. Hooftplein Commissioned by the Municipality of Rotterdam
1920–21

Berlage designed the environmental site, today unrecognizable, for the Spiekman Monument, dedicated to the Socialist leader of Rotterdam. He conceived a quiet, finished urban space in the vicinity of the Spangen neighborhood. During the years, Oud and Brinkman were building a important series of low-income apartment buildings there.

386. Study of the plan and elevation.

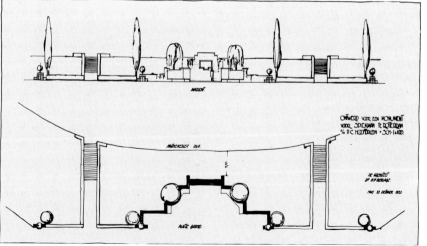

386

With L.N. Holsboer
Commissioned by the Municipapity
of Utrecht
1920–24

Designed by Berlage, acting as a consultant, and by L.N. Holsboer, director of the city's public works office, the town plan of Utrecht was drawn up to extend the city's boundaries. They had been fixed in 1911, but a request for expansion was made in 1918.

The plan was submitted in October 1920. It had to deal with the problems of a city situated at the crossroads of the country's infrastructures. For this reason, it had to interweave road development and residential expansion in continuity with the historic center of the city.

It also had to take into account an expected future population of 450,000, compared to the population of 140,000 in 1920. The new neighborhoods were designed for habitation by mixed social groups. They were distributed to link up the fringes of peripheral expansion to the northwest, west, and south and alternated with industrial development areas. They form a pattern enclosed by a first ring of infrastructures. This was achieved by excavating canals, by laying out road axes linking the existing ones, and by shifting the railway lines and station. Based on experiences tested in the plans for Amsterdam South and The Hague, the neighborhoods were structured by creating a hierarchy in the road system. The principle axes, with diagonals converging in the squares, which were focal points, formed the framework of the system. The dense secondary network followed often irregular routes. It interacted with the primary network, creating always-varied block alignments and breaking the monotony of serial expansion. The singling out of a series of buildings to be used for public functions and distributed at strategic points within the neighborhoods provided the occasion to redefine the vast areas of the historic center. The careful division of parks and finished green areas gave the city breathing space. The largest area of green was concentrated in the southeastern area of the city and housed sports facilities.

The plan for the Oog in Al garden-complex was submitted to Berlage for an opinion in 1918 as part of his consultantship. He was initially paid 2,500 florins for the plan of the neighborhood, which referred back to the plan conceived by A.H. op ten Noord, Holsboer's predecessor until 1918. Berlage rationalized the picturesque layout of the neighborhood, located immediately to the south of the new station. It was built in the following years.

The report attached to the plan was published in 1921 in the special town-planning issue of the *Tijdschrift voor Volkshuisvesting* It suggested systematically abolishing existing land-use restraints wherever they might be prejudicial to the objectives if the town plan. This was the case, for example, of the line of military forts surrounding Utrecht to the east.

The plan was revised in 1924. It was submitted in July and approved in December. It eliminated the suffocating boundary of forts through the insertion of another ring-road, which linked up with the route planned to the northwest. The external vehicular ring thus created connected radially at strategic points to the one in the most immediate vicinity of the city, modifying the previous design of connections between military forts.

In the revised plan, the construction program also underwent some changes. These affected the completion of several neighborhoods and variations in the layout of several blocks. Simultaneously, the necessity of linking the Utrecht town plan to a broader, regional planning dimension was debated. The comments of D. Hudig, secretary-director of the Nederlandsch Institute voor Volkshuisvesting en Stedebouw, appearing in the institute's publication in 1925, suggested this course of action.

Bibliography: Berlage 1921, *Toelichting* . . . ; red. 1922, *De uitbreiding* . . . ; Blijstra 1969; also *Gedrukte Verzameling Gemeente Utrecht* 1921, 111, and 1924, 174; M.J.W. Roegholt, *Het stadsgewest*, Wassenaar, 1925, pp. 191–97.

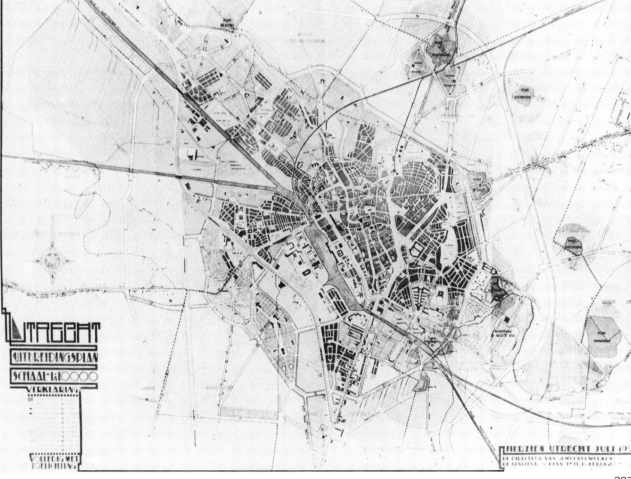

387

387. *Drawing of the plan, second draft, July 1924.*

With A.D.N. van Gendt and W.N.
van Vliet
The Hague, Raamweg/
Groenhovenstraat/Burnierstraat
Commissioned by
the De Nederlanden van 1845
Insurance Company
1920–27

The second building for the insurance company in The Hague is one of Berlage's few mature works in which his experimentation with new materials was realized constructively. The ideal premise to this was laid in his intervention at the VI International Congress of Architects in Madrid in April 1904. Foreseeing the systematic adoption of reinforced concrete, he exhorted architects to study its "artistic forms" in order to remain masters of their profession.

The plot on which the edifice was built measures over 5,000 square meters. It lies to the north of The Hague, between Raamweg and Groenhoverstraat, not far from the Henny House (1912). It was purchased by the company in 1919. Berlage conceived the plans between 1920 and 1922, with the assistance of the Van Gendt engineering studio and of Van Vliet. The executive plan was ready in 1924, when the insurance company's improved financial situation permitted construction to begin. It was completed three years later.

The principal façade extends some 80 meters along the Groenhovenstraat; the side façades measure some 40 meters. In the rear, the courtyard of the building is bisected by a projecting volume on axis with the principal façade. There is a typing room on the ground floor and a lunchroom on the first floor. The layout is based on the principle of bilateral symmetry and fully corresponds, according to the architect himself, to the interior requirements of the building. A revolving door leads to the entrance atrium, which houses a bicycle storeroom and is directly connected to the basement. The atrium leads to the hall. This is a double-height space in the shape of a Greek cross inscribed

in a square. It is lit directly from above. In the May 1927 project, which shows the variations made during construction, the inside corners of the hall are chamfered and the outside triangular sectors have been made into offices for the public. Large work spaces are located to the left and right of the hall. They are large courtyards illuminated by exterior skylights and interior glass diffusion velaria. The organization of the office is free, following American examples. A summer cooling system to support the air-conditioning system is based on the evaporation of jets of water sprayed onto the skylights. The offices of the division supervisors are located on the long exterior side of the courtyards. Along an even more peripheral band, served by a longitudinal hallway, are the offices of the management and the administration, which face out of the main façade. The upper floor houses the Fatum en Labor, an affiliate of the insurance company. It is reached via the stairways to the sides of the entrance. The working spaces are L-shaped, to optimize the lighting. The small foyer, set between the stairways, looks onto the hall on the ground floor and leads to a meeting room, which is revealed by the polygonal apse on the main façade. Directly above the meeting room, the multilobate plan of the smaller second floor houses the offices of the company's top management.

On the exterior, the structural grid of coarse concrete highlights the orthogonal lines of the façades. The infills of the stereometric oriel windows of the stairwells are of glass-concrete material; those of the opaque parts are in red brick, with a darker brick used for the coping bands. In both cases, they are surrounded by glazed black brick contiguous to the exposed concrete structure.

The ground floor is recessed along a good portion of the façade. Paired pilasters enclose the compressed serial oriel windows of the openings, with

a double interaxis contrasting with the upper spans. A diagonal tension in the façade marks the passage to the end bays. The link between pilasters and beams, orthogonally in sympathy with the supporting frames of the projecting first floor, is traced by al-

lusive capitals—recessed corbels with chamfered edges, which are accentuated even more over the principal entrance.

Compared to the articulated partition of the ground floor, the upper floor maintains a substantial conti-

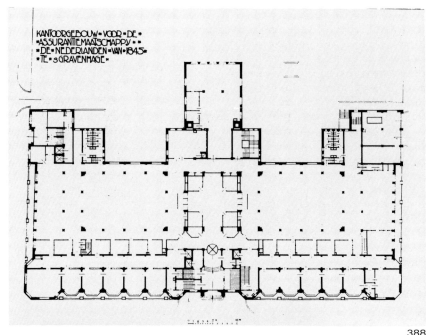

388

388. Plan of the ground floor.

389. Meeting room, contemporary photograph.

389

nuity in the projecting façade. The small individual pilasters double the cadence of the openings. Their connection with the small horizontal corbel (a thin shadow under the coping) is ended by a sharp dentate blade corresponding to the lower floor, which is used to house the baldacchino. The infills of the upper exterior squares of the façade module repeat on the surface the rhythm of the oriel windows below and visually enhance the slim pilasters.

The unusual dentelled link between vertical and horizontal structures, roughly drawn in several sketches of the first project of the Municipal Museum of The Hague, is constantly reiterated in the interior of this edifice and assumes an extraordinary plastic energy in relation to the flat plastered surfaces of the walls. One result is an evocation of an archaic image of a threshold in the passage between the hall and the office courtyard.

The meeting room is dressed with a low, emerald-cut wainscoting and furnished with pieces designed by Berlage, as is the office of the top management directly above. This office corresponds to the major projection of the main façade—the semi-hexagonal oriel window of the entrance, which is strengthened in its supporting ribs. In contrast, the solutions of the corners are contained to stress the preeminence of the horizontal span. The 45-degree chamfered corner houses a window on the parterre. At the center of the niche on the upper floor a plinth supports a brick pilaster strip, which repeats the red–black color contrast of the whole building. The niche is crowned by a clock.

Some critics accused Berlage of anachronism because of the stereotomic treatment of a plastic building material like reinforced concrete. Another faction reacted, maintaining that the architect intended to build an edifice of "tectonic beauty." Berlage replied indirectly to the contro-

versy. In a lecture delivered at the Sorbonne in 1923, he declared: "The most important factor in the evolution of architecture in Holland is the victory of the new decoration over the old, a victory won by force."

In 1933, plans for a radical extension over the entire plot were proposed by W. Dyuff. In 1954, an additional floor was coherently added to the building by W.M. Dudok.

Bibliography: Hana 1925–26; E.J.B. 1927; Sangster 1927; Van Moorsel 1927; Wattjes 1927, *Gebouw* . . . ; Zwart 1927, *H.P. Berlage* . . . ; also cfr. *Het Bouwbedrij* 1927, 8, p. 179.

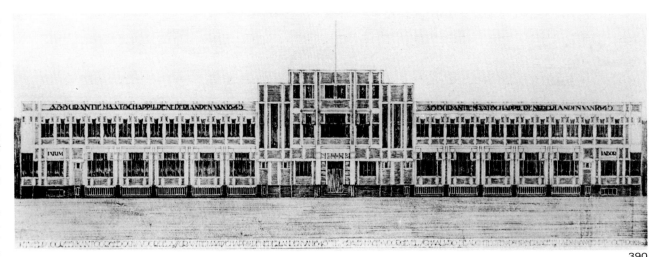

390

391

390. Main façade, October 1922.

391. Exterior, contemporary photograph.

231

With A.C. Burgdorffer (1921), H.S. de Roode (1926)
Rotterdam
Commissioned by the Municipality of Rotterdam
1921 and 1926

In his lessons in the *Stedenbouw*, published in 1914, Berlage declared: "The art of town planning in every age has always agreed on at least one principle: that of not erecting a monumental edifice in the center of a square."

Berlage received this commission in 1921. He was to be the consultant to A.C. Burgdorffer, city director of public works. Berlage's commission was the nineteenth awarded by the local government for the design of an area whose size, and the preexisting historic buildings on the site, seemed to pose serious limits. The area was the vast Hofplein, at the end of the Coolsingel, in the vicinity of the central station. Berlage's plans and models were ready at the end of 1921 and were put on public display.

The theoretical foundation of the project was the assumption that the site was the center of the city's traffic pattern because of its key position in terms of the historic old town. For Berlage, the historic shape of the square could not be disregarded. Designed as an ellipse, with the focal points coalescing the principal bands of traffic, the new square was shifted decidedly to the south after demolition of a building complex. The ancient Delft gateway, originally in the center of the area, was inserted in the northern face. It was also set apart from the edifices in the project to exalt its monumental volume and to give the square two points of access. On the southern face Berlage placed a gateway-edifice, yet another variation on a theme dear to his heart. It had the same function in the layout as the Delft gateway and was marked by a clock tower. On the west side, Berlage designed a monument to the city. Around it was a rotunda distributing arriving traffic. On the extreme east side, on the principal axis of the ellipse, a tall building completed the square. The building lay just beyond

the line of the railway viaduct and the station. This was to be the second point of traffic distribution in the square.

The significance of the urban locus of the square for the modern city was defined in the Hofplein's monuments. The symbology of the monument to the city showed Venus, bearer of beauty and patron of Rotterdam, holding the scepter of Mercury atop the globe of the earth, a harbinger of commercial prosperity. The image of the tower, on the other hand, was "in the American spirit." Just as "the ancient city developed the spiritual square in the cathedral," Berlage explained in his presentation of the project, "the secular square had the royal palace and the social square the town hall."

In 1922 a stormy debate broke out in the specialized journals and also among the public. Berlage's design had numerous champions. Behrens spoke in favor of it in his lectures on his impressions of the Netherlands upon his return to Germany in October 1922. But alternative proposals and critical comments were also advanced. In the end, the city government came out against the plan, judging it too costly and fearing the consequences, including the demolition of some 300 residences.

In February 1926, exactly five years later, Berlage was requested to design a new project as consultant to H.S. deRoode, director of the office of public works. It was understood that the cost of this project would have to be limited. The second version of the plan was submitted in October 1926 and was compensated with an honorarium of 7,000 florins. In his new plan, the basic assumption of the Hofplein as the bipolar center of traffic and certain solutions from the first plan remained.

Unable to reconstruct continuous fronts on the long sides of the square, Berlage introduced an exedral con-

struction to surround the Delft gateway on the north side of the square. The exedra was segmented at the extremities, thus relating to the surrounding urban fabric. There were two portals in the center of this exedra, one for incoming traffic, the other for outgoing traffic. On the south side the end bay of the block between Coolsingel and Haagscheveer was reconstructed, but the idea of the tower behind the railway viaduct was abandoned.

Because of the cost of expropriation and of the new construction, not even Berlage's second plan for the

392. Model of the first project, view from southwest.

393. Drawing of the plan, first design.

392

393

Hofplein was realized. And the wavering conduct of the city government was certainly also a factor.

Accompanied by violent polemics (worth mentioning are M. Stam and the counterplan of "Opbouw"), the city government awarded new commissions to solve the problem of the Hofplein. The twenty-first plan, designed by W.G. Witteveen, head of the city's town planning since 1924, was approved in 1928. It called for the removal of the Delft gateway to another site. The debate over the Hofplein dragged on through the 1930s. But the most dramatic event occurred in May 1940: the entire center of Rotterdam was razed to the ground by the Luftwaffe, opening a new chapter in town planning affairs—and not only in regard to Rotterdam—through the immediate resumption of discussion over reconstruction.

394. *Perspective sketch from the west, first design.*

395. *Perspective sketch from the east, first design.*

396. *Aerial perspective view from the southwest, second design.*

394

395

396

Bibliography: Berlage 1922, *Het Hofplein . . .* ; Berlage 1922, *Ontwerp . . .* ; Berlage 1922, *Slotbeschouwing*; Bakker Schut 1922; De Clercq 1922; Granpré Molière 1922; Kromhout 1922; Meischke and Schmidt 1922; Mieras 1922; Oud 1922; Plate 1922; red. 1922, *Het Hofplein . . .* ; Tinbergen 1922; Van Beek 1922; Van der Mandele 1922; Verhagen 1922; Walenkamp 1922; Berlage 1923, *Entwurf . . .* ; Van den Berg and Scheffer 1924; Zwart 1926; Stam 1927; A.O. 1928; Witteveen 1928; Otten 1929; also cfr. *Bouwkundig Weekblad* 1922, 20; *Tijdschrift voor Volkshuisvesting* 1922, 3; *Stadbaukunst* January 1923; *Wendingen* 1923, 3; *Tijdschrift voor Volkshuisvesting en Stedebouw* 1927, 2.

Studies for the Construction Plan of the De Esch Polder

Rotterdam East
1921–22

397. Study of the layout.

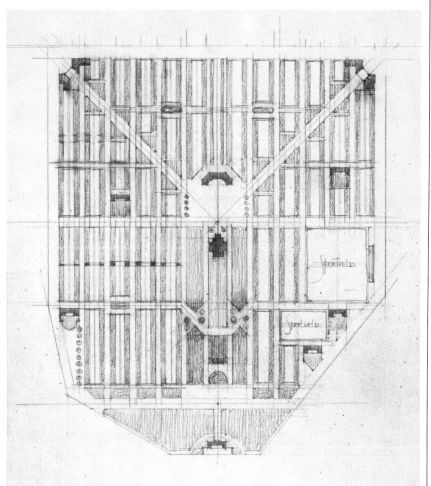

397

Studies for Dwellings

1922

Among the drawings in Berlage's archives, type B (May 1922), a row house, shows a one-family residence. The covered surface area was 39 square meters. The house slept six people and was composed of a ground floor and an attic with windows. Type C (June 1922) was the double residence for four families. It had four floors, and the plan referred back to the models adopted for the De Arbeiderswoning Building Society in 1911.

398. Study of the plan and elevation.

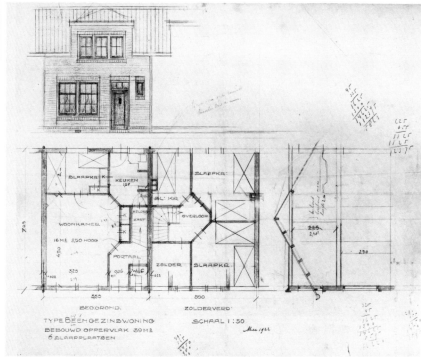

398

Consultantship for the Town Plan of Batavia

Project for a Cafè-Restaurant

Commissioned by the Municipality of Batavia (today Djakarta, Indonesia) 1923–25

In February 1923, Berlage embarked on the steamship *Grotius* in Genoa on a voyage to the Dutch Indies (Java, Bali, and Sumatra). He was given a triumphal welcome and delivered lectures on the "idea of architecture" and "the architectural history of Amsterdam." During his stay, the municipal government of Batavia, where in 1913 he had built the headquarters of the De Nederlanden van 1845 Insurance Company, asked him to make a critical appraisal of the city's town plan. At the same time, the governor asked him to write a report on the thorny question of restoration of the monumental complex of the ancient temples of Prambanan. After an on-the-spot investigation, Berlage wrote the report. Tasks of this sort were not new to him. He had been hired as a town-planning consultant to numerous cities, including Haarlem, Gouda, Delft, and Nijmegen.

Bibliography: Berlage 1923, *Brieven . . .* ; Karsten 1923; Van der Boom 1925; Berlage 1931, *Mijn . . .* ; Passchier 1984.

399. Travel sketch, Bali, May 20, 1923.

The Hague, Stadhouderslaan/ Adriaan Goekooplan 1924

The café-restaurant was to be sited in an area immediately north of the municipal museum Berlage had designed. It was drafted in two versions, dated July and October 1924, respectively. Both projects entailed a two-story building with exterior garden, but the plans and composition of the volumes differed. The first version was more traditional. Two lateral volumes pivoted around a small octagonal hall, illuminated by a lantern with a cupola on the top of the roof. These volumes are also united by a low covered veranda.

The second version had flat and sloping roofs. This building was also of tripartite composition but, through the cunning application of molding, the geometry of the whole was amalgamated in the plan. A frequent motif was the square chamfered to 45-degrees and sunk at the points. The stairwells were arranged in a double pair and mutually rotated 90-degrees. They intersected the margins of the plan orthogonally and projected beyond the volume of the edifice.

Bibliography: Blijstra 1971.

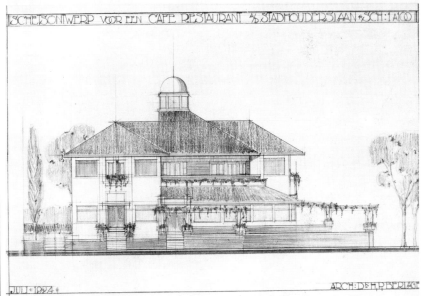

400. Study of the façade.

399

400

With P. Zwart
The Hague, Hofweg/
Lange Vijverberg
Commissioned by the Municipality
of The Hague
1924–25

volume of the small tower. It features alternating surfaces of glass-concrete material under a monolithic cap. The vertical infills between the openings are in exposed brick.

Bibliography: Wattjes 1926; also cfr. *Architectura* 1923, 21; *Bouwkundig Weekblad* 1923, 24 and 26.

Between 1924 and 1925, Berlage renovated the Gevangenpoort, where Hofweg and Lange Vijverberg meet along the historic basin of the Vijverberg. He was assisted by P. Zwart, a collaborator in his studio from 1921 to 1927, and later a famous Dutch graphic designer. The work began after the conclusion, in the preceding years, of the function of this very central and representative area of the city. In 1922 a construction plan was submitted calling for partial interment of the Vijverberg. The press and professional groups reacted immediately. The Bond van Nederlandsche Architecten, the principal professional association, called on Berlage to state his opinion, since he had been consultant to the city on "the implementation of the plan" since 1916. The critic Mieras believed that construction in this area was neither indispensable nor desirable.

Berlage's proposal for renovation of the area was limited to the head of the basin. The street was to be widened slightly and the promenade was to be redesigned by creating semi-hexagonal profiles of the corners protruding toward the water. Berlage also designed a commemorative column for erection. In the open space at the end of Lange Vijverberg, the monument to Johann de Witt was surrounded in an eccentric position by a trilobate platform that marked the parking area. Berlage placed a traffic divider in Buitenhof. This pier was also to be a station for public vehicles and trams and was to be fitted out with greenery and benches. Berlage also added a reinforced concrete kiosk with public toilets and flower and newspaper stands on the pier. The segmented volume of the small but elegant construction originated in the elevated projection in the plan, an outgrowth of two linked octagons. The flat roofs acts as a hanging garden. Detached from it is the compact

401

401. Drawing of the plan.

402. Buitenhof, contemporary photograph.

402

Amsterdam West, Mercatorplein
Commissioned by the Consortium
of Private Construction Companies
of Amsterdam West and Hoofdweg
1924–27

Berlage designed a swastika-shaped
itinerary of lanes for the green space
at the center of Mercatorplein. It alluded to the dynamism of the motor
traffic around it and to the design of
the Turbinenplatz, which had been
inspired by Sitte. The north–south
direction of the square functioned as

a symmetrical axis for the design of
the façades of the two central blocks
on the long sides, Two edifices with
portals were positioned at the northeast and southwest extremities of the
short sides. Each of the edifices was
flanked by a high tower on the axis
running parallel to the Hoofdweg. A

403. Layout of the square.

404. Perspective view from the south.

The story of the Mercatorplein was
part of the renewed construction activity facilitated by the government.
The brusque about-face in government policy under the growing pres-
sure of the post-war economic crisis,
after five years of legislative and financial backing of the Wonigwet for
the housing sector, resulted in an exceptional growth in residential construction in 1921, with lasting effects.
Although the grants were actually
reduced in 1921, the incentives were
still appealing. In 1922 a *bouwcombi-
natie*, coordinated by the entrepre-
neur H. van der Schaar, proposed an
agreement to the city government for
the construction of some 6,000 residences in the Amsterdam West area.
In certain respects, their proposal
departed from construction regulations. One of the terms to receive allocation of the "prizes" was the use
of reinforced concrete for the structures. The purpose was to test rational construction techniques. But
another of the terms was the use of
exposed brick on the outer infills in
order to assist the traditional brick
industry. Abolition of the incentive
scheme in 1923 damaged the consortium's economic status. This forced
the city government to act against its
own wishes and guarantee a 13-mil-
lion-florin grant in January 1924. Besides Berlage, numerous architects
were associated with the project.

Berlage's involvement was actually
limited to the Mercatorplein, the key
square in the project that was crossed
by the area's principal traffic arteries,
and to the curtains of four surrounding blocks. Berlage intended to ele-
vate the space to the dignity of a
square by designing construction
curtains based on the monumental
elevation of the towers, while the
porticoed arrangement of the ground-
level areas was designed to promote
the social function of the square.

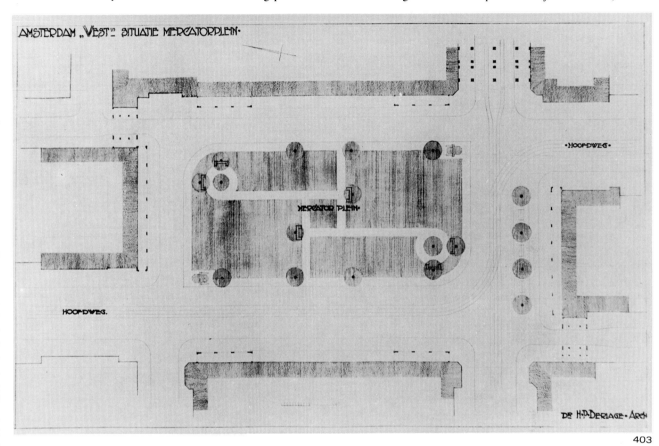

403

HET · MERCATORPLEIN · IN · AMSTERDAM-WEST.

404

third edifice with a portal passing above the Jan Evertsenstraat on the northwest side was not built, so Berlage intervened in the square only. The monumental accentuation of the trapezoidal reinforced concrete architrave on the portal, crowned by a polygonal oriel window projecting from the bare brick wall, highlights the towers. A different modulation of the façade corresponds to the recessing of the central portions of the east and west curtains. The continuous bands of cement balconies, moved by a reiterated triangular projection and protected by a metal railing, are repeated on the three stories above, emerging from the exposed brick façades. An alternation of pairs of small square and parahexagonal windows marks the attics, into which paired and characteristically Dutch corbels of the tackles to lift domestic weights are hammered. They are decorated with elegant spiral irons reminiscent of butterfly antennas. A band of glass-concrete elements stacked up at 45-degrees eases the transition from the residential floors and the corbelled shelter of the portico, providing light to the ground-floor shops.

The articulated volumes of the towers of the two portalled buildings sum up the different design solutions conceived between 1924 and 1926. They also make one of Berlage's convictions explicit: "The sense of spatial unity [of squares] is guaranteed by the important buildings and their relative heights." Built between 1925 and 1927, Berlage's work on Mercatorplein unfortunately was mutilated in the northern tower and in the ground-level design, deflating the tension to define a "locus" of the contemporary city, the square, which was implicit in the architect's commitment. Leaving aside the moral inspirations, he believed that "to construct was to serve" the community.

Bibliography: J.B. 1926; red. 1926, *Amsterdam-West*; also cfr. *Tijdschrift voor Volkshuisvestig en Stedebouw* 1922, p. 246; *Tijdschrift voor Volkshuisvestig en Stedebouw* 1924, p. 66; *Het Bouwbedrijf* 1924, 6; *De Groene Amsterdammer* August 22, 1925; *Bouwkundig Weekblad Architectura* 1927, 13; *Het Bouwbedrijf* 1927, 1; *Wendingen* 1927, 6–7; *Tijdschrift voor Volkshuisvestig en Stedebouw* 1928, 7.

405

406

407

Study-project for the Headquarters of the Rijksverzekeringsbank

Amsterdam South, Stadionweg/ Apollolaan
Commissioned by
the Rijksverzekeringsbank
1925–26

Between 1925 and 1926, at the same time Berlage was overseeing construction of the Christian Science Church and the new De Nederlanden building in The Hague, he was also designing the headquarters of the Rijksverzekeringsbank, a public social welfare institute. It was to be located in the southern part of Amsterdam, facing the plot of land reserved for the Kunstenaarshuis in the second version of the town plan for that part of the city.

The Berlage archives conserve numerous studies of plans dating between May 1925 and June 1926 that testify to the elaborate design process. The last draft shows a rhomboidal plan. The corner entrances were skilfully placed, inverting the directional grid. The solution for the rear of the building was peculiar. It was to be reserved for residences and to be autonomous of the main block of the building, in the plan and in its vertical elevation. In the layout, the work spaces for the 1,000 bank employees were located in the perimetral bands of the rhomboid. A monumental stairway inserted in a triangular grid prefigured a pentagonal prism. Two rectangular courts, juxtaposed to form an L-shape compared to the principal symmetrical axis, are interior voids in the volume. They illuminate the interior spaces from the first floor up.

Headquarters of the Amsterdamsche Bank

With J.B. Ouëndag and W.B. Ouëndag, Jr.
Amsterdam, Rembrandtsplein 47
Commissioned by the Amsterdamsche Bank
1926–32

In 1926 Berlage, who had been involved with the Rijksverzekeringsbank project for a year, was asked to join the Ouëndag architectural firm to work on the project of the Amsterdamsche Bank, to be built in the center of the city adjacent to Sanders' Panopticum, built in 1881–82.

It is hard to know exactly what Berlage contributed to this building.

On the basis of documentary evidence, his work was probably limited to certain problems in the design and plan of the corner on the Rembrandtsplein because of the attention reserved for the "tower" as an urban marker. A perspective plan in the Berlage archives showed a spherical crown on the tower. During construction, the rounded corner in the plan on the Amstelstraat was also eliminated.

Bibliography: J.P.M. 1927; red. 1927, *Het nieuwe . . .* ; ouendag 1932; Smets 1932; Van Haersma Buma and Kroner 1932.

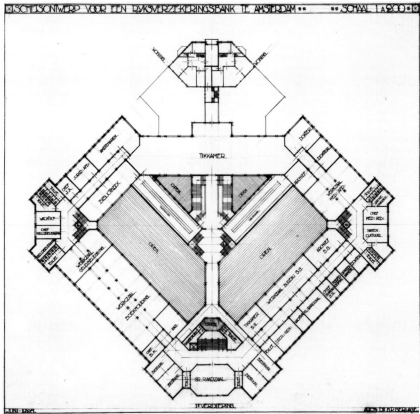

408

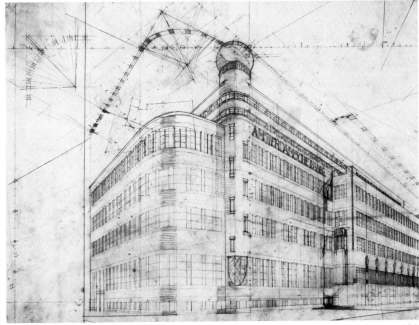

409

410

409. *Perspective study for the corner.*

410. *Present state.*

405. *Perspective study for the edifice with tower.*

406. *Perspective study for the edifice with tower.*

407. *The edifice with tower on the north, contemporary photograph.*

408. *Study of the plan for the first floor.*

With P. Zwart (for the interiors)
The Hague, 1 A. Bickerweg
Commissioned by the Church
of Christ Scientist
1925–26

William Gray Purcell, Berlage's American friend, propagandized the principles of the Christian Science Church in a letter dated May 1918. He wrote: "I think you will be interested to know that in America the new spirit has touched religion and produced a faith expressing itself with the simplicity of primitive Christianity but taking full account of modern intellectual equipment and world machinery. . . . The Christian Science began here in 1866, was practically unheard of until the '90s and now commands the support of our best citizens and best minds (and hearts). I connected myself with this body of spiritual workers shortly after I saw you last. . . . There are three Christian Science Societies in your country. I believe you would be interested in the type of citizens who are found associated with this movement, which is so essentially democratic in the broadest application of that word."

The results of this active proselytism were immediate. In a short note to the council of the Christian Science community in The Hague, in December 1922, Berlage specified his honorarium of 1,700 florins for the general plan of a church whose construction costs would come to over 2,000 florins. In a letter dated May 1925 that was part of a frequent exchange of correspondence with Purcell, Berlage wrote: "In return of to the sending of your plan, which gived me an idea of the extension of those churches in America, I posted my design at your address, as the entire scheme was realized before the receipt of yours, and construction has begun. You will see that my plan does not agree with some points you outlined. But you should reckon first with the fact, that we in our country, in general, can not dispose of as large finantial possibilities as in yours and of course not at the beginning of the development of a new religious

movement, which expresses not the general spirit of Holland. And secondly, that the meanings about some details are depending on local customs and views. The church which seats 700 will be completed at a cost of not yet 100.000. I studied your plan, and do not like it. For it seems to me to respond to the American sense. I hope you will criticise mine in regard with the necessary limitations and Dutch views." [sic]

Inaugurated on Christmas Day, 1926, the complex is composed of three edifices with independent volumes connected in the plan. The large church structure seats a congregation of 700 in the galleries and parterre. There is a Sunday school for 200 children, an elongated edifice to the right of the church. The residence has Nordic sloping roofs (those of the other edifices are flat) and is an annex to the left of the low structure built of reinforced concrete in front of the church. The exterior is dressed in tight exposed yellow brick. The structure of the plastered interior is revealed by the design of the frame. The possibilities offered by the variations in height of the plot are exploited to articulate the interior levels. A centrifugal tension and the clock tower mark the layout. The square outside the church rises slightly toward the entrance atrium of the church, which is recessed from the street. A T-shaped stairway leads through a large vestibule to the entrances of the church hall. As in a chinese box, the passage revolves around the small rooms of the officiants, placed around the spiral staircase of the tower. The orthogonal lines of the walls of the church hall run from a fulcrum just outside the the church and inflect diagonally. Two hallways follow these directions and lead to the stairs to the upper balcony, which seats about 200. The elaborate plan of the church hall (cfr. Bock 1983, p. 134) comes from the joining of two different small squares at the opposite points of the large central square, which is rotated 45 degrees and is complicated by chamfering. On the exterior, the dominant volume of the church pivots around the tower, which also highlighted by the copper-green color of the roof. The volume spreads out like a fan and

reveals the complexity of the plan, despite the severe treatment of the façades. The trellis-covered terrace of the school is located at the level of the church-hall pavement. The school faces only onto the canal and is composed of a rectangular space divided into boxes on the long sides. The vestibule is slightly rotated compared to the school. It is located on a lower level and has an independent entry from the street. The complex is closed off by a wall in full brick, a visual extension of the parapet of the adjacent bridge. In the design of certain elements (the lamp set into the corner, toward the canal; the tower crown), Berlage proved he was a master of a typically Dutch decorative geometrism. But the references to Wright are evident in the controlled explosion of the volumes, in the sections of the plan, and in the variety of voids despite the prevalence of solids. The relationship between the solidity of the brick wall and the

energy of the L-shaped glass-cement bands, which diffuse natural light, is also significant. In a letter dated March 1925 Purcell counseled Berlage "to flood the church with daylight, and with artificial light, as this religion stands for enlightenment as opposed to the dusky mysticism of the old theology." Berlage turned the interior design of the church to the talented Piet Zwart. His work in this building was praised by contemporaries for the "Zakelijkheid" of the materials: industrial rubber for most of the floors and shiny tiles lining the hallways and on the pulpit. The nude metal of the music-stands and the organ pipes stands out in contrast to these materials. The only precious element in the design is the colored glass skylight inscribed in the triangle traced by the ribs of the ceiling, although the symbolic meaning prevails over the decorative.

411. Plan at the level of the church hall.

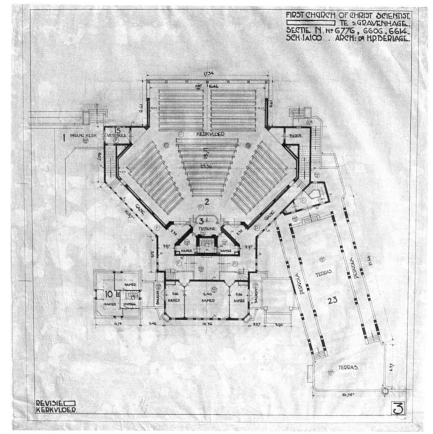

411

Bibliography: Berlage 1925, *Het plan* . . . ; G. 1927; Van Rood 1927; Wattjes 1927, *Christian.* . . .

412. *Detail of the roof of the church hall, present state.*

413. *Principal frontage, contemporary photograph.*

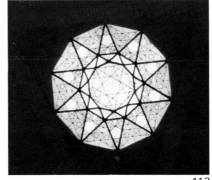

412

413

With E.F. Strasser and B. Wille
Moscow, Red Square
1926

"That is the beginning of the general revolution for which Russia gave the signal," wrote Berlage to his friend and confidant William Gray Purcell in November 1918, referring to the collapse of the central European empires and the formation of the people's republics. Before he went on to the subject of his project for the Pantheon of Mankind, he added: "The conception which I myself have always supported and which is of a socialistic nature will be realized."

In the years immediately afterward, Berlage progressively intensified his measured political commitment. In November 1919 he was among the subscribers to the heterogeneous league of Socialist-Revolutionary Intellectuals, founded by the anarchist Bart de Ligt, which was dissolved in 1922. He also participated in the stormy meetings of the Social Democratic left wing held in Amsterdam's "De Rode Leeuw," next to his De Beursbengel on the Damrak. In 1921 he founded, with Gerrit Rietveld, the association "Holland-Russia." In May of the same year he delivered a lecture entitled *The Crisis and Art*, which was published in the second edition of *Studies over bouwkunst, stijl en samenleving*". In this lecture, he affirmed that society's ills, and war, their perverse offspring, were inevitable consequences of capitalist development; the revolutionary crisis underway would bring about a society in which the very reasons for the crisis would disappear. Nevertheless, Berlage believed, even the most revolutionary spirit is unconsciously influenced by tradition.

It was precisely the meditated legacy of tradition which shaped Berlage's project for Lenin's mausoleum. The design was conceived in unclear circumstances. The dossier of documents in the Berlage archives includes the 1926 presentation, signed "Architekten E.E. Strasser und B. Wille

unter dem Starken Kunstlerischen Einfluss von Berlage." Strasser was the son-in-law and associate, with Wille, of Berlage's studio in the Hague.

Berlage was probably invited to submit a project to oppose the one by Russian Academician A.A. Ščusev before the definitive approval of Ščusev's mausoleum, erected provisionally for the funeral and reconstructed a first time in oak in May 1924. Berlage's passionate commitment has no known outcome. Ščusev's mausoleum was constructed between 1927 and 1930 in sumptuous stone materials to replace the temporary monument.

Berlage defined the strong image of a symmetrically planned mausoleum right next to the high walls of the Kremlin in the area of Red Square between the Spasskaja and Nikolskaja towers. His design was not immune

414

414. Perspective study of the entire complex.

415

416

to influences from Garnier in a measured dialogue with its surroundings. The volume of the central structure of the mausoleum rises in large steps, assuming a form reminiscent of mechanical gears, and is crowned by a tholos. In the background the Spasskaja tower is framed by two thin smokestack-towers buttressed by spurs toward the walls, which terminate in crystalline urns held by slim legs.

The symmetrical promenades at the sides of the central structure terminate in the porticoed pavilions of the entrance end bays. They have the effect of horizontally expanding the dimensions of the complex on a grand scale. Inside, the open galleries are longitudinally marked by the rhythmic sequence of pilasters and continuous balustrades. Toward the outside, a lower base runs around a portico whose façade on the square evokes the profile of a factory with the serrated skyline of shed roofing. The squat exterior pilasters of the galleries are linked to the triangular architraves of the portico by means of progressive projections. These are repeated in the transition from the intrados to the plane of the facade. This was a variation of an intuitive concept Berlage had formally tested in the first design for the Municipal Museum and in the second building for the De Nederlanden van 1845 in the Hague. To reinforce the rootedness of the construction in this low base, the plinth of the pilasters was compressed pyramidally. In a preliminary study illustrated by an interior view the same motifs are repeated, although not completely worked out. The design of the roofing is also different.

The attachment of the symmetrical wings to the mausoleum, from which a smaller structure projects to the left, is mediated by a stereometric volume. It is occupied by two flights of steps in a series that ascend to the upper level. Continuation of the itinerary, organized on staggered planes inside high balustrades, assumes a sinuous band form around the cell holding the sarcophagus.

The funerary ambiance of the octagonal plan, inscribed in the semicircle of the itineraries, is separated—but not closed off from—the surrounding space and seems almost suspended in an atemporal dimension. The steps leading to the bare naos descend through thresholds framed by monolithic triangular pilasters outlined by salients progressively projecting toward the exterior. At the center of the naos is the sarcophagus with Lenin's corpse, inside a stepped cruciform frame sunk into the pavement. The stepped pyramidal octahedron of the roof covering is truncated. Perhaps a transparent surface covers it, in predictable contrast with the shadow of the itinerary that is crossed with blades of light passing through narrow vertical openings in the wall.

The rejection of the proposal in no way hampered Berlage's opinion of Russia. He and a group of associates from the "Nederland-Nieuw Rusland" traveled to Russia in the summer of 1929. In Moscow and other cities, Berlage delivered a lecture on modern architecture. In 1930, the *Bouwkundig Weekblad* published his impressions of the trip. This travel writing was a constant in Berlage's experience. His impressions of his trips to the United States in 1911 and to the Dutch colonies in 1923 were important precedents. His travel sketches were another constant. On this trip, he attempted to grasp the essence of the Russian building tradition. The sketches counterpoint the cautious opinion Berlage expressed on modern Soviet architecture. Significantly, the conclusion of his impressions was his sonnet *aan de Wolga.* The sonnet begins with an eloquent eulogy of the regenerative power of the "great water," in whose depths are preserved elevated things. In the final verses, a subtle fear replaces it: "Dat moeder Wolga eens beleeft het uur./ Waarop haar kinderen zich koesteren aan cultur?" ("May Mother Volga still live in that hour/ when her children will still be nourished by her culture?").

415. Sketch of the central structure.

416. Sketch of the tholos.

With C. Biemond
Amsterdam South, between
Weesperzijde and Amsteldijk,
at the end of today's Vrijheidslaan
Commissioned by the Municipality
of Amsterdam
1926–32

Berlage foresaw the construction of a new bridge on the Amstel River to link the city's eastern zone with the newly expanding southern zone as one of the keystones of the second version of the Amsterdam South town plan, dating around 1916. The aerial view of the eastern segment of the plan defines with precision the image of the bridge added onto the new layout of the west bank of the river. In the report accompanying the plan, the "bridge square" is illustrated as a perspective fulcrum, with a hotel to the south and a building for the "De Hoop" oar company north of the Bridge.

Berlage received the commission to design the bridge ten years later, in 1926. He submitted his work to the competent municipal offices in 1927, giving an estimated cost of 1,600,000 florins. In substance, Berlage based his design on the idea that the bridge would form an architectural backdrop at the end of the city, since beyond it lay the country landscape. Toward this end, the northern areas of the banks (Amsteldijk to the west and Weesperzijde to the east) were elevated approximately three meters with earthworks. The ramps at the extremities of the bridge lead to the promenades along the river and to the boat depots under the terraces. In his project for the eastern bank, Berlage designed the Schollenbrug, a bridge along Weesperzijde, at the conclusion of the promenade, which was built together with the main bridge. Berlages's study for a headquarters for an aquatic sports club, the "Amstel Paviljoen," is contemporary with his bridge design. He designed the clubhouse with G.J. Rutgers. Signed by Berlage in 1927, the perspective view of the pavilion depicts an elongated edifice on the water that echoes Wright's work. It was placed on the same site as the one

in the aerial view of the town plan. A water club designed by J.J. van der Linden was finally constructed on that site in 1953.

The bridge is over 100 meters long and some 23 meters wide. It has five spans and is supported by massive connections on the banks. The central

balancing span is asymmetrical. It has a cabin for the lifting systems and a small tower with a complex design to control the river traffic. From the side toward the city, the tower appears to be a sort of lighthouse. On the shaft of the tower is a seven-meter-high allegorical relief by Hildo Krop, the

municipal sculptor. It represents the natural genius of the Amstel, the patronymic protector of the city, controlled by the *dam* (bank), rising from the water. The construction of the Berlage brug, immortalized in an amateur film by W. Scheffer, was completed in 1932 with the assistance

417

418

of C. Biemond, chief of the bridge department of the city public works office. Few variations were made during construction. The lantern crowning the lighthouse tower was eliminated. A smaller sculpture was moved to the upper part of the tower shaft. The reinforced concrete-and-iron structure was built as designed and dressed in brick and stone. The balancing span was built of iron and wood.

Bibliography: Red. 1927, *De nieuwste* . . . ; Zwart 1927, *De Amstelbrug* . . . ; red 1930–31, *Dr. Berlage's* . . . ; Berlage 1932, *De nieuwe* . . . ; Biemond 1932; Van Ravensteyn 1932; De Boer and Evers 1983.

417. *View of the model from the north; in the right foreground, the Amstel Paviljoen.*

418. *Perspective view of the Amstel Paviljoen.*

419. *Present state.*

420. *Perspective view of the small tower for the traffic controller, first version.*

419

420

With Schut
Commissioned by the Municipality
of Groningen
1927–28

Usquert
Commissioned by the Municipality
of Usquert
1928–30

Designed by the municipal director of public works with Berlage's consultantship, the town plan of Groningen was based on the enhancement of the infrastructural network in support of the newly expanding areas of the city. Two types of constructions—open and closed—further qualified only as residential and industrial were designed. Two concentric ring roads were connected radially to a dense network of secondary roads that converged in the center of the old city, where Berlage had built the Villa Heymans in 1893–95. The task of containing urban expansion was accomplished by the new railway line to the south. To the east, a system of canals supports the industrial belt that circles the city except for the southern area, surrounding a residential neighborhood. The green zones screen the construction areas, filling the empty spaces. A park with sports facilities, with winding paths and a picturesque pond, was designed to the southwest.

The municipal council of Usquert, a town with a population of 2,000 in the northern part of the province of Groningen, began to consider construction of a new town hall in 1926. Before a suitable plot of land had been purchased, a city employee submitted a general plan, which was rejected.

Berlage was contacted in 1928. The reasons were unclear, but it is certain that city officials—in particular, the mayor, T.E. Welt, and the socialist commissioner, J. Geerling—had very clear ideas about the building program and, naturally, costs. They granted Berlage free rein in regard to the architectural aspects. Their letter was received in the Hague studio by the architect E.E. Strasser, Berlage's son-in-law and partner. He forwarded it to Ascona, Switzerland, where the old master was resting after participating in June at the first meeting of CIAM, at La Sarraz, where he had delivered a paper entitled *Der Staat und der Widerstreit in der modernen Architektur*. Berlage expressed his interest in a letter from Ascona, but he accepted the commission only in August, on his return to the Netherlands. In September he sent a first version of his design, which could be termed elementary bordering on the banal. The municipal council expressed its "pleasurable and favorable impression," although questions were raised over the size of the design, which some deemed excessive, and its cost. In December, Berlage sent more detailed drawings and a cost projection. He reduced this projection by 20 percent to ease the concerns of the council. In the first version, the project showed a square plan. at the center was a large vestibule lit by a tower skylight. The building was based on a module of 110 centimeters, the same used in the contemporary second design of the Municipal Museum in The Hague. This module was based on the size of the brick chosen for the

construction—5.5 x 11 x 22 centimeters. The structure of the town hall had an almost cubical form, with a simple, symmetrical layout. Dissatisfied with this solution, Berlage designed a second version, in which he broke the continuity of the wall, partially recessing the eastern and

northern façades. On the west side, two volumes rose from the main structure. In this second version, the vestibule under the tower was still at the center of the building, but the entrance was shifted toward the corner and the stairwell projected slightly to the south. A third version

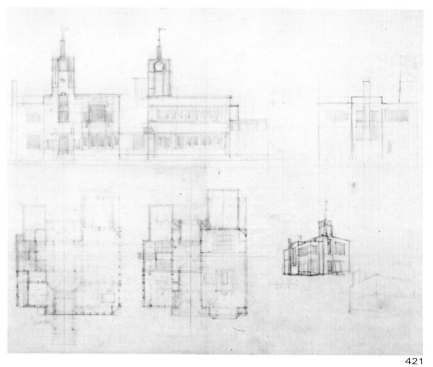

421

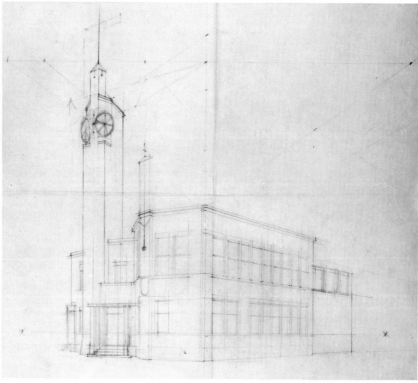

422

confirmed the progressive liberation from the original conception of the layout, although the arrangement of the rooms remained rigid. The entrance and the tower were both moved to the center of the eastern—street—façade. The tower was more elongated and dominated the image of the building. The windows were arranged in long rows. In the fourth version the entrance was rotated, as was the balcony of the mayor's office and the tower, to make them perpendicular to the transverse axis of the street and to solve the problematic siting of the building. In the fifth and final version the mayor's study was modified, with part of it shifted under the council meeting room. The balcony flanked the tower, and the eastern wall turned at an obtuse angle. The interior spaces surrounding the vestibule were arranged coherently. The vestibule was also used as a waiting room. The bicycle storeroom, the jail cell, and the bathroom were on one side; the archives were on the other. Both sides project on the plan.

This tormented process confirms the extreme attention Berlage gave to defining the image of the project, even in small commissions. A tower was certainly needed to mark the presence of the town hall, which was located on the outskirts of town and was no greater in volume than the villas around it. For Berlage, the importance of the tower evidently went beyond this simple need and took on a symbolic significance. In fact, he offered to pay out of his own pocket for the work of raising the tower even higher after the municipal council rejected his proposal. During construction, Berlage controlled every detail, choosing the colors of the bricks, of the roof tiles, and of the interiors. He designed the garden, the clock on the tower, the flagpole, the bench in the vestibule, and many other objects in the interior design. The structure was built of reinforced concrete, with flat roofs. It was faced in brick woven into different designs. Construction was completed in April 1930, and the town hall was inaugurated in the presence of the architect. (H.V.B.)

Bibliography: Karstkarel and Terpstra 1980; Taverne 1980.

421. Study of the plan and elevations, first version.

422. Perspective layout, second version.

423. Main façade.

423

With J. Limburg
The Hague, Spui and Groenmarkt/
Kerkplein
Commissioned by the Municipality
of The Hague
1929

In 1918, Berlage was consulted about a project for a new town hall of The Hague. He proposed siting it in the Alexanderveld, north of the historic center, and attached plans to his report that reformulated the idea advanced in the 1908 town plan. Berlage returned to this project in 1929, again at the request of the municipal council, with the assistance of J. Limburg. This time he proposed two sites in the historic center. Plans, perspective sketches, and a cost estimate of some 50,000 florins are preserved.

The Groenmarkt plan was designed in two versions. It called for a pair of buildings with a courtyard flanked and connected to the old town hall by an aerial passageway. In one version, the block that separates the area of the project from Buitenhof was to be demolished to allow a single square to extend out to the Hofvijver. Berlage had redesigned that block in 1924–25. He had worked in the area

on the Chamber of Deputies in 1920. In the second version, only one portion of the block was to be demolished; the rest became the perspective focus of the corner tower of the new building.

In the Spui plan, sited south of Binnenhof, the town-hall layout juxtaposed in a T-plan two edifices with courtyards. One of the courtyards was a basin of water. This version was preferred by Berlage and by the municipal authorities, because it was freer from the constraints imposed by preexisting constructions. The entrance was placed between Spui and Kalvermarkt, fencing off two green areas and establishing a path that led to the high tower marking the complex. This was accomplished by means of two triangular basins. A second version was identical in compositional principles but was planned for a smaller plot.

Bibliography: Red. 1923, *Dr Berlage over het . . .* ; red. 1926, *De Stadhuisbouw . . .* ; Blijstra 1971; also cfr. *De Amsterdammer* 1935, 3053.

424. Perspective sketch of the Plan Groenmarkt.

Utrecht, Wittevrouwensingel/
Nachtegaalstraat
Commissioned by
the De Nederlander van 1845
Insurance Company
1929–30

425. Present state.

424

425

Commissioned by the A. Bruinsma
Construction Company
1929–30

In 1929, a competition for the construction of two areas of Amsterdam
South was announced. These areas
were the districts of Allebéplein and
Minervaplein. The program was
drawn up by the municipal office of
public works. It specified that the
competing construction companies
had to name the architects to design
the plans for the squares in agreement
with the municipal council. The
companies were also to pay the architects' fees. Departures from the
building regulations and changes in
the alignments were permitted so
long as they were architecturally ad-
vantageous and did not obstruct
traffic. Certain binding uses were also
laid down for the areas. A public
building was to be constructed in the
Allebéplein and garages in the eastern
and western blocks of the Minervaplein. The sketches of the design, accompanied by a descriptive report,
were all that was required for the first
phase of the competition and were
to be submitted by July 1, 1929.
Some of the most illustrious Dutch
architects took part in the tender.
The commission chose Blaauw for
Minervaplein and Boterenbrood for
Allebéplein, setting off a storm of
controversy in the specialized press,
with letters of protest over the selection guidelines written by the rejected
architects.

Berlage died on August 12, 1934
in The Hague. He was 78 years old
and did not live to see his last masterpiece—the Municipal Museum in
The Hague—completed. On August
16, in accordance with his last will
and testament, his body was cremated
at Velsen.

Bibliography: cfr. *Bouwkundig Weekblad Architectura* 1930, 15 and 1932, 2.

426

426. Perspective sketch of the Minervaplein.

Berlage wrote a lot throughout his life—there is still a mass of yet unpublished material—and, more importantly, he gave many lectures. He wrote for many periodicals, both in the Netherlands and abroad. The most significant Dutch professional reviews, *Bouwkundig Weekblad* and *Architectura*, regularly featured his articles, as well as such other culturally important publications as *De Kroniek* and *De Beweging*. He also published around fifteen books, mostly collections of essays, some of which were an editorial success, with several reprints.

This catalogue includes more than 180 texts, listed in chronological and, within each year, alphabetical order. Minor texts are also listed, such as brief presentations of designs or reports from a jury co-authored by Berlage. Although this bibliographical list tries to be the most complete as yet, it is still possible that some titles should be added, especially after further research in the press.

Since this catalogue was established for research purposes, it did not seem suitable to include a long inventory of manuscripts (mostly some ten lectures and a few curious literary works—theater pieces and poems) and other unpublished material (a very large correspondence, travel diaries, and other private papers), which are kept in different archives and need further work to organize and compare them.

The notes are limited to essential information. A quick glance will confirm that which we stated above: A good portion of Berlage's writings, certainly the most relevant portion and almost all the books, is based on his conferences. The general bibliography includes the many press notices about a lecture by Berlage only when they contain a summary, sometimes fairly analytical. They are the following: Rieber, 1898; Walle, 1898; editorial, 1899, "Verslag . . ."; Walenkamp, 1904; editorial, 1912, "De Berlage . . ."; Van Dessel, 1913; Schwagermann, 1913–1914; editorial 1915–1916; Wegerif, 1916; editorial, 1917, "Lezing . . ."; editorial, 1922, "De Redevoering . . ."; editorial, 1932, "De Schrikbeelden . . ."; editorial, 1932, "Dr. H.P. Berlage . . .". Aside from Berlage's theoretical criticisms, the specific list of his writings is rather limited. The introduction to the only existing anthology (Van Bergeijk, 1985) considers this aspect of his work in details.

1883

"Amsterdam en Venetië," in *Bouwkundig Weekblad* III, 34, August 23, pp. 217–219; 36, September 6, pp. 226–228, and 37, September 13, pp. 232–234.

The subtitle explains: "Remarks on the present transformations in Amsterdam."

"De St. Pieterskerk te Rome," in *Bouwkundig Weekblad* III, 5, February 1, pp. 26–28, and 6, February 8, pp. 33–35.

Historic and architectural analysis of St. Peter's Basilica in Rome.

1884

"De retrospectieve kunst," in *Bouwkundig Tijdschrift* IV, 30, pp. 77–78.

On the history of architecture and crafts, in connection with the International Exhibition on export and colonial trade held in Amsterdam in 1883, where a series of interiors inspired by models from the 16th and 17th century were presented—Berlage referred several times to the "Jan Steen Room"; the article was then featured in *Rapport over de bouwkunst op de Internationale Koloniale- en Uitvoerhandeltentoonstelling te Amsterdam 1883*, Van Munster, Amsterdam 1885, pp. 77–88.

"Het Volksoffiehuis aan de Ruyterkade," in *Bouwkundig Weekblad* IV, 24, June 11, p. 161.

Presentation of the design, signed Sanders and Berlage, for the working-class café "De Hoop" promoted by the Maatschappij voor Volkskoffiehuizen, on the occasion of the café's inauguration.

"Gottfried Semper," in *Bouwkundig Weekblad* IV, 21, May 22, pp. 142–146.

The subtitle indicates that the article was drawn from a biographical profile by Herman Hettner, published in his *Illustrierte Monatshefte* in 1879 and featured in *Kleine Schriften* after the author's death. See also *idem*, 1903.

1885

"Bij de plaat," in *Bouwkundig Weekblad* V, 5, February 7, p. 29.

Presentation of the headquarters of the Focke and Meltzer Co. In Amsterdam, signed by Sanders and Berlage.

1886

"Bij de plaat," in *Bouwkundig Weekblad* VI, 32, August 7, p. 190.

Presentation of the design of the villa Scheffer in Weesp, signed by Sanders and Berlage.

"De Dom te Milaan," in *Bouwkundig Weekblad* VI, 21, May 22, pp. 124–127.

Lecture on the history of the Italian Gothic and the Duomo in Milan, held at the headquarters of the Maatschappij tot Bevordering der Bouwkunst on May 14, 1886. "Bouwkundig Weekblad" is the association's journal. The lecture was given on the occasion of the announcement of the competition for the Duomo's new façade in *Bouwkundig Weekblad* 1886, VI, 16, April 17, pp. 96–97.

"De Plaats die de Bouwkunst in de moderne Aesthetica bekleedt," in *Bouwkundig Weekblad* VI, 27, July 3, pp. 161–163, and 28, July 10, pp. 169–172.

Review of the "place of architecture in modern aesthetics," relating the opinions of Kant, Schelling, Schopenhauer, Solger, Krause, Hegel, Trahndorf, Weisze, Schleimacher, Deutinger, Vischer, Krichman, Von Zimmermann, Von Köstlin, Fechner, and Lotze; a sort of hotchpotch.

"Indruk van de Jubileumtentoonstelling te Berlijn," in *Bouwkundig Weekblad* VI, 34, August 21, pp. 203–207.

In his "impressions of the Jubilee Exhibition in Berlin," which opened on May 23, Berlage leaves detailed descriptions to critics and gives a general account, mostly of the building and its architecture section, where Semper, Wagner, Schmitz, Neckelmann, and Lipsius were among the architects exhibited.

1887

"Ingezonden brief aan de redactie," in *Bouwkundig Weekblad* VII, 45, November 5, p. 275.

The letter to the editor, signed by Berlage and Klinkhamer, is dated November 2, 1887; it is a response to a note published in the same review (44, October 29, p. 272) concerning the polemical discussion around the issue of municipal subsidies for the Quellinus school of arts and crafts in Amsterdam, where Berlage was to teach until 1896.

1888

"Bij de plaat," in *Bouwkundig Weekblad* VIII, 39, September 29, p. 239.

Presentation of the design, signed by Sanders and Berlage, for a "kiosk" of the streetcar company Noord-Hollandsche Tramwegmaatschappij in Amsterdam.

"Een Reijse door Noord-westelijk Frankrijk," in *Bouwkundig Weekblad* VIII, 13, March 31, pp. 81–84; 14, April 7, pp. 87–90,, and 15, April 14, pp. 94–97.

Lecture on "a trip in the northwest of France," in Normandy in particular, in search of the Gothic. The lecture was held at the Amsterdam headquarters of the Maatschappij tot Bevordering der Bouwkunst on March 16, 1888.

"Het Sanatorium te Baarn," in *Bouwkundig Weekblad* VIII, 14, April 7, p. 87.

Presentation of the design, signed by Sanders and Berlage, of a sanatorium.

"Rapport," in *Bouwkundig Weekblad* VIII, 21, May 26, p. 136.

Jury's report, signed by Berlage, H.J. Wolter, and H. Moen, on a competition announced by Maatschappij tot Bevordering der Bouwkunst in 1887.

1889

"Blijde inkomsten en steden in Feesttooi," in *Bouwkundig Tijdschrift* IX, 35, pp. 23–35.

Lecture on the history of commemorative installations. It was given at the general assembly of the Maatschappij tot Bevordering der Bouwkunst, held on May 26, 1887, on the occasion of the commemorative festivities organized for King Willem III in 1887. Berlage illustrated with L.W.R. Wenkebach and G. Müller the 1887 *Geillustreerde Feestgids*, published for the occasion by H. Binger, a fellow member of the Breero Club. Some of Berlage's drawings were published again in *Bouwkundig Weekblad* III, 1887, 17.

1892

"De Kunst in stedenbouw," in *Bouwkundig Weekblad* XII, 15, April 9, pp. 87–91; 17, April 23, pp. 101–102; 20, May 14, pp. 121–124, and 21, May 21, pp. 126–127.

Lecture on "art in urban planning," held in Rotterdam on December 10, 1891, in The Hague on the 28th of the same month, and again at the Amsterdam headquarters of the Maatschappij tot Bevordering der Bouwkunst on March 25, 1892 (cfr.: *De Opmerker* XXVI, 1891, pp. 408–409; *Bouwkundig Weekblad* XII, 1892, pp. 8 and 85). This is his personal interpretation of Camillo Sitte's *Der Städtebau nach seinen Künstlerischen Grundsätzen*, published in 1899.

"Zur Praxis des Preisrichteramtes bei öffentlichen Wettbewerbungen," in *Bouwkundig Weekblad* XII, 3, January 16, pp. 15–17.

Translation edited by Berlage of an article by K. Henrici "on juries in public competitions," published in *Deutsche Bauzeitung* 1891, December 24, pp. 623–624.

1893

"Het Kantoorgebouw der Algemeene Mij. voor levensverzekering en lijfrente te Amsterdam," in *Architectura* I, 43, October 28, pp. 186–187.

Presentation of the design for the building of De Algemeene insurance company in Amsterdam.

"Is het schoone in de kunst ideaal of reëel, subjectief of objectief?," in *Bouwkundig Tijdschrift* XIII, 39, pp. 25–29.

Lecture on "beauty in art" held on May 28, 1892, at the national congress on architecture promoted for the 25th anniversary of the Maatschappij tot Bevordering der Bouwkunst.

"Prijsvragen," in *Architectura* I, 42, October 21, pp. 180–181.

Report, signed by Berlage and J.Th.J. Cuypers, of the jury for a competition for a "buffet in a hall, with boiserie" announced by "Architecture et Amicitia" in 1892.

"Rapport der Jury," in *Bouwkundig Weekblad* XIII, 39, September 30, pp. 239–241.

Report, signed by Berlage, E. Gugel, and J. Verheul and dated September 23, of the jury for a competition for the headquarters in Haarlem.

1893–1901

J. van den Vondel, *Gijsbreght van Aemstel*, De Erven F. Bohn, Haarlem, 2 vols.

Berlage worked on a monumental edition of the dramatic masterpiece of 17th-century Dutch literature and designed the staging. L. Simons wrote the introduction, B. Zweers was responsible for the music, and A.J. van Derkinderen did the illustrations. Since 1638, every month of January, the municipal theater presents the tale of Amsterdam's valiant defense by Gijsbreght of Aemstel.

1894

"Bouwkunst en impressionisme," in *Architectura* II, 22, June 2, pp. 93–95; 23, June 9, pp. 98–100; 24, June 16, pp. 105–106, and 25, June 23, pp. 109–110.

Lecture on "Architecture and Impressionism" with the motto inspired by Goethe, "The master reveals himself in the art of limiting himself." It was held on November 1893 at the "Bouwkunst en Vriendschap" in Rotterdam, and on March 28, 1894, at "Architectura et Amicitia" in Amsterdam (cfr.: *De Opmerker* XXVIII, 1893, pp. 363–364 and 367–368, and XXIX, 1894, pp. 102–103 and 201–202; *Architectura* II, 1894, pp. 53 and 113. Commentary by W.C. Bauer).

"Het Karakter van moderne bouwwerken," in *Bouwkundig Weekblad* XIV, 12, May 19, pp. 82–83.
Answer to the annual queries from the Maatschappij tot Bevordering der Bouwkunst on "the lack of character in 19th-century buildings" and on "the modern" in architecture.
"Kunst en samenleving," in *De Amsterdammer* February 11.
Article on "art and society."
"Verbouwing van 'Arti et Amicitiae'," in *Premie-Uitgave*, Vereeniging tot Bevordering van Beeldende Kunsten, Amsterdam, undated.
Presentation, written with A.C. Bleys, of the renovation design for the headquarters of "Arti et Amicitiae" in Amsterdam. Berlage did the illustrations.

1895
"Alweer," in *De Kroniek* I, 28, July 7, p. 219.
On the new main post-office in Amsterdam, a Neo-Renaissance work by C.H. Peters. The article was written for the column "Architecture"
"De Architectuur en de Pers," in *De Kroniek* I, 20, May 12, p. 156.
On "architecture and the press." on the same page, "Een Vooruitgang, for the column "Architecture."
"Den Heer A. Pit," in *De Kroniek* I, 49, December 1, p. 388.
In the column "Architecture." Response to A. Pit's observations on the concept of style; "style is independent from the choice of construction materials."
"Een Vooruitgang," in *De Kroniek* I, 20, May 12, p. 156.
Response to the news published in *Nieuws van den Dag* of the reconstruction of the Rondeel Hotel; in the column "Architecture."
"Iets over Goethiek," in *Architectura* III, 17, April 27, pp. 70–72; 18 May 4, pp. 73–76; 21, May 25, pp. 86–87; 23, June 8, pp. 93–95, and 24, June 15, pp. 97–98.
Lecture held on April 3, 1895 at the headquarters of "Architectura and Amicitia" in Amsterdam; on the "theme of the Gothic," it takes up again the themes developed in a lecture held at the Amsterdam headquarters of the Maatschappij tot Bevordering der Bouwkunst in November 28, 1890 (cfr. *Bouwkundig Weekblad* X, 1890, p. 304).
"Ijzer en steen," in *De Kroniek* I, 46, November 10, pp. 362–363.
On "iron and stone," in the column "Architecture"; Pit's observations on this article provoked the response

"Den Heer A. Pit."
"Kritiek," in *De Kroniek* I, 16, April 14, p. 123.
On architectural criticism in the column "Architecture"; several recent buildings.
"Kritiek," in *De Kroniek* I, 32, August 4, pp. 250–251.
Again on Peters's new post office near the Dam (v. *Alweer*) for the column "Architecture."
"Over Architectuur," in *De Kroniek* I, 2, January 6, pp. 9–10.
"I am convinced that architecture should move in the direction indicated by architects who know how to make logical arrangements": Style, form, and construction, however, depend on "the most powerful criterion of judgment, that of the right feeling." In the column "Architecture."
"Over Architectuur," in *De Kroniek* I, 8, February 17, pp. 58–59.
Notes on an article on "architecture and the public" published in the column "Architecture" in *De Opmerker* on January 12, 1895.
"Over de toekomst der Architectuur," in *De Kroniek* I, 27, June 30, pp. 210–211.
On the "future of architecture," in the column "Architecture."
"Rapport van Beoordeeling," in *Architectura* III, 19, May 11, pp. 79–80.
Report, signed by Berlage, J.Th.J. Cuypers, and J. Ingenhol, of the jury for the competition for "public baths in a large city."
"Schouwburgen," in *Bouwkundig Weekblad* XV, 2, January 12, pp. 7–10; 3, January 19, pp. 16–19, and 6, February 9, pp. 36–40.
Lecture on theaters held at the Amsterdam headquarters of the Maatschappij tot Bevordering der Bouwkunst on October 12, 1894: introduction; acoustics and orchestra; scenes and stage settings of the *Gijsbreght van Aemstel* (see 1893–1901 and Rebel-Benschop, 1981).
"Uit een voordracht," in *De Kroniek* I, 26, June 23, p. 202
Excerpts of a lecture; in the column "Architecture."

1895–1896
"Over Architectuur," in *Het Tweemaandelijksch Tijdschrift* I, 1895, July 6, pp. 417–427, and II, 1896, January 3, pp. 202–235.
"Claims that designing should not be done in terms of style. In this manner, an authentic architecture can be achieved, comparable to that of the Middle Ages, an architecture that is

a purely utilitarian art" (G. Fanelli 1968, p. 149). Quotes at length from J.E. van der Pek's "Bouwen in Stijl, in *De Amsterdammer* 1895.

1896
"Architectuur en versieringskunst," in *De Kroniek* II, 67, April 5, p. 108.
On "architecture and the decorative arts"; in the column "Architecture."
"De Arbeiderswoningen aan de gedempte Lindengracht," in *De Kroniek* II, 98, November 8, pp. 360–361.
On a housing complex of 32 low-income apartments built by J.E. van der Pek on Lindengracht in Amsterdam in 1896 (cfr. *Bouwkundig Weekblad* XVI, 1896, 41), in the column "Architecture."
"Een fraai boek," in *De Kroniek* II, 74, May 24, pp. 162–163.
On a "pretty book," in the column "Decorative Arts": About the book *De Kunstnijverheid*, for which the provincial council of Antwerp had organized a competition; the Dutch version was edited by A.W. Weissman
"Een nieuw gebouw," in *De Kroniek* II, 104, December 20, pp. 408–409.
On the administrative building of the Simplex bicycle factory in Amsterdam, a work by J. van Straaten; in the column "Architecture."
"Een nieuw tijdschrift," in *De Kroniek* II, 65, March 22, pp. 92–93.
On a new review, "Maandschrift voor Versieringskunst," in the column "Decorative Arts."
"Fransche Teekenaars," in *Bouwkundig Weekblad* XVI, 31, August 1, pp. 189–191; 32, August 8, pp. 195–198; 35, August 29, pp. 213–216 and 36, September 5, pp. 219–220.
Review of French illustrators, of posters in particular (Cheret, Toulouse-Lautrec, Dorne, Steinlen, and Lebejaz).
"Tentoonstelling te Haarlem," in *De Kroniek* II, 58, February 2, p. 34.
On an exhibition in Haarlem, in the column "Decorative Arts."
"Volkskunst," in *De Kroniek* II, 78, June 21, pp. 202–203.
On folk art, in the column "Decorative Arts."

1897
"Dr. P.J.H. Cuypers," in *De Kroniek* III, 125, May 16, p. 153.
For the seventieth birthday of the master of 19th-century Dutch architecture. On Cuypers, see the recent *P.J.H. Cuypers en Amsterdam*, Cahiers NDB 6, Staatsuitgeverij, The Hague, 1985, edited by G. Hoogewoud, J. Jaapkuyt, and A. Oxenaar, with an up-to-date bibliography.

"Dr. P.J.H. Cuypers," in *Eigen Haard* 21, May 22, pp. 333–335.
See the article in *De Kroniek* in the same year.
"Duitsche Architectuur," in *De Kroniek* III, 113, February 21, pp. 59–60.
On German architecture, in the column "Architecture."

1898
"De Beurs te Amsterdam," in *Bouwkundig Weekblad* XVIII, 14, April 2, pp. 99–102.
Lecture on the history of the Stock Exchange buildings held in Amsterdam on April 1, 1898, for the Maatschappij tot Bevordering der Bouwkunst and "Architectura et Amicitia."
"De Nieuwe St. Bavo te Haarlem," in *De Kroniek* IV, 176, May 8, p. 148.
On the new church of St. Bavo in Haarlem, in the column "Architecture."
"Drijwerk van F. Zwollo," in *De Kroniek* IV, 187, July 24, p. 241.
On the craft work of F. Zwollo, in the column "Decorative Arts." Although this article is featured in the catalogue by Thijs, 1956, it was probably written by M.A.J. Bauer and signed "B." On Zwollo, see *Frans Zwollo Sr. 1872–1945*, exhibition catalogue, Museum Boymans-van-Beuningen, Rotterdam 1982; bilingual text in Dutch and German.
"Over Architectuur," in *De Kroniek* 191, September 11, p. 295.
On Belgian Art Nouveau and Van de Velde, in the column "Architecture."

1900
"Een nieuw produkt," in *De Kroniek* VI, 263, January 7, p. 5.
A new technique in ceramics of the Rozenburg Co. in The Hague, in the column "Decorative Arts."
"H.J. de Groot. Iets over ontwerpen in architectuur," in *De Kroniek* VI, 303, October 13, p. 326.
On De Groot's text on architectural design, excerpted from "Architectura." For De Groot, a scholar in architectural design and drawing who influenced a whole trend in the Dutch architectural culture, see his fundamental *Driehoeken*, Amsterdam, 1896, with J.M. de Groot, and *Iets over ontwerpen in architectuur*, Maassluis 1900.

1901
"De Nieuwe Beurs te Amsterdam," in *De Ingenieur* XVI, November 9, pp. 722–726.
On the new Stock Exchange in Amsterdam: introduction to the visit of the members of the Royal Institute

of Engineering, followed by a meeting on September 10, 1901.

1903

"Gottfried Semper," in *Architecture* XI, 6, February 7, pp. 46–47; 7, February 14, pp. 54–55; 8, February 21, pp. 62–63; 9, February 28, pp. 70–72; 10, March 7, pp. 79–80, and 11, March 14, pp. 88–89.

Lecture on Semper held at "Architectura et Amicitia" on October 29, 1902. Semper was one of Berlage's spiritual masters. On Semper and Berlage, see Singelenberg, 1976.

"Het Gebouw der Algemeene te Leipzig," in *Architectura* XI, 16, April 18, pp. 125–126.

Presentation of the design for the building of De Algemeene insurance company in Leipzig.

1904

"Architectonische toelichting tot het plan van uitbreiding der Stad Amsterdam tusschen Amstel en Schinkel," in *Gemeenteblad van Amsterdam* I, pp. 876 and 1725.

Report on the first development plan for the south of Amsterdam; see also *Gemeenteblad van Amsterdam* 1905, II, pp. 14–57, for the discussion at the municipal council on January 11, 1905, and 1906, p. 774, for the approval of the plan on September 22, 1906.

Over Stijl in bouw- en meubelkunst, A.B. Soep, Amsterdam, undated, 130 pp. ill.; W.L. & J. Brusse, Rotterdam 1908², 131 pp., 38 ill. by the author; 1917³, 143 pp., 38 ill.; 1921⁴, 176 pp., 38 ill., 50 photographs.

In 1902 Soep asked Berlage for a text provisionally entitled *Handwerk en Kunst*, and published two years later with the title *Over Stijl in bouw- en meubelkunst*, which was Berlage's first book. It is a brief history, influenced by Semper, of the "evolution in style" of furniture and its social and cultural context.

"Programma van de eereprijsvraag," in *Architectura* XII, 47, November 19, pp. 382–383.

A competition for a government office in Haarlem was announced on the occasion of the fiftieth anniversary of "Architectura et Amicitia," the terms of which were signed by Berlage and L.H.E. van Hylckema Vlieg.

"Thema behandeld op het Congres te Madrid," in *Architectura* XII, 21, May 21, pp. 163–164.

Paper read at the VI International Congress of architects held in Madrid in April 1904, which P.J.H. Cuypers

took part. "Reinforced concrete will probably cause a major evolution in architecture; architects must, therefore, study its artistic forms now if they want to keep control over their art." The French version of the text was published in 1906.

"Vóór-Historische Wijsheid," in *Architectura* XII, 45, November 5, pp. 365–366, and 47, November 19, p. 385.

Response to the article with the same title by H. Walenkamp, in *Architectura* 1904, XII, 41, October 8, pp. 333–336, on "the significance and aesthetic role of the duodecimal system." Walenkamp responded in No. 46, November 12, p. 376, and Berlage responded in turn in the No. 47.

1905

"Beschouwingen over stijl," in *De Beweging* I, 1, January, pp. 47–83; published also separately, *idem*, s.i., 36 pp.; included in *Studies over bouwkunst, stijl en samenleving* 1910, pp. 45–76.

The "remarks on style" take a phrase by A. Verwey as a motto: "In our time, balance is really modern." Dutch version of *Gedanken über Stil in der Baukunst*, published in the same year.

"Feestrede," in *Architectura* special issue, pp. 4–6.

Article for the commemorative issue published for the fiftieth anniversary of "Architectura et Amicitia."

Gedanken über Stil in der Baukunst, Julius Zeitler Verlag, Leipzig, 53 pp. ill.

Lecture on "style in architecture" held at the Museumverein in Krefeld on January 22 and 23, 1904. "Truth in construction as an essential factor of good architecture. Architecture as the art of enclosing space ("*Raumschliessung*"). The function of the walls as elements enclosing space can only be achieved through a flat decoration" (G. Fanelli, 1968, p. 151). This an updated version of the text *Gottfried Semper* of 1903.

"Huizen van De Bazel," in *De Kroniek* XI, 544, May 27, p. 166.

Note on De Bazel's Viruly houses, in Willemspark, Amsterdam. For De Bazel, see A.W. Reinink, *K.P.C. de Bazel - architect*, Universitaire Pers, Leiden, 1965, with bibliography, and "K.P.C. de Bazel," in M. Bock ed., *Architectura 1893–1918*, exhibition catalogue, Architectuurmuseum, Amsterdam 1975¹, pp. 71–92, with anthology and bibliography.

"Over de waarschijnlijke ontwikkel-

ing der architectuur," in *Architectura* XIII, 29, July 22, pp. 239–240; 30, July 29, pp. 247–248; 31, August 5, pp. 259–260; 32, August 12, pp. 266–267; 33, August 19, pp. 273–274; 36, September 9, pp. 303–304; 41, October 14, pp. 379–381; published in the small volume by J. Waltman Jr., *idem*, Delft, 1905, 38 pp.; included in *Studies over bouwkunst, stijl en samenleving* 1910, pp. 77–104.

Lecture on the probable development of architecture, held at "Architectura et Amicitia" on March 22, 1905.

1906

"Gebouw ten dienste der Arbeiderscoöperatie 'Voorwaarts' te Rotterdam," in *Architectura* XIII, 47, November 24, pp. 387–388.

Presentation of the design for the workers' cooperative "Voorwaarts" in Rotterdam.

"Influence des procédés modernes de construction dans la forme artistique," in *6e Congrès International des Architects. Comptes-Rendus*, Madrid 1906, pp. 174–176.

Cfr. "Thema . . ." from 1904.

"K.P.C. de Bazel," in *Elsevier's* XVI, 32, pp. 73–87.

On De Bazel, on whom he had written an article in 1905. Berlage also wrote an *in memoriam* in 1923–1924.

1907

"Baukunst und Kleinkunst," in *Kunstgewerbeblatt* XVIII, pp. 183–188 and 241–245; updated in the Dutch version, *Beschouwingen over Bouwkunst en hare ontwikkeling* 1911, pp. 17–35.

Lecture on "architecture and minor arts" held in Hamburg.

"Ter Herinnering," in *De Kroniek* XI, October 19, p. 9.

Article for the review's commemorative issue.

1908

"Concertzalen," in *Toonkunst* IV, 1 and 4; also in *Muzikale Brieven* 1911, I, June, pp. 26–43, and in *Architectura* 1911, XIX, 13, April 1, pp. 98–101; 14, April 8, pp. 106–108, and 15, April 15, pp. 114–117; included in *Beschouwingen over bouwkunst en hare ontwikkeling* 1911, pp. 83–102.

Lecture held in Delft on the theme of the concert hall, in connection with the design of the Beethovenhuis.

"Eenige beschouwingen over de Klassieke Bouwkunst," in *De Beweging* IV, 8, August, pp. 115–134; included in *Beschouwingen over bouwkunst en hare ontwikkeling* 1911, pp. 1–16.

Remarks on "classical architecture" are the theme of a lecture at the annual meeting of the association of

high-school teachers.

Grundlagen und Entwicklung der Architektur, W.L. & J. Brusse, Rotterdam, and Julius Bard, Berlin, VI + 122 pp., 29 ill.; published in parts in Czech, 1911, and in Dutch and English, 1912.

Four lectures from a course on interior design taught at the Kunstgewerbe Museum in Zürich in 1907, on the invitation of J. de Praetere. "Simple geometric principles are the basis of architecture. Reference to Semper's ideas. Quotes from Sheraton. . . . Interesting illustration showing the application of geometric systems in the works of Berlage and De Bazel." (G. Fanelli 1968, p. 152. Cfr. also editorial 1907).

"Slotvoordracht: Samenvatting," in AA.VV., *Voordrachten over bouwkunst*, Maatschappij voor goede en goedekoope lectuur, Amsterdam, undated, pp. 341–394, also published separately, 55 pp., 24 ill. Reissued by *Onze Kunst* with different illustrations by Berlage and the title "Over Architectuur; included in *Studies over bouwkunst, stijl en samenleving* 1910, with the title "Opmerkingen over bouwkunst, pp. 197–225.

Report on the lectures held at "Architectura et Amicitia" in 1907–1908 by Van der Pek (principles and values of architecture), Kromhout (Islamic art), Leliman (classical architecture), J.Th.J. Cuypers (medieval architecture), Weissman (Renaissance), Walenkamp (present and future of architecture), and Berlage (conclusion and summary).

1909

"Alfred Messel," in *De Beweging* V, 8, August, pp. 113–116.

Article *in memoriam* on the German architect who died that year.

"Architektur," in *Wissen und Leben*, pp. 528–543.

Article on architecture in the Zürich review.

"Het Uitbreidingsplan van 's-Gravenhage," in *Bouwkunst* I, 4–5, July-October, pp. 97–144; reissued separately, *idem*, 48 pp., ill.; included in *Beschouwingen over bouwkunst en hare ontwikkeling* 1911, pp. 43–80.

The first part, "Stedenbouw (pp. 98–120) brings together a course on urban planning that Berlage taught first at "Practische Studie" in Delft, in the winter 1908–1909, and later in Düsseldorf, in German, in the spring 1909. The second part (pp. 120–144) presents the development plan for The Hague (this part is condensed in the 1911 edition).

"Kunst en Maatschappij," in *De Beweging* V, 11, November, pp. 20166–186, and 12, December, pp. 229–264; included in *Studies over bouwkunst, stijl en samenleving* 1910, pp. 1–44.
Lecture on "art and society" held at the Studentenleesgezelschap voor Sociale Lezingen in Amsterdam. The motto is taken from Schoenmaekers's (the theosophist friend of Mondrian) "Het Geloof van den nieuwen mensch, the same as in *Kunst en Gemeenschap*, published in 1911: "Ours is an earthly religion."
"Over Architektuur," in *Onze Kunst* VIII, July, pp. 21–29 and August, pp. 60–69; issued separately, *idem*, 20 pp., ill.
See "Slotvoordracht: Samenvatting," 1908.
Rapport over de Amsterdamsche parken en plantsoenen, J.H. de Bussy, Amsterdam, 46 pp.
Report on open spaces written for the Amsterdam Housing Council by a commission that included Berlage and J. van Hasselt among its members.
"Über Städtebau," in *Neudeutsche Bauzeitung*, pp. 393–397 and pp. 408–410.
Lecture on urban planning held in Düsseldorf. See "Het Uitbreidingsplan . . ." 1909.
1910
L. Zwiers, *Burgerlijke bouwkunde: houtconstructies*, Van Mantgem & De Does, Amsterdam 1910², 544 pp., ill.
For the second revised edition, Berlage wrote the preface to Zwiers's handbook on wooden construction.
"Der Haagsche Stadterweiterungsplan," in *Der Städtebau* VII, 5, pp. 49–53 and ill. 25–28, and 6, pp. 65–67.
German version of the second part of "Het Uitbreidingsplan . . ." 1909.
"Iets over de Moderne Duitsche Architectuur en de Brusselsche Tentoonstelling," in *De Beweging* VI, 11, November pp. 151–156 and reissued in *Bouwkundig Weekblad* XXX, 46, 1910, November 12, pp. 542–543; included in *Beschouwingen over bouwkunst en hare ontwikkeling* 1911, pp. 37–42.
On the German participation in the Brussels World Fair in 1910; cfr. R. Breuer, ed., *Deutschlands Raumkunst und Kunstgewerbe auf der Weltausstellung zu Brüssel 1910*, J. Hoffmann, Stuttgart, undated.
Studies over bouwkunst, stijl en samenleving, W.L. & J. Brusse, Rotterdam, 126 pp., 20 ill. by J. Briedé; 1922², 153 pp., 20 ill.

Fundamental collection of essays: "Kunst en Maatschappij" 1909; "Beschouwingen over stijl" 1905; "Opmerkingen over bouwkunst" 1908 (original title, "Slotvoordracht: Samenvatting").
In the second edition, the essay "De Crisis en de kunst," 1922, was also included.
1911
"Architektuur en omgeving," in *De Beweging* VII, 6, June, pp. 225–234; published in part in *Architecture* XIX, 1911, pp. 215–216, with the title, "Berlage's Beschouwingen."
On the results of the competitions for the Bismarck mausoleum in Bingerbrück-Bingen—Gropius and Mies van der Rohe were among the many competitors—and for a Swiss national mausoleum. Discussion on "architecture and environment."
Beschouwingen over bouwkunst en hare ontwikkeling, W.L. & J. Brusse, Rotterdam, 121 pp., 26 ill. by J. Briedé.
Fundamental anthology of essays: "Eenige beschouwingen over klassieke bouwkunst" 1908; "Bouwkunst en kleinkunst" 1907 (original title, "Baukunst und Kleinkunst"); "Iets over de Moderne Duitsche Architectuur en de Brusselsche tentoonstelling" 1910; "Stedenbouw" 1909 (see "Het Uitbreidingsplan van 's-Gravenhage" 1909); "Concertzalen" 1908; and the lecture, "Over Baksteenbouw."
"Het artikel van den Heer J. de Meijer over 'Concertzalen'," in *Architectura* XIX, April 29, pp. 131–132.
Response to the article by J. de Meijer, "Concertzalen," in *Architectura* XIX, 17, April 22, pp. 123–125; cfr. Berlage, *Concertzalen*, 1908.
"Kantoorgebouw voor de Assurantie Mij. Tegen Brandschade en op het Leven 'De Nederlanden van 1845' te Rotterdam," in *De Bouwwereld* X, 42, October 18, pp. 333–335.
Presentation of the design for the building of De Nederlanden van 1845 insurance company in Rotterdam.
"Kunst en Gemeenschap," in *De Beweging* VII, 12, December, pp. 225–238; published in German and English in 1912; included in *Een drietal lezingen in Amerika gehouden* 1912, pp. 1–13.
Lecture on "art and the community."
"Über moderne Baukunst," in *Zeitschrift des Österreichischen Ingenieur- und Architecten Vereines* LXII, 21, pp. 321–326.
Lecture on modern architecture, full of philosophic quotes, held in Vienna

at the Österreichisches Ingenieur- und Architecten Verein.
"Základ a Vyvoj moderní Architektury," in *Styl*, pp. 62 sq. Cfr. *Grundlagen* . . . 1908.
1912
"Amerikaansche Reisherinneringen," in *De Beweging* VIII, 6, June, pp. 295–300; 7, July, pp. 47–56; 8, August, pp. 105–121; 9, September, pp. 278–287; 10, October, pp. 46–61; published as a book, *idem*, W.L. & J. Brusse, Rotterdam, 1913, 48 pp., 16 ill.
Memories of Berlage's trip to America in 1911.
"Art and the Community," in *The Western Architect* XVIII, 8, August, pp. 85–89.
Lecture held in America, English version of "Kunst en Gemeenschap 1911."
Een drietal lezingen in Amerika gehouden, W.L. & J. Brusse, Rotterdam, 43 pp.
Collection in Dutch of the three lectures given in America, at Harvard: "Kunst en Gemeenschap," 1911; "Grondslagen en Ontwikkeling der Architektuur," 1912; "Over moderne architektuur, 1912."
"Foundations and Development of Architecture," in *The Western Architect* XVIII, 9, September, pp. 96–99, and 10, October, pp. 104–108.
Lecture given in America; English version of a part of *Grundlagen* . . . 1908.
"Grondslagen en Ontwikkeling der Architektuur," in *De Beweging* VIII, 1, January, pp. 17–35; included in *Een drietal lezingen in Amerika gehouden*, 1912, pp. 15–30.
Cfr. *Grundlagen* . . . 1908.
"Kunst und Gemeinschaft," in *Wissen und Leben* VI, pp. 168–183, 232–242, 307–314, and 360–369.
German version of "Kunst en Gemeenschap 1911."
"Modern Architecture," in *The Western Architect* XVIII, 3, March, pp. 29–36.
Lecture given in America, English version of "Over moderne architektuur 1912."
"Neuere Amerikanische Architektur," in *Schweizerische Bauzeitung* LX, 11, September 14, pp. 148–150, and 12, September 21, pp. 165–167.
Summary of the lecture on the "new American architecture" (the skyscraper, Sullivan, and Frank Lloyd Wright) held at the Swiss Ingenieur- und Architekten Verein in Zürich, on March 30, 1912. A brief editorial completes the text in No. 13,

September 28, p. 178. Cfr. "De Berlage avond . . .," editorial, 1912. English translation in Gifford, 1966, pp. 606–616.
"Over Moderne Architektuur," in *De Beweging* VIII, 2, February, pp. 45–59; included in *Een drietal lezingen in Amerika gehouden* 1912, pp. 31–43.
Based on the text of a conference on the significance of modern architecture around 1905, revised and used several times, such as in *Über moderne Baukunst* 1911.
"Waar zijm wij aangeland?" in *De Beweging* VIII, 4, April, pp. 1–13; reissued in *Bouwkundig Weekblad* XXXII, 1912, 14, April 6, pp. 160–161,, and 15, April 13, pp. 170–179; *partim* in *Architectura* XX, 1912, 8, February 24, p. 64.
On a series of unresolved issues in the debate on architecture in the Netherlands (the issue of the Dam in Amsterdam, the theater in The Hague, the quadrennial exhibition).
1913
Bouwkunst in Holland, Maatschappij voor goede en goedkoope lectuur, Amsterdam, undated, 32 pp., 20 ill.
Popular lecture on the history of Dutch architecture (text pp. 3–9), held at the Vereeniging tot het houden van Voordrachten met licht in Amsterdam.
"Landhuis te Baarn," in *Bouwkundig Weekblad* XXXIII, 11, March 15, pp. 125–126.
Presentation of the design for the villa Salomonson at Baarn.
"Reisherinnering," in *De Beweging* IX, 12, December, pp. 298–305.
On the Swiss châlet, to discuss the relationship between architecture and environment.
"Reisindruk," in *De Beweging* IX, 7, July, pp. 78–85.
Reflections on German architecture and exhibition pavilions following Berlage's visit to the international Baufach Ausstellung in Leipzig.
1913–1914
"L'Art et la Société," in *Art et Technique* 1913, I, 6, September, pp. 95–112; 7/8, October/November, pp. 113–132; 1914, 10, January, pp. 157–163; 11, February, pp. 169–182; published in a book, *idem*, Editions Tekhné, Brussels 1921, 44 pp., 93 ill.
1914
"Over moderne architectuur," in *Vlaamsche Arbeid* IX, pp. 1–17; issued separately, *Vlaamsche Arbeid*, Antwerp, undated, 17 pp.
Cfr. "Über moderne Baukunst" 1911, and "Over moderne architektuur"

1912.

"Stedenbouw," in *De Beweging* X, 3, March, pp. 226–247; 4, April, pp. 1–17; 5, May, pp. 142–157, and 6, June, pp. 263–279.
Four lectures on urban planning given in Delft for the student association "Practische Studie"; cfr. Schwagermann, 1913–1914.

"Vertreter des Holländischen Werkbundes H.P. Berlage," in Herman Muthesius, ed., *Die Werkbund Arbeit der Zukunft*, E. Diederichs Verlag, Jena 1914, pp. 16–20.
Contribution to Muthesius's book on the Werkbund: Berlage pleads the cause of a Dutch Werkbund. See also W. Penaat, "De Deutsche Werkbund en een Hollandsche Driebond," in *Bouwkundig Weekblad* 1914, pp. 339–341, 356–358, and 364–365; J. Gratama, "De Duitsche Werkbond en zijn betekenis voor Nederland," in the same review, 1914, pp. 311–315; and the *Driebond* issue of *Architectura* 1917.

1915

"Berlage over Bruggen-bouw," in *Bouwkundig Weekblad* XXXV, 15, April 17, p. 118.
Article on the Wagenbrug in The Hague, taken from *Algemeen Handelsblad*: At a meeting of the municipal council in The Hague, the councilman for Public Works, J. Kok, read a letter by Berlage (quoted in full here) on the rebuilding of the Wagenbrug bridge.

"Bij de Afbeeldingen. Amsterdam zuid," in *De Nieuwe Amsterdammer* 47, November 20.
Presentation of the aerial perspectives illustrating the development plan for the south of Amsterdam.

Het Pantheon der Menschheid. Afbeeldingen van de ontwerpen, W.L. & J. Brusse, Rotterdam 26 pp., ill. 1929².
Presentation of the plans for an idealistic Pantheon of Mankind, with a postscript in verse by H. Roland Holst-van der Schalk. Editions with English and French translation of the poem. See also chapter VI in *Schoonheid in samenleving*, 1919.

"Jury-Rapport," in *Prijsvraag voor het ontwerpen van een Tuinstadwijk*, Amsterdam.
Report signed by Berlage and A. Keppler of the jury for the competition for a garden-neighborhood promoted by the Sociaal-Technische Vereeniging van Democratische Ingenieurs en Architecten. See also *Bouwkundig Weekblad* 1914, p. 126.

"Over het boek van Dr. M. Eisler," in *De Beweging* XI, 3, March pp. 161–172; issued also separately, *idem*, 12 pp.
Review of the book by Eisler, *Die Geschichte eines holländischen Stadtbildes* 1914, on the urban history of Haarlem.

1916

"De Verhouding van de Bouwkunst tot de Maatschappij," in *De Beweging* XII, 1 January, pp. 1–14.
Lecture on "the relationship between architecture and society" held in Amsterdam at "Architectura et Amicitia," on November 20, 1915.

"Een Reis naar Kopenhagen," in *De Beweging* XII, 7 July pp. 1–16.
Impressions from a trip to Copenhagen and Denmark.

"Het Uitbreidingsplan Amsterdam-Zuid," in *De Bouwwereld* XV, 9, March 1, pp. 65–68; 10, March 8, pp. 75–77, and 11, March 15, pp. 84–86.
Report on the development plan of the South of Amsterdam.

"Stedenbouw," in L. Zwiers, ed., *Bouwkundig Woordenboek*, Van Holkema & Waunderf, Amsterdam, 2 vols., 685 + 611 pp., ill., pp. 398–402 vol. II.
Berlage wrote the column "urban planning" in the dictionary of architecture by Zwiers.

1917

"Baukunst und Religion," in *Die Tat* 7, pp. 615–621.
On "architecture and religion." On page 615, he announced that he was preparing a book for E. Diederichs Publishing in Jena, entitled *Kunst und Gesellschaft*. See "Kunst en Maatschappij" 1909.

"P.J.H. Cuypers," in *Architectura* XXV, 19, May 12, p. 146.
Berlage wrote a brief homage, opening with a motto from Goethe, in a booklet issued for P.J.H. Cuypers's 90th birthday.

"Memorie van toelichting," in *Gemeenteblad van Amsterdam* I, pp. 901–914.
Report on the second development plan for the south of Amsterdam, dated March 1915; reproduced in Fraenkel, 1976, pp. 97–106.

1918

"Aantekening," in *De Beweging* XIV, 2, February, pp. 98–99.
Note on the Comité Néerlando-Belge d'Art Civique.

"Het werk van den architect A.J. Kropholler," in *Levende Kunst* I, 2, February, pp. 21–37; issued also separately, *Enkele Landhuizen en Interieurs door A.J. Kropholler*, 16 pp.

On the villas and interiors by Kropholler.

"Over Normalisatie in de Uitvoering van de Woningbouw," in *De Beweging* XIV, 6, June, pp. 387–403; included in *Normalisatie in Woningbouw*, W.L. & J. Brusse, Rotterdam, pp. 21–50.
Brusse's book puts together the programmatic report by J. van der Waerden (pp. 1–20) at the congress on housing held in Amsterdam on February 11 and 12, 1918, and the lecture on standardization in construction given by Berlage at "Architectura et Amicitia," which draws on his brief contribution to the Congress. Cfr. the note by Van Bergeijk in Casciato, Pannini, and Polano, 1979. See also Z. Gulden, "Dr. Berlage en de normaliseering der woningen," in *Bouwkundig Weekblad* 1918, 40; P.J. Hamers, "Normalisatie?" in *Bouwkundig Weekblad* 1918, 44; J.J.P. Oud, "Bouwkunst en normalisatie bij den massabouw," in *De Stijl* 1918, 7; AA.VV., *Normalisatie in den woningbouw*, Amsterdam 1920.

"Toorop's monumentale kunst," in *Wendingen* I, 12, December, pp. 19–23.
Contribution to the *Festschrift* for the sixtieth birthday of J. Toorop.

1919

"Aan de redactie van La Cité," in *La Cité* 1, p. 6.
Letter to the editors of the Belgian magazine.

"De Restauratie in ambachts- en nijverheidskunst," in *Jaarboek van Nederlandsche ambachts- en nijverheidskunst*, W.L. & J. Brusse, Rotterdam 1919, pp. 56–59.
Article on restoration in crafts in the first yearbook of the VANK.

Schoonheid in Samenleving, W.L. & J. Brusse, Rotterdam, 168 pp., ill.; 1924².
"Perhaps the most philosophical and systematic book by Berlage (the chapters reveal a certain consistency, although there is an amount of free association)" (Van Bergeijk 1985, p. 47); the last chapter is devoted to the Pantheon of Mankind. Illustrations by Berlage and annotated bibliography.
Van Doesburg published a polemical response, 1920.

"Tot een Afscheid," in *De Beweging* XV, 12, December, pp. 321–322.
Memorial for the closing of the review, to which he had contributed since 1907.

1920

"De historische ontwikkeling der

ruimte," in *Bouwkundig Weekblad* XLI, 3, January 17, pp. 11–17.
This is the 3rd chapter of *Schoonheid in samenveling* 1919, followed by a review of the book signed S.

"Een Plan voor de Kralinger Bosschen," in *De Nieuwe Amsterdammer* 291, July 30.
On the new plan by Klijnen, Granpré Molière, and Verhagen for Kralinger Bosschen in Rotterdam.

"Het ontwerp voor het Gemeentemuseum te 's-Gravenhage," in *Wendingen* III, 11–12, November-December, pp. 3 and 6–7.
Booklet on the museum in The Hague, with a presentation of the museum's design.

"Inleiding," in J. Wils, ed., *Volkswoningbouw*, Haagsche Kunstkring, Den Haag, undated.
Introduction to an album devoted to five low-income housing complexes (20 ill., drawings by J. Wils, cover by V. Huszar), reviewed in *Bouwkundig Weekblad* 1920, 22.

1921

"Een Woord vooraf," in J. Wils, ed., *Arbeiderswoningen in Nederland*, W.L. & J. Brusse, Rotterdam, 1921, XXIII + 156 pp., ill.
Very brief introduction to a catalogue of working-class housing complexes. Beside Berlage, A. Keppler and W. Kromhout contributed essays. Reviewed by Oud, 1921.

"Frank Lloyd Wright," in *Wendingen* IV, 11, pp. 3–8; *partim*, reissued in *De Bouwwereld* XXI, 1922, 45, November 8, pp. 355–356.
Essay on Wright in a special issue devoted to the American architect; an English version was published by the same journal in 1926.

"Toelichting ontwerp uitbreidingsplan gemeente Utrecht 1920," in *Tijdschrift voor Volkshuisvesting* II, special issue on urban planning, December 22, pp. 8–21.
The article by Holsboer and Berlage on the plan of Utrecht is on pp. 10–21.

1922

"De Crisis en de kunst," in *Ter Waarheid* pp. 75–80; *partim* included in *De Bouwwereld* XXI, 1922, 27, July 5, pp. 208–209; issued also separately, *idem*; included in the second edition of *Studies over bouwkunst, stijl en samenleving* 1910.
Lecture on the consequences of the World War and the advent of a new society, with illustrations drawn from the design of the museum in The Hague. The lecture was held in May

at the Studentengezelschap voor Sociale Lezingen in the Leiden Volkshuis.

"Het Hofpleinvraagstuk te Rotterdam," in *De Bouwwereld* XXI, 5, February 1, pp. 36–41.
On the first plan for the Hofplein in Rotterdam: It puts together the commission's line and the report by Berlage and Burgdorffer; see "Toelichting . . ." 1921, and "Ontwerp van het Hofplein te Rotterdam" 1922.

"Ontwerp van het Hofplein te Rotterdam," in *Rotterdamsch Jaarboekje* pp. XLVII-L; issued as a booklet, W.L. & J. Brusse, Rotterdam, 24 pp., ill., text pp. 3–20.
Presentation of the first plan for the Hofplein in Rotterdam, designed by Berlage with H.C. Burgdorffer, the city's director of Public Works. Reviewed by G. Versteeg in *Klei* 1922, pp. 179–181.

"Slotbeschouwing," in *Bouwkundig Weekblad* XLIII, 4, January 28, p. 36.
Official remarks, signed by Berlage and Burgdorffer, to the municipal commission in Rotterdam on the issue of the Hofplein.

1922–1923

"Het schoone stadsgezicht," in *Winterboek van de Wereldbibliotheek*, W.L. & J. Brusse, Rotterdam, pp. 109–115.
Article on the aspect of the city "as an expressive synthesis of artistic values," in the winter catalogue of Brusse's Wereldbibliothek, with sketches by Berlage.

1923

"Bij het graf van K.P.C. de Bazel," in *Bouwkundig Weekblad* XLIV, 50, December 15, pp. 500–501.
Brief contribution to the commemorative issue on De Bazel, who died in 1923, published with the editorial team of "Architectura."

"(Brief aan de Vereeniging van Bouwkundigen)," in *Indisch Bouwkundig Tijdschrift* XXVI, 9, p. 165.
Letter for the twenty-fifth anniversary of the Vereeniging van Bouwkundigen.

"(Brieven van de Indische Reis)," in *Het Vaderland* April 28, June 16, July 7, July 27, and August 25.
Travel letters from Berlage's trip to the Dutch Indies; one letter was published in *Indisch Bouwkundig Tijdschrift* 1923, XXVI, 15, pp. 305–306.

"(De Klerk)," in *Architectura* XXVII, 38, December 29, p. 230.
Article *in memoriam* of De Klerk, who died in 1923. On De Klerk, see S. Shulof Frank, *Michel de Klerk*, Ph. D.

dissertation, Columbia University 1969; Fanelli and Godoli 1982; W. de Wit, *The Amsterdam School*, The MIT Press 1983, with an updated bibliography.

"Entwurf für die Umgestaltung des Hofpleins in Rotterdam," in *Stadtbaukunst alter und neuer Zeit* 15, January, pp. 225–232.
German version of "Ontwerp van het Hofplein te Rotterdam, 1922.

Inleiding tot de kennis van de ontwikkeling der toegepaste kunst. Een cultuurstudie van deze tijd, W.L. & J. Brusse, Rotterdam, 77 pp., 92 ill.
Cycle of five lectures given to the students of the Nederlandsche Handelshoogeschool in Rotterdam: "Introduction to the knowledge of the evolution in arts and crafts." Review by Th. van Rijn in *De Hollandsche Revue* 1924, pp. 240–275.

"K.P.C. de Bazel," in AA.VV., *Karel Petrus Cornelis de Bazel*, Vereeniging Ambachts-en Nijverheidskunst, Amsterdam, undated, p. 19.
Contribution to a memorial volume devoted to De Bazel and promoted by the VANK. Cfr. "Bij het graf . . . ," also 1923.

1924

"De Ontwikkeling der Moderne Bouwkunst in Holland," in *Wil en Weg* II, May 16, pp. 559–565; May 17, pp. 588–594; June 18, pp. 626–634; included in *idem*, Maatschappij voor goede en goedkoope lectuur, Amsterdam 1925, 90 pp., 65 ill.
Lecture, often repeated, on the development of Dutch modern architecture. The lecture was held at the Sorbonne, Paris, on November 27, 1923. Berlage designed the cover and graphics of the booklet edition. Excerpts in French were published in *L'Architecture vivante* 1923, 2, fall-winter.

"De Bazel en De Klerk," in *De Socialistische Gids* IX, 1, January, pp. 25–28; issued also separately, *idem*, Ontwikkeling, Amsterdam, 6 pp.
Reflections on De Bazel and De Klerk, both of whom died in 1923, and to whom Berlage had devoted other articles.

"De Europeesche Bouwkunst op Java," in *De Ingenieur* XXXIX, 22, May 31, pp. 399–408; issued also separately, *idem*, Belinfante, The Hague, 28 pp., 35 ill.
Lecture on colonial architecture in Java, held at the Koninklijk Instituut van Ingenieurs on April 8, 1924.

1925

"Het plan der 'First Church of Christ

Scientist'," in *Architectura* XXIX, October 10, pp. 360–363 and in *Bouwkundig Weekblad* XLVI, 41, October 10, pp. 487–490.
Presentation of the design for the Church of Christ Scientist in The Hague.

1926

"Frank Lloyd Wright," in *Wendingen* VI, 6, pp. 79–85.
English version of the 1921 text, in the famous series of booklets of "Wendingen" devoted to the American architect; presently in *The Work of Frank Lloyd Wright*. The Wendingen edition, reprint, Bramhall House, New York 1965, introduction by Frank Lloyd Wright.

"(Lambertus Zijl)," in *Architectura* XXX, 26, June 26, p. 301.
Brief homage to the sculptor Zijl on the occasion of his sixtieth birthday. On Zijl, cfr. R.W.P. de Vries J., *Lambertus Zijl*, Bussum 1946, and M. Broekhuis, "Ideologie in steen," in *Nederlands Kunsthistorisch Jaarboek* 34 (1983), pp. 195–226.

"Roland Holst," in *Architectura* XXX, 28, July 10, pp. 325–326.
On the occasion of Roland Holst appointment as director of the Rijksakademie voor Beeldende Kunsten.

1927

"Aan den Heer Burgemeester der Gemeente Heemstede," in *Bouwkundig Weekblad Architectura* XLVIII, 13, March 26, pp. 117–118.
Report, signed by Berlage, H. van der Kloot Meyburg, and B. Hoogstraten, to the mayor of Heemstede.

"(Het nieuwe raadhuis te Hilversum)," in *Bouwkundig Weekblad Architectura* XLVIII, 42, October 15, p. 376.
Brief untitled article in the special issue edited by Wijdeveld for the completion of W.M. Dudok's municipal building in Hilversum.

"Toelichting van Dr. Berlage en den Directeur van Gemeentewerken op het 2e Hofplein-ontwerp," in *Bouwkundig Weekblad Architectura* XLVIII, 5, pp. 41–45.
Presentation, signed by Berlage and Burgdorffer, of the second plan for the Holfplein in Rotterdam; cfr. "Ontwerp . . . ," 1922.

1928

"Der Staat und der Widerstreit in der modernen Architektur," in M. Steinman, ed., *CIAM Dokumente 1928–1939*, Basel 1979, pp. 24–25.
The text of Berlage's contribution to the first Congrès International d'Architecture Moderne at La Sarraz was

published in part in the book on CIAM edited by Steinmann.

"Glaskunst," in AA.VV., *Leerdam. 50 jaar Glasindustrie*, W.L. & J. Brusse, Rotterdam 1928, 135 pp., ill., pp. 14–20.
Article on "the art of glass" for the book commemorating the fiftieth anniversary of the glass company Leerdam. De Lorm, Copier were also among the contributors.

"Le Plan de la ville moderne," in *La Vie urbaine* VII, pp. 1193–1214.
On modern urban planning.

"R.N. Roland Holst," in *Bouwkundig Weekblad Architectura* XLIX, 48, December 1, pp. 378–379.
On the occasion of Roland Holst's sixtieth birthday, on whom he had written an article in 1926.

1929

"Bolsward en het ontwerp van het Groene Kruisgebouw door ir. J. de Bie Leuveling Tjeenk," in *Bouwkundig Weekblad Architectura* L, 30, 27 July, pp. 233–237.
On the Bolsward issue, Berlage supports the design by C.J. Wierda against the Schoonheidscommissie.
(Article) in AA.VV., *Vank Jubileum orgaan, Nederlandsch Vereeniging voor Ambachts- en Nijverheidskunst*, 38 pp., p. 28.
Very brief article on the occasion of the 25th anniversary of the VANK. P. Zwart and J. de Meyer are among the other contributors to this commemorative booklet.

"Een Russische Kultuur," in AA.VV., *Kultuur en wetenschap in het nieuwe Rusland*,, undated, pp. 9–10.
Preface to a collection of essays, edited by R.N. Roland Holst, J. Hoogcarspel, and P. Alma, on "culture and science in the new Russia," promoted by the Dutch branch of the Internationale Arbeidershulp; now in *VH 101* 1972, 7–8, spring-summer, p. 200 (French translation).

"Het architectorale karakter," in *W.A. van Konijnenburg*, Martinus Nijhoff, The Hague.
On the "architectural character" of the paintings by Van Konijnenburg.

"Nieuwe Strevingen in de Kerkelijke Bouwkunst," in AA.VV., *Religie en Bouwkunst*, De Tijdstroom, Huis ter Heide, pp. 62–78.
Article on new trends in religious architecture in the proceedings of the second congress "Religion and architecture," held near the Oolgaardhuis in Arnhem on July 10–11, 1929. The congress was organized by the Centrale Commissie voor het Vrijzinning

Protestantisme. Berlage, G. Feenstra, J. Havelaar, G.S. Sirks, and W.J. Wegerif were among the participants. R. Miedema wrote the introduction.

"Aan de Wolga," in *Nieuwe Rusland* July-September; also in H.C. Pieck, *Zwart en Wit uit het Roode Rusland*, Scheltens and Giltay, Amsterdam, p. V.

The sonnet "Aan de Wolga" was published in the review of the Holland-Russia association, which was founded by Berlage and G. Rietveld in 1921. It serves as an introduction—following J.M. Burgers's preface—to Pieck's book on the Soviet Union.

1930

"Indrukken van Rusland en zijn bouwkunst 'oud en nieuw'," in *Bouwkundig Weekblad Architectura* LI, 5, February 1, pp. 33–40, and 9, March 1, pp. 73–79.

Impressions from a trip to Russia, on architecture in particular. It ends with the sonnet, "Aan de Wolga." Travel sketches by Berlage. See editorial, "Dr. H.P. Berlage . . . ," 1932.

1931

Mijn Indische reis. Gedachten over cultuur en kunst, W.L. & J. Brusse, Rotterdam 147 pp., 36 ill. by the author.

In 1923, Berlage kept a diary of his trip to the Dutch Indies (February 28 - June 25), published as a book in 1931. See "Brieven . . . ," 1923, and

"De Europeesche . . . ," 1924. Reviewed by C. de Graaf in *Bouwkundig Weekblad Architectura* 1932, pp. 211–214.

"Naar een internationale Werkgemeenschap, een plan met 16 illustraties, door H.Th. Wijdeveld," in *Bouwkundig Weekblad Architectura* LII, 35, August 29, pp. 309–313.

Discussion of H.Th. Wijdeveld's ideas of an "international working community," published as a booklet by C.A. Mees, Santpoort 1931.

1932

"Bouwkunst en Socialisme," in AA.VV., *Socialisme, Kunst, Levensbeschouwing*, Van Loghum-Slaterus, Arnhem, pp. 55–77.

Article on "architecture and socialism," published in the proceedings of the symposium held in The Hague in 1930, with texts by H. van Treslong, M. Lobstein, G.H. van Senden, W. Banning.

"De Nieuwe Amstelbrug," in *Bouwkundig Weekblad* LIII, 22, May 28, pp. 182–183.

Presentation of the design for a new bridge on the Amstel in Amsterdam, the "Berlage Bridge." Followed by Biemond, 1932.

Speech given on the occasion of his receiving the RIBA award, in J. de Bie Leuveling Tjeenk, "De Uitreiking van de gold medal van de RIBA aan Dr. Berlage," in *Bouwkundig Weekblad*

Architectura LIII, 11, March 12, pp. 88–89.

Berlage was presented with the RIBA award by R. Unwin on March 7, 1932. The report on the ceremony, including Unwin's speech, was completed in the No. 12, on March 19, p. 100. The original English text by Berlage was published in the *Journal of the Royal Institute of British Architects* XXXIX, 1932, 10, March 19, in the article "The Royal Gold Medal," pp. 374–376, and in *The Architects and Building News* CXXIX, 1932, 3299, March 11, pp. 330–331, in "Presentation of the Royal Gold Medal."

"Er kome geen nieuwe cultuur, zonder levensstijl," in *Vooruit* February 13.

Interview in which Berlage expressed unfavorable opinions on the Nieuwe Zakelijkheid, published by the The Hague edition of the socialist newspaper *Het Volk*. Quoted in its entirety by Duiker, 1932.

1933

"Kunst en Broederschap," in H.P. Berlage and H. Roland Holst-van der Schalk, *Broederschap in de Levenspraktijk*, Servire, Den Haag, pp. 35–54.

Collection of the lectures by H. Roland Holst-van der Schalk and Berlage on "art and brotherhood," held at the meeting of the Broederschapsfederatie on May 21–22, 1932, at the School voor Wijsbegeerte in Amers-

foort.

"Over Bouwkunst," in *VAEVO. 1908–1933*, pp. 33–35.

Article on architecture in the book illustrating "the results of the work and trends of the first twenty-five years" of the Vereeniging tot bevorderinng van het Aesthetisch Element in het Voortgezet Onderwijs.

1934

Het Wezen der bouwkunst en haar geschiedenis, Volksuniversiteit Bibliotheek 62, De Erven F. Bohn N.V., Haarlem, VI + 228 pp., 201 ill.

Summary history of architecture, from the Assyrians to the 19th century; it was authorized by Berlage in May 1934 and published after his death.

"(Willem Kromhout)," in *Bouwkundig Weekblad Architectura* LV, 19, May 12, p. 170.

Very brief article devoted to Kromhout.

1939

"De Mening van Dr. H.P. Berlage over het boek van J.C. Slebos," in J.C. Slebos, *Grondslagen voor aesthetiek en stijl*, Ahrend & Zoon, Amsterdam, p. 5.

Berlage's views on Slebos's book devoted to the "basis of aesthetics and style," published after his death.

Bibliography

This bibliography comprises almost 400 titles, updated to 1985, and features the most significant range in the literature on Berlage. Further items could also be included on each subject, as can be seen from a list of almost 500 titles on the Stock Exchange in A.W. Reinink, 1975—certainly an extreme example, but to the point. Specific bibliographical references are given at the end of each essay in the catalogue of works. Titles are set in chronological and—within each year—alphabetical order of authors. If the author is the same for several items (as in the special case of the AA.VV. and the editorials), the texts are put in alphabetical order of titles.

The most significant items are annotated: A quick glance at the bibliography reveals the evolution in Berlage's popularity. Interest in his work rose slowly in the early 1890s, to culminate with the extraordinary wealth of comments around his Stock Exchange. Among others, AA.VV. 1916, *De Invloed . . .* , AA.VV. 1916, *Dr. H.P. Berlage en zijn werk*, T. Landré 1916, M. Eisler 1919, J. Gratama 1925, and J. Havelaar 1927, testify to the constant and loyal attention given to his work in the early 20th century—with few dissenting voices. In 1916, the master's sixtieth birthday was celebrated in different publications.

The friendly commemoration of 1934—see AA.VV., *H.P. Berlage ter gedachtenis* and AA.VV., *Dr. H.P. Berlage 1856–1934*—was followed by years of fall from grace. The threat of demolition of the Stock Exchange in the late 1950s gave rise to a renewed interest. This was followed in turn by a flourishing critical literature in the 1970s—linked to the 1975 exhibition—with such fundamental studies as P. Singelenberg 1972; AA.VV. 1975, *H.P. Berlage 1856–1934*; M. Bock, K. Broos, P. Singelenberg 1975; M. Bock 1983. Aside from the texts mentioned above, which form the basic critical material, the other significant general texts are the following: L. Simons 1898; W. Vogelsang 1904; K. Sluyterman 1905; J.L.M. Lauweriks 1907; A.W. Weissman 1909; T. Landré 1910; G. Versteeg 1914; AA.VV. 1916, *Dr. H.P. Berlage Nzn . . .* ; A.J. Kropholler 1916; A. Behne 1922; H. Sörgel 1925; J. Gratama 1916; W. Kromhout 1926; J.M. van der Mey 1926; editorial 1926 (on the occasion of Berlage's seventieth birthday); AA.VV. 1928; and, after the Second World War: Grassi 1961; P. Singelenberg 1969; and M. Bock 1975. Aside from some collective publications, the most meaningful memorial articles written when Berlage died in 1934 were signed by A.J. Kropholler, L. Lionni, J.P. Mieras, J.J.P. Oud, C. van Eesteren, S. van Ravesteyn, and J. Wils.

A few reading suggestions will help in a thematic approach to the bibliography. Fanelli's two books, published in 1968 and 1978, provide the framework of modern Dutch architecture as well as fundamental analytical tools. On the general issue of mass construction, see: D.J. Grinberg 1977; M. Casciato, F. Panzini, S. Polano 1979; H. Engel and J. de Heer 1984; in the particular case of Berlage, see: H. Searing in AA.VV. 1975, *H.P. Berlage 1856–1934*; M. Bock in M. Bock, Broos, P. Singelenberg 1975. Bock presents an analysis of the the role of building materials in Berlage's architecture. On the issue of urban planning, see: K.P.C. de Bazel in AA.VV. 1916, *Dr. H.P. Berlage en zijn werk*; M.J. Granpré Molière in AA.VV. 1934, *H.P. Berlage ter gedachtenis*; Blijstra 1970; M. Bock in M. Bock, Broos, P. Singelenberg 1975; F.F. Fraenkel 1976; E.J. Hoogenberk 1980; F. de Jong 1985. G. Semper's influence on Berlage is analysed in P. Singelenberg 1976. A. W. Reinink studied the relationship with Viollet-le-Duc in 1970 and 1982. On the issue of Berlage and the architecture in the United States, see: L.K. Eaton 1956; A.W. Reinink 1970; D. Tselos 1970; L.K. Eaton 1972; AA.VV. 1975, *Americana*. H. Searing 1982, and H.P. Rovinelli 1984, focused on the links with the Amsterdam School. On the issue of the arts in Berlage's architecture, see: A. Verwey 1898; J. Veth 1900; J.L.M. Lauweriks 1903; K. van Leeuwen 1906; R.N. Roland Holst in AA.VV. 1916, "Dr. H.P. Berlage en zijn werk; and both Th. van Rijn and A. Verwey in AA.VV. 1934, *H.P. Berlage ter gedachtenis*. On the issue of Berlage's work in the field of design and interior architecture, see: J.G. Veldheer 1901; W. Vogelsang 1903; J.F. Staal in AA.VV. 1916, *Dr. H.P. Berlage en zijn werk*; AA.VV. 1917, 1921, *Jaarboek*; C. van der Sluys 1921; C. de Lorm 1923; J. Wils 1923; J. Havelaar 1924; J. de Jong 1929; both J. Eisenloeffel and H. Wouda in AA.VV. 1975, *H.P. Berlage 1856–1934*; M. Boot in AA.VV. 1975, *H.P. Berlage 1856–1934*; F. Liefkes 1975; F. Leidelmeijer and D. van der Cingel 1975, as well as the comprehensive review in AA.VV. 1985, and R. Ramakers 1985. Illustrations of furniture, fixtures, and objects designed by Berlage are scattered throughout the basic bibliography given here, but they can also be found in several other specialized books and reviews, among others cfr. "De Architect," plates 285, 555, 570, 581. For works in glass, see: A.D. Copier in AA.VV. 1934, *H.P. Berlage te gedachtenis*; H.C. Haarman-Engelberts 1980; and A. van der Kley-Blekxtoon 1984; for the graphic arts, see: A.C. Strasser-Berlage in AA.VV. 1934, *H.P. Berlage ter gedachtenis* and E. Braches 1973—for the *Gijsbreght* of 1893–1901, see: E. Braches 1971; and L. Rebel-Benschop 1981.

1884

J. Kok, "Karakter en stijl der Amsterdamsche Beurs," in *Bouwkundig Weekblad* IV, 51, December 17, pp. 338–339.

Editorial, "Prijsvragen," in *Bouwkundig Weekblad* IV, 46, November 12, pp. 303–304.

Editorial, "Prijsvraag voor den bouw van eene nieuwe Beurs te Amsterdam. Rapport van de internationale jury and "De Beursplannen," in *Bouwkundig Weekblad* IV, 49, December 3, pp. 319–325.

1885

J.R. de Kruijff, "De Beursprijsvraag," in *Bouwkundig Weekblad* V, 26, July 4, pp. 161–164, and 27, July 11, pp. 167–168.

Editorial, "Beursgebouw te Amsterdam," in *Bouwkundig Weekblad* V, 50, December 19, pp. 311–312.

Editorial, "Bij de plaat," in *Bouwkundig Weekblad* V, 45, November 14, p. 278.

Editorial, "De Beurs-Prijsvraag," in *Bouwkundig Weekblad* V, 22, June 6, pp. 137–138.

Editorial, "Het Rapport der jury over de Beurs-ontwerpen," in *Bouwkundig Weekblad* V, 22, June 6, p. 142.

Editorial, "Het Winkelhuis der Firma Focke en Meltzer," in *Bouwkundig Weekblad* V, 46, November 21, pp. 284–285.

C.T.J.L. Rieber, "De Beurs-prijsvraag," in *Bouwkundig Weekblad* V, 23, June 13, pp. 143–145, and 25, June 27, pp. 158–159.

1887

J.R. de Kruijff, "Knollen voor citroenen," in *Bouwkundig Weekblad* VII, 21, May 21, pp. 126–128.

Editorial, "Prijsvragen," in *Bouwkundig Weekblad* VII, 28, July 9, p. 169.

1888

Editorial, "Prijsvragen," in *De Opmerker* XXIII, 40, October 6, p. 32.

Editorial, "De Domgevel te Milaan," in *De Opmerker* XXIII, 42, October 20, pp. 335–336.

1889

C.T.J.L. Rieber, "De Bekroning der Nederlandsche Bouwkunstenaars te Parijs," in *Bouwkundig Weekblad* IX, 40, October 5, pp. 235–236.

1890

M. (H.C. Müller?), "Ontwerp voor een Mausoleum. H.P. Berlage. Architect. Bijschrift," in *De Architect* I, text on the plates 7–9, 17; already in a letter presumably by H.C. Müller, in *Amsterdammer* March 19, 1889.

1891

J.R. de Kruijff, ed., "Prae-adviezen van het bestuur der Maatschappij over de antwoorden der Afdeelingen op den gestelde vragen," in *Bouwkundig Weekblad* XI, 20, May 16, pp. 118–121.

Editorial, "Tafel 51," in *Architektonische Rundschau* VII, 7, s.n.

(C.T.J.L.) R. (Rieber), "De nieuwe Beurs te Amsterdam," in *Bouwkundig Weekblad* XI, 4, January 24, p. 22, and 5, January 31, pp. 28–29.

1893

A.N. Godefroy, "Voordracht," in *Architectura* I, 12, March 18, pp. 46–48.

1894

M.K., "Een merkwaardig bouwwerk," in *Algemeen Handelsblad* April 22 and 27.

J. Kok, "Het nieuwe gebouw voor de "Algemeene te Amsterdam," in *Bouwkundig Weekblad* XIV, 9, April 28, pp. 59–60.

R. (Rieber), "Bij de plaat," in *Bouwkundig Weekblad* XIV, 34, October 20, p. 217.

1895

Editorial, "Berlage's expositie," in *Architectura* III, 5, February 2, p. 21.

Editorial, "De Amsterdamsche Beurskwestie," in *Architectura* III, 24, June 15, p. 100.

1896

A.W. de Flines, "Beursbouw," in *Architectura* IV, July 25, pp.120–121.

L., "Het Gebouw der Maatschappij Arti et Amicitiae te Amsterdam," in *Bouwkundig Weekblad* XVI, 40, October 3, pp. 244–245.

Editorial, "Beursbouw," in *Architectura* IV, June 13, pp. 97–98; September 26, pp. 156–157; October 3, p. 162.

Editorial, "De Amsterdamsche Beurs," in *De Opmerker* XXXI, October 3, pp. 315–318.

1897

A.J. van Derkinderen, "Beursbouw 1219–1897," in *De Amsterdammer* July 11.

Editorial, "Het in aanbouw zijnd hoekhuis Raadhuisstraat en Herengracht te Amsterdam," in *Bouwkundig Weekblad* XVII, 42, October 16, p. 308.

1898

J. Cuypers, "De Beursbouw," in *Architectura* VI, 11, March 12, pp. 45–46.

W. Kromhout, "De nieuwe Beurs," in *Amsterdamsche Courant* March 16.

J.B.L. (Lambeek) Jr., "De Nieuwe Koopmansbeurs te Amsterdam," in *Architectura* VI, 12, March 19, pp. 50–52.

Editorial, "De nieuwe Koopmansbeurs te Amsterdam," in *Bouwkundig Weekblad* XVIII, 12, March 19, p. 83.

R. (Rieber), "De Beurs te Amsterdam," in *Bouwkundig Weekblad* XVIII, 15, April 9, pp. 109–112.

L. Simons, "Holländische Baukunst: H.P. Berlage," in *Dekorative Kunst* I, 7, pp. 20–29.

H.J. Walle, "Vergadering," in *Architectura* VI, 14, April 2, pp. 58–59; 15, April 9, pp. 61–63; 16, April 16, pp. 66–67; 17, April 23, pp. 69–71.

A. Verwey, "Bijdragen tot de versiering van de nieuwe Beurs," in *Het Tweemaandelijksch Tijdschrift* III, 2, pp. 183–212; also in *Orspronkelijk Dichtwerk*, Amsterdam 1938, vol. II, pp. 730–735.

J.E. van der Pek, "De nieuwe Beurs," in *Algemeen Handelsblad* March 17.

1899

A.W. Weissman, "Het Beursontwerp," in *De Opmerker* XXXIII, March 26, pp. 97–100.

Editorial, "Vereenigingsgebouw voor den Alg. Nederl. Diamantbewerkers-Bond te Amsterdam," in *Bouwkundig Weekblad* XIX, 26, July 1, p. 207.

Editorial, "Verslag der 1100e gewone vergadering," in *Architectura* VII, November 9, pp. 388–389.

1900

Neubauten in Holland: Amsterdam Haag Rotterdam, Berlin.

J. Veth, *De Muurschilderingen van Der Kinderen in het Trappenhuis van het Gebouw der Algemeene Maatshappij van Levensverzekering en Lijfrente te Amsterdam*, Amsterdam.

1901

J.G.V. (Veldheer), "Das neue Künstlerhaus in Amsterdam," in *Dekorative Kunst* IV, 5, pp. 197–203.

1902

J.H. Schorer, "Bijdrage tot de ontwikkeling der Amsterdamsche Architectuur. De nieuwe Beurs," in *Bouwkundig Weekblad* XXIII, June 7, pp. 215–216.

1902–1903

H. von Poellnitz, "Die neuesten Kunstrichtungen in der Architektur Amsterdams," in *Deutsche Bauhütte* VI, pp. 30–31 and 172.

H. Walenkamp, "De nieuwe Beurs," in *De Amsterdammer* 1326, November 23; 1328, December 7; 1329, December 14; 1903, 1336, February 1; 1337, February 8.

1903

P.J.H. Cuypers, "De nieuwe Beurs van Amsterdam," in *Bouwkundig Weekblad* XXIII, 23, June 6, p. 236.

K.P.C. de Bazel, "Enkele opmerkingen naar aanleiding van den Amsterdamschen Beursbouw," in *De Kroniek* IX, June 13, pp. 189–190.

L. (Lauweriks), "De Opening der nieuwe Beurs," in *Architectura* XI, 22, May 30.

J.L.M. Lauweriks, "De nieuwe Beurs," in *Architectura* XI, 39, September 26, pp. 309–311; 40, October 3, pp. 317–318; 41, October 10, pp. 327–328; 42, October 17, pp. 333–335; 43, October 2024, P. 341; 45, November 7, pp. 357–358; 46, November 14, pp. 365–366; 47, November 21, pp. 375–376; 48, November 28, pp. 382–383; 50, December 12, pp. 397–398; 51, December 19, pp. 405–407; 52, December 26, pp. 413–417.

J.L.M. Lauweriks, "Toorop's sectielen in de nieuwe Beurs," in *Architectura* XI, 49, December 5, p. 390.

R. Neter, "H.P. Berlage's neue Börse in Amsterdam," in *Innen-Dekoration* pp. 189–196.

Editorial, "De nieuwe Beurs te Amsterdam," in *De Bouwwereld* II, 21, May 27, pp. 161–162.

Editorial, "De Neubau der Niederländischen Lebensversicherungsgesellschaft am Augustus-Platz zu Leipzig," in *Zentralblatt für das Deutsche Baugewerbe* II, pp. 459–462 and 467–470.

Editorial, "Het Leipziger gebouw der Algemeene Maatschappij van Levensverzekering en Lijfrente," in *De Bouwwereld* II, 12, March 25, p. 92.

E. Redelé, *De nieuwe Beurs te Amsterdam en de Proletariërs (Toorop, Derkinderen, Berlage)*, Amsterdam.

L. Simons, "De Bouwkunst als toekomst-kunst," in *De Gids* 7; also published as a booklet.

W. Vogelsang, "Hollandsche gebruikskunst; 't Binnenhuis, De Woning, Arts and Crafts," in *Onze Kunst* II, pp. 19–23.

W. Vogelsang, "H.P. Berlage's Neubau der Amsterdamer Börse," in *Dekorative Kunst* VI, August, pp. 401–421.

1904

Editorial, "Het Uitbreidingsplan van Amsterdam," in *De Opmerker* XXXIX, 47, November 19, pp. 369–370.

J.H.W. Leliman, "De Uitbreiding van Amsterdam," in *De Bouwwereld* III, 45, pp. 353–356; 46, pp. 361–366; 47, pp. 373–376; 48, pp. 381–

383; 49, pp. 387–390.

W. Vogelsang, "H.P. Berlage," in *Moderne Bauformen* 10, pp. 71–77; Czech translation in *Volné Sméry* 1906, pp. 285–288.

H. Walenkamp, "Het 'materialisme' der moderne Bouwkunst," in *Architectura* XII, 32, August 6, pp. 263–264.

H. Walenkamp, "De nieuwe uitbreidingsplannen der stad Amsterdam," in *Architectura* XII, 41, October 8, pp. 336a–336b.

H. Walenkamp, "Voordracht Berlage over het nieuwe uitbreidingsplan van Amsterdam," in *Architectura* XII, 47, November 19, pp. 384–385.

A.W. Weissman, *De Beurs te Amsterdam, 1835–1903*, Amsterdam.

1905

K. Sluyterman, "H.P. Berlage Nzn.," in *Elsevier* XXIX, pp. 3–21.

W.N. van Vliet, "De Gebouwen der Algemeene Maatschappij van Levensverzekering en Lijfrente aan het Damrak te Amsterdam," in *De Bouwwereld* IV, 24, June 14, pp. 189–191; 25, June 21, pp. 198–199; 26, June 28, pp. 203–204.

1906

AA.VV., *Internationale Prijsvraag der Carnegie-Stichting. Het Vredespaleis te 's-Gravenhage*, Elsevier, Amsterdam, 74 lose plates.

J.H.W. Leliman, "De Amsterdamsche Beurs-Calamiteit," in *De Bouwwereld* V, 15, April 11, pp. 113–115.

J.H.W. Leliman, "De Vredespaleis-prijsvraag," in *De Bouwwereld* V, 24, June 13, pp. 185–187; 26, June 27, pp. 201–204; 28, July 11, pp. 217–219; 30, July 25, pp. 237–239; 39, September 26, pp. 305–307; 46, November 14, pp. 361–363.

J.H.W. Leliman, "Het Beursrapport," in *De Bouwwereld* V, 37, September 12, pp. 289–292, and 49, December 5, pp. 385–386.

Editorial, "Wahrheit und Konstruktion als Schmuck," in *Architektonische Rundschau* XXII, 9, September, pp. 65–69.

K. van Leeuwen, "De Muurschildering van A.J. Der Kinderen voor de nieuwe Beurs," in *Jonge Kunst* 11, March, pp. 165–168, and 12, April, pp. 180–183.

1907

P. Klopfer, "Über H.P. Berlage," in *Deutsche Bauzeitung* 60, pp. 423–424.

J.L.M. Lauweriks, "Die neue holländische Architektur," in *Kunst und Künstler* VII, pp. 551–558.

Editorial, "Raumkunst und Architektur," in *Schweizerische Bauzeitung* IL, 24, June 15, pp. 293–297; 25, June 22, pp. 303–306; 26, June 29, pp. 317–318.

1908

J.G. (Gratama), "De Architectuur van het Beethovenhuis," in *Bouwkundig Weekblad* XXVIII, 48, November 28, pp. 946–950; 51, December 19, pp. 1004–1006.

W. Hutschenruyter, *Het Beethovenhuis*, S.L. van Looy, Amsterdam, 38 pp.

Editorial, "Dagteeken- en Kunstambachtsschool voor meisjes," in *De Bouwwereld* VII, 24, June 10, pp. 186–188.

Editorial, "Het Beethovenhuis," in *Architectura* XVI, 50, December 12, pp. 429–430.

C.J.S., "Het Beethovenhuis," in *Bouwkundig Weekblad* XXVIII, 48, November 28, pp. 945–946.

1909

Editorial, "Dagteeken- en Kunstambachtsschool voor meisjes," in *Architectura* XVII, 35, August 28.

P.H.S. (Scheltema), "Het Uitbreidingsplan van 's-Gravenhage," in *De Opmerker* XLIV, 26, June 26, pp. 201–203; 27, July 3, pp. 209–211.

A.W. Weissman, "Berlage, Hendrik Petrus," in Thieme-Becker, *Allgemeines Lexicon der bildenden Künstler*, Leipzig, vol. III, p. 420.

1910

T. Landré, "H.P. Berlage," in *Onze Kunst* IX, 17, pp. 73–102, and in *L'arte flamande* 1910, pp. 137ff and 169ff.

1910–1911

W. van Diedenhoven, "Het nieuwe boek van Berlage," in *De Samenleving* pp. 28–31, 62–65, and 91–95.

1911

Editorial, "Bayreuth te Scheveningen," in *Bouwkundig Weekblad* XXXI, 2, January 14, p. 24.

Editorial, "Het gegoten huis te Santpoort," in *Architectura* XIX, 18, May 6, pp. 141–142.

Editorial, "Het Wagner-theater te Scheveningen," in *Bouwkundig Weekblad* XXXI, 3, January 21, p. 30.

Editorial, "Het Wagner-theater te 's-Gravenhage," in *De Bouwwereld* X, 2, January 11, p. 16.

Editorial, "Criticized Dutch Architect Criticizes New York Architecture," in *The New Yorker Herald* November 12.

1912

C. Engelen, "Vier boeken van H.P. Berlage," in *De Boekraal* 8–9, pp. 281–294.

Editorial, "Berlage gepasserd," in *Bouwkundig Weekblad* XXXII, 25, June 22, pp. 302–303.

Editorial, "De Bazel over Dr. Cuypers-Berlage," in *Bouwkundig Weekblad* XXXII, 31, August 3, pp. 373–374.

R. (editorial), "De Berlage Avond en Berlage's Voordracht over Amerika," in *Architectura* XX, 5, February 3, pp. 34–35.

H. Robbers, ed., *Het Kunstenaarshuis te Amsterdam*, Verbond van Nederlandsche Kunstenaars-Vereeningen, Amsterdam, undated, 31 pp.

1913

A. Moen., "Het doodvonnis over 'Parkwijck' uitgesproken," in *Architectura* XXI, 4, January 25, p. 22.

W. van der Pluijm, "De Beurs te Amsterdam 1903–1913," in *Architectura* XXI, 21, May 24, pp. 170–171.

H. van Dessel, "Bouwmeester Berlage te Brussel," in *De Bouwgids*, pp. 53–55.

1913–1914

C.H. Schwagermann, ed., "Het aesthetisch gedeelte van stedenbouw," in *Bouwkundig Weekblad* XXXIII, 51, December 20, pp. 627–629; XXXIV 1914, 1, January 3, pp. 6–8; 2, January 10, pp. 16–20; 9, February 28, pp. 98–100; 10, March 7, pp. 116–118; 11, March 14, pp. 125–128; 12, March 21, pp. 137–140; 16, April 18, pp. 186–189; 17, April 25, pp. 198–202.

1914

Hahn, "Die neue Börse zu Amsterdam," in *Bau-Rundschau* 31, July 30.

G. Versteeg, "Berlage's werken," in *Klei* January 15.

1915

J.B. von Loghem, "Tentoonstelling van Architectura et Amicitia, in het Stedelijk Museum te Amsterdam," in *De Nieuwe Amsterdammer* December 11.

1915–1916

Editorial, "Voordrachten over Bouwkunst," in *Bouwkundig Weekblad* XXXVI, 31, November 27, pp. 230–233; 32, December 4, pp. 238–240; 33, December 11, pp. 247–248; 34, December 18, pp. 254–255; 35, December 25, pp. 262–264; 1916, 36, January 1, pp. 267–271; 37, January 8, pp. 277–278.

1916

AA.VV., *De Invloed van Dr. Berlage op de ontwikkeling der nederlandsche bouwkunst*, in *Bouwkundig Weekblad* XXXVI, 44, February 26, pp. 322–328; 45, March 4, pp. 330–335. Among the many architects who answered the question on "Berlage's influence on Dutch architecture": De Bazel, Limburg, Van Loghem, Van der Pek, Slothouwer, Vogelsang, Wegerif, M. Brinckman, Brouwer, Buskens, Granpré Molière, De Klerk (whose response is fairly polemical), Van der Steur, and Versteeg.

AA.VV., *Dr. H.P. Verlage en zijn werk*, W.L. & J. Brusse, Rotterdam 132 pp. + 164 ill. *Festschrift* for Berlage's sixtieth birthday, with mostly laudatory texts; this is the first significant monograph, with a catalogue of the works, a bibliography, and a valuable illustrated repertory. It features essays by A. Verwey (Berlage's philosophy, pp. 1–13), J. Gratama (Berlage's work, pp. 24–51, an essay which was to be updated in 1925), K.P.C. de Bazel (Berlage's urban planning, pp. 52–56), J.F. Staal (Berlage's furniture, pp. 57–66), R.N. Roland Holst (sculpture and painting in Berlage's architecture, pp. 67–76), W. Vogelsang (the evolution in Berlage's work, pp. 77–104), J. Kalf (Berlage, architect in a period of transition, pp. 105–117). Graphics by S.H. de Roos; Brusse published most of Berlage's books.

AA.VV., *Dr. H.P. Berlage. 21 Febr. 1856–1916*, booklet for Berlage's sixtieth birthday published by *Architectura* XXIV, 8, February 19, pp. 58–60. Articles by J. de Meijer, Candidus, J.F. Staal and H.Th. Wijdeveld.

A.W. Bos, "Uitbreidingen van Amsterdam," in *De Ingenieur* XXXI, pp. 965–969.

A.E. Brinckmann, "Grundlagen und Entwicklung der Architektur," in *Neudeutsche Bauzeitung* VI, pp. 460–467.

J. de Meijer, "Dr. Berlage's 'Parkwijck," in *Architectura* XXIV, 15, April 8, p. 113.

P. de Vooys, "Het Berlage Boek," in *De Beweging* pp. 72ff.

M. Eisler, "H.P. Berlage und sein Erweiterungsplan Amsterdam Süd," in *Der Städtebau* 10–11, pp. 112–115.

H. Hoste, "Dr. H.P. Berlage, 21 februari 1856–1916," in *De Telegraaf* February 20.

A.J. Kropholler, "Dr. H.P. Berlage," in *Bouwkundig Weekblad* XXXVI, 43, February 19, pp. 314–315.

T. Landré, *Dr. H.P. Berlage Nzn.,*

Hollandia, Baarn, 48 pp.
Brief monograph on Berlage, published also in *Mannen en Vrouwen van Betekenis*, the review directed by Pijzel.

J.H.W. Leliman and Sluyterman, *Het Moderne Landhuis in Nederland*, The Hague 1916[1], rev. ed. 1922[2].

J.J.P. Oud, "De Moderne en Modernste Bouwkunst," in *Bouwkundig Weekblad* XXXVI, 46, March 11, pp. 341–343.
Response to De Klerk's views on Berlage, see AA.VV. 1916, *De Invloed*. . . .

Editorial, "Het Uitbreidingsplan zuid der Gemeente Amsterdam," in *Bouwkundig Weekblad* XXVI, 44, February 26, p. 328.

J. van Epen, "Dr. H.P. Berlage," in *Bouwkundig Weekblad* XXXVI, 43, February 19, pp. 315–316.

J.B. van Loghem, "Gevraagde kritiek op: Dr. H.P. Berlage en zijn werk," in *Bouwkundig Weekblad* XXXVI, 3, May 20, pp. 29–31.

R.A. van Sandick, "Dr. H.P. Berlage," in *De Ingenieur* pp. 168ff.

A.H. Wegerif, "Met Dr. Berlage naar Denemarken," in *Architectura* XXIV, pp. 154–155.

1917

AA.VV., *Driebond nummer*, special issue of *Architectura* XXV, 39–40, October 6, pp. 2–43.

C.H. Blaauw, "Dr. H.P. Berlage en zijn werk," in *Architectura* XXV, 2, January 13, pp. 10–11.

J.H.W.L. (Leliman), "Het Uitbreidingsplan Amsterdam-Zuid," in *De Bouwwereld* XVI, 33, August 15, pp. 253–256; 34, August 22, pp. 261–263.

Editorial, "Amsterdam. Het Uitbreidingsplan-Zuid," in *Architectura* XXV, 32, August 11, pp. 243–249.

Editorial, "Lezing Dr. H.P. Berlage," in *Bouwkundig Weekblad* XXXVIII, 42, October 20, pp. 244–245; from "Het Vaderland."

1918

A.J. Kropholler, "Dr. Berlage's kantoorgebouw te Londen," in *Wendingen* I, 5, May 30, pp. 11–15.

J. Stübben, "Die südliche Stadterweiterung von Amsterdam," in *Deutsche Bauzeitung* 14, pp. 65–68; 16, pp. 73–75; 17, pp. 77–79.

T. van Doesburg, "Moderne bouwkunst bij noodwoningen in gewapend beton," in *De Stijl* I, 8, June, p. 96.

1919

M. Eisler, *De Bouwmeester H.P. Berlage*, Kunst in Holland, 7, Hölzel, Vienna, undated, 23 pp., 10 plates.

Brief monograph with lose plates, as part of a series on Dutch art. There is also a German edition.

J.J.P. Oud, "Dr. H.P. Berlage und sein Werk," in *Kunst und Kunsthandwerk* XXII, 6–8, January, pp. 189–228.

J. Wils, "De hedendaagsche stroomingen in de bouwkunst," in *De Beweging* XV, pp. 84–98 and 257–268.

1920

J.H.W. Leliman, *Het Stadswoonhuis in Nederland gedureende de laatste 25 jaren*, The Hague 1920[1]; 1924[2].

J.P.M. (Mieras), "Algemeene beschouwingen," in *Bouwkundig Weekblad* XLI, 43, October 22, pp. 277–278; 52. December 25, pp.20 289–290.

1920–1921

T. van Doesburg, "De Taak der nieuwe architectuur," in *Bouwkundig Weekblad* XLI, 50, December 11, pp. 278–280; 51, December 18, pp. 281–285; 1921, XLII, 1, January 8, pp. 8–10.

1921

AA.VV., *Ontwerpen voor de Verbouwing en Uitbreiding van het Gebouw van de Tweede Kamer der Staten-Generaal*, album of lose plates with a booklet published as a special issue of *Bouwkundig Weekblad* July 16.

A. Boeken, "Over Berlage en zijn museumontwerp voor Den Haag," in *Elsevier* 41, p. 209–211.

J. Hoogenboom, "Een Opmerking over het Haagse museum-plan," in *Bouwkundig Weekblad* XLII, 30, July 23, pp. 195–196.

Jaarboek van Nederlandsche Ambachts- en Nijverheidskunst, VANK, Rotterdam.

J.P.M. (Mieras), "Het Ontwerp voor de Haagsche Musea-gebouwen van Dr. H.P. Berlage," in *Bouwkundig Weekblad* XLII, 3, January 15. pp. 13–17; 4, January 22, pp. 23–29.

J.J.P. Oud, "Naar aanleiding van 'Arbeiderswoningen in Nederland'," in *Tijdschrift voor Volkshuisvesting* III, 1, pp. 130–132.

C. van der Sluys, *Binnenhuiskunst*, Amsterdam, 2 vols.

H.E. van Gelder, "Bij de Museumontwerpen," in *Mededeelingen van den Dienst voor Kunsten en Wetenschappen der Gemeente 's-Gravenhage* III, 1, January, pp. 71–81.
The same review published in the following years many articles on the museum in The Hague, signed by Van Gelder, D.F. Slothouwer, and P. van Aanroy.

H.E. van Gelder, "Het Haagsche museumontwerp," in *De Bouwwereld* XX, 6, February 9, pp. 42–46; 7, February 16, pp. 50–52.

C.M. van Moorsel, "Aanval," in *Bouwkundig Weekblad* XLII, 4, January 22, p. 33.

1922

P. Bakker Schut, "Het Hofpleinvraagstuk," in *Weekblad voor gemeentebelangen*, pp. 33–34.

A. Behne, "Holländische Baukunst in der Gegenwart," in *Wasmuth's Monatshefte für Baukunst* VI, 1–2, pp. 1–33.

I.K. Bonset (T. van Doesburg), "Archachitektonika," in *Mécano* 3.

S. de Clercq, "Dr. Berlage's Hofpleinplannen," in *Elsevier* 43, pp. 209–211.

M.J. Granpré Molière, "Het nieuwe Hofplein te Rotterdam," in *Bouwkundig Weekblad* XLIII, 5, February 4, pp. 44–46.

V. Huszar, "Over de moderne toegepaste kunsten," in *Bouwkundig Weekblad* XLIII, 7, February 18, pp. 59–69.

W. Kromhout, "Een Plan voor het Hofplein," in *De Bouwwereld* XXI, 7, February 15, pp. 54–57.

J.C. Meischke and Schmidt, "Het Hofplein van Dr. Berlage," in *Bouwkundig Weekblad* XLIII, 4, January 28, pp. 26–36.

J.P. Mieras, "Algemeene beschouwingen," in *Bouwkundig Weekblad* XLIII, 28, March 15, pp. 274–276.

J.J.P. Oud, *Het Hofplein-plan van Dr. Berlage*, Stedebouw 1, Nederlandsch Istituut voor Volkshuisvesting, Zwolle and H.D. Tjeenk Willink & Zn., Haarlem, 19 pp.

A. Plate, "Eenige opmerkingen over het Hofpleinontwerp," in *De Ingenieur*, pp. 141–146.

Editorial, "Het Hofplein te Rotterdam," in *De Bouwwereld* XXI, 19, May 10, pp. 146–147.

Editorial, "Nieuwe Museum in Den Haag," in *De Bouwwereld* XXXI, 42, October 18, p. 331, from "Het Vaderland."

Editorial, "De Redevoering van Dr. Berlage te London," in *De Bouwwereld* XXI, January 11, pp. 14–16; from "Garden Cities and Town Planning."

Editorial, "De Uitbreiding van Utrecht," in *Tijdschrift voor Volkshuisvesting* III, 11, November 15, pp. 198–302.

S.C. Tinbergen, "Het Rotterdamsche Hofpleinvraagstuk," in *De Bouwwereld* XXI, 5, February 1, pp. 33–35.

J. van Beek, "Berlage's Hofplein," in *De Bouwwereld* XXI, 5, February 1, pp. 43–44, from "Maasbode."

K.P. van der Mandele, "Het Hofpleinplan-Berlage," in *De Bouwwereld* XXI, 10, March 8, p. 83, from *Voorwaarts*.

P. Verhagen, "Dr. Berlage's plan voor het Hofplein," in *De Gids* 1, pp. 277–284.

H.J.M. Walenkamp, "Dr. Berlage Hofpleinontwerp," in *De Amsterdammer*, pp. 2333 and 2335.

1923

F. Berckelaers, "Bij de Ontwerpen van Dr. Berlage," in *Het Overzicht* 15, March-April, pp. 42 and 44–49.

H. Cleyndert, "Het plan-Berlage voor Amsterdam-zuid en zijn noodzakelijke herziening," in *Tijdschrift voor Volkshuisvesting en Stedebouw* IV, 9, September 15, pp. 251–258.

C. de Lorm, *Het gezellige binnenhuis*, Rotterdam 1923[1], 1926[2].

T. Karsten, "Een Indisch oordeel over Dr. Berlage," in *De Bouwwereld* XXI, 23, June 6, pp. 181–182, from *Locomotief*.

Editorial, "Dr. Berlage over De Bazel," in *De Telegraaf* December 1, morning edition.

Editorial, "Dr. Berlage over het Haagsche Raadhuis," in *De Bouwwereld* XXII, 8, February 21, pp. 60–61.

J. Wils, *De sierende elementen van de bouwkunst*, Rotterdam.

1924

J. Havelaar, *Het moderne meubel*, Rotterdam 1924[1], 1928[2].

J.H.C. van den Berg and L.S.P. Scheffer, *Iets over Utrecht's uitbreiding en Utrechtsche woning-complexen der laatste jaren*, Stedebouw 2, Nederlandsch Instituut vor Volkshuisvesting, Haarlem-Zwolle.

J.G. Wattjes, *Nieuw Nederlandsche Bouwkunst*, Amsterdam 1921[1], 1926[2], rev. ed. 1929[3].

1925

J. Gratama, *Dr. H.P. Berlage bouwmeester*, W.L. & J. Brusse, Rotterdam, XLVII + 187 pp.
List of works, bibliography and rich collection of pictures. Gratama's essay, pp. XI–XXXIX, is a revised version of the one published in the 1916 *Festschrift*.

H. Sörgel, "Holländische Architekten-Charakterköpfe: H.P. Berlage," in *Baukunst*, pp. 102–103.

A. van der Boom, "De Reisschetsen van bouwmeester H.P. Berlage," in *Op de Hoogte*, pp. 295ff.

J.A.G. van der Steur, "Eerepromotie Dr. H.P. Berlage," in *Bouwkundig Weekblad* XLVI, 5, January 31, pp. 81–85.

C.A. van der Velde, *De A.N.D.B. Een overzicht van zijn ontstaan, zijne ontwikkeling en zijne beteekenis*, Amsterdam; particularly ch. XVI, "Het Bondsgebouw," pp. 302–312.

1925–1926

H. Hana, "Berlage's kantoorgebouw 'De Nederlanden' te 's-Gravenhage," in *Wil en Weg*, pp. 294ff.

1926

J.B. (Blaauw), "Amsterdam West," in *Architectura* XXX, 47, November 20, pp. 525–527.

J. Gratama, "Berlage zeventig jaar," in *De Telegraaf* February 21.

J. Gratama, "Dr. H.P. Berlage architect," in *Maandblad voor beeldende kunsten*, pp. 143ff.

W. Kromhout, "H.P. Berlage, 1856–1926," in *Nieuwe Rotterdamsche Courant* February 20.

J.J.P. Oud, *Holländische Architektur*, Bauhausbücher 10, Albert Langen, Munich, 85 pp.; rev. ed. 1929².

J.M. van der Mey, "Berlage 70 jaar," in *Het Volk* February 20.

J.G. Wattjes, "Kiosk op het Buitenhof te Den Haag," in *Het Vaderland* December 22.

P. Zwart, "Het vereenvoudigde Hofpleiplan," in *Het Vaderland* December 22.

Editorial, "Amsterdam-West," in *Architectura* XXX, 26, June 26, p. 304.

Editorial, "De Stadhuisbouw te 's-Gravenhage," in *Bouwkundig Weekblad* XLVIII, 17, April 24, p. 178.

Editorial, "Dr. H.P. Berlage, architect, 1856–21 Februari 1926," in *Bouwkundig Weekblad* XLVII, 8, February 20, pp. 73ff.

Editorial, "Huldigung van Dr. Berlage," in *Architectura* XXX, 29, July 17, p. 337.

1927

P. Bakker Schut, "Het Uitbreidingsplan 's-Gravenhage West," in *Tijdschrift voor Volkshuisvestin en Stedebouw* VIII, March 3, pp. 61ff.

E.J.B. (Belinfante), "Het nieuwe kantoorpaleis te 's-Gravenhage van "De Nederlanden van 1845," in *De Hollandsche revue*, pp. 230ff.

G., "Het nieuwe kerkgebouw van First Church of Christian Scientist te 's-Gravenhage," in *Buiten* p. 376.

J. Havelaar, "Berlage's werken," in *Opgang* pp. 698ff.

J. Havelaar, *Dr. H.P. Berlage*, Ned-erlandsche Bouwmeesters 3, Van Munster's, Amsterdam, undated, 36 pp.

Essay on Berlage as part of a series devoted to contemporary Dutch architects (W. Kromhout, P. Kramer, A.J. Kropholler).

J.P.M. (Mieras), "Het nieuwe kantoorgebouw van de Amsterdamsche Bank te Amsterdam," in *Bouwkundig Weekblad Architectura* XLVIII, 11, March 12, pp. 100–103.

Editorial, "De nieuwste Amstelbrug," in *Bouwkundig Weekblad Architectura* XLVIII, 2, pp. 19–21.

Editorial, "Het nieuwe gebouw van de Amsterdamsche Bank," in *Het Bouwbedrijf*, pp. 155ff.

H. Sangster, "Het nieuwe kantoorgebouw van 'De Nederlanden'," in *De Ingenieur*, pp. 313ff.

M. Stam, "M-Kunst," in *i 10* 1, 2, pp. 41–43.

C.M. van Moorsel, "De Nederlanden van 1845' van Dr. H.P. Berlage," in *Maandblad voor beeldende kunsten*, pp. 183ff.

C.M. van Moorsel, "Dr. P.J.H. Cuypers en Dr. H.P. Berlage," in *Opgang*, pp. 348ff.

C.M. van Moorsel, "Het nieuwe gebouw van de Nederlanden in Den Haag," in *Bouwkundig Weekblad Architectura* XLVIII, 17, April 23, pp. 153–155; 22, May 28, pp. 203–204.

A.M. van Rood, "First Church of Christian Scientist te 's-Gravenhage. Architect Dr. H.P. Berlage," in *Bouwkundig Weekblad Architectura* XLVIII, 49, December 3, pp. 424–426.

J.G. Wattjes, "Gebouw 'De Nederlanden van 1845'," in *Het Bouwbedrijf*, pp. 179ff and 266ff.

P. Zwart, "De Amstelbrug van H.P. Berlage," in *Het Vaderland* January 29.

P. Zwart, "H.P. Berlage, De Nederlanden van 1845," in *Het Vaderland* March 4.

1928

AA.VV., *Beursherdenking*, monograph for the twenty-fifth anniversary of the Stock Exchange published in *Bouwkundig Weekblad Architectura* IL, 21, May 26, pp. 161–168; 22, June 2, pp. 174–175.

Articles by S. Theiss, H. van de Velde, R. Mallet Stevens, B. Taut, T. Oestberg, P. Behrens. J. Hoffmann, E. Mendelsohn, K. Moser, E. Sundhal, and I. Tengbom; the No. 22 also includes R.N. Roland Holst's text of May 28, 1928.

J.F. de Balbian Verster, "De Breero-Feesten en de Breero-Club (1885–1890)," in AA.VV., *Jaarboek van het Genootschap Amstelodamum*, XXV, pp. 195–220.

J. Duiker, "Visie op nieuwe cultuur," in *De Telegraaf* May 26.

A.O. (Otten), "Het Hofpleinplan te Rotterdam," in *Bouwkundig Weekblad Architectura* XLIX, 6, February 11, pp. 41–44.

Editorial, "Berlage en de eerbied voor de traditie in de kunst," in *Studien* II, pp. 144ff.

Editorial, "Uit boek en blad," in *Opgang*, p. 368.

M. Stam, "Der Zusammenbruch der Monumentalität in Rotterdam," in *ABC* II, 4, pp. 44ff.

W.G. Witteveen, "Het Hofplein te Rotterdam," in *Tijdschrift voor Volkshuisvesting en Stedebouw* IX, 4 April, pp. 74–80.

P. Zwart, "De Betekenis van Berlage's Beurs," in *Het Vaderland* May 27.

P. Zwart, "De Haagsche museumbouw," in *Het Vaderland* June 23.

1929

J. de Jong, *De Nieuwe Richting in de Kunstnijverheid, in Nederland*, W.L. & J. Brusse, Rotterdam, XIV + 113 pp., 287 ill.

A. Otten, "Het Hofplein te Rotterdam," in *Bouwkundig Weekblad Architectura* L, 9, March 2, pp. 65–67.

Editorial, "Het nieuwe Museum te 's-Gravenhage," in *Eigen Haard*, pp. 966ff.

J.B. van Loghem, "De Plannen van Dr. H.P. Berlage voor het nieuwe museum te 's-Gravenhage," in *Nieuwe Rotterdamsche Courant* November 24.

J.B. van Loghem, "Moderne architectuur," in *Nieuwe Rotterdamsche Courant* July 19.

P. Zwart, "Berlage's ontwerpen voor het Gemeentemuseum," in *Het Vaderland* December 10.

1929–1930

C.M. van Moorsel, "Een nieuw museumplan voor Den Haag," in *Roomsch-Katholiek Bouwblad*, pp. 130ff.

1930

H. van der Kloot Meyburg, *Bouwkunst in de stad en op het land*, Rotterdam, rev. ed. 1930³.

1930–1931

Editorial, "Dr. Berlage's Amstelbrug," in *Roomsch-Katholiek Bouwblad*, p. 342, from *De Telegraaf*.

1931

H.T. Zwiers, "Het nieuwe Museum te 's-Gravenhage van Dr. H.P. Ber-lage," in *Bouwkundig Weekblad Architectura* LII, 1, January 3, pp. 1–6.

1932

C. Biemond, "Het ontwerp voor de Berlagebrug," in *Bouwkundig Weekblad Architectura* XLIII, 22, May 28, pp. 183–187.

J. Duiker, "Dr. Berlage en de 'Nieuwe Zakelijkheid'," in *De 8 en Opbouw* III, 5, pp. 43–51.

W.B. Ouëndag, "De Amsterdamsche Bank te Amsterdam," in *Bouwkundig Weekblad Architectura* LIII, 48, November 26, pp. 425–431.

J.J.P. Oud, "De "Nieuwe Zakelijkheid in de Bouwkunst," in *De 8 en Opbouw* III, 23, November 10, pp. 223–228.

Editorial, "De Schrikbeelden van levensacrobatiek, beton ijzer, glas, asphalt, enz.," in *Klei*, p. 197.

Editorial, "Dr. H.P. Berlage over Rusland," in *Roomsch-Katholiek Bouwblad* III, 13, January 28, pp. 196–198.

F.C. Smets, "De Climatiseering installaties," in *Bouwkundig Weekblad Architectura* LIII, 48, November 26, pp. 438–440.

G.J. van Haersma Buma and F.R. Th. Kröner, "Omschrijving . . . ," in *Bouwkundig Weekblad Architectura* LII, 48, November 26, pp. 432–437.

S. van Ravensteyn, "De nieuwe Amstelbrug van Berlage," in *Gemeenschap*, pp. 338ff.

1932–1933

Editorial, "Uitsprachen van Dr. H.P. Berlage over het Nieuwe Bouwen," in *Roomsch-Katholiek Bouwblad*, pp. 11 ff.

1932–1935

Moderne bouwkunst in Nederland, W.L. & J. Brusse, Rotterdam, 20 vols.

With Dudok, Gratama, Hulshoff, Van der Kloot Meyburg, Staal, and Luthmann, Berlage is the editor of a series documenting modern Dutch architecture.

1933

Editorial, "Utrecht, let op U saeck!" in *Bouwkundig Weekblad Architectura* LIV, 43, October 28, pp. 371–372.

1934

AA.VV., *H.P. Berlage ter gedachtenis*, commemorative booklet published by *Bouwkundig Weekblad Architectura* LV, 51, December 22, 54 pp.

Articles by A. Verwey, H.P. Bremmer, E.E. Strasser, A.D. Copier, J. Eisenloeffel, W.A. van Konijnenburg, J. Langejan, H.E. van Gelder, K. Kuiler, A. van Baalen, A.M. Hammacher, J.B. van Loghem,

J.J.P. Oud, F.R. Yerbury, M.J. Granpré Molière, R.N.20Roland Holst, A.C. Strasser-Berlage, Th. van Rijn, H. Wouda, D. Roosenburg, and J.A.G. van der Steur.
AA.VV., *Dr. H.P. Berlage 1856–1934*, commemorative booklet published by *De 8 en Opbouw* V, 18, September 1, pp. 149–158.
Articles by J.J.P. Oud, J. Duiker, H. Nuyten, J.B. van Loghem, G. Rietveld, S. van Ravensteyn, and B. Merkelbach.
O.B. de Kat, "Mannen van heden. Dr. H.P. Berlage, architect van het nieuwe Gemeentemuseum te 's-Gravenhage," in *Op de Hoogte*, pp. 246ff.
A.J. Kropholler, "In memoriam Dr. H.P. Berlage," in *Maanblad voor beeldende kunsten*, pp. 177ff.
L. Lionni, "H.P. Berlage è morto," in *Casabella* 83, November, pp. 2–3.
J.P. Mieras and A.P. Smits, "H.P. Berlage, commemorative booklet published by *Bouwkundig Weekblad Architectura* LV, 33, August 18, pp. 337–348.
J.J.P. Oud, "H.P. Berlage," in *L'Architecture d'aujourd'hui* V, 34–35, p. 245.
Paulsen, "Dr. H.P. Berlage zum Gedächtnis," in *Wasmuth's Monatshefte für Baukunst* XVIII, 10, October, pp. 494–496.
Editorial, "Beteekenis van Berlage," in *De Tijd* August 13.
Editorial, "Bij den dood Dr. H.P. Berlage," in *Eigen Haard*, pp. 527ff.
Editorial, "Dr. Hendrik Petrus Berlage. Baanbreker voor onze moderne bouwkunst," in *De Telegraaf*, *and in Algemeen Handelsblad* August 13.
Editorial, "Dr. H.P. Berlage overleden–'The grand old man' der bouwkunst," in *Het Vaderland* August 13.
Editorial, "Dr. H.P. Berlage en zijn Beursgebouw," in *Het Vaderland* August 13.
Editorial, "Dr. H.P. Berlage," in *Amstelodamum*, p. 70.
Editorial, "Dr. H.P. Berlage overleden. Schepper van de moderne architectuur in ons land," in *De Maasbode* August 13.
Editorial, "In memoriam Berlage," in *De Hollandsche Revue*, pp. 403ff.
Editorial, "In memoriam Berlage," in *Klei* p. 134.
J. Slagter, "Bij het heengaan van Berlage," in *Elsevier* 88, pp. 211ff.
C. van Eesteren, "In memoriam Dr. H.P. Berlage," in *Tijdschrift voor*

Volkshuisvesting en Stedebouw XV, 9 September, pp. 135–137.
V.H., "Dr. H.P. Berlage," in *Neerlandia* p. 135.
G.W. van Heukelom, "Ter Herdenking–Dr. H.P. Berlage 1956–1934," in *De Ingenieur* pp. 325ff.
S. van Ravesteyn, "Berlage 1856–1934," in *Gemeenschap* p. 569.
A. Verwey, "Architect Dr. H.P. Berlage," in *Nieuwe Rotterdamsche Courant* August 13, evening edition.
C. Verwey, "Bij den dood van Berlage," in *De Smidse* September, pp. 1ff.
C. Veth, "In memoriam–Dr. H.P. Berlage," in *De Socialistische Gids*, pp. 629ff.

1934–1935
J. Baanders, "Anno 1897," in *Roomsch-Katholike Bouwblad*, p. 22.
A.J. Kropholler, "Dr. Berlage en zijn werk als bouwmeester," in *Roomsch-Katholiek Bouwblad*, pp. 18ff.
C.M. (van Moorsel), "Het nieuwe Gemeentemuseum in Den Haag," in *Roomsch-Katholiek Bouwblad*, pp. 385ff.
J. Wils, "Dr. H.P. Berlage. In memoriam," in *De Delver* 1.

1935
L. Artz, "Das neue Gemeindemuseum im Haag," in *Wasmuth's Monatshefte für Baukunst* XIX, pp. 257ff.
J.J. de Gelder, "De nieuwe gemeentelijke musea van 's-Gravenhage en Rotterdam," in *Oudheidkundig Jaarboek* IV, 4, pp. 9–10 and 88–95.
G. Friedhoff, "De nieuwe musea in Den Haag en Rotterdam," in *Elsevier* 90, December, p. 383.
D. Jansen, "Het Haagsche Gemeente-Museum," in *Weekblad voor C. en C.* 32, pp. 4ff.
E. Persico, "L'ultima opera di Berlage," in *Casabella* VIII, 93, September, pp. 4–7.
J.H. Plantenga, "Eenige opmerkingen," in *De Gids* 4, October, pp. 94ff.
A. Plasschaert, "Het Haagsche museum geopend," in *De Amsterdammer* 3027, p. 12; 3028, p. 7.
E.E. Strasser, "Het nieuwe Gemeente-museum te 's-Gravenhage," in *Bouwkundig Weekblad Architectura* LVI, 31, August 3, pp. 317–324.
H.E. van Gelder, "Het nieuwe Gemeentemuseum te 's-Gravenhage," in *Gudheidkundig Jaarboek* IV, 4, pp. 61ff.
D.S. van Zuiden, "Ons nieuwe museum aan de Stadhouderslaan," in *De Haagsche Gids*, pp. 53ff.
A.N. Zadoks, "Le Musée de La Haye," in *Beaux-Arts* 135, pp. 1ff.
J.S. Zwrtendijk, "Twee nieuwe mu-

sea: Den Haag en Rotterdam," in *Maanblad voor beeldende kunsten* August, pp. 259ff.

1935–1936
J.W. (Wils), "Twee musea," in *De Delver*, p. 33.

1936
J. Slagter, "De Inrichting der nieuwe musea in Den Haag en Rotterdam," in *Elsevier* 92, p. 238.

1938–1940
A. Romein, "Hendrik Petrus Berlage. Bouwmeester der Beurs," in J. and A. Romein, *Erflaters van onze beschaving Nederlandse gestalten uit zes eeuwen*, Amsterdam-Antwerpen 1938–40[1]; 1959[8], rev. ed., pp. 842–864.

1940
AA.VV., *J.F. Staal*, in *Bouwkundig Weekblad Architectura* 25, special issue devoted to J.F. Staal, in particular the articles by A. Boeken and R.N. Roland Holst.

1941
"Hendrik Petrus Berlage," in *Nederland bouwt in baksteen 1800–1940*, exhibition catalogue, Museum Boymans, Rotterdam, pp. 13–17.

1943
Repertorium betreffende de Nederlandsche monumenten van geschiedenis en kunst, Nederlandschen Oudheidkundigen Bond, 's-Gravenhage, 2 vols.
Very useful bibliography; a third volume was published in 1950.
J.G. Wattjes with F.A. Warner, *Amsterdams bouwkunst en stadsschoon (1306–1942)*, Amsterdam.

1946
J.P.M. (Mieras), "De Raadsvoordracht voor het bouwen van de nieuwe Beurs te Amsterdam volgens het ontwerp Berlage 1896–9 sept.–1946," in *Bouwkundig Weekblad* LXIV, September 3, pp. 203–204.

1948
L. van der Waals, "24 Schetsen. Zwervende en reizende toch thuis," in *Nijgh & Van Ditmar*, Rotterdam-The Hague, 28 pp., 24 tipped-in plates.

1953
J.P.M. (Mieras), "Op de inwijding van de Beurs van Berlage," in *Bouwkundig Weekblad* LXXI, May 12, pp. 149–150, and June 9, pp. 185–186.
J.J. Vriend, "De Beurs als bouwkunstig monument," in *Algemeen Handelsblad* May 23.

1956
L.K. Eaton, "Sullivan and Berlage," in *Progresive Architecture* XXXVII, pp. 138ff.
D. Minderman, "Dr. H.P. Berlage,"

in *Taak en Tolk* XXXI, 5, June, pp. 4–9.
W. Thijs, *De Kroniek van P.L. Tak*, Wereld-Bibliotheek, Amsterdam-Antwerp, 362 pp. With annexes.
S. van Deventer, *Kröller-Müller. De geschiednis van een cultureel levenswerk*, D. Tjeenk Willink & Zn., Haarlem, 156 pp.; Sam van Deventer Stichting, Arnheim 1984, reprint.

1959
Editorial, "Een Discussie over Berlage's Beurs," in *Bouwkundig Weekblad* LXXVII, 9, February 28, pp. 99–109, and LXXVII, May 23, pp. 249–260.
Editorial, "Eredità dell'Ottocento: H.P. Berlage strutturalista," in *L'architettura–cronache e storia* 49, November, p. 487.
P. Singelenberg, "Eenige beschouwingen over de Beurs van Berlage," in *Bulletin K.N.O.B.* XII, series VI, pp. 131–144.
On the history of the Stock Exchange, with english summary. First publication by one of the most significant Berlage scholar.
J.J. Vriend, *Architectuur van deze eeuw*, Amsterdam.

1960
A.J. Kropholler, "Over Berlage, de Beurs en baksteen," in *Baksteen* 3, May, pp. 11–14.
J.J.P. Oud, "Preferenties," in *Elsevier* 19, March.
H.P.L. Wiessing, *Bewegend portret*, Amsterdam, in particular pp. 159–161.

1961
G. Grassi, "Immagine di Berlage," in *Casabella continuità* 249, March, pp. 38–46.
Essay on Berlage's idea of architecture; in the same issue, an editorial, "Un architetto e una città: Berlage ad Amsterdam," p. 37, and "Preferenze" by Oud (translated from *Elsevier* 1960) p. 53. Grassi's text is followed by an anthology of texts freely collected from Berlage in 1910, "Studies over bouwkunst, stijl en samenling: Arte e società," pp. 47–49, "Previsioni sull'evoluzione dell'architettura," pp. 50–51, and "Considerazioni sullo stile," pp. 51–52.

1963
P. Singelenberg, "Berlage's Monument voor Verleden en Toekomst uit 1889," in AA.VV., *Album Discipulorum J.G. van Gelder*, Haentjens Dekker & Gumbert, Utrecht, pp. 143–154.
P. Singelenberg, "Het bijzondere van

'De Algemeene'," in *Heemschut* XL, 2, March, pp. 33–34.

J.J. Terwen, "De Beurs van Berlage, schakel van de Nederlandse bouwkunst," in AA.VV., *150 jaar Koninkrijk der Nederlanden*, Amsterdam-Rotterdam, pp. 156–161.

1966

L. Gans, *Nieuwe Kunst. De Nederlandse Bijdrage tot de Art Nouveau*, Oosthoek's, Utrecht.

D. Gifford, ed., *The Literature of Architecture*, New York, English translation of Berlage 1912, "Neuere amerikanische Architektur," pp. 606–616.

1968

G. Fanelli, *Architettura moderna in Olanda 1900–1940*, Marchi & Bertolli, Florence, 371 pp. (revised Dutch edition, *Moderne architectuur in Nederland 1900–1940*, Cahiers NDB 2, Staatsuitgeverij, The Hague, 1978[1]; 1981[2], 368 pp.).
Fundamental tool for the study of Dutch architecture between 1900 and 1940. Chronological general bibliography, annotated (842 titles in the Dutch edition), biography, and catalogue of the works, with the relevant bibliography of another 90 architects. English summary. For Berlage, see pp. 57–63 (pp. 58–80 in the Dutch edition) and pp. 184–188 (pp. 236–239 in the Dutch edition) of the biographies.

1969

R. Blijstra, *2000 jaar Utrecht*, A.W. Bruna and Zoon, Utrecht-Antwerp, 427 pp.

P. Singelenberg, *H.P. Berlage*, Meulenhoff, Amsterdam, 31 pp. 32 pp. of plates.

1970

R. Blijstra, "Stedebouw 1900/1940 in 's-Gravenhage," in *'s-Gravenhage* XXV, 12, December pp. 1–52.

A.W. Reinink, "American Influences on Late Nineteenth-Century Architecture in the Netherlands," in *Journal of the Society of Architectural Historians* XXXIX, 2, pp. 163–174.

A.W. Reinink, "Berlage en Viollet-le-Duc: enkele aantekeningen over de 'muur' van de Beurs," in AA.VV., *Opstellen voor H. van der Waal*, Scheltema and Holkema, Amsterdam and Leiden, pp. 156–163.

D. Tselos, "Richardson's Influence on European Architecture," in *Journal of the Society on Architectural Historian* XXIX, 2, pp. 156–162.

1971

R. Blijstra, "Berlage in 's-Graven-hage," in *'s-Gravenhage* XXVI, 12, December, pp. 1–52.

E. Braches, "Over Derkinderen's Gijsbreght van Aemstel," in *Open* III, pp. 3–16.

1972

L.K. Eaton, *American Architecture Comes of Age*, The MIT Press, Cambridge, Mass., and London.

A.W. Reinink, "'Nieuwe kunst' en neoklassicisme: enkele architectuurtheoretische parallelen," in *Nederlands Kunsthistorisch Jaarboek* 23, Fibula-Van Dishoek, Bussum, pp. 455–472.

P. Singelenberg, *H.P. Berlage. Idea and Style. The Quest for Modern Architecture*, Haentjens Dekker & Gumbert, Utrecht, 274 pp., 136 pp. of plates.
First critical monograph on Berlage, in which his work is analyzed up to the Amsterdam Stock Exchange: training, education in Zürich, trip to Italy, partnership with Sanders, early works (in particular the buildings for the De Algemeene and the De Nederlanden), the Stock Exchange (four central chapters), the villa Henny, the headquarters of the ANDB. The last part is a study of exchanges and influences, but also the complex roots of Berlage's aesthetic and architectural body of theories. English text; bibliography and wide documentation.

1973

E. Braches, *Het boek als Nieuwe Kunst 1892–1903*, Oosthoek's, Utrecht, 555 pp.

1974

J.D. Braksma, "Drie vroeë pretoriase kerkbouw. 3. Die Christ Church," in *De Arte* XVI, pp. 18–30.

1975

AA.VV., *Americana*, exhibition catalogue, Rijksmuseum Kröller-Müller, Otterlo, 112 pp.

AA.VV., *H.P. Berlage 1856–1934. Een bouwmeester en zijn tijd*, Nederlands Kunsthistorisch Jaarboek 25, Fibula-Van Dishoek, Bussum, 366 pp.
Collection of essays on Berlage: P. Singelenberg discusses the museum in The Hague (pp. 1–89, issued also separately), M. Boot writes about the Villa Henny (pp. 91–131), H. Searing, about housing (pp. 133–179), F.F. Fraenkel, about the development plan for the south of Amsterdam (pp. 181–275), and G. Hoogewood, about the competition for the Amsterdam Stock Exchange in 1884 (pp. 277–365).

R. Blijstra, *Over Haagse architectuur*, Uitgave van het Gemeentebestuur van 's-Gravenhage, The Hague 1975, 155 pp.

M. Bock, "Berlage: een monument opblazen," in *Museumjournaal* XX, 4, August, pp. 146–154.

M. Bock, K. Broos, and P. Singelenberg, ed., *H.P. Berlage, bouwmeester 1856–1934*, Haags Gemeentemuseum, The Hague, 96 pp.; 1979[2].
Catalogue of the exhibition organized by the Gemeentemuseum in The Hague. Essays by P. Singelenberg (social and cultural context, aesthetic theories, works between 1878 and 1934) and M. Bock (building materials, urban planning, housing). Catalogue of the works.

E. Godoli, "Hendrik Petrus Berlage e la 'Nieuwe Kunst'," in AA.VV., *Situazione degli studi sul Liberty*, ed. by R. Bossaglia, C.20Cresti, V. Savi. Proceedings of the international conference at Salsomaggiore Terme, CLUSF, Florence, pp. 215–227.

G. Hoogewoud, "De Amsterdamse Beurskwestie," in *Wonen-TA/BK* 2, January, pp. 5–16.

F. Liefkes, "Eetkamer-ameublement van Van de Velde en Berlage," in *Bullettin van het Rijksmuseum* XXIII, 1, pp, 16–28.

A.W. Reinink, *Amsterdam en de Beurs van Berlage*. Cahiers NDB, 1, Staatsuitgeverij, The Hague, 157 pp.
Monograph on the public reaction and contemporary critics to the Amsterdam Stock Exchange. Complete bibliography including almost 500 titles, pp. 145–155.

1976

AA.VV., *Museumplein*, exhibition catalogue, Kunsthistorisch Instituut der Universiteit, Amsterdam.

F.F. Fraenkel, *Het Plan Amsterdam-Zuid van H.P. Berlage*, Canaletto, Alphen aan den Rijn, undated, 416 pp.

J. Peet, "De Traditie van land en volk, een ideologie in het r-k bouwblad," in *Plan* VII, 2, February, pp. 17–32.

P. Singelenberg, "Sempers Einfluss auf Berlage," in AA.VV., *Gottfried Semper und die Mitte des 19. Jahrhunderts*, Birkhäuser Verlag, Basel and Stuttgart, pp. 308–314.

1977

D.J. Grinberg, *Housing in the Netherlands 1900–1940*, Delft University Press, Delft, 144 pp.

1978

AA.VV., *Kunstenaren der idee. Symbolistische tendenzen in Nederland, ca.* 1880–1930, exhibition catalogue, Haags Gemeentemuseum, The Hague.

G. Fanelli, *Architettura Edilizia Urbanistica Olanda 1917/1940*, F. Papafava, Florence, 786 pp.
Detailed documentation and rich illustration about Dutch architecture between the two World Wars.

D.J. Meijers, "De democratisering van schoonheid," in AA.VV., *Kunst en Kunstbedrijf. Nederland 1914–1940*, Nederlands Kunsthistorisch Jaarboek 28, Fibula-Van Dishoek, Haarlem, pp. 55–104.

R.W.D. Oxenaar and W.G. Quist, *Rijksmuseum Kröller-Müller*, Kröller-Müller Stichting, Otterlo, 21pp., 1981[2].

Editorial, "Baarnse Badhotel wel degelijk ontworpen door Berlage," in *Baarnsche Courant* August 23, p. 2.

1979

AA.VV., *Architettura Socialdemocrazia Olanda 1900/1940*, Arsenale, Venice, 61 pp. (partial Dutch translation, *Nederlandse Architektuur in internationaal perspektief 1900/1940*, Ekologische Uitgeverij, Amsterdam 1981).

C.L. Anzivino and E. Godoli, *Ginevra 1927: il concorso per il palazzo della Società delle nazioni e il caso Le Corbusier*, Modulo, Florence.

M. Casciato, F. Panzini, S. Polano, ed., *Funzione e senso. Architettura-casa-città. Olanda 1870–1940*, Electa, Milan, 221 pp.; new rev. ed., *Olanda 1870–1940. Casa, città, architettura*, Electa, Milan 1980[2] (Dutch translation, *Architektuur en volkshuisvesting. Nederland 1870–1940*, SUN, Nijmegen 1980).
On pp. 62–67 (pp. 58–63 in 1980 ed.), Italian translation of Berlage's "Normalisatie in Woningbouw" 1918, with an introductory note by H. van Bergeijk, commenting also the excerpts published by Grassi 1961.

J. Kroes, *Het Paleis aan de laan. De geschiednis van het bondsgebouw van de A.N.D.B.*, Industriebond N.V.V., Amsterdam.

1980

AA.VV., *Nooit gebouwd Nederland*, Grafisch Nederland 1980, Koninklijk Verbond van Grafische Ondernemingen, Amsterdam, 104 pp.

H.C. Haarman-Engelberts, "Glasserviezen van Leerdam," in *Antiek* XIV, 9, pp. 553–566.

E.J. Hoogenberk, *Het Idee van de Hollandse stad*, Delftse Universitaire Pers, Delft, 247 pp.

P. Karstkarel and R. Terpstra, "On-

twerp- en bouwproces van Berlages raadhuis," in *Plan* XI, 4, pp. 28–32.
P. Panerai, J. Castex, and J.C. Depaule, *Formes urbaines: de l'îlot à la barre*, Dunod, Paris.
M. Singelenberg-van der Meer, *Nederlandse keramiek- en glasmerken*, De Tijdstroom, Lochem, rev. ed. 1985², 125 pp., useful bibliography about ceramics and glass.
E. Taverne, ed., *Het Raadhuis van Berlage in Usquert*, exhibition catalogue, Groninger Museum, Groningen 1980, 60 pp.
C. van de Ven, *Space in architecture*, Van Gorcum, Assen, 278 pp.
1981
Amsterdamse gebouwen 1880–1980, Het Spectrum, Utrecht-Antwerp, 323 pp.
Updated architectural guide of Amsterdam 1880–1980; the guide edited by H.J.F. de Roy van Zuydewijn, is also useful: *Amsterdamse bouwkunst 1815–1940*, J.H. de Bussy, Amsterdam, undated, 215 pp.
H. Jellema, ed., *Bergen aan zee badplaats sinds 1906*, Pivola, Schoorl, 144 pp.
L. Rebel-Benschop, "Berlage en de Gijsbreght," in *Wonen-TA/BK* 22, November, pp. 10–12.
1982
K. Broos, *Piet Zwart 1885–1977*, exhibition catalogue, Haags Gemeentemuseum, The Hague and Van Gennep, Amsterdam, 96 pp.
J. de Heer, "De Geest der neogotiek," in *Plan* XIII, 7–8, July-August, pp. 30–37.
G. Fanelli and E. Godoli, *Wendingen 1918–1931. Documenti dell'arte olandese del Novecento*, Centro Di, Florence, 151 pp.
Italian translation of Berlage's article on Frank Lloyd Wright, published by *Wendingen* 1921, pp. 133–134.

A.W. Reinink, "Nouveaux aspects de l'influence de Viollet-le-Duc aux Pays-Bas," in AA.VV., *Actes du Colloque International Viollet-le-Duc*, Nouvelles Editions Latines, Paris, pp. 289–293.
H. Searing, ed., "Berlage or Cuypers? The Father of Them All," in AA.VV., *In Search of Modern Architecture*, The MIT Press, Cambridge, Mass., pp. 226–244.
H. Searing, "Berlage, H.P.," in *Macmillan Encyclopedia of Architects*, The Free Press, New York, pp. 185–189.
T. van Velzen, ed., *Het Haags Gemeentemuseum*, Haags Gemeentemuseum, The Hague, 36 pp.
1983
M. Bock, *Anfänge einer neuen Architektur*, Staatsuitgeverij, The Hague, and Franz Steiner, Wiesbaden, 420 pp.
Main critical monograph on Berlage, with that of P. Singelenberg of 1972. Examines Berlage's contribution to the Dutch architectural culture at the end of the 19th century as well as his works (plans, designs, texts), revealing the rich contemporary background up to the turn of the century. Text in German; analytical picture documentation, bibliography, and reprint of Berlage's significant text of 1894, "Bouwkunst en impressionisme.
N. de Boer, "De magere erfenis," in *Wonen-TA/BK* 7, April pp. 9–19.
W. de Boer and P. Evers, *Amsterdamse bruggen, 1910–1950*, Amsterdamse Raad voor de Stedebouw, Amsterdam, 112 pp.
F. Leidelmeijer and D. van der Cingel, *Art nouveau en art déco in Nederland*, Meulenhoff/Landshoff, Amsterdam 191 pp.

S. Polano, "Berlage svuotato," in *Casabella* 489, March, p. 24.
F. Smit, "Berlage, Dudok, Weeber. Den Haag in de onvoltooid verleden tijd," in *Wonen-TA/BK* 1, January, pp. 10–26.
1984
H. Engel and J. de Heer, "Stadsbeeld en massawoningbouw," in *O. Ontwerp Onderzoek Onderwijs* 7, fall, pp. 10–22.
C. Passchier, "Architecten en het bouwen in voormalig Nederlands-Indië," in *Plan* XV, 8, August, pp. 5–11.
H.P. Rovinelli, "H.P. Berlage and the Amsterdam School 1914–1920: Rationalist as Expressionist," in *Journal of the Society of Architectural Historian* XLIII, October 3, pp. 256–264.
A. van der Kley-Blekxtoon, *Leerdam glas 1878–1930*, De Tijdstroom, Lochem-Gent, 112 pp.
1985
AA.VV., *Industrie & Vormgeving in Nederland 1850/1950*, exhibition catalogue, Stedelijk Museum, Amsterdam, 318 pp.
AA.VV., *Rijksmuseum Kröller-Müller*, Johan Enschedé en Zonen, Haarlem. Second revised edition, in Dutch, English, German, and French, 159 pp.
F. de Jong, ed., *Stedenbouw in Nederland. 50 jaar Bond van Nederlandse Stedenbouwkundigen*, De Walburg, Zutphen, 318 pp.
J. de Vries, "Albert Verwey en de beeldende kunst," in *Jong Holland* I, 1, February, pp. 7–26.
M. Gunnink, *St. Hubertus. Het jachthuis van H.p. Berlage voor de familie Kröller-Müller gelegen in het Nationale Park De Hoge Veluwe*, Kröller-Müller Stichting, Otterlo, 69 pp.; also in English, *St Hubertus's Lodge. Designed by H.P. Berlage, architect for the Kröller-*

Müller family.
S. Polano, "Amsterdam Sud 1900–1917. L'urbanistica di Berlage," in *Casabella* 511, March pp. 38–49.
R. Ramakers, *Tussen kunstnijverheid en industriële vormgeving: de Nederlandsche Bond voor Kunst en Industrie*, Reflex, Utrecht, 135 pp.
F. Schulze, *Mies van der Rohe. A Critical Biography*, The University of Chicago Press, Chicago and London, 355 pp.
P. Singelenberg, "Berlage in Londen. Holland House in Bury Street (1914–1916)," in AA.VV., *Bouwen in Nederland*, Leids Kunsthistorisch Jaarboek 1984, III, Delftsche U.M., Delft, pp.20407–425.
H. van Bergeijk, ed., "Hendrik Petrus Berlage. Architettura urbanistica estetica, Zanichelli, Bologna, 272 pp.
Essay on Berlage's theoretical production, with a discussion of the sources and the milieu. Anthology of Berlage's texts in Italian translation: "Amsterdam en Venetië" 1883; "De Plaats die de bouwkunst in de moderne aesthetica bekleedt 1886; "Gottfried Semper" 1903; "Het Uitbreidingsplan van 's-Gravenhage" 1909; "Über moderne Baukunst" 1911; "Amerikaansche Reisherinneringen" 1912; "Stedenbouw" 1914; "De Bouwkunst als maatschappelijke kunst," from *Schoonheid in samenleving* 1919; "Bouwkunst en socialisme," from AA.VV., *Socialisme, Kunst, Levenbschouwing*, 1932. Catalogue of Berlage's writings and bibliography.
C. van der Hoeven and J. Louwe, *Amsterdam als stedelij bouwwerk. Een morfologies analyse*, SUN, Nijmegen, 160 pp.
J. Willink, "Bremmer en het blijvende in de kunst," in *Jong Holland* I, 3, September, pp. 50–57.